PROPERTY AND JUSTICE

Property and Justice

J. W. HARRIS

OXFORD
UNIVERSITY PRESS

OXFORD

UNIVERSITY PRESS

Great Clarendon Street, Oxford OX2 6DP

Oxford University Press is a department of the University of Oxford.
It furthers the University's objective of excellence in research, scholarship,
and education by publishing worldwide in

Oxford New York

Athens Auckland Bangkok Bogotá Buenos Aires Cape Town
Chennai Dar es Salaam Delhi Florence Hong Kong Istanbul Karachi
Kolkata Kuala Lumpur Madrid Melbourne Mexico City Mumbai Nairobi
Paris São Paulo Shanghai Singapore Taipei Tokyo Toronto Warsaw
with associated companies in Berlin Ibadan

Oxford is a registered trade mark of Oxford University Press
in the UK and in certain other countries

Published in the United States
by Oxford University Press Inc., New York

British Library Cataloguing in Publication Data
Data available

Library of Congress Cataloging in Publication Data
Harris, J. W.
Property and justice / J. W. Harris.
p. cm.
Includes bibliographical references.
1. Property. 2. Justice. I. Title.
K720.H37 1996
346.04—dc20
[342.64] 96-8683
ISBN 0-19-825957-3
ISBN 0-19-925140-1 (Pbk.)

1 3 5 7 9 10 8 6 4 2

Printed in Great Britain
on acid-free paper by
Bookcraft Ltd., Midsomer Norton, Avon

For

Jose and Hugh

Preface

People everywhere invoke 'justice' in political and ethical controversies and in criticizing and applying the law. Against that, two and a half millennia of speculative thought have yielded no agreement about what justice is. Indeed, in addition to diametrically opposed conceptions of justice, there are those who say that justice does not exist. They recommend us to close our ears to its every-day invocation, since it does and can have no objectively knowable meaning, and hence no bearing on our practical concerns. Rather, it is a cloak for naked promotion of the interests of particular individuals or groups.

Such disagreements and scepticism about justice are familiar enough. More surprisingly, there is no concensus, and there is also scepticism, about the concept of property. All societies have property institutions of one kind or another. We all make plans and enter into transactions which take for granted the blindingly obvious fact that property institutions exist. We also, from time to time, disagree on moral and political grounds about how property institutions ought to be designed and about how property should be allocated among us. Yet when speculative thought is brought to bear on the subject, it appears that the very idea of property is so malleable that, again, there is no agreement about what it is and, believe it or not, there are sceptics who deny that there is any such thing as property.

The concern of this book is strictly 'practical', in the ordinary, rather than the philosophic, sense of that term. Political and legal decisions have to be made about questions of property distribution and property-institutional design. In reaching them, the claims of 'justice' cannot be ignored. Property has to be confronted with justice. Given the diversity of understanding and scepticism about both concepts, I have been forced to go back to the drawing-board as to each.

In Part I of the book I attempt to set out the nature of property institutions. I take account of the complexities which are commonly papered over in purely philosophical appraisals of the subject, whilst at the same time abstracting from the dead weight of detail which is, inevitably, the practising lawyer's every-day concern. In this Part it has been necessary to rein in the tendency of the concept of property to balloon in such a way that disagreements about the justice or injustice of property would be without intelligible focus. In Part II I take as my starting-point a minimalist conception of justice from which we may begin to address the normative cogency of what I call 'property-specific justice reasons'. I have then gone on to quarry from the tradition of western political philosophy those claims about just human association which have a bearing on property institutions. I have had the temerity to filter out the dross from the gold, using for that purpose the posited minimalist conception of justice.

The upshot consists of a mix of morally viable property-specific justice reasons. I offer them to all those concerned with political and legal questions about distribution and property-institutional design. They are relevant to such questions because it is these same property-specific justice reasons which, I shall argue, support a moral right of every citizen of a modern State that his society should provide a property institution, but only one which is structured so as to take account of what justice does indeed require.

Hence the day-to-day property questions which confront the political reformer, the lawyer, or the judge ultimately implicate a more fundamental question. Supposing we agree, minimally, that justice makes the following demands: people should not be treated differently on the basis that some kinds of human beings are inherently inferior to others; some degree of autonomous choice should be accorded to everyone; and unprovoked invasions of bodily integrity should be banned. Does it follow that the external resources of the world ought to be brought within the domain of some kind of property institution? There is nothing intuitively obvious about the answer to that question. It requires detailed examination, which this book seeks to provide. Step by step, eliminating false leads as we proceed, we arrive at an answer, which is, yes.

J. W. HARRIS
Keble College, Oxford
March, 1996

Acknowledgements

I began the research for this book when I was the holder of a British Academy research readership from 1990 to 1992. I was also awarded a grant by the British Academy to meet the cost of preparing the first draft. I wish to express my gratitude to the Academy for this invaluable support, and also to the Warden and Fellows of Keble College, Oxford, for granting me research leave to hold this readership.

Some sections of the book are based on papers delivered at conferences or as occasional lectures. An earlier version of Chapter 7, dealing with private and non-private property, was presented at the W. G. Hart workshop, held at the Institute of Advanced Legal Studies in the University of London in 1993 and attended by participants from many parts of the world. This paper was subsequently published in the *Law Quarterly Review* ((1995) 111 *LQR* 481). Some of my discussions of the notion of self-ownership, which appear in Chapters 11 and 17, formed the basis of lectures delivered at Keble College, the University of Hong Kong, and a workshop on human rights at Griffiths University in Brisbane—subsequently published in the *Oxford Journal of Legal Studies* ((1996) 16 *OJLS* 55). I greatly benefited from discussions provoked on all these occasions.

The opening chapters of the book were read by Professor Bernard Rudden of Oxford, who offered valuable criticisms. Professor Stephen Munzer, of the University of California Los Angeles, has been kind enough to read the bulk of the first draft. I am greatly indebted to him for his generosity with his time and his detailed comments and suggestions. Needless to say, I alone am responsible for all the arguments and conclusions which the book contains.

I should also like to thank my wife, Jose, and my son, Hugh, who have endured with patience the distraction from family concerns which the preparation and writing of this book have involved.

Contents

Part I

What is Property?

Part II

Is Property Just?

Cases

PART 1

What is Property?

1

Introduction

(i) THE UBIQUITY OF PROPERTY

Property is a legal and social institution governing the use of most things and the allocation of some items of social wealth. 'Social wealth' comprises all those things and services for which there is a greater potential total demand than there is a supply.

As an institution, property is a complex organizing idea. Through social learning and interaction, it is made available to the individual as a point of reference intervening between the brute facts of his situation, on the one hand, and his claims, desires, projects, and plans, on the other hand. Its complexity is twofold. It resides partly in the fact that the institution comprises many elements, from determinate prescriptive or permissive rules to open-ended principles of exclusive use and allocation. Its complexity resides also in the fact that the package of elements it contains varies enormously in time and place and is nowhere static for long.

Despite its complexity, property, as an organizing idea, is very old and is now worldwide. The oldest written records attest to it. Few primitive peoples, whose societies have been researched by anthropologists, have turned out to lack any conception of it.[1] In the modern world, any normal person will have heard of it, from childhood up.

In the modern world, the institution of property is everywhere embodied in law. That is to say, the various organs of government deploy it, officially, as part of the mechanism for controlling the use of things and as part of the mechanism for supervising or directing the allocation of wealth. The role played by property in forwarding these endeavours varies according to the cultural and ideological backgrounds of different political communities. At a minimum, the use of chattels of small value (which are numerically most of the tangible 'things' that there are) and the spending of residual income are governed by rules and principles of property law. In most jurisdictions, the compass of property is much more extensive, reaching to the use of most

---

[1] See A. Irving Hallowell, 'The Nature and Function of Property as a Social Institution', in Hallowell, *Culture and Experience* (U. Pa. Press, 1955), ch. 12, and works there cited; and Lawrence C. Becker, 'The Moral Basis of Property Rights', in J. Rowland Pennock and John W. Chapman (eds.), *Property* (Nomos XXII, NYUP, 1980), 187, and works there cited at 198 ff.

valuable things, such as houses and factories, and to the allocation of a substantial part of social wealth.

Nowhere is property the only mechanism for controlling the use of things
or the exclusive device for wealth-allocation. There are commonly laws controlling abuse of the atmosphere, but the air, above a certain height, is not
parcelled out into thing-like units subject to the institution of property. A
considerable proportion of social wealth is allocated *in specie* through the
form of public services, such as education and health-care, without benefit of
property.

Property is a social institution as well as a legal institution. Members of
societies make assumptions and claims, and defer to the claims of others,
against a background in which the institution of property is taken for granted.
They have done so throughout recorded history. The historical origins of
property, like those of other major social institutions such as marriage, kinship, contractual bargains, and criminal responsibility, are not recoverable
from our primeval past. When property becomes a legal as well as a social
institution depends on whatever heuristic conditions we care to stipulate for
the emergence of legal systems. If there is no 'law' until the emergence of
official agencies prefiguring those of the modern State, like courts and legis-
latures, then property was merely a social institution before such agencies
came into being to give official recognition to property rules and principles. In
any event, the social dimensions of property continued, and continue, alongside its legal dimensions. Countless assumptions and claims are informed by
the idea of property without reference to official agencies of the law. Furthermore, the open-ended nature of many proprietary principles entails that, even
when embodied in law, their official interpretation and implementation often
interact with current social understandings of them.

Property has a dual function, since it governs both the use of things and the
allocation of items of social wealth. It is in this duality of function that its
controversiality principally resides. It is one thing to say that a society ought to
afford to an individual the use of some resource. It is another to say that the
individual should be armed with power over others by virtue of a capacity to
dictate the use of the resource. 'Property' encompasses both.

The aim of this study is to enquire into those reasons which, allegedly,
justify property institutions, and in their light to investigate some particular
questions of institutional design and concrete questions of resource-allocation.
For such questions to have a focus we must first get a grip on what kind
of institutions property institutions are. What are their essential, and what
their typical, features? Faced with the complexities to which reference has
been made, the most promising enquiry procedure seems to be the following. We shall describe imaginary societies in which property institutions are
alternatively absent and present. We shall compare those features which, from
this perspective, appear essential to such institutions with elements present in

the property institutions familiar in modern societies, especially in English law.

To anticipate our conclusions, it will emerge that the essentials of a property institution are the twin notions of trespassory rules and the ownership spectrum. By 'trespassory rules' is meant any social rules, whether or not embodied in law, which purport to impose obligations on all members of a society, other than an individual or group who is taken to have some form of open-ended relationship to a thing, not to make use of that thing without the consent of that individual or group. The most hallowed such trespassory rule embodies the commandment 'thou shalt not steal'. Legal trespassory rules may be supported by criminal or civil sanctions, or both. In modern legal systems, they protect privileged relationships to land, chattels, money, and various sorts of ideational entities. As Bentham put it, the paradigm type of a property law is: '"Let no one, Rusticus excepted", (so we will call the proprietor) "and those whom he allows meddle with such or such a field"'.[2]

By 'the ownership spectrum' is meant the open-ended relationships presupposed and protected by trespassory rules. All attempts in the history of theorizing about property to provide a univocal explication of the concept of ownership, applicable within all societies and to all resources, have failed.[3] Yet property talk, lay and legal, deploys ineliminable ownership conceptions. The ownership spectrum ranges from what I shall call 'mere property' to 'full-blooded ownership'. Any relationship along the spectrum will be called an 'ownership interest'. Sophisticated property institutions contain elaborate conditions of title whereby individuals or groups are vested with ownership interests and thereby slot into the protection of trespassory rules.

All ownership interests comprise some use-privileges and some control-powers. Ownership interests in the upper half of the spectrum also comprise powers of transmission. Transmissibility is only a necessary feature of an ownership interest in the case of money.

The items on the ownership spectrum are united in three respects only. First, they all involve a juridical relation between a person (or group) and a resource. Secondly, the privileges and powers which they comprise are open-ended—that is, they cannot be concretely listed. Thirdly, they authorize self-seekingness on the part of the individual or group to whom they belong.

From this core of trespassory rules and the ownership spectrum many other elements typically to be found in property institutions build out. We shall discuss property-limitation rules, expropriation rules, and appropriation rules, all of which presuppose that there are ownership interests to be restricted or re-allocated. We shall investigate varieties of trespassory rules which have created ownership interests in ideational entities, or vested non-ownership proprietary interests in persons, or secured quasi-ownership interests to public

[2] Jeremy Bentham, *Of Laws in General* (Athlone Press, 1970), 177.
[3] See Tony Honoré, *Making Law Bind* (Clarendon Press, 1987), chs. 8 and 10.

agencies. Non-ownership proprietary interests lack the second above-mentioned feature of ownership interests, *viz.*, open-endedness. Quasi-ownership interests represent variable mixes of elements modelled on ownership interests and those derived from the functions discharged by the particular agency. They lack the third of the above-mentioned features of ownership interests, *viz.*, self-seekingness. We shall also consider the multiplicity of devices for hiving off the allocation of wealth which stems from the control powers and powers of transmission inherent in ownership interests. Cashable rights, like bank accounts and shares, are brought within the purview of property institutions by being subjected to expropriation and appropriation rules in the same way that money and other resources are. All this institutional scaffolding will be seen to rest on the twinned pillars of trespassory rules and the ownership spectrum.

(ii) THE ELUSIVENESS OF PROPERTY

Property is ubiquitous and complex, socially important and controversial. Yet any general notion of property is notoriously elusive. Political philosophers who have dealt with it are not obviously discussing the same thing, and what lawyers mean by it seems to be something different again.

One tradition of political philosophy sought to explicate that relationship between a person and a thing (conceived of as paradigmatic of property) and to explore its moral foundations—property as rights to things. Today political philosophers ask whether unequal distributions of property can be justified—property as wealth. Does anything unite these senses of property, the one which begins with the individual and some feature of the physical environment, and the other which conceives of property as a social cake capable of being sliced up in different ways? A third tradition explored the connections between property and independence within civil society. Does that enquiry have in mind property in things, or holdings of property (including money), or both? To add to the problem, political philosophers have always contrasted private property with common property, and sometimes with State property. Anthropologists and historians have added notions of collective property, group property, tribal property, and communal property. Is there anything in the term 'property' which makes all these expressions branches of a common conceptual tree?[4]

---

[4] See, generally, Richard Schlatter, *Private Property: The History of an Idea* (George Allen & Unwin, 1951); Lawrence C. Becker, *Property Rights: Philosophic Foundations* (Routledge & Kegan Paul, 1977); Allan Ryan, *Property and Political Theory* (Basil Blackwell, 1984); Andrew Reeve, *Property* (Macmillan, 1985); Jeremy Waldron, *The Right to Private Property* (Clarendon Press, 1988); Stephen R. Munzer, *A Theory of Property* (CUP, 1990); James Grunebaum, *Private Ownership* (Routledge, 1991); John Christman, *The Myth of Property* (OUP, 1994); James Penner, *The Idea of Property in Law* (OUP, forthcoming).

Further mystifications arise when, in pursuit of a variety of theoretical projects, 'property' is extended beyond the sphere of resource-holdings. Philosophers have for centuries advised us that we have property in our own bodies.[5] Social theorists of our day insist that welfare entitlements and jobs are in some sense 'property'.[6] The literature of modern economics includes references to 'property' wherein propertization is a function of internalizing externalities into the decisions of economic actors.[7] Is there anything, could there be anything, which constitutes an essence of propertiness underlying all these uses?

The practising lawyer is not concerned with these problems. She consults legal materials and advises her clients about property transactions. If she looks to English textbooks and manuals, she will usually find that they deal with property piecemeal—real property, personal property, intellectual property, and so forth.[8] She does not limit her advice to matters contained in textbooks which have 'property' on the title page. She may be concerned with tax planning in order to preserve as much as possible of her clients' 'property' (property as wealth) from the inroads of the revenue. Or she may be concerned with aspects of planning law which restrict the uses her client may make of his 'property' (property as things). It is not her business to speculate whether any uniting idea underlies the 'property law' in the textbooks and these other contexts in which law has a bearing on 'property'. She may occasionally come across a statute or a constitutional provision or some doctrine of case law which deploys the term 'property' dispositively—one legal consequence follows if some jural entity constitutes 'property' and another if it does not. Such questions she will settle *ad hoc*, depending on the statutory, constitutional, or doctrinal context.

For all this elusiveness of the idea of property, all of us (philosophers, lawyers, and ordinary folk) seem to share an intuitive sense of what property is. We get by in daily life with a range of conventional property talk which has no problems in 'knowing' who owns a particular book or a car or a house or a £10 note. Otherwise we could not borrow or lend or sell, or use things without consulting other people's preferences. Must we assume that there is a radical disconnection between this conventional property talk and its background

[5] See Ch. 11, sect. (ii) below.

[6] See, e.g., Charles A. Reich, 'The New Property' (1964) 73 *YLJ* 733 (discussed in Ch. 9, sect. (iii)(b) below). C. B. MacPherson, *Property: Mainstream and Critical Positions* (Basil Blackwell, 1978), chs. 1 and 12 and 'Capitalism and the Changing Concept of Property', in E. Kamenka and R. S. Neale (eds.), *Feudalism, Capitalism and Beyond* (Edward Arnold, 1975) (discussed in Ch. 9, sect. (iii)(d) below; Joseph W. Singer, 'The Reliance Interest in Property' (1988) 40 *Stan. LR* 611 (discussed in Ch. 8, sect. (ii)(b) below).

[7] See Harold Demsetz, 'Toward a Theory of Property Rights' (1967) 57 *Am. Econ. R* 347; and the literature surveyed in Yoram Barzel, *Economic Analysis of Property Rights* (CUP, 1989). Definitions of 'property' specially tailored to economic analysis are discussed in Ch. 9, sect. (iii)(a) below.

[8] For an exception, see F. H. Lawson and Bernard Rudden, *The Law of Property* (2nd edn., Clarendon Press, 1982).

assumptions, on the one hand, and the theoretical agenda of philosophy or the *adhoc*ness of legal practice, on the other?[9] Or should we adopt a position of comfortable scepticism? 'Property' means nothing in particular and those who seek to justify or condemn it, or to decry or applaud any particular distribution of it, engage in sound and fury signifying nothing.[10]

We might explain away conventional property talk as ideological myth-making, reflecting some psychological need or covert political power play. Or we might simply dismiss it as an inexplicable but uninteresting mystery. But we would have to be careful to avoid joining in. We would need to steel our-selves against taking any part in those political controversies which argue for or against distributions of property within societies or families or which advo-cate or oppose State as opposed to private ownership or which debate the justice of expropriation and compensation. We should also, if we are serious about our scepticism, police our own use of property talk to ensure that it is always tongue-in-cheek, engaged in just to placate the unenlightened and never seriously meant. These are feats beyond most property-sceptics.

Or we could recognize that, for better or for worse, there are ubiquitous institutions of a certain kind which form the background for conventional property talk. Sophisticated uses of 'property' could be seen in their light and either accommodated or left aside by appropriate stipulations. The object would be to identify the institutions so that a special sub-class of moral con-cerns, property-specific justice reasons, can be assessed and, in the light of that assessment, particular questions of distribution and of institutional design can be addressed. That is the project attempted in this book.

(iii) TERMINOLOGY

A few minor terminological points may be worth making at the outset. They concern the use of the word 'property' itself and some other associated terms.

We have said that 'property' refers to a ubiquitous human institution. We have also said that this institution is an organizing idea. This does not entail that the institution, in its entirety, or even broad features of it, are con-sciously brought to mind in daily life. On the contrary, when people's claims, desires, plans, and projects are shaped by reference to this organizing idea they typically present to themselves only the bearing of the institution upon some

---

[9] Such an assumption appears, e.g., in Bruce A. Ackerman, *Private Property and the Constitution* (Yale UP, 1977), ch. 2.

[10] That is the conclusion of Thomas C. Grey, 'The Disintegration of Property', in Pennock and Chapman (eds.), n. 1 above, 69. For effective criticism of this essay, see Munzer, n. 4 above, 31–5. Scepticism about property is also announced by Kevin Gray, 'Property in Thin Air' (1991) 50 *CLJ* 252; but in his case it is difficult to understand what it is he supposes he is sceptical about, as he offers his own definition of the essence of 'propertiness' as power to exclude.

particular resource. In concrete situations it is usually 'ownership' which is the organizing idea.[11]

There are a host of linguistic conventions for indicating that the relationship so singled out confers on a person privileges and powers, somewhere along the ownership spectrum, which are peculiar to him or her. Their grammatical forms diverge even between different European languages. In English, one may speak of 'owning', 'having', 'having got', 'possessing', 'being entitled to', 'being invested with', 'being endowed with', something; or of a thing 'belonging to' someone; or simply of its being 'his' or 'hers'.

No light is thrown on the nature or justifiability of property institutions by examining linguistic usages of this kind as such for they are all, taken in isolation, ambiguous. Every one of them may be used to designate relationships which have nothing to do with ownership interests. The verb 'to own' may be used synonymously with 'to acknowledge', as where someone 'owns' another as his leader or his king.

Personal possessive pronouns, in particular, are deployed in many non-property contexts. 'My', 'yours', 'his', or 'hers' may signify relationships which have nothing to do with owning.[12] In context, it will usually be clear enough whether such expressions are being used in a property-invocational sense or not. Even a child will not confuse the sense of 'my' as between: 'It's my ball!' and 'she's my teacher'. However, there are contexts where the ambiguity persists. If a car park attendant asks: 'Is this your car, madam?' Is he making an enquiry about ownership, or only seeking to find out who is the driver?

This ambiguity in personal possessive pronouns may be exploited for comic ends. Take the following passage from Charles Dickens's novel *Dombey & Son*:

'I beg your pardon, ma'am,' said Florence . . . 'is this Captain Cuttle's house?'
'No,' said Mrs. MacStinger. . . .
'Perhaps you can have the goodness to tell us where Captain Cuttle lives, ma'am, as he don't live here.'
'Who says he don't live here?' retorted the implacable MacStinger. 'I said it wasn't Cap'en Cuttle's house—and it ain't his house—and forbid it that it ever should be his house—for Cap'en Cuttle don't know how to keep a house—and don't deserve to have a house—it's my house—and when I let the upper floor to Cap'en Cuttle, oh, I do a thankless thing, and cast pearls before swine!'[13]

Mrs MacStinger was, of course, just being awkward. She was, nevertheless, accurately invoking a property institution, on the assumption that Captain Cuttle was a mere lodger with no open-ended set of use-privileges or control-powers over the top floor, whilst she was either the freeholder or the

[11] See Ch. 5 below.
[12] This point is made by Frank Snare, 'The Concept of Property' (1972) 9 *Am. Phil. Q* 200.
[13] Charles Dickens, *Dombey & Son* (Chapman and Hall Ltd, 1892), ii, ch. 3 (64–5).

leaseholder of the house. As we shall see, both freehold and leasehold estates carry ownership interests.[14]

Context is usually enough to make plain whether or not a property institution is being invoked. It will never be necessary, though it will usually be sufficient, to employ some such expression as 'it's my property!' It has often been remarked that English usage of the word 'property' itself has changed over the centuries. It is only since about the seventeenth century that the word 'property' has been standardly applied to the thing which is the object of an ownership interest. An older usage refers to some of the relationships between persons and resources along the ownership spectrum as 'a property in' the thing in question. Borrowing from this latter usage, we shall speak of relationships at the lower end of the spectrum as 'mere property'.

But again, little is to be gained by tracking usage of the word 'property' any more than by reflection on other, ambiguously proprietorial epithets. Etymologically, the word derives, ultimately, from the Latin *proprius*, and is correctly deployed in contexts which have nothing to do either with rights or with the things over which rights are asserted.[15] It may simply signify that a quality is 'proper to' something or, in older usage, someone. We speak of 'properties' of a gas or of a structure.

The old *Book of Common Prayer*, speaking of God, avows that his 'property is always to have mercy'. Modern versions of the communion service substitute the word 'nature' for 'property'. The story goes that a radical preacher once bemused his congregation by referring to the Church as a body 'whose nature is always to have property'.

None of these other usages of the word causes practical ambiguities. Whereas 'my' is problematic, 'my property' is clear enough. It is the least ambiguous way of asserting an ownership interest. However, the usage of the term 'property' to stand for things rather than rights over things is frequently decried. Jeremy Bentham disliked it.

It is to be observed, that in common speech, in the phrase *the object of a man's property*, the words *the object of* are commonly left out; and by an ellipsis, which, violent as it is, is now become more familiar than the phrase at length, they have made that part of it which consists of the words *a man's property* perform the office of the whole.[16]

What does it matter? One reason commonly advanced for deploring the thing-property usage is that it is often the case that several persons may have

[14] See Ch. 5, sect. (iii) below.

[15] See Kenneth Minogue 'The Conception of Property and its Contemporary Significance', in Pennock and Chapman (eds.), n. 1 above, 11–12; and Charles Donahue jr. 'The Future of the Concept of Property Predicted from its Past', *ibid*. 28, at 31.

[16] J. Bentham, *An Introduction to the Principles of Morals and Legislation* (J. H. Burns and H. L. A. Hart (eds.), Athlone Press, 1970), 211 n. 12. This much-cited comment appears in ch. xvi, Division of Offences, in which Bentham sets himself the task of dividing the whole of the law into categories of offences, each of which is to be given a distinct label. To this end, he engages in terminological stipulations.

rights simultaneously subsisting over the same object. That is certainly true. But if one of those rights (or bundle of rights) differs from the rest in that it consists of an open-ended set of use-privileges and control-powers (an owner-ship interest), it does no harm to refer to the object as that person's 'property'. Another objection, infused with the learning derived from the English law of estates in land, insists that there may be successive ownership interests in the same resource. Indeed there may be. However, the time frame of ascriptions of 'property' to the resource may none the less indicate the ownership relation which is the present subject of concern. A third objection invokes relativity of title. Yet we can speak of an object being someone's 'property', when we assert that someone has a present ownership interest in it, even when it is the case that that someone can support his claim to be the owner only against one class of disputed claimants and not against another.

It is only if ownership interests never really exist in modern law that property-thing usage ought to be seen as misleading and something whose extraordinary persistence needs to be explained away. We shall investigate various kinds of scepticism about ownership in Chapter 8. Suffice it to say for the moment that contemporary lay and legal assumptions are not sceptical about it. They take it to be axiomatic that people can own things and one way of indicating this assumption is by referring to the thing owned as 'property'.

C. B. MacPherson recognized this modern usage and made two odd claims about it. The first is that it is not likely to outlast the twentieth century.[17] As a prophecy, that seems highly implausible. We have only a few years to wait to find out whether he was right. The second is that the usage—calling things 'property'—is confined to laymen and is not shared by philosophers or lawyers.[18] Whether contemporary philosophers are always so guarded in eschewing the modern usage may be open to doubt, but certainly lawyers are not. Reported cases are replete with references to 'the property' being im-proved, or damaged, or allowed to deteriorate. Legislation similarly speaks of things as well as of rights as 'property'. Parliament has recently enacted the Property Misdescriptions Act 1991, which penalizes house agents for mis-describing things (houses and flats), not rights.

The point about legal usage is that it often deals with aspects of property institutions which are not directly concerned with the old paradigm of an ownership interest in a tangible object protected by trespassory rules. We shall investigate ideational entities and hived-off parcels of wealth-potential which come within the purview of modern property institutions.[19] In relation to such things, the word 'property' hovers between the bundle of rights in question and some reified entity of which the rights are constitutive. And does it matter? If a layman owns shares or a copyright or a broadcasting franchise and we quiz

---

[17] C. B. MacPherson, *Property: Mainstream and Critical Positions* (Basil Blackwell, 1978), 7.

[18] Ibid., 2–3.

[19] See Ch. 4 below.

him to explain whether 'property' is the totality of the rights vested in him or some abstract entity comprised of these rights, he may invite us to take our pick.

Lawyers are concerned with definitions of the word 'property' in particular contexts. A constitution may restrict the State's right to take 'property'. A statute may authorize a divorce court to reallocate 'property', or stipulate formalities for the transfer of 'property', or impose a tax on 'property'. We shall meet some of these contextual definitions later on.[20] It would, however, be foolish to attempt a universal definition of the word 'property' such that it would enable conclusions to be read off from any constitutional or statutory provision which employed the term. How could one possibly assume, in advance of contextual enquiry, that all and only that which is 'property' for the purpose of constitutional provisions is also 'property' for the purposes of divorce jurisdictions, formality rules, and revenue law? Deductions from purportedly universal definitions of the word 'property' are to be deplored.

At the same time it is possible to get a grip on the essential features of those universal institutions known as property institutions. If it were not, a vast swathe of argument, in the history of political philosophy and in everyday political controversy, would be without focus. That will be our preliminary task. We wish to identify those features of social organization to which property-specific justice reasons apply. That objective is in no way impeded if the word 'property' is applied alternatively either to rights or (when ownership interests are in question) to the object in respect of which such interests exist.

One claim may be made at this stage in defence of the modern property-thing English usage. If property institutions are justifiable at all, then one facet of moral discourse is appropriately resource-centred ('lumpy'). Social wealth, those things and services as to which there is a greater demand than there is a supply, is there to be allocated. If property institutions contribute to a just allocation, the totality of that wealth will be parcelled out, one way or another, between individuals, groups, and public agencies. Whatever the moral criteria for such parcelling, it will entail references to separated items. The separated items may be referred to as objects, resources, assets, or (tangible or intangible) 'things'. Those terms we shall employ more or less interchangeably.

It is undoubtedly true that the term 'property' is most discriminatingly employed when it refers to rights or bundles of rights, but that its usage also to refer to things (objects, assets, resources) in which ownership interests are thought to subsist is an implicit, and understandable, recognition of this essential lumpiness of property talk. For all his fussy objection to this usage, Bentham was, as we have seen, well aware that the paradigm of a property law was a trespassory rule relating to a specific thing.

'Property' is today used by lawyers and laymen alike to designate resources to which ownership interests pertain. Lawyers often, and laymen sometimes,

[20] See Ch. 4, sect. (iv) and Ch. 9, sect. (iii)(c) below.

also use the word 'property' or the phrase 'proprietary interest' to refer to rights over things, rather than to the things themselves. We take on board both usages—property as things and property as rights over things—when we speak of property institutions.

Finally, an ambivalence encountered in theoretical discussions of property institutions should be noted. When commentators make conceptual claims about 'the nature of property', they are sometimes referring to the institution as a whole and sometimes specifically to 'ownership'—an ambivalence which can lead to misplaced conceptual cavilling.[21] The twin foundations of a property institution are, as we shall argue, trespassory rules and the ownership spectrum. One of the essential pillars should not be confused with the entire edifice.

Our discussion throughout will be institution-focused. What kind of institution is a property institution? Can such institutions be justified? If so, what should they be like?

(iv) PRE-ANNOUNCED CONCLUSIONS

At the end of Part I of this book it will be suggested that, for general theoretical purposes, 'property' should be conceived of as comprising items which are either the subject of direct trespassory protection or separately assignable as parts of private wealth. More expansive definitions of 'property' fail to demarcate the subject-matter of property-specific justice reasons.

By the end of Part II we shall reach the conclusion that every citizen of a modern State has a moral background right that his or her society maintain or introduce a property institution with certain features. The right derives from a mix of property-specific justice reasons and calls for these same reasons to be taken into account in questions of distribution and property-institutional design. Some philosophic dead wood must be cut away, especially the notions of 'self-ownership' and 'personhood-constituting', and the contentions that all questions of distribution or property-institutional design can be subsumed under either 'equality of resources' or 'social convention'. The surviving property-specific justice reasons include the *prima facie* normative status of all ownership freedoms, privacy, convention-dependent conceptions of labour-desert, and pragmatic recognition of the wealth-creating potential of incentives

[21] See, e.g., Bruce A. Ackerman, *Private Property and the Constitution* (Yale UP, 1977), 99 n. 11, commenting on Frank Snare, 'The Concept of Property' (1972) 9 *Am. Phil. Q* 200. Ackerman notes Snare's claim that certain kinds of rules—punishment rules, damage rules, and liability rules—are peripheral to the concept of property. Snare is wrong, says Ackerman, because such rules are 'entirely independent' of the concept of property. In fact, what those rules are independent of is the concept of 'ownership'. Snare was seeking to analyse the concept of a property institution and to that concept, as we shall see, trespassory rules are essential.

and markets and of the contribution to political culture of independent holdings of wealth—all to be assessed in the light of the community's obligation to discharge citizens' basic needs and the pervasive danger of illegitimate domination.

The background right is historically situated. It does not have the same ahistorical status as do rights not to be subjected to unprovoked violence to the person. There are no natural rights to full-blooded ownership of the world's resources.

Good faith implementation of the moral background right may or may not achieve a threshold of justice for a property institution. If it does, the trespassory rules of the institution are, *prima facie*, morally binding. Murder, assault and rape are always moral wrongs. Theft is morally wrong only when this justice threshold is attained.

2

Imaginary Societies

(i) FOREST LAND

In Forest Land, the members of a tribe live together in a communal dwelling constructed of wood, grass, and leaves. They subsist, throughout the year, on fruits and roots which they gather from the forest which surrounds them and on such grubs, birds, and small animals as they can catch. Although any of them may pick up a stone or a stick from the abundant supply of the forest to make a kill, they have no artefactual weapons or tools. There are customary social rules about many matters, policed by informal social pressure. Many of these rules relate to how members of the tribe are to treat one another, but some concern how they are to behave in relation to the communal dwelling and to the natural environment. No one may urinate or defecate indoors. There is a rota governing obligations to carry out repairs to the dwelling. There are rules of taboo prohibiting the killing of certain sacred animals. Formal acts of adoration directed towards the sun and certain sacred trees and sites are obligatory at particular times of the year.

There is no property in Forest Land. The content of the rules includes no reference to any such idea. The rules are for the most part specific, stipulating the performance of, or refrainment from, concrete actions; but even to the extent that they embody open-textured notions—'deliberate' killing, 'reverential' obeisance, 'weather-proof' repair—these relatively abstract notions are never filled out in social interpretation by reference to any such conception as that a thing is proper to, is the peculiar province of, belongs to, a particular individual or group or to the community as a whole.

Since the Forestlanders' social arrangements employ no conception of ownership, it is apparent that they have no institution of 'private property'. What must be stressed is that no other conception of property would be of service to the tribesmen in their internal interpretation and application of their rules. A visiting anthropologist might describe the rules they have relating to treatment of the physical environment as a system of 'common property'. To make this idea intelligible to the tribesmen the anthropologist would first have to explain what 'property' is. He might tell them that in other societies there are trespassory rules protecting ownership interests, that there are things people can own and others can steal. When he said that they had 'common property', he meant that no such ownership rights or trespassory protection was part of their social conventions. The conception of private property is in this way logically prior to that of common property.

Perhaps the Forestlanders would be intrigued by the anthropologist's information. However, so long as they were happy not to change the regime they have, they could find no use for the idea of 'common property' or for that of any other conception of property in the regulation of their own affairs. Whether or not some obligatory repair had met their standard of being 'weather-proof', or whether or not some required act of obeisance had been truly 'reverential', would not turn on the interpretation of any proprietary conceptions. 'Property', for them, is simply not an organizing idea.

(ii) STATUS LAND

Status Land resembles Forest Land, except that its inter-personal and environmental rules are structured and interpreted around an organizing idea which the Forestlanders lacked. That is the notion of status. There is an established system of sexual pair-bonding. Customary rules dictate that the male partner may commit some acts of personal violence towards the female partner and towards children springing from their sexual union which otherwise would fall foul of a general prohibition upon such activities. He is, as well, subjected to positive obligations of support and maintenance peculiar to his status, and armed with a status-dependent authority. There is as well a hereditary tribal chief and a class of duly initiated priests. The chief is empowered to give directions as to the rotation of duties over maintenance of the communal dwelling and he is endowed with a unique mystical competence to provide authentic solutions to disputes. The priests control the discharge of the proper acts of obeisance towards sacred trees and sites and they are required to acquire healing skills which they must put at the service of the sick. Both chief and priests are exempted from obligations of maintenance of the communal dwelling.

The conception of status thus underpins some of the inter-personal and environmental rules of the tribe. Particular individuals who fulfil the status conceptions occupy roles—those of 'husband', 'father', 'chief', or 'priest'. Any disputed interpretation of a relevant rule is referred to these organizing ideas. But there is still no institution of property.

The visiting anthropologist may impart some curious information to the Statuslanders. In other places, he may tell them, conceptions of status and of individual roles are connected with ownership interests over material resources. In fact, he may say, there are societies in which it would be inconceivable that a person could fit a status and discharge a role if he were not the owner of material wealth of some kind. If the Statuslanders could understand him, they would be able to show that things were different with them. Status and property are, elsewhere, intimately interconnected organizing ideas but, as it happens, they have the one without the other.

The anthropologist may persist: 'Ah, but you do have a conception of property. Look at the relations between husbands and their wives and children. Now in other places, as I say, people are conferred open-ended use-privileges and powers of control over material resources which others are prohibited from stealing. That relationship to the resource is what they call "property". I note that inter-personal rules of yours prohibit everyone from committing acts of violence against women and children unless those persons are their husbands or fathers. Therefore, you must already recognize that husbands own their wives and children.'

The baffled Statuslanders might ponder on this. In so far as they could be brought to grasp what this alien institution, property in material resources, amounted to, they might concede that there was some analogy between ownership interests and marital and parental privileges. Or they might conclude that it was quite different. Ownership interests, in relation to material things, seem to postulate a base-line of: 'Do what you please with the thing', whereas their status relations had a spiritual and ethical base-line of paternalistic love and nurture. However that might be, when it came to the implementation of their status conceptions, as part of their internal social organization, they proposed to go on as before without drawing analogies between, or otherwise being influenced by, these strange notions of property to which the anthropologist had tried to draw their attention.

Status, as an organizing idea, has, in the history of the world, often been intimately connected with property. It is not logically dependent on any proprietary conception.

(iii) RED LAND

Red Land is a modern country committed to the uncompromising socialisation of all resources. Like Forest Land and Status Land, it has rules governing inter-personal relations and rules structuring labour. But of course, the latter are far more elaborate since they relate to the production and distribution of artefacts of many kinds and to the provision of a far wider range of services. Its inhabitants are frugal in their demands on material products so that, in relation to many basic needs, the society commands an abundance. All the food, clothing, and furniture that she may want may be taken at will by any citizen from communal stores, although she is prohibited from misusing these things or parting with them to others. There is no money and no system of barter or exchange.

So far as unique items are concerned—like specific dwellings or library books—there is a system of licensing and rationed use. An applicant is granted privileges of use over these things by an appropriate bureaucrat or committee on suitable terms stipulating the mode of enjoyment. These licensed privileges of use are protected by trespassory rules. During the subsistence of the licence, everyone but the licensee is prohibited from meddling with the dwelling or the library book in any way which might frustrate the licensed use. However, questions whether the terms of any licence have been infringed, or disputes about whether a trespassory rule has been broken, are not resolved by reference to any notion that, during the persistence of the licence, the item is, in any open-ended sense, 'her' house or 'his' book. Such questions and disputes are settled according to the spirit of the licence, having regard to the general goals of fraternal living. Disputes may always be resolved in favour of a 'trespasser' by a retrospective termination of the licence if the relevant committee or bureaucrat takes the view that his was the greater need.

Notwithstanding the existence of trespassory rules, there is no property institution in Red Land. No conception of 'property' is deployed in the application and interpretation of Red Land rules. No appeal is ever made to a licensee's self-seeking say-so.

Of course, since Red Land is a modern country, its inhabitants will be aware that in other places there are property institutions. They may express the distinctiveness of their system of social organization by describing it as one of 'State property' or 'collective property'. The factories, the hospitals, the farms, the mines, and the houses are 'owned' by the State, for they are not owned by anyone else. To facilitate the discharge of productive and management objectives, there may be trespassory rules delimiting the circumstances in which citizens have access to industrial machinery, hospital operating theatres, or government offices. Yet, when questions arise as to how managers or officials or citizen committees should discharge their various functions, no reference need ever be made to any notion of State ownership. There is no question of an official warding off some criticism of a decision by answering that he represents the State, the State is the owner of some resource, and therefore it, through him, is at liberty to make what decisions it pleases. All such questions are appropriately resolved by reference to the purpose for which a particular productive enterprise has been established, in fulfilment of the goals of collective living.

Red Land trespassory rules confer on licensees of dwellings and library books, and on officials discharging certain functions, what we shall call 'protected non-property holdings'. Trespassory rules are a necessary, but not a sufficient, condition for the existence of property institutions since in all such institutions open-ended ownership conceptions, of one kind or another, structure resource-use and wealth-allocation. If the notion of ownership interests had never arisen in the world, there would be no point in describing the Redlanders' rules as a system of 'State property'. So far as the internal operation of the system is concerned, they have no property institution. The conception of 'private property' is logically prior to that of 'State property' or 'collective property', as it is to that of 'common property'.

(iv) CONTRACT LAND

Contract Land is like Red Land, except that the discharge of obligations and the allocation of goods are not exclusively governed by the goals of collective living to which the citizens are committed. As a supplement, it is accepted that some duties and some allocations should be made pursuant to contracts freely entered into. As in Red Land, trespassory rules do not confer either on citizens or on officials open-ended claims over things. However, there is no literal abundance, relative to wants, of food, clothes, furniture, and so on. Such things are obtained from communal stores through bargains freely made between individuals and community representatives in exchange for services rendered to the community. Licences to occupy dwellings are obtained in the same way. There is no money.

Each contractor offers to the community some service which he or she can perform and receives in exchange defined use-privileges. Contracts may in terms allow for a contractor to re-allocate some or all of the use-privileges to others, either as a gift or by way of sub-contract, but the notion of property never intervenes. A man who is granted the use of a loaf of bread may be expressly permitted, under the terms of his contract, to eat it or allow his dependants to eat it or to exchange the privilege to do either of these things with another person for defined use-privileges over something else or for services. Where a man contracts for the use of a pair of trousers, the contractual terms may be relatively non-specific, perhaps permitting 'reasonable use'; but such open-textured terms will not, in case of dispute, be interpreted by reference to any notion of open-ended use-privileges. Like the licensees in Red Land, those who contract for dwellings will have the terms of their licences construed without benefit of open-ended possessory claims, although, unlike their Red Land counterparts, no revocation in breach of contract by the community will be permissible even if that would better promote the goals of collective living to which their society is committed. They have espoused, like Redlanders, an ideal of social co-operation which cannot tolerate private property but, unlike Redlanders, they suppose that a particular range of autonomous choice associated with contract should be preserved.

There is no property institution in Contract Land. Since it is a modern country, its citizens will know that in other places when people make contracts they often exchange money for other things which the seller owns and thereby themselves become owners. Like the Redlanders, however, they have contrived to institute a society which dispenses with ownership interests. They have done that, let us suppose, because of the evils of fetishism, wealth-disparity and domination-potential which follow in the train of private property—evils we consider in Chapter 14 of this book.

Now a philosopher may take the Contractlanders to task in the following terms: 'So long as you retain service contracts, you have not succeeded in eliminating property. Here's the proof. There have been societies in which people owned other people as slaves. That is not so in Contract Land, so you must own yourselves. If you own yourselves, you must also own all your work potential. Therefore, if you permit individuals to enter into contracts to perform services for the community, you are empowering them to transmit property (that is, part of the work potential they own) to the community. So you have a property institution.'

This extraordinary argument is, as we shall see, the common coin of a wide range of political philosophers. The Contractlanders are unlikely to be impressed. Contract is a distinct organizing idea from property. When they enter into service contracts with the community or with each other, what they are required to do depends on the terms of the contract. Interpretation of the terms is not mediated through any such notion as that the purchaser of their services has an open-ended set of legitimate demands on them analogous to the ownership of things that other societies permit.

Contract Land is an imaginary society. It requires an even greater exercise of the imagination to envisage it than do any of our other imaginary societies. In the history of the world contract, as an organizing idea, has been even more intimately connected with property than has status. Perhaps there has never been a real society which recognized the institution of contract which did not also recognize that people could own things or money. For all that, contract and property are logically distinct organizing ideas.

(v)　WOOD LAND

Wood Land society is similar to that of Forest Land, except that its population has expanded, and its members have begun to range over wider areas to collect food and to kill game and it has evolved techniques for manufacturing some types of artefacts—weapons, traps, skinning tools, and grass ropes. In addition, different kinship groups within the tribe have erected hunting lodges at a distance from the central dwelling to accommodate their members on over-night expeditions.

Individuals who make weapons, traps, tools, or ropes are recognized to have a special relationship to these objects. There are trespassory rules which impose obligations on all other members of the tribe not to take or use these objects without the permission of the manufacturer. Manufacturers are required, in some circumstances, to allow other tribe members to have free use of the objects and are forbidden from destroying or wasting them. Within these limits, the manufacturers are entitled to make any use of the things and to dictate how or when they are to be used by others. They commonly allow their objects to be used either gratuitously or in return for food, services, or bartered use of others' implements.

The hunting lodges are also the subject of trespassory rules which prohibit members of other kinship groups from entering them without the permission of the erecting group, unless permitted to do so. The lodges, once erected must not be pulled down so long as they are serviceable to any, and permission to enter must not be denied to any tribe member if that would endanger his life. Subject to these restrictions, erecting groups may use the lodges as they see fit and dictate the terms of entry to others. They frequently allow entry to out-kin tribesmen who are not *in extremis*, sometimes out of benevolence, sometimes in fulfilment of some reciprocal arrangement, and sometimes in exchange for food contributions or for services like carrying water or helping with repairs.

The institution of property exists in Wood Land in artefacts (which are the subject of individual property) and in relation to hunting lodges (which are the subject of kinship-group property). Within the parameters set by particular limitation rules, the use-privileges and control-powers exercisable over these things by the manufacturers or the erecting groups are open-ended. Should a question arise as to the rightness of some use or control over uses by others which is not covered by a limitation rule, it is settled by appeal to the relationship, protected by trespassory rules, between the manufacturer and the object, or between the erecting group and the lodge. They will have some term to express that relationship. We shall call it 'mere property'. It comprises an open-ended set of use-privileges and control-powers. However, there is no question of the individual manufacturers or the kinship-group erectors being able to transfer, *en bloc*, the privileges and powers vouchsafed to them to other individuals or groups in such a way that the transferees will step into the protection afforded by the trespassory rules. Wood Land 'mere property' is at the lower end of the ownership spectrum.

(vi) PINK LAND

Pink Land society is similar to that of Red Land, except that the licences to use scarce items are in rather different terms. Instead of being revocable at will by the authorities, they are for fixed terms—years in the case of dwellings, weeks in the case of library books—subject to forfeiture only if the dwellings or the books are seriously damaged or abandoned by the licensees. Furthermore, unlike both Red Land and Contract Land, the terms of the licences do not seek to spell out in detail the uses which may be made of the licensed things. They take this form: for the duration of the licence to an individual, the dwelling (or book) is his or hers to do with as he or she pleases, including permitting use to others, so long as it is not damaged or abandoned. It is to this open-ended relationship, rather than to the terms or purposes of the licence, that reference is made when interpreting the trespassory rules.

Brown is the licensee of a dwelling. If Jones enters Brown's garden to prevent Brown from painting his (Brown's) front door in garish colours, the answer is, straightforwardly, that it is Brown's door and his painting does not constitute serious damage or abandonment, and hence Jones had no excuse for his trespass. In Red Land, it would have been necessary to determine whether a colour scheme which was offensive to neighbours conflicted with a proper understanding of fraternal solidarity. In Contract Land, the question might be whether such activity contravened an express or implied term as to 'reasonable' use.

A similar contrast would arise if, say, Brown made use of his licensed scientific textbook exclusively as a source of quotations for his idiosyncratic poetry. In Pink Land it is taken for granted that he can do this since, for the duration of the licence, the book is his to use as he pleases. In Red Land, would such use be non-fraternal? in Contract Land, would it violate the terms of the contractual licence?

In Pink Land there is conferred on licensees both an open-ended range of uses and powers to control uses by others. Citizens may share their licensed dwellings (or books) with anyone they choose, as temporary guests or more permanent cohabitees (or co-users). Licensees commonly avail themselves of this power, sometimes out of friendship, sometimes subject to an informal understanding concerning mutual favours, sometimes as part of explicit bargains in return for services or swapped facilities with other licensees. They are not, however, empowered to substitute anyone else as licensee.

The institution of property exists, to an exiguous extent, in Pink Land as regards licensed objects. As in Wood Land, the relationship between person and thing functions as an organizing idea in the internal operation and interpretation of the rules. Again, this relationship is that of 'mere property'.

3

Minimal Structure

We shall return to the imaginary societies (described in the last chapter) from time to time in order to bring to light structural features present in property institutions and, later, as points of reference for some of the property-specific justice reasons which have been canvassed in the tradition of western political philosophy and which are part of the staple of everyday political debate. Some preliminary lessons may be derived from our move from the first four non-property societies to the fifth and sixth which exhibited property institutions, albeit in a very restricted degree. They concern scarcity, trespassory rules, and the dual functions of property institutions (use-control and wealth-allocation). We shall see what follows from this duality of function in relation to the spectrum from mere property to full-blooded ownership. We shall pass on to other elements of the minimal structure of all real-world property institutions, especially property-limitation rules, expropriation rules, appropriation rules, and title conditions.

(i) SCARCITY

The first lesson concerns the contrast between the connections of scarcity to wealth, on the one hand, and scarcity to property, on the other hand. Where there is an abundance of resources, that is, more of them available for instant use than all those seeking to exploit them may desire—as was the case with sticks and stones in Forest Land and Status Land, and food and clothing in Red Land—there is no wealth to be allocated. Such things contribute to the well-being of individuals but they are not part of social wealth as such. Social wealth comprises all those things and services regarding which distributive choices have to be made.

That does not mean that items off the list of social wealth are immune from social regulation. There were environmental rules in Forest Land, and in Red Land citizens were banned from misusing the abundant consumable goods. Such regulations and bans constitute instances of what we shall call 'property-independent prohibitions'. They were not selectively addressed to 'owners', because there were none in those societies. Only an outsider would insist on calling such prohibitions a system of 'property' law.

In real societies, there is a plenitude of sunlight and air. The modern interventionist State may be called on to take a host of environmental measures in relation to these things. These may include, as well as property-independent prohibitions, anti-pollution rules specifically addressed to owners of other resources (what we shall call 'property-limitation rules'). Further, the fostering of programmes for the production of electricity from wind-power or sunlight may have the effect of creating ownership interests over generating resources. Nevertheless, sunlight and atmospheric oxygen are not themselves part of social wealth in the sense that they must be allocated between competing claimants. (It may be otherwise with clouds whose distribution can be affected by weather-control technology.[1])

The significance of the scarcity requirement resides in this. If a particular resource is not scarce, or ceases to be scarce, allocation mechanisms do not have to be invented or kept in being. Where a resource really is abundant, it will normally be pointless to carve out parcels of exclusivity through the operation of trespassory rules (although, as we shall see, that is not true in the case of ideas transferred from the private to the public domain[2]). In that sense, it is normally a necessary condition of a resource being subjected to a property institution that it be scarce and hence an item of social wealth.

However, it is not a sufficient condition. The resource may be allocated to individual or group use through arrangements that do not employ a property institution. That was the case with the scarce chiefly and priestly services in Status Land, with commodities generally in Contract Land, and with scarce items subjected to licences in Red Land.

In real modern societies many services, which involve demands on scarce physical or human resources, are allocated without benefit of property institutions. If free hospital care is provided for citizens who need it, some agency of the society decides that the citizen is ill enough to require such care and he or she is then admitted to hospital, granted temporary use of a bed and bedding, supplied with requisite medicines and bandages, and allowed a share of the services of medical and other staff. At no point does the patient have a proprietary relation to any of these things. For even an exiguous notion of property to interpose between desire and socially approved choice, an individual's proper use of a thing must be partly mediated through a (possibly constrained, but at the same time open-ended) notion of private domain. (Of course, the agency supplying the service may itself be vested with either what we shall call a 'quasi-ownership interest',[3] or a 'protected non-property holding'.[4])

(ii) TRESPASSORY RULES

A second lesson to be drawn from the moves between our imaginary societies is that trespassory rules, like scarcity, are a necessary but not sufficient

[1] See 'Who Owns the Clouds?' (anonymous note) (1948) 1 *Stan. LR* 43.
[2] See Ch. 4, sect. (i) below.   [3] See Ch. 7, sect. (iii)(b) below.
[4] See Ch. 7, sect. (v) below.

condition for property. If it is accepted within a society that people should have private domains over any things, like the artefacts and hunting lodges in Wood Land, then such acceptance must necessarily be manifested through trespassory rules. Nothing could be owned if nothing could be stolen (or otherwise wrongfully interfered with). The term 'trespassory rules' is used here stipulatively and in a very wide sense. It encompasses all rules which, by reference to a resource, impose obligations (negative or positive) upon an open-ended range of persons, there being excepted some privileged individual, group, or agency. Rules of this kind may be enforced only by informal social pressure, or by legal sanctions (civil or criminal). The simplest kind of trespassory rules impose negative obligations on all the world save a privileged possessor or possessors. The most venerable example is 'Thou shalt not steal'. Recall also Bentham's paradigm: '"Let no one, Rusticus excepted", (so we will call the proprietor) "and those whom he allows meddle with such or such a field."'[5]

Ownership interests may be protected by civil or criminal trespassory rules, or by both. Civil protection may be afforded by granting to owners rights to sue for damages or for injunctive relief or to claim restitution should the trespasser have gained possession. In modern English law, for example, ownership of chattels is protected both by rules of the law of tort[6] and by prohibition of theft[7] and criminal damage.[8] Estates in land (carrying ownership interests) are protected by the right to recover possession which derives from the old law of ejectment. Further civil protection of ownership interests in land is provided by the torts of trespass and nuisance and criminal protection by the offences of criminal damage and burglary and the criminal prohibition of eviction of residential occupiers.[9] When in *Donoghue* v. *Stevenson*[10] Lord Atkin laid the foundations for the modern tort of negligence in English law, he announced a generalized duty not to cause foreseeable injury 'to the consumer's life or property'.[11]

All the foregoing examples presuppose ownership interests in things as the object of protection. As we shall see, such interests range, especially in the case of land, along a spectrum from mere property to full-blooded ownership. The category of obligors covered by trespassory rules is always open-ended, but need not be limitless. They may not include good-faith purchasers. There are many other variants of trespassory rules to which reference will be made in the next chapter, such as those protecting non-ownership proprietary interests over tangible things, and those creating ownership interests in ideational entities.

Nevertheless, as the imaginary Red Land example reveals, there could, in theory, be trespassory rules and yet no property institution. (As we shall see,

---

[5] Jeremy Bentham, *Of Laws in General* (Athlone Press, 1970), 177.
[6] Now contained in the Torts (Interference with Goods) Act 1977.
[7] Theft Act 1968.   [8] Criminal Damage Act 1971.
[9] Criminal Law Act 1977, Pt. 2.   [10] [1932] AC 562.
[11] *Ibid*. 599.

instances of 'protected non-property holdings' may occur even in real societies.[12]) Red Land licensees were protected by trespassory rules, and there were
trespassory rules restricting access to factories, hospitals, and government
offices. However, what amounted to a trespass was not dependent on any
notion of the thing belonging, even temporarily, to a licensee or on any notion
of the State 'owning' the communal assets. No such notions entered into disputed questions about what licensees or State officials might properly do. The
internal application and interpretation of the society's rules and principles for
fraternal collective living made no reference to ownership relations, for there
were none in Red Land. Only an outsider would insist that its trespassory rules
constitute a system of 'property' law.

The idea of a proprietary relationship entailing an open-ended set of use-
privileges and control-powers, that is, some version of an ownership interest,
is a separate and indispensable element of a property institution.

(iii) PRIVILEGED USE AND WEALTH-ALLOCATION

Perhaps the most important moral to be drawn from our imaginary societies
concerns the dual functions of the institution of property, as governing both
the use of things and the allocation of items of social wealth. Much that is
controversial about the institution arises from this duality of function. If the
maker of a tool, in Wood Land, or the licensee of a dwelling, in Pink Land, is
free, within limits, to use the tool or the dwelling as he pleases on the basis
that it is 'his', the same positive relation also gives him a (limited) power of
wealth-allocation *vis-à-vis* his fellows.

The Wood Land tool is a scarce object, that is, it is a member of a class of
objects as to which the totality of use-demands exceeds the supply. It is thus
an item of social wealth. The social rules which allocate open-ended use-
privileges to its maker also empower him to make concrete allocations of use
to others. This power invests him as an agent of wealth-distribution. An item
of social wealth is also part of his private wealth. Furthermore, this allocative
power makes his own use-privileges into mutable wealth. Instead of allowing
others to use the tool for reasons of benevolence or whim, he may trade use-
privileges for other scarce things or services. If his tool is sufficiently scarce
and sufficiently valued by others, he may even become a modest accumulator
of private wealth. As the sole disposer of a wondrous cooking pot, he might
gain unlimited access to the humbler artefacts of others, get all his food-
gathering and preparation done for him, and trade pot-use for exemption from
communal labour.

So, too, with the Pink Land dwelling-licensee. We have assumed that dwellings in Pink Land are unique. Of course, if there were an abundance of

[12] See Ch. 7, sect. (v) below.

indistinguishable dwellings, they would be off the agenda of wealth and property. But a dwelling must at least be locationally unique, and we have assumed that demand for the use of any particular dwelling exceeds supply so that the licensing system was necessary. The Pink Land licensee, for the duration of the licence and within limits, is free to use the place as he will. This entails that he may permit dependants, cohabitees, guests, and lodgers some use of it. He thus becomes the agent for the allocation of some portions of social wealth. His mere-property interest confers on him some power to affect the lives of others. If he trades exercises of his powers for other scarce services or things, his bundle of privileges and powers is partly transformed into mutable and/or accumulatable private wealth—although the absence of a medium of exchange and of any power to make outright transfers of his licence sets severe limits to this process.

Thus, even mere-property interests exhibit the dual functions of use-control and wealth-allocation. With ownership interests higher up the spectrum, and even more when institutional mechanisms are devised for hiving off wealth-potential, the latter function assumes increasing significance.

(iv) HALF PROPERTY

Property institutions are imaginatively dispensable, as the Forest Land, Status Land, Red Land, and Contract Land examples show.[13] Can we invent a social setting which displays a 'half-property' institution? That would be one in which privileged use is distributed, via trespassory rules, according to a possessive relationship between persons and things, but the relationship would carry no wealth allocation potential. We shall see that in real-world property institutions use-privileges, on the one hand, and mutable and accumulatable wealth, on the other hand, are very commonly separated and vested in different persons. The shareholders in a public company or the beneficiaries under a large trust have private wealth—cashable claims on scarce resources—without necessarily having any substantial use-privileges over the items vested in the company or the trustees. The wealth-potential of property may be hived off.[14] Our present question is whether we can imagine an institution of half-property where there would be no such hiveable element.

Surely we can. The social rules of Wood Land/2 would permit a tool-maker exclusive use of what he had made, but ban him from ever permitting another the use of it. The Pink Land/2 licences would stipulate that the licensee may do anything he pleases in or to the dwelling for the duration of the licence but on pain of forfeiture if he ever allowed a co-resident to cross his threshold. Or perhaps Wood Land/3 rules would permit the tool-maker to grant gratuitous

---

[13] See also William Morris's *Nowhere* discussed in Ch. 18 below.
[14] See Ch. 4, sect. (ii) below.

concessions of use to others, and only bargaining or reciprocal understandings involving such concessions would be beyond the pale. Perhaps Pink Land/3 licensees would be able to take lodgers if they wished, but on pain of forfeiture if there was any arrangement whereby the lodger did the washing up.

Something approaching Pink Land/2 licences are not unknown in real systems. The interest created by an English statute (the Matrimonial Homes Act 1967) has been so understood. The House of Lords had issued a controversial common law ruling: although a wife by virtue of her status had a right to remain in occupation of a matrimonial home owned by her husband as against him, that right ought not to be regarded as binding on any purchaser from him and so ought not to be admitted into the category of property rights.[15] Parliament reversed that ruling by enacting the 1967 Act. The Act enabled spouses to register occupation rights. Once registered, such rights bind purchasers. In *Wroth* v. *Tyler*,[16] Megarry J analysed the nature of the right so created. He concluded that, although a spouse's occupation right would be protected against successors, she was given no affirmative control over who else should live in the dwelling. She herself could not be turned out, but she could not insist that other members of her family be allowed to continue to reside with her.

It is common enough for tenancy agreements to contain specific prohibitions on sub-letting parts of the demised premises or against taking lodgers. Such prohibitions are needed precisely because, in their absence, the ownership interest conferred by a tenancy includes open-ended powers of control as well as open-ended use-privileges. The unusual features of the right analysed in *Wroth* v. *Tyler* is that, in its nature and without specific limitation, it did not carry any such powers. If there had ever been an institution in which all resources allocated to individual use involved rights of this kind—a person might use the resource as he liked but not allow use to another—the institution would differ from typical property institutions in that it would be performing only one of the dual functions of such typical institutions. It would regulate use without allocating social wealth as private wealth. For that reason, it may be called a half-property institution.

(v) MERE PROPERTY

A half-property system of this kind is imaginable, but it would be just that, a 'half-property' system. The idea of property comprises the notion that something that pertains to a person is, maybe within drastic limits, his to use as he pleases and therefore his to permit others to use gratuitously or for exchanged favours. That is all that is entailed by what is here called 'mere property'. It

[15] *National Provincial Bank Ltd.* v. *Ainsworth* [1965] AC 1175.
[16] [1974] Ch. 30.

embraces some open-ended set of use-privileges and some open-ended set of powers of control over uses made by others. The former, without the latter, amounts to half property. If there were any societies in which mere property was never afforded to any individual or group over anything, they would lack even the minimal form of a property institution.

This conclusion is fully compatible with the truth to which we have already alluded—that property institutions diverge enormously in the range of elements they comprise.[17] This divergence encompasses, as well as variable limits on uses, varieties of restrictions on transmissibility. The sorts of property we imagined in Wood Land and Pink Land entailed nothing approaching free transmissibility. It was not supposed that the Wood Land tool-maker could exchange the tool itself for services or things, only temporary concessions as to its use. The Pink Land licensees had no power to transmit their licences as a total bundle of rights to others, either *inter vivos* or on death. They enjoyed merely the power to give away or exchange privileges abstracted from the bundle, that being inherent in the notion that, for the duration of the licence, the dwellings were theirs. Wealth accumulation would obviously be greatly inhibited in either society in any case by the absence of a monetary exchange medium. All that Wood Land tool-makers and Pink Land licensees have is an exiguous proprietary relationship to their things, but that is enough to make them minuscule agents for wealth-allocation and minuscule potential wealth-accumulators, as well as recipients of open-ended use-privileges over parts of social wealth.

(vi) FULL-BLOODED OWNERSHIP

The position of the Wood Land artefact-makers and the Pink Land licensees is a million miles removed from that of the typical owner in modern societies. At the upper end of the ownership spectrum stands a relationship between a person and some resource such that the rules of the property institution are premised on the assumption that, *prima facie*, the person is entirely free to do what he will with his own, whether by way of use, abuse, or transfer. We shall call this paradigm 'full-blooded ownership'.

The premise gives rise to a *prima facie* presumption only. Rules of all legal systems include what we shall call 'property-limitation rules' and 'expropriation rules' whereby ownership privileges and powers may be curtailed or taken away. The presence of such rules does not contradict the possibility of full-blooded ownership.[18] On the contrary, they may presuppose it—although they may also presuppose ownership interests lower on the ownership spectrum.

Writers on the subject of property frequently cite the following passage from

---

[17] See Ch. 1, sect. (i) above.
[18] For the contrary view, see Ch. 14, sect. (i)(a) below.

the beginning of book 2 of Blackstone's *Commentaries*, and then go on to point out its inadequacies in view of the many restrictions on property rights to be found in modern societies:

There is nothing which so generally strikes the imagination and engages the affections of mankind, as the right of property; or that sole and despotic dominion which one man claims and exercises over the external things of the world, in total exclusion of the right of any other individual in the universe.[19]

Yet, as Frederick Whelan has shown,[20] the *Commentaries* are replete with examples in which the law imposes limitations on what owners may do, rights of use availing against owners, and instances in which property is subject to forfeiture or escheat. Blackstone, the lawyer, was perfectly familiar with property-limitation and expropriation rules. Blackstone, the legal philosopher, summarizes the political culture which he considered owed its legitimacy to conventional acceptance of the common law, by speaking of the 'absolute' right to property 'inherent in every Englishman'. But this absolute right 'consists in the free use, enjoyment, and disposal of all his acquisitions, without any control or diminution, save only by the laws of the land'.[21]

Full-blooded ownership of things entails a relationship between a person (or persons) and a thing such that he (or they) have, *prima facie*, unlimited privileges of use or abuse over the thing, and, *prima facie*, unlimited powers of control and transmission, so far as such use or exercise of power does not infringe some property-independent prohibition. This definition refers only to privileges and powers. It is common for juristic expositions to include claim-rights and duties within the concept of ownership. As we shall argue in Chapter 8—where the even commoner onslaught on the very idea of person–thing relations is addressed—claim-rights and duties are conferred or imposed by rules which presuppose ownership interests and are not, analytically, integral to ownership conceptions.

Full-blooded ownership is the other end of a spectrum from the mere property enjoyed by Wood Land tool-makers and Pink Land licensees. The upper end of the spectrum encompasses more use-privileges than do stages lower down. As to use-privileges, the gradation is uninterrupted. However, the wider powers inherent in ownership as one moves up the spectrum pass a significant point of discontinuity where transmission of the owner's entire bundle of privileges and powers becomes permissible. He who has mere property can exchange particular uses for favours and in that sense 'exploit' his powers. A vastly more important exploitation potential is available to the individual who can trade the thing he owns.

---

[19] Sir William Blackstone, *Commentaries on the Laws of England* (16th edn., J. Butterworth and Son, 1825), Book 2, 1.
[20] Frederick H. Whelan, 'Property as Artifice: Hume and Blackstone', in J. Rowland Pennock and John W. Chapman (eds.), *Property: Nomos XXII* (NYUP 1980), 101 at 114–25.　　　　　　　　　　　　　　　　　　　　　　　[21] *Commentaries*, Book 1, 138.

Any ownership interest entails some power over the lives of others. That power is immeasurably increased when, as an attribute of his ownership, a person may substitute another as the beneficiary of the range of trespassory protection he enjoys. Powers of exchange, sale, and *inter vivos* gift and, finally, testamentary freedom may be severally or collectively attributes of different ownership interests. Unrestricted testamentary freedom, for example, was largely unknown to medieval common law.[22]

As we shall see in the next chapter, the ownership spectrum has been applied, within modern property institutions, to ideas (intellectual property), to money, and to cashable rights. In the case of money, the use-privileges and powers of control inherent in full-blooded ownership are insignificant compared with the powers of transmission inherent in that relationship; and, in the case of cashable rights, power of transmission is the only element of the ownership bundle which applies.

Ownership interests, at any point on the spectrum, entail both open-endedness and permitted self-seeking. One cannot produce a definitive catalogue of the uses that a person may make of a thing, or of the control-powers he may exercise in respect of it, if his relation to it consists of an ownership interest rather than some non-ownership proprietary interest. He may also, within the terms of the relevant property institution, defend any use or exercise of power by pointing out that, as owner, he was at liberty to suit himself. Authorized self-seekingness is a feature of an ownership interest.

Some things are not the subject of proprietary rights at all, there being no trespassory rules relating to them—like the oxygen in the air and the light of the sun. To them the term 'common property' is sometimes applied.[23] Other things are subjected to trespassory rules, but without self-seeking ownership interests being conferred on individuals or groups. (This is, as we shall see in Chapter 7, the case with State or public property where 'quasi-ownership' interests are vested in agencies discharging public functions; or where, exceptionally, 'protected non-property holdings' place resources altogether beyond the domain of property.)

Where ownership interests do exist, the outer boundary of the control-powers entailed by them is reciprocally related to the trespassory rules which protect them. Taking photographs of an attractive residence may constitute no civil wrong against its owner, if the prevailing conception of ownership includes no power directly to control that particular use of it. If a society's conception of ownership encompassed no power of testation, persons who took over a deceased's assets would commit no wrong merely because it was known that the deceased had not wished them to succeed him.

Ownership interests in some kinds of resources come low down on the ownership spectrum because most uses of the resource are not banned to

[22] See George W. Keeton and L. C. B. Gower, 'Freedom of Testation in English Law' (1935) 20 *Iowa LR* 326.   [23] See Ch. 7, sect. (iv) below.

others. Provided, however, that an open-ended set of use-privileges and control-powers is reserved by some degree of trespassory protection, there is still an 'owner'. The English Court of Appeal has ruled that, although the private owner of a road dedicated as a highway could not interfere with the rights of members of the public to pass and repass, he was entitled to an injunction to prevent a racing tout from walking up and down the road to make notes about race horses being trained on the plaintiff's adjoining land.[24]

[T]he soil of the highway belonging to the plaintiff he has a right to ask for what purpose the defendant entered on to it, whether for the purpose of using it in the ordinary and reasonable way in which a highway may be used or for the purpose of doing that which amounted to an interference with the plaintiff's legal use of his own land.[25]

So far as the content of the relevant protective trespassory rules is fixed, the perimeter of ownership control-powers is established. (It will often be that both are contested, when the property-specific justice reasons supporting the ownership interest have to be weighed against other values, a matter to which we return when discussing ownership as a principle.[26]) Within that perimeter, ownership serves as an irreducible organizing idea.[27] Where trespassory protection runs out, the owner cannot dictate uses. Within the compass of that protection, his use-privileges and control-powers are inferred, not from the content of the trespassory rules, but from the prevailing conception of the ownership interest itself, anywhere along the spectrum from mere property to full-blooded ownership. Property-limitation rules and expropriation rules impinge upon this situation.

(vii) PROPERTY-INDEPENDENT PROHIBITIONS

Ownership, at its fullest, does not entail even *prima facie* privileges or powers to act in ways which contravene prohibitions whose addressees are not specifically designated as owners. If deliberate homicide is prohibited, it would never be even a *prima facie* defence that the murderer was using his own dagger. If incitement is an offence, it is nothing to the purpose whether or not an accused hired a criminal with his own money. If deliberate deceit is banned as a means of inducing binding contracts, it is no kind of answer for the fraudster to protest that the deceptions were inscribed on his own note paper.

Such prohibitions are not limitations on property. Their impact does not depend on whether someone is an owner or not.[28] They merely exhibit the

---

[24] *Hickman* v. *Maisey* [1900] 1 QB 752.   [25] *Ibid.* 759, *per* Romer LJ.
[26] See Ch. 6, sect. (i) below.   [27] See Ch. 5, sect. (i) below.
[28] A similar point is made by Fitzgerald, Nozick, and Waldron—see P. J. Fitzgerald (ed.), *Salmond on Jurisprudence* (12th edn., Sweet and Maxwell, 1966), 249; Robert Nozick, *Anarchy, State and Utopia* (Blackwell, 1974), 171; Jeremy Waldron, *The Right to*

obvious point that human relations are governed by institutions other than property, such as criminal law and contract.

An anthropologist visiting Forest Land might wish to make a tally of its universalized social rules. He might decide to draw a line between those rules which prescribe how members of the tribe are to behave towards one another and those which prescribe how they are to deal with features of the environment (the communal dwelling, sacred sites, and so on). Perhaps he might choose to call the latter 'property' rules. There would be nothing amiss in adopting such a label, provided the anthropologist was careful to avoid its alien implications. For the tribesmen themselves, no feature of the external world is 'proper to' any individual or group, there being no trespassory rules. If they go in for rule-categorizations of any kind, such classifications cannot make use of the foreign conception. For them, both the terms 'property-limitation rules' and 'property-independent prohibitions' would be unintelligible. We employ them and distinguish them because in real societies both are present.

(viii) PROPERTY-LIMITATION RULES

We have argued that 'trespassory rules', in the wide sense we have stipulated for that expression, are a necessary, but not a sufficient, requirement of property institutions. They are the only kind of rules which are tied, conceptually, to the idea of a property institution. Yet property institutions also typically comprise, as part of their minimal structure, other varieties of property rules, for which we shall employ the labels 'property-limitation rules', 'expropriation rules', and 'appropriation rules'. Even in our imaginary Wood Land and Pink Land societies, where only mere-property interests were recognized, there were rules limiting or providing for the forfeiture of ownership interests.

Property-limitation rules and expropriation rules are not strictly necessary requirements of property institutions. One could have a version of a property institution in which owners were literally free to do anything they liked to or with their things and where their neighbours must just watch out for themselves, and where there was no power in others or in the State to strip them of their ownership interests. They would simply be subject to obligations flowing from property-independent prohibitions which apply to everyone. However, no such system exists today and probably none ever did.[29] Although their content and scope varies in time and place, we may say that any property

---

Private Property (Clarendon Press, 1988), 32–3. None of these authors draws attention to the theoretical and practical implications of the distinction between property-limitation rules and property-independent prohibitions mentioned in sect. (xiii) of this Chapter.

[29] For property-limitation rules and expropriation rules in Roman law, see W. W. Buckland and Arnold D. McNair, *Roman Law and Common Law* (2nd edn. revised by F. H. Lawson, CUP, 1952), 94–6; Peter Birks, 'The Roman Law Concept of Dominium and the Idea of Absolute Ownership' (1986) *Acta Juridica* 1 at 12–13, 16–19.

institution must, in practice, comprise property-limitation rules and expropriation rules as well as trespassory rules. Appropriation rules must also have been
present in any society which recognized something approaching full-blooded
ownership in any assets, to counteract disorderly scrambles to secure control
of things which had become ownerless; and appropriation rules will be
indispensable to any community which purports to discharge an obligation to
meet the basic needs of citizens by conferring on them ownership interests in
money or other resources.[30] ('Property-duty rules' and 'property-privilege
rules' bulked large in feudal societies, but, as we shall see, constitute an eccentric anachronism in the modern world.)

An important feature of all complex property institutions resides in property-
specific limitation rules whereby *prima facie* normative claims founded on the
prevailing ownership conception are overridden. Property-limitation rules,
unlike property-independent prohibitions, are premised on the assumption that,
but for the restrictions they contain, the owner would be free to act in a certain
way. Some positive or negative mode of using a thing which would otherwise be
privileged to X by virtue of his ownership interest in it is negated by the
imposition of a corresponding negative or positive duty, enforceable by civil or
criminal sanctions or by both. Or the exercise of some power, otherwise inherent
in ownership, is qualified or curtailed.

In common law systems, a landowner's use-privileges are limited by the tort
of nuisance. He is, *prima facie*, entitled to do what he likes on and with his
own land, but not if that would cause unacceptable harm to his neighbours—
sic utere tuo ut alienum non laedas. Successful invocation of this maxim
requires a plaintiff to show 'not only that he has sustained damage, but that the
Defendant has caused it by going beyond what is necessary in order to enable
him to have the natural use of his own land'.[31] 'The effect is that, if the user is
reasonable, the defendant will not be liable for consequent harm to his neighbour's enjoyment of his land.'[32]

The special rule known as the rule in *Rylands* v. *Fletcher* makes a landowner liable to his neighbour even for an isolated escape of noxious substances: 'the person who for his own purposes brings on his land and collects and
keeps there anything likely to do mischief if it escapes must keep it at his
peril'.[33] In civil law systems, there is a generalized idea of 'abuse of rights'.
One has rights, *qua* owner, but anti-social exercise of them is not allowed.[34]

[30] See Ch. 15, sect. (ii)(b) below.
[31] *West Cumberland Iron and Steel Company* v. *Kenyon* [1879] 11 Ch. D 782 at 787,
per Brett LJ.
[32] *Cambridge Water Co.* v. *Eastern Counties Leather Plc.* [1994] 2 AC 264 at 299, *per*
Lord Goff.
[33] [1866] Exch. 265 at 279, *per* Blackburn J.
[34] H. C. Gutteridge, 'Abuse of Rights' (1933–5) 5 *CLJ* 22. F. H. Lawson, *Negligence in
the Civil Law* (Clarendon Press, 1950), ch. 12. It is uncertain to what extent such a
doctrine was known to Roman law—see Buckland and McNair, n. 29 above, 96–9.

Such rules are not property-independent prohibitions because the measure of the wrongfulness of the conduct they proscribe is allegedly harmful exercise of ownership privileges or powers. The defendant to a common law action for the tort of private nuisance, for example, is either an occupier of land who is claimed to have acted as occupying owners ought not to act, or else some other party who, for one reason or another, is said to be responsible for just such an excess.[35] (We shall see that ownership interests of varying magnitudes are incidents of legal estates in land.[36]) In contrast, if X sticks a knife in Y neither X's culpability nor the appropriate sentence for his crime implicates any question about what it is fit for owners to do with their possessions.

In modern States, environmental conservation rules impose drastic limits on ownership privileges and powers. In English law, no substantial change of use ('development') is permitted without planning permission from a public authority.[37] Ownership use-privileges are overridden where there is a public interest in conservation.[38] Public regulation has superimposed restraints on deleterious uses going well beyond those flowing from the common law of nuisance.[39]

The English legal conception of ownership evolved to encompass a power of free testation over the entirety of a person's wealth, in contrast to most civil law systems where ownership does not comprise such freedom in respect of that which is the heir's *legitima portio*. However, since the enactment of the Inheritance (Family Provision) Act 1938, this power has been liable to be overridden where, in the view of a court, a deceased has made inadequate provision for certain dependants.[40]

Ownership in all modern systems comprises powers to make contracts governing the use or transmission of property. But everywhere some limitations are imposed on the exercise of such powers, for example, by denying them to minors or to those suffering from mental disability. During this century, radical restrictions have been imposed on ownership-transmission freedoms to curtail the development of excessive monopolies over industrial enterprises. Occasionally, the exercise of ownership powers to contract is made obligatory, thus removing the option not to exercise them from the owner's control-powers, as when owners of enterprises which make services available to the public are required to enter into legal relations with anyone who wishes to avail himself of the service.[41]

---

[35] *Harris* v. *James* (1876) 45 LJQB 545 (landlord liable for tenant's lime-burning where land let expressly for that purpose). *Mint* v. *Good* [1951] 1 KB 517 (landlord liable for nuisance caused by ill repair of wall where responsibility for repairs lay on landlord).

[36] See Ch. 5, sect. (iii) below.   [37] Town and Country Planning Act 1990.

[38] Planning (Listed Buildings and Conservation Areas) Act 1990.

[39] Planning (Hazardous Substances) Act 1990, Environment Act 1995.

[40] The jurisdiction is now contained in the Inheritance (Provision for Family and Dependants) Act 1975 as amended. See Ch. 11, sect. (iv)(c) and Ch. 14, sect. (i)(b)(1) below.

[41] If the rights and duties arising from such an obligatory exercise of power are set out in detail in statute law, a court may rule that the relationship is not contractual, but purely statutory, in character—*Norweb Plc* v. *Dixon* [1995] 3 All ER 952 (DC).

There would be no property-limitation rules in our imaginary propertyless societies, although there could be many property-independent prohibitions. Thus Red Land and Contract Land could have speed-limit rules, or rules banning dangerous driving or forbidding anyone to drive who had not passed an appropriate test. But there could be no rules requiring 'owners' of vehicles to take steps to ensure that they were roadworthy, since there were no owners in those societies.

Property-limitation rules differ from property-independent prohibitions either in that they are specifically addressed to persons with ownership interests, or in that the standard of wrongdoing assumes that, but for the rule, someone would, as owner, be entitled to use a resource in the way proscribed. All property-limitation rules presuppose ownership interests.

(ix) PROPERTY-DUTY RULES AND PROPERTY-PRIVILEGE RULES

Ownership is commonly said to carry obligations. In our foregoing description of property-limitation rules, we have encompassed within the one category both rules which remove privileges and powers from the prevailing conception of ownership by imposing negative restraints, and those which have the same effect by positively requiring the owner to use his assets or exercise his powers in a particular way. The latter variant, those which impose property-specific positive obligations, may be treated as a distinct category of property-duty rules. Nothing crucial to the understanding of the structure of property institutions turns on this. Either way, such rules presuppose ownership interests somewhere along the ownership spectrum.

Nevertheless, in what follows rules restraining ownership freedoms, whether by the imposition of negative or positive obligations, will be referred to as 'property-limitation rules'. The reason is that, in practice, separation would be arbitrary. The law of nuisance or the rule in *Rylands* v. *Fletcher*, for example, may be viewed either as denying to the owner some use which, but for legal restraints, he would be permitted to make of his land, or as positively requiring him to use the land in a way which does not harm his neighbour. Property-limitation rules, of either variant, are focused on the relationship entailed in the ownership interest between a person and a resource. The criminal law imposes duties upon factory owners to fence dangerous machinery. Under our stipulation, this is a property-limitation rule. Its effect is to deprive owners of a power of control (to decide whether or not safety guards should be installed), which was, *prima facie*, inherent in their ownership interests. It would be implausible to understand the rule to be based on the assumption that, as owners, they had no say-so over this matter in the first place.

There can, however, be property-duty rules which would not be instances of property-limitation rules as we have defined them. Obligations could be imposed on owners of assets as such which had nothing to do with the exercise of any ownership privileges or powers over the asset in question. Such were a characteristic of feudal law. Someone with a limited ownership interest in land deriving from his position within the feudal hierarchy might, as holder of such an interest, be required to perform personal services of various kinds to his superior lord not directly connected with the use of the land over which his limited ownership interest subsisted. There was a time when only persons vested with property holdings were required to perform jury service. Even today, vestiges of the ideology of high Toryism can be encountered, whereby social rules impose obligations on the wealthy to undertake public service. That the rich have personal moral obligations to the less fortunate, though uncrystallized in the form of social rules, has always been an aspirational feature of critical morality.

Property-privilege rules have also, in various social contexts, played an important legal and social role. They, too, presuppose ownership interests. They were also part of feudal law. Until the latter part of the nineteenth century, voting rights were property-based. In modern life, the idea that anyone, because he owns property, has preferential privileges unconnected with the use-privileges and control-powers inherent in his ownership interests is, to say the least, uncongenial.

Property-duty and property-privilege rules, as distinct from property-limitation rules, play an insignificant role in modern property institutions. Everyone is prohibited from doing certain things to or with animals or cars—property-independent prohibitions. Owners of certain dangerous or diseased animals, or owners of cars, are required to take certain steps which limit their ownership freedoms in relation to these things—property-limitation rules. It would be a strange proposal to suggest that owners of dogs (or of cars), and no-one else, should be required to undertake military service or should be given privileged access to higher education.

(x) EXPROPRIATION RULES

Another set of rules which presuppose ownership interests are those whereby part or all of the privileges and powers constituting a person's ownership of something may be stripped from him against his will. In the private law of most systems, what a person owns may be taken away from him as a means of enforcing payment of his debts in processes of civil execution or bankruptcy. Rules of criminal law invariably provide for sanctions by way of fines or confiscation. (Confiscation of the proceeds of crime has, in English law, recently been elevated to the status of a major weapon in the armoury of the criminal justice system in the context of drug trafficking and other large-scale criminal activity.[42]) Modern systems of family law empower courts to take ownership interests from one spouse and to vest them in another or to require financial or other provision for dependants.[43] By virtue of the development over the last century and a half of the doctrine of proprietary estoppel, common law systems have evolved an equitable jurisdiction whereby courts can wholly or partly divest owners of property in favour of those who have relied on expectations created by the owner's conduct.[44] (Exercises of judicial discretion under these family law provisions or by virtue of proprietary estoppel implicate explicit invocation of property-specific justice reasons and will be referred to in appropriate contexts in Part II of this book.) Most significantly of all, the governments of modern States have asserted the power, enshrined in law, to tax money and other property-holdings owned by citizens, and to purchase property-holdings compulsorily.

The functions served by these various types of rules are, of course, extremely diverse. We shall refer to them collectively as 'expropriation rules' because they have in common the assumption that divestable ownership interests exist in things (tangible or ideational) or in money or in cashable rights.

Needless to say, the label 'expropriation' is meant to carry no derogatory flavour. If property institutions are justifiable at all, then at least some of the rules whereby what a person owns may be taken from him against his will are justified. As we shall see, justice has inevitable costs.[45] At this stage we make only the point that this very significant category of rules, like property-limitation rules, is, analytically, an outwork from the core conceptions of the ownership spectrum and trespassory rules.

(xi) APPROPRIATION RULES

Another category of rules which presupposes ownership interests consists of those rules which confer such interests over resources on individuals or groups. We shall call these 'appropriation rules'. They may constitute no more than the counterpart of expropriation rules, as in the case of the family law rules referred to above which empower courts to take property from one person and give it to another on divorce or death; or those rules which govern the circumstances in which a person loses ownership of a chattel and another gains it by virtue of its becoming a fixture annexed to land or an accession to another's chattel, or where it loses its identity by virtue of being processed into the creation of a new chattel. In such cases the same rule may be looked on indifferently as an appropriation or an expropriation rule. The former label

---

[42] Drug Trafficking Act 1994; Criminal Justice Act 1988, Part VI; Proceeds of Crime Act 1995.
[43] See Ch. 11, sect. (iv)(c) and Ch. 15, sect. (ii)(c) below.
[44] See Ch. 14, sect. (i)(b)(1) below.   [45] See Ch. 15, sect. (i) below.

may seem preferable where the social purpose of the rule is taken to be exclusively the advancement of the welfare of the person who receives the ownership interest, as where tenants of dwellings are given enforceable powers to purchase long leases or freeholds from their landlords.

Other kinds of appropriation rules govern assets which, but for their impact, would be ownerless. The most obvious example of the latter are rules of succession to the property of deceased persons who have either died intestate or who, as to the asset in question, have no power of testation. They include also rules governing initial conditions of title, such as those which confer ownership on finders in some circumstances, or the ancient common law rule which accords ownership over treasure trove to the Crown.

In modern States, appropriation rules are among the devices employed to discharge the community's responsibility to meet the basic needs of citizens. Such needs may be catered for without ownership interests of any kind being conferred. But alternatively, as we shall see, they may be met by according mere property interest in dwellings or by payments of money.[46]

(xii) TITLE CONDITIONS

'Title', as a term of art, refers to the conditions, within a particular property institution, which must be satisfied before a person can slot into the protection of its trespassory rules. In Wood Land, the creation by a tool-maker was the condition which triggered the protection of his 'mere property' in the tool. In Pink Land, it was the grant of a licence over a dwelling or a library book. Once ownership powers come to include free transferability, *inter vivos* or on death, the fact that some transactions have taken place appears among conditions of title. In the interests of determinacy and public order, a property institution may designate as sufficient conditions of title long possession of something over which an ownership interest is claimed or long user as to a non-ownership proprietary interest. In modern law, systems of public registration are employed as the appropriate conditions of title for some property interests in land and ideas. If . . . is true of X, then X is entitled to the protection of the property institution's rules in relation to ownership over a *res* (a tangible or ideational thing or a sum of money or a cashable right), or to some other proprietary interest, where the blank is to be filled in by some such conditions as creation, long possession or long user, transactions, or registration.

'Title', in the sense in which it refers in this way to whatever conditions for slotting into the protection of trespassory rules an institution may lay down, is to be distinguished from many other uses of this word and cognate terms.[47] In particular, 'title' is sometimes used as a synonym for ownership, and English

[46] See Ch. 15, sect. (ii) below.
[47] See Bernard Rudden, 'The Terminology of Title' (1964) 80 *LQR* 63.

usage employs cognates of these nouns interchangeably. Nothing is to be gained by investigating such linguistic phenomena. For our purposes it is enough to say that title conditions of some kind, as well as trespassory rules and ownership interests, are a necessary feature of a property institution. What a person may do in relation to a thing as to which he has trespassory protection depends on the prevailing concept of ownership. Whether X is such a person depends on the conditions of title specified within the institution. Later in this book we consider whether there are any natural conditions of title, that is, facts about the world from which it follows, in justice, that X ought to be accorded some conception of ownership and the protection of trespassory rules.

(xiii) OVERLAPPING RULE-CATEGORIES

Distinctions have been drawn in this Chapter between trespassory, property-limitation, expropriation, and appropriation rules. These distinctions bring to light different functions served by rules of property institutions. All such rules presuppose ownership interests by protecting them, limiting them, taking them away, or conferring them.

It is apparent, however, that there is not, in all cases, a one-for-one correlation between rule and function. The law of private nuisance contains rules which both protect the ownership interests of land-owners and limit the use-privileges of other land-owners—that is, they serve both as trespassory and as property-limitation rules. Matrimonial law empowers courts to transfer property between spouses on divorce so that the rules conferring such jurisdiction serve both as expropriation and appropriation rules. As we shall see, that principle which prohibits the taking of property without compensation may be triggered by some kinds of property-limitation rules as well as by expropriation rules.[48] It is the fact that they presuppose ownership interests which makes all such rules property rules, whether or not they discharge more than one function in relation to such interests.

Much more important is the distinction between all these varieties of property rules and property-independent prohibitions. Failure to make that distinction entails serious theoretical and practical disadvantages.

Rules prohibiting inter-personal violence are among those we have called 'property-independent prohibitions'. Supposing one took the view that, because violent assaults can be committed with things and the weapons used might happen to be owned by the offender, such rules should be regarded as restrictions on ownership and hence property rules. It would follow that any society which restricted inter-personal violence would, for that reason alone, exhibit a property institution. Justificatory or disjustificatory arguments about property could not be disentangled from arguments about the rightfulness of

---

[48] See Ch. 6, sect. (iii) below.

banning homicide or assault. Anyone who supposed that there was a root-and-branch objection to property institutions of all kinds could be misrepresented as claiming that killing is never wrongful.

In Part II of this book, we shall begin with a minimalist conception of justice which includes prohibitions on violence, and ask whether there are legitimate moves from that starting-point towards justifications of trespassory rules which protect ownership interests in resources—that is, property-specific justice reasons. If all restraints on action are property rules, 'property' can never be the subject of distinct social appraisal or evaluation. Yet, as we shall see in Chapters 8 and 9, there are theorists who make this conflation with just this consequence.

In particular, theorists have deployed a spurious notion of what we shall call 'totality ownership'—a person is 'owner' only if he is free to do anything he likes with that which he is said to own, including using it as a weapon. Armed with that conception, it is easy to show that there are not, and never have been, any owners;[49] and also that ownership, as a conception, suffers from inherent contradictions.[50] To avoid all such theoretical pitfalls, the distinction between property-limitation rules and property-independent prohibitions is essential.

The distinction has practical implications as well. Much of environmental law consists of property-limitation rules—restrictions on what people would otherwise be free to do by virtue of ownership interests. We may wish, however, for reasons of environmental protection to ban certain kinds of conduct universally so that the question of whether a wrongdoer has or claims an ownership interest is entirely irrelevant—property-independent prohibitions. A measure of environmental protection may misfire precisely because the legislature has chosen the wrong category of rule.

For an illustration of this, consider the decision of the House of Lords in *Southern Water Authority* v. *Nature Conservancy Council*.[51] Section 28 of the Wildlife and Countryside Act 1981 made it an offence for any 'owner' or 'occupier' of land (designated as a site of special scientific interest by the Nature Conservancy Council) to carry out on the land operations proscribed by the Council without giving notice to the Council. The House ruled, with regret, that this provision imposed no sanction on someone who entered on to land for a few weeks only solely for the purpose of undertaking the proscribed operations. Even less could the provision be held to penalize the notorious 'fly-tipper', who deposits rubbish in the countryside.[52] The notice requirements and the juxtaposition with 'owner' showed that an 'occupier', within the section, was 'someone who, although lacking the title of an owner, nevertheless stands in such a comprehensive and stable relationship with the land as to be, in company with the actual owner, someone to whom the mechanisms can sensibly be made to apply'.[53] The provision had to be construed merely as a property-limitation rule rather than as a property-independent prohibition.

[49] See Ch. 8, sect. (ii)(b) below.   [50] See Ch. 14, sect. (i)(a) below.
[51] [1992] 3 All ER 481.   [52] *Ibid.* 489, *per* Lord Mustill.   [53] *Ibid.* 488.

4

Building upon the Minimal Structure

Since it has been possible for things to be stolen whilst at the same time owners could more or less use and dispose of them as they pleased, the minimal structure of property institutions has been in place. Title conditions, property-limitation rules, expropriation rules, and appropriation rules, of one kind or another, have existed, all presupposing the core twinned conceptions of trespassory rules and the ownership spectrum.

Modern legal systems have erected sophisticated structures upon these universal elements. The details in the case of any one system occupy volumes of codes, constitutions, statutes, regulations, cases, commentaries, treatises, and textbooks. Our principal aim of confronting property with justice would be swamped were we to embark on too much detail. Yet some sketch of these lawyerly sophistications must be attempted. Too often works on political philosophy concerned with justificatory or disjustificatory arguments about property have blenched before this array of juristic invention. Without enmiring our discussion in too much detail, we need an approximate grasp of what modern property institutions are really like.

The following sketch takes common law systems in general, and English law in particular, as examples. It is suggested that the basic features of the property superstructures of modern systems will differ in terminology and detail rather than in kind. The topics to be investigated are intellectual property, features of property institutions resulting from the separation of wealth from use, and non-ownership proprietary interests. We shall conclude by suggesting, provisionally, that an item comes within the scope of a property institution (that it is a 'proprietary' interest) if either it is subject to specific trespassory protection or if it is separately transmissible as part of a person's private wealth.

(i) INTELLECTUAL PROPERTY

Conceptions of property arose, historically, in relation to tangible things, at some point along the ownership spectrum. Modern legal systems have attached the same conception, within temporal limits, to ideational entities.

How has this been possible given that, as suggested in the last chapter, for an item to be brought within a property institution it must not only be subjected to trespassory protection and be the subject of an ownership interest but must also, normally, be scarce? Ideas, as a totality, are potentially infinite. Any particular idea may be scarce in the sense that there are more people who could make use of it if they knew of it than those to whom it is disclosed. So scarcity is not a function of the relation of a property system to the surface of the earth, as in the case with land, nor of the relation of needs and demands to productive capacity, as in the case with most chattels. It is a function of publicity. An idea which is and always has been in the public domain was never scarce. Such an idea has no place within property institutions. A newly invented idea may be one of which many others, apart from its inventor, would wish to make use if they knew about it.

Once an idea is fully in the public domain, it ceases to be scarce and in that sense an item of social wealth which must be allocated between competing claimants. An ideational entity differs from a tangible object in that mere uses of it are not naturally competitive. If you eat a bun, I cannot eat it too. If you dig out a plot of land for a swimming pool, I cannot build a house upon the same plot at the same time. But we may all, simultaneously, make any use we please of the abstract proposition that the angles of a triangle add up to 180 degrees. You may now be communicating that geometrical truth to your children as an educational device; she may be employing it as part of a mathematical thesis; I am using it to illustrate the present discussion. We none of us thereby tread on each other's toes. The abstract entity is incapable of being exclusively occupied by anyone, and it will never wear out or be destroyed through use. The same is true of any ideational entity. How could such things become the subject of ownership interests?

The answer is that, in the case of those ideational entities which are comprised within intellectual property, the law creates artificial scarcity. The common law evolved trespassory rules to protect the right of an author or composer of any literary, artistic, or scientific work to withhold knowledge of it from others. Even if use of such knowledge did not constitute a wrong arising out of a personal relationship between the alleged wrongdoer and the inventor, it would nevertheless be subject to the sanction of damages or injunction. That way, the author or composer was granted an ownership interest, not merely in a particular artefact (a chattel), but in the ideas comprised within the literary, artistic, or scientific work.

Yates J put the matter this way:

Ideas are free. While the author confines them to his study, they are like birds in a cage, which none but he can have a right to let fly: for, till he thinks proper to emancipate them, they are under his own dominion. It is certain every man has a right to keep his own sentiments, if he pleases: he has certainly a right to judge whether he will make them public, or commit them only to the sight of his friends. In that state, the manuscript is in every sense his peculiar property; and no man can take it from him, or make any use of it which he has not authorised, without being guilty of a violation of his property. And as every author or proprietor of a manuscript has a right to determine whether he will publish it or not, he has a right to the first publication; and whoever deprives him of that priority is guilty of a manifest wrong; and the Court have a right to stop it.[1]

Once the idea, upon being made public, ceases to be scarce, the law, through such devices as copyright, design right, patents, trade marks, and so forth, surrounds it with trespassory rules prohibiting unauthorized use. The rules may impose civil or criminal sanctions. They are invariably codified in statutory form.[2] The common law tort of passing off may also be invoked to protect commercial property in a designation which has not been registered as a trade mark. It has been held, for example, that wine producers enjoy a monopoly over the use of the word 'champagne' sufficient to sustain an injunction against the marketing of a non-alcoholic drink labelled 'Elderflower Champagne'.[3]

The law takes an intangible thing and builds around it a property structure modelled on the structure which social and legal systems have always applied to some tangible things.[4] By instituting trespassory rules whose content restricts uses of the ideational entity, intellectual property law preserves to an individual or group of individuals an open-ended set of use-privileges and powers of control and transmission characteristic of ownership interests over tangible items.

The conditions which trigger the obligations imposed by the trespassory rules—whether mere invention, publication, or entry in some public register —vary from one kind of subject-matter to another, as does the degree of abstractness of the ideational entities they protect. It is a commonplace, for example, that whereas registered patents protect the content of newly invented ideas capable of industrial application copyright law protects only the form of literary expression (not its substance). One who makes use of another's patented invention may be liable to sanctions if it can be shown that he was exploiting the substance of the idea comprised in the patent. To do so is a

[1] *Millard* v. *Taylor* (1769) 4 Burr. 2303 at 2379.

[2] See e.g., the Copyright, Designs and Patents Act 1988, Pt. I, Chaps. 2 and 6 (copyright), Part III, Chap. 2 (design right); the Patents Act 1977 ss. 60–71 (patents); the Trade Marks Act 1994, ss. 9–21, 92 (trade marks).

[3] *Tattinger* v. *Allbev Ltd* [1994] 4 All ER 75.

[4] For a useful summary of the emergence of intellectual property in continental Europe, see Boudewijn Bouckaert, 'What is Property?' (1990) 13 *Harvard Journal of Public Policy* 775, 789 ff. Bouckaert himself disapproves of attributing the label 'property' to these rules on the ground that, since scarcity in this field is artificial, the justifications for intellectual property must be different from those which support property in tangible things. He apparently adheres to a Lockean natural rights theory and supposes that the 'property' label should reflect this ethical base. Contrast the views of Justin Hughes, 'The Philosophy of Intellectual Property' (1988) 77 *Geo LJ* 287. Hughes argues that the 'property' label is appropriate for intellectual property because two familiar arguments for property, those connected with labour and personality, apply to it with even greater cogency than they apply to property in material resources. It will be argued in Pt. II of this book that the justifications for intellectual property are indeed different from those applicable to other forms of property. Nevertheless, for the reasons given in the present chapter, the 'property' label is entirely appropriate.

'trespass' on his part. But it is no trespass, within copyright law, to employ for one's own purposes the substance of the information, reflections, opinions, or emotive reactions contained in a literary composition so long as one does not reproduce the form in which they are expressed. Yet nothing unites one copy of a literary work to another except an abstract idea of some kind. Two printed volumes (distinct chattels) are only copies of 'the same book' by virtue of a mental abstraction which reifies 'the book'. Two inscriptions of a brand name on different items of merchandise are, similarly, examples of 'the same trade mark' by a mental reification of associative connections. It is just that in the case of patent law we abstract at a deeper level, reaching below forms of expression to substantive ideational content.

Thus, in the case of all intellectual property some ideational abstraction or other is made the reference point for trespassory rules which ban some kind of uses of the abstract entity to all except a privileged proprietor. As with other property, the outer perimeter of ownership interests in intellectual property is fixed by the relevant trespassory rules.[5] For example, in the case of English copyright, section 16 of the Copyright, Designs, and Patents Act 1988 lists five general classes of acts in relation to a work which the owner of the copyright has the exclusive right to do, and the doing of which by anyone else without the owner's licence constitutes an infringement: copying the work; issuing copies of it to the public; performing, showing or playing the work in public; broadcasting the work or including it in a cable programme service; and making an adaptation of the work. 'Pirating', that is, distributing copies to the public without licence, is, it has been held, 'akin to theft' and should be punished accordingly.[6] Special classes of cases are exempted, such as 'fair dealing' for the purposes of research or private study, or for the purposes of criticism, review, or reporting.[7] 'Fair dealing', it has been held, is a matter of degree and impression.[8] Most importantly, trespassory protection is restricted to a certain time span (extended in 1995 from fifty to seventy years from the author's death).

Within these limits a private domain is reserved. It consists of an open-ended set of use-privileges, control-powers, and powers of transmission. The exclusive rights listed in section 16 of the 1988 Act in relation to copyright point to actions on the part of others which are *prima facie* banned. They do not tally up all the privileges and powers of the owner. It is not specifically enacted that the copyright owner may (if he chooses) license only members of his family to make copies, or transact only with publishers whose politics match his own, or keep the work unpublished until some turn in public affairs which makes it topical and profitable, or read passages from it aloud at a

---

[5] See Ch. 3, sect. (vi) above.   [6] *R.* v. *Carter*, *The Times*, 13 Jan. 1992 (CA).
[7] Copyright, Designs and Patents Act 1988, ss. 29 and 30.
[8] *Hubbard* v. *Voster* [1972] 2 QB 84; *BBC* v. *British Satellite Broadcasting Ltd* [1991] 3 All ER 833.

charity bazaar. He may do these and countless other things with the work because he is its owner.

We show in the next chapter that ownership interests in general function as irreducible organizing ideas. The same is true of the open-ended set of privileges and powers over an ideational entity reserved by the trespassory rules of intellectual property. It would be extraordinary if it had not itself come to be described as 'ownership' of the intangible entity. The word 'property' is used to indicate such ownership interests and also lesser non-ownership proprietary rights carved out of them—such as licences to use patents—just as that word is employed to cover ownership interests and non-ownership proprietary interests over tangible things. Furthermore, the much condemned (but actually harmless) usage, whereby 'property' is employed to refer to the object of an ownership interest in the case of tangible items,[9] is also common in the context of intellectual property (as in the above citation from Yates J). Mechanisms for hiving off wealth-potential, for instance by granting shares in companies in whom ownership interests are vested, apply in much the same way whether those corporate ownership interests subsist in tangible or ideational entities.

If X owns a patent, a copyright, or a trade mark, she is free to use it in any self-seeking way she pleases and to control uses by others within the perimeter of protection set by the appropriate trespassory rules; and she has powers of transmission, *inter vivos* or on death, similar to those which the law affords to owners of other proprietary items. Expropriation rules, upon bankruptcy or for taxation, apply in much the same way. Property-limitation rules are likely to be different, since 'anti-social' uses of what one owns are not normally subtracted from a totality of *prima facie* use-privileges where the subject is ideational rather than tangible.

Whether the rationale for creating intellectual property differs from justifications appropriate to other forms of property we have yet to consider. But given that a society's laws have been extended to include those trespassory rules which create artificial scarcity in unpublished and published ideas, and given that the protected private domains are absorbed within the familiar rules of the property institution which already obtain over land and goods, it is not surprising that the resulting structure is viewed as itself an extension of the property institution. Only if the notions of using abstract things as one likes, and controlling use of them by others, were altogether incomprehensible would that extension not have occurred. Social intercourse is, however, replete with references to mental entities. Supposing the whole process to be justifiable, its property terminology is appropriate.

Whether intellectual property could have emerged in the absence of property over tangible resources constitutes an unanswerable counterfactual speculation. Supposing in Forest Land, where the notion of owning anything was unknown, some gifted bard had complained when others sang his songs

---

[9] See Ch. 1, sect. (iii) above.

without his leave, and that his fellow tribesmen had concurred in creating a prohibition against that being done. Would the Forestlanders have evolved some property-like terminology in respect of songs although they had none applicable to chattels or land? We, who have been infused with ownership ideas respecting solid objects from childhood, cannot make the mental empathetic leap needed even to guess at the answer. Be that as it may, intellectual property was created historically always in societies in which advanced property institutions over tangible resources were entrenched, and, to varying degrees, absorbed the existing mental frameworks of those institutions.

(ii) THE SEPARATION OF WEALTH FROM USE

So far we have been concerned with property in tangible things and in ideational entities, along the ownership spectrum, created by trespassory rules. Such property, we have seen, involves both use-privileges and control-powers and commonly powers of transmission as well. As we have also seen, to the extent that an 'owner' has powers of control and transmission, he is an agent for the allocation of social wealth.[10] If he can, so far as his powers go, determine the allocation of advantages over scarce resources, within whatever property-limitation rules obtain, he may use these powers for his own benefit. Hence, by virtue of such powers, items of social wealth are also part of his private wealth.

Yet many facets of property institutions have no direct bearing on use-privileges over things and no direct connection with trespassory rules. How does this come about? It is because the power to allocate social wealth, that is, private wealth, may be, through the operation of a variety of instrumentalities within a property institution, separated from use-privileges over things?

(a) Money

A pre-legal social system may, and all mature legal systems do, empower owners of things to trade their bundles of privileges and powers for tokens of exchange which may themselves be traded either for similar bundles of privileges and powers over other things or for services. Such physical tokens—coins, banknotes—constitute 'money' in its most restricted legal sense, which encompasses only those chattels that must be accepted by creditors as 'legal tender' in discharge of debts. 'Money', as an abstract economic conception, includes much of what will hereafter be referred to as 'cashable rights'—as when economists discuss the 'money supply' or when, in conventional usage, a person is said to have 'money in the bank'. In either sense, as we shall see, 'money' is property.

[10] See Ch. 3, sect. (iii) above.

F. A. Mann offered the following definition of money in the more restricted sense (money as chattels). 'It is suggested that, in law, the quality of money is to be attributed to all chattels which, issued by the authority of the law and denominated with reference to a unit of account, are meant to serve as universal means of exchange in the State of issue.'[11]

In English law, such chattels consist either of minted coins or of Bank of England notes (the latter constituting legal tender even though they are in form promissory notes).[12] Tokens of this kind are protected by trespassory rules, especially the prohibition of theft, in the same way as other chattels. That is enough to subject them to the institution of property.

Such tokens differ from other chattels in two ways. First, it would be possible for a property institution to recognize a non-transferable ownership interest in an ordinary chattel. It would be a contradiction to say of a token both that it was 'money' and that it could not be transferred. It is true that tokens which are legal tender may also, in the context of particular transactions, play the role of commodities where, for example, coins are sold and bought as curios or for a price which reflects the commercial value of the metal out of which they are made. A property institution might ban such transactions. But monetary tokens cannot serve as a medium of exchange if exchange is not permitted. In their case, transferability is a conceptual component of ownership.

Secondly, although monetary tokens are subject to open-ended use-privileges, these are insignificant compared with the power to allocate social wealth which money affords. For what it is worth, an owner has, subject to any property-limitation rules debarring defacing of tokens, an open-ended set of use-privileges over his monetary tokens. He may turn his coins into ornaments or paper his walls with banknotes. There is a scene in a play by Jean Anoulh in which the disillusioned man of wealth and the poor heroine share a cathartic experience by tearing up banknotes. As she tears the last note Isabelle says: '*Voilà pour les pauvres! Nous les avions oubliés*'.[13]

The power to allocate enjoyment over scarce resources is what gives money its distinctive character. Hence the ambivalence in usage between 'money' as chattels and 'money' as including cashable rights. A man who presently enjoys ownership privileges and powers over few tangible things, but at the same time has ready access to a large quantity of monetary tokens, is wealthy.

Usage, both lay and legal, varies on the matter of whether money is 'property'. Investment advisers debate whether, at particular seasons, it is wise to retain one's wealth in the form of money, or rather to invest it in 'property'. On the other hand, 'property' is sometimes used synonymously with 'wealth'. Members of the 'propertied classes' do not drop in and out of that status

---

[11] F. A. Mann, *The Legal Aspect of Money* (5th edn., Clarendon Press, 1992), 8.
[12] *Ibid*. 16–18.
[13] Jean Anouilh, *L'Invitation au château* (La Table Ronde) Act 4, p.t. 200.

depending on whether their assets are currently in liquid form or are tied up in ownership interests in land and goods. Sometimes English statutes deem it necessary to define 'property' as including money[14] and sometimes they pre-suppose that money is 'property' by, for example, referring to a disposition of 'any sum of money or other property'.[15]

General statements about criminal sanctions commonly include fines as a form of deprivation of 'property', as when Sir James FitzJames Stephen in his *History of the Criminal Law* described criminal law as 'a collection of threats of injury to life, liberty and property'.[16] On the other hand, in the context of constitutional prohibitions against taking property without compensation, the word 'property' could not be understood to include money, as to give compensation for taking money would merely be to give back what had been taken. Such provisions have never been understood to restrain legislative authority to impose fines or taxes.[17]

Such shifts in usage may be related to the fact that, in the case of money, the use-control function of property institutions is insignificant in comparison with their wealth-allocation function. Sometimes, money is conceived of as property as well as wealth, and sometimes as a form of wealth other than property. As we shall see, some political philosophers have hiccoughed over just this ambiguity.[18]

Traditionally, theorists sought to justify ownership interests in things. Modern theorists of distributive justice concern themselves with allocation of wealth. Our enquiry is directed towards everything that comes within the reach of property institutions. Such institutions always apply trespassory rules and the ownership spectrum to some things and, so far as modern instances are concerned, always facilitate the hiving off of wealth through monetary tokens and other instrumentalities to be discussed. Any abstract item of wealth may be brought within the scope of some of the institution's rules—especially expropriation and appropriation rules. That is enough to warrant using the label 'property', as we shall see, even for cashable rights. In the case of monetary tokens, there is as well the fact that they have always been subjected to the trespassory rule against stealing in the same way as any other chattels. The coins and notes in my pocket are owned by me and can be stolen by anyone except me. (The same is true of other chattels which, whilst not constituting legal tender, are used for the purpose of drawing on cashable rights—such

[14] e.g. the Theft Act 1968, s. 4(1), and the Drug Trafficking Act 1994, s. 62(1).

[15] Inheritance (Provision for Family and Dependants) Act 1975, s. 8(1).

[16] Sir James FitzJames Stephen, *History of the Criminal Law of England* (Macmillan, 1883), ch. 18, 106.

[17] See the concession of Council arguing for a wide interpretation of such a provision in *Belfast Corporation* v. *O.D. Cars Ltd* [1960] AC 490 at 508. The no-taking-without-compensation principle is discussed in Ch. 6, sect. (iii) below.

[18] See our discussion of MacPherson in Ch. 9, sect. (iii)(d), Waldron in Ch. 13, sect. (iv), and Proudhon in Ch. 16, sect. (i)(a) below.

as cheques, credit cards, book tokens, luncheon vouchers, and so on. They exhibit, in varying degrees, the second peculiarity of chattels which are monetary tokens, namely, that ownership use-privileges are of insignificant importance compared with their role in allocating wealth.)

Thus, despite contextual shifts in usage, any general enquiry into the basic structure and justification of property institutions must regard money as property.

(b) Cashable rights

The institution of contract is as universal as that of property. It is an important adjunct to property as a means of allocating social wealth. In Chapter 2 we imagined a society, Contract Land, in which contract was substituted altogether for property as a means of wealth-allocation. That was a society without money or ownership interests in any other assets which none the less sought to respect individual choice and did not aspire to outright socialization of all aspects of collective living. Whether property institutions are justifiable precisely because they inherently facilitate choices which no merely contractual regime could do is a question discussed in Chapters 13 and 14 of this book.

At any rate, Contract Land stands apart from all historical experience. Bargaining and contracting in most situations take property for granted. In modern legal systems, the majority of contracts presuppose the institution of property. The contractor on one side at least offers to transmit something over which he has ownership privileges and powers, especially money.

1. Choses in Action

Furthermore, the institutions of contract and property intersect in ways which enable the wealth-allocating function of a property institution to be dissociated from its use-control function. Some contractual rights may be traded for money or other property. In the terminology of English law, they are 'choses in action'. Where this is the case, the rightholder has the same control over the allocation of social wealth that the money equivalent of his rights would provide, and for that reason his rights are themselves commonly treated as a species of property. They are subjected to expropriation rules, like taxation, criminal confiscation, execution of judgments, and bankruptcy, in the same way as other forms of property. If they involve unqualified claims to the payment of money, like bank accounts, the rights themselves are, commercially and even in some legal contexts, treated as 'money'—even though, as we have seen, 'money', as a legal-technical concept, is confined to chattels which are legal tender.[19] As reified entities, they may be made the subject of direct trespassory protection. In modern English law, bank balances may be stolen.[20]

[19] See the discussion of 'bank money' by F. A. Mann, n. 11 above, 5–7.
[20] *Chan Man-Sin* v. *R.* [1988] 1 All ER 1. They are also 'property' which may be dishonestly obtained by deception—*R.* v. *Quick, The Times*, 18 Aug. 1993.

Furthermore, restitutionary remedies have been devised whereby the monetary value of such rights is protected, so long as it can be distinctly identified, against a wide class of intermeddlers other than good-faith recipients for value.[21]

The bundles of contractual rights which, by virtue of their transmissibility, are thus turned into property may be more complex, especially shares in corporate enterprises. Where contractual rights are not assignable for value, as is the case in English law with most contracts for personal services, their wealth-allocative function is limited to the control which the rightholder has over the corresponding obligations of his contractee: he has the power to enforce, release, or vary the performance of some scarce service. Where they are so assignable, he has as well the broader range of ownership powers which the money equivalent of his rights will afford. It is their cashability which brings assignable contracts within the purview of property institutions in a way non-assignable contracts are not.

Cashable rights, which are treated as property, are usually, but need not be, founded in contract. For example, it has been held that the term 'intangible property' in the English Theft Act[22] comprises assignable export quotas granted by government. In consequence, such quotas could be stolen.[23]

Assignable contractual rights to money represent the purest form, within property institutions, of the separation of wealth-allocation from use-control. So long as they remain uncashed or unassigned, they entail no privileged use over any items (tangible or ideational). However, even before the modern extension of criminal and restitutionary protection to their monetary value, trespassory rules were a necessary background for even this facet of the institution of property. Such rules protect the money and other proprietary subject-matters into which the rights, by assumption, can be translated.

Other assignable contractual rights may or may not confer privileged use over things. Shares in companies consist of rights to money (dividends when declared and a share in the company's residuary assets on dissolution), and rights to vote in company resolutions. Only remotely does this entail privileged use over assets, in that, in theory, a majority of shareholders might resolve that company assets be allocated to their use. Partnership contracts and some kinds of contracts relating to land do entail privileged use. However, of assignable contracts generally it may be said that the wealth-allocation, rather than the use-control, function of property is usually dominant and sometimes all that is present.

2. Business Goodwill

By extension of the notion that that which is cashable is property, the 'goodwill' associated with a business enterprise may be treated as a proprietary

---

[21] *Re Hallett's Estate* (1880) 13 Ch.D 696.   [22] Theft Act 1968, s. 4(1).
[23] *Attorney-General of Hong Kong* v. *Nai-Keung* [1988] Cr. LR 125.

entity for the purposes of some of the rules of a property institution. If an expropriation rule imposes a tax on the capital value of assets owned by an enterprise, its goodwill may feature as a distinct balance-sheet item. Goodwill may also be invoked as a distinct item of property in connection with constitutional principles banning the taking of property without compensation. In one case[24] the Privy Council had to decide whether legislation prohibiting the provision of pilot services by anyone other than employees of a public port authority amounted to the compulsory acquisition without compensation, contrary to the constitution of Malaysia, of the 'property' of a partnership which had previously employed licensed pilots. The Board held that the non-assignable rights to employ pilots were not property, but that the goodwill, being something which the partnership might have sold to a purchaser, was property.[25] (As we shall see, *ad hoc* definitions of 'property' for the purpose of such constitutional provisions warrant circumspect treatment.[26])

'Goodwill' is one of the many fuzzy perimeter applications of property institutions. Cashable rights are central features of modern property institutions in a way that business goodwill is not. Goodwill is not itself the subject of trespassory protection. You can steal a bank account, but acting in such a way as to diminish the value of a competitor's business goodwill is not of itself wrongful. If manufacturer X copies the goods of manufacturer Y without infringing a registered patent or trade mark and without leading the public to believe that the goods he supplies are Y's goods (which would constitute the tort of passing off), Y is without redress since the common law will not recognize a monopoly in the article itself.[27] Choses in action may be conceptually divorced from the subject-matter out of which they arise and, as such, traded or subjected to expropriation or appropriation rules. The balance-sheet item represented by goodwill cannot be dissociated from the underlying enterprise to the same extent. Unlike shares in a company, business goodwill is not separately assignable.

3. Trusts

Another instrumentality for separating use-privileges from wealth is the sub-institution of the trust, employed by systems which derive from English common law. All the property subject matters hitherto discussed—land, chattels, intellectual property, and choses in action—may be vested in a person or persons on trust for others. Civil trespassory rules directly protect the domain of the trustee since it is he who has *locus standi* to seek redress should they

---

[24] *Government of Malaysia* v. *Selangore Pilot Association* [1978] AC 337.

[25] The majority of the Board took the view that this property had not been compulsorily 'acquired' because the authority itself would have no power to sell the goodwill.

[26] See Ch. 9, sect. (iii)(c) below.

[27] *British Leyland Motor Corp. Ltd* v. *Armstrong Patents Co. Ltd* [1986] AC 577; *Re Coca-Cola Co.'s Applications* [1986] 2 All ER 284; *Reckitt and Colman Products Ltd* v. *Borden Inc.* [1990] 1 All ER 873.

be infringed; and it is the trustee in whom ownership privileges and powers are *prima facie* vested. Nevertheless, the rules of the sub-institution and the remedies it provides are designed to guarantee that every one of these owner-ship privileges and powers is exercised, not for the trustee's benefit, but for that of the beneficiaries. In addition, beneficiaries have certain direct remedies against strangers who intermeddle with trust property. The upshot is that the beneficiaries enjoy, as part of their private wealth, the totality of ownership privileges and powers vested in the trustee.

The interests of beneficiaries under private trusts take many forms. They are regarded as proprietary in nature (in common law, but not civil law, sys-tems),[28] by virtue of the fact that they are the subject of generalized, but not unlimited, trespassory protection. They are enforceable against recipients of the trust property with actual or constructive notice of their existence. They may be enforced against 'volunteers' (those who receive the trust property otherwise than for value) even if the latter had no notice of them, so long as their subject matter is identifiable.[29] They are not protected against 'equity's darling' (a *bona fide* purchaser for value of the trust property without notice). Thus, trespassory protection is open-ended, equity's darling being the recog-nized exception.

Beneficiaries' interests are also often freely alienable as part of the bene-ficiaries' private wealth, and so would count as 'property' on that ground alone, like any other cashable rights. That is not so in the case of protective trusts ('spendthrift trusts'), under which someone is entitled to receive the income of a fund but any purported disposition of his entitlement (or his bankruptcy) entails the termination of his interest and its replacement by other trust pro-visions. Furthermore, under the modern discretionary trust each individual beneficiary has no cashable entitlement and for that reason his rights to call for due administration of the trust are not regarded as proprietary interests for the purposes of tax law.[30] Nevertheless, the totality of the beneficiaries are regarded as the collective owners of the wealth-potential represented by the trust property. Beneficiaries who are all *sui juris* may, in English common law, by their unanimous decision bring the trust to an end and alienate the assets in any way they choose.[31] That rule is a recognition that collective equitable ownership prevails over the court's duty to respect and enforce the wishes of

---

[28] The European Court of Justice has held that the right of a sole beneficiary absolutely entitled under a trust of an apartment in France is not a 'right *in rem*' for the purposes of Art. 16(1) of the Convention on Jurisdiction and the Enforcement of Judgments in Civil and Commercial Matters 1968 (which confers exclusive jurisdiction over rights *in rem* in immovable property on the courts of the country in which the property is situated)—Case C–294/92 *Webb* v. *Webb* [1994] ECR I–1717.

[29] *Re Diplock* [1948] Ch. 465.

[30] *Gartside* v. *IRC* [1968] AC 553. *Pearson* v. *IRC* [1981] AC 753.

[31] *Saunders* v. *Vautier* (1841) 1 Cr. and Ph. 240; *Re Chardon* [1928] Ch. 464; *Re Smith* [1928] Ch. 915.

the settlor who created the trust. Under the Variation of Trusts Act 1958, this principle has been extended both to protective trusts and to situations in which the beneficiaries are not *sui juris*, the court being empowered to stand in the shoes of persons who are under incapacity, unascertained or unborn, for the purpose of joining in an exercise of collective equitable ownership.[32]

The trust institution has been adapted to serve many goals. Express trusts may impose duties to forward public or private purposes, as well as to serve the interests of particular individuals. The only obligation uniting trusts for individuals and trusts for purposes is the negative duty on the trustee not to use his ownership privileges and powers for his own benefit.[33]

Charitable trusts involve what we shall call 'quasi-ownership interests', because the privileges and powers which they entail, though modelled on those inherent in prevailing ownership conceptions, lack the crucial characteristic of ownership interests proper. They cannot be exercised by those in whom they are vested in a self-seeking way.[34]

Assets which are held on private trusts are usually the subject of ownership interests since the trustees may exercise their privileges and powers in the self-seeking interest of their beneficiaries. They are not constrained, as quasi-owners of State or public property are, by the imperative to discharge some public function. In that sense, an asset subjected to a private trust is within the domain of genuine ownership relations.

The only exception is represented by those unusual cases where, for a time, the equitable interest is in abeyance, the trustees being required or permitted to apply assets towards the discharge of a purpose but no-one being vested with a self-seeking power of decision.[35] There are other contexts in which the equitable interest is said to be in abeyance although the person in whom legal title is vested is not, technically, a trustee. He may be an executor administering the estate of a deceased person,[36] a trustee in bankruptcy or a company acting through its liquidator.[37] In all these contexts—private purpose trusts, unadministered estates, the estates of bankrupts, and companies in course of liquidation—the legal owners' privileges and powers are constituted by an amalgam derived partly from ownership and partly from the particular private law regime. They are vested with quasi-ownership interests. For the time being, no-one has the self-seeking prerogative characteristic of ownership interests proper.

---

[32] J. W. Harris, *Variation of Trusts* (Sweet and Maxwell, 1975).

[33] We leave here to one side those 'constructive trusts' which are sometimes imposed upon property-owners as a technical means of enforcing a particular non-contractual and non-tortious personal obligation, where even this basic trust-defining negative obligation is absent.

[34] See Ch. 7, sect. (iii)(b) below.

[35] *Re Thompson* [1934] Ch. 342; *Carreras Rothmans Ltd* v. *Freeman Mathews Treasure Ltd* [1985] Ch. 207.

[36] *Commissioner of Stamp Duties (Queensland)* v. *Livingstone* [1965] AC 694.

[37] *Ayerst* v. *C. and K. (Construction) Ltd* [1975] 2 All ER 537.

(iii) NON-OWNERSHIP PROPRIETARY INTERESTS

Our discussion of the imaginary societies yielded the conclusion that the core idea of a property institution resides in the twinned conceptions of trespassory rules and the ownership spectrum. We have seen how property institutions build out from this core by applying the spectrum to ideational 'things' made artificially scarce through the creation of special kinds of trespassory rules, and, most importantly, by hiving off the wealth-potential of the spectrum. Another characteristic out-work of property institutions consists in the recognition of non-ownership proprietary interests. When a person is vested with such an interest over a resource, his relationship to it does not involve an open-ended set of use-privileges and control-powers. For example, it is in English law an essential negative characteristic of an easement that it does not involve that open-ended set of possessory privileges and powers which is the hallmark of an estate.[38] Nevertheless, the rights comprised within such an interest are protected against all-comers. Such protection is afforded by a special class of civil trespassory rules, sanctioned by damages or injunctive relief. Such rules do not outlaw any use of the resource not authorized by the holder of the interest, as is typically the case with ownership interests. They do, however, in one way or another, ban such uses of the resource as would frustrate the limited rights entailed by the interest.

The content of non-ownership proprietary interests is not open-ended, but the range of persons who may fall under obligations by virtue of them is open-ended. In the traditional legal terminology, such interests rank with ownership interests in being 'rights *in rem*' as distinct from 'rights *in personam*'. What this entails is that, for such an interest to exist, a property institution must contain appropriate trespassory rules imposing general obligations not to frustrate it.

A property institution's recognition of non-ownership proprietary interests typically presupposes the ownership spectrum in two ways. First, the range of protection specifically includes successive owners. For a claim over a resource to count as a proprietary interest it must be enforceable, *inter alios*, against all who acquire ownership interests. Secondly, one of the transactional powers characteristically contained within conceptions of ownership is that of creating specific instances of non-ownership proprietary interests.

If a person's relationship to a thing, tangible or ideational, falls somewhere towards the upper end of the ownership spectrum, he has an extensive set of open-ended use-privileges and wealth-allocation powers. He may, as we have seen, be divested of some elements of this bundle by property-limitation rules. But he may also be so divested by his own contract or concession, even though the entire bundle is not transferred. Mere contract or concession represents an

---

[38] *Copeland* v. *Greenhalf* [1952] Ch. 488; *Grigsby* v. *Melville* [1973] 1 All ER 385, affd. [1973] 3 All ER 455.

exercise of an ownership power and does not, of itself, introduce new elements into the property institution. However, by virtue of specialized trespassory rules forming part of the institution, particular species of contracts or grants gain a distinctively proprietary status. If a particular category of contract or grant conferring some specific use-privilege over the thing, or some determinate monetary claim out of the wealth-potential of its exploitation, is protected by trespassory rules, not merely against the contractor or grantor, but against the world in general including succeeding owners, the contract or grant creates a non-ownership proprietary interest.

Non-ownership proprietary interests may also arise independently of the exercise of transactional power. They may result from expropriation rules which, *pro tanto*, divest an owner of part of his bundle of use-privileges and control-powers. Such is the case, for example, when the rules of a property institution enable easements or servitudes to be acquired by prescription over land, or when rights of detention over chattels are conferred as a means of enforcing debts.

(a) Non-ownership Proprietary Interests in Land

In the nature of the case, parcels of land are the objects most susceptible to proprietary rights other than ownership. There are three common types: rights to enjoy some extracted category of the use-privileges which *prima facie* are comprised within ownership; rights to deny to the owner the enjoyment of some of his ownership privileges; and rights to subtract some monetary value out of the wealth-potential of the land. The first, in English law, take the form of positive easements such as rights of way, and various kinds of *profits à prendre*, like the right to take fish or game. They are protected by trespassory rules in that civil relief, by way of damages or injunction, is afforded the right-holder against all-comers to the land. The second set, which are similarly protected, take the form of natural rights to support of land by neighbouring land and to non-interference with water running in defined channels, certain negative easements which prevent building to obstruct light or removing buildings which provide support for other buildings, and the nineteenth-century invention of restrictive covenants affecting freehold land. As all English law students learn, it was the innovative granting of injunctive relief against successors to freehold land, i.e. the creation of a new trespassory rule for their protection, which turned restrictive covenants into proprietary interests.[39] The third group is represented by mortgages and charges of various kinds. In English law, their creation and operation are hedged about with truly bewildering and obscuring complexities. But in essence they confer on

---

[39] *Tulk* v. *Moxhay* (1848) 2 Ph. 774. It was not until later, however, that the contours of the interest were retrospectively settled (see, e.g., *Re Nisbet and Potts' Contract* [1905] 1 Ch. 391, affd. [1906] 1 Ch. 386; *London County Council* v. *Allen* [1914] 3 KB 642).

mortgagees and chargees rights to money enforceable, in the last resort, by sale of the property into whoever's hands its ownership has passed.

(b) Non-ownership Proprietary Interests in Other Resources

The potentiality exists, within property institutions, for subjecting both chattels and intellectual property to all three varieties of non-ownership proprietary interests. Whether any particular institution has done so depends on what trespassory rules it happens to have evolved. Given the transitory durability of most chattels, it will usually be unnecessary to have devised trespassory rules to protect minor abstractions of use-privileges or of rights to control use-privileges; but systems for affecting mortgages of valuable chattels are worth having. Proprietary entities which are themselves the result of abstraction of wealth-potential, like shares in companies and other cashable rights, are not susceptible of the first two kinds of non-ownership proprietary interests since they do not carry use-privileges at all, but they can be mortgaged or charged.

(c) Tenurial Incidents

English law also retains a few eccentric non-ownership proprietary interests from its feudal past. As we shall see in the next chapter, it is an incident of an estate that its holder enjoys ownership privileges in relation to land, either at present, or, in the case of reversions on leaseholds, when the reversion falls in. The classical feudal land law predated the emergence of leasehold estates. At that time the freehold tenant of land enjoyed a dual relationship with the land he held. He had an open-ended ownership interest,[40] protected by trespassory rules enmeshed within the medieval writ system of real actions and actions for recovery of seisin. But he was also under a duty to provide services of some kind to his tenurial superior, that duty being inherent in his relationship to the land.[41]

The superior lord himself—who (so far as freehold land was concerned) became always in practice the king after the Statute *Quia Emptores* 1290—was also vested with a proprietary interest in relation to the land, a lordship. That lordship was no more inconsistent with the tenant's present ownership interest than is the modern State's power of eminent domain.[42] However, in classic feudal theory, a future ownership interest in the land itself was an incident of a lordship, just as it is today an incident of a reversion on a lease; for the lord would be vested with open-ended ownership privileges and powers by the prevailing trespassory rules should the inferior estate escheat. In

[40] For rejection of the contention that the tenurial system was incompatible with 'ownership', see Ch. 5, sect. (iii) and (vii)(b) below.

[41] For 'property-duty rules', see Ch. 3, sect. (ix) above.

[42] See Sir Frederick Pollock and F. W. Maitland, *History of English Law* (CUP, 1911), ii, 3–4.

modern English land law, surviving tenurial incidents—the result for the most part of the conversion of copyholds into freeholds in 1925—carry no such potential ownership interests in relation to the land itself. They entail defined non-ownership proprietary interests. If a freeholder dies intestate and without intestate successors, his land comes to the Crown, no longer by virtue of escheat inherent in the Crown's paramount lordship, but by reason of a special appropriation rule governing all *bona vacantia*.

(d) The *Numerus Clausus*

Assume that a society has evolved both a conception of ownership fairly high up along the ownership spectrum and also the institution of free contracting. An owner is then blessed with a substantial open-ended set of use-privileges and powers of exploitation, and he may contract that another shall be free to exercise any of them or control the exercise of any of them. It does not follow that he can, at pleasure, vest another with a proprietary interest as regards any part of his ownership bundle. Smith may contract with Sykes not to use his (Smith's) grand piano to play pop music. But Smith and Sykes may not be able, by any contract between themselves, to impose obligations on other persons, such as subsequent owners of the piano. For that to be possible their society would have to have instituted a trespassory rule protecting that kind of personal negative servitude over chattels, a conception rejected in English law.[43]

Non-feudal legal systems characteristically delimit the kinds of non-ownership proprietary interests which may be created. Bernard Rudden has described this generalization as the phenomenon of the *numerus clausus*.[44] Furthermore, such systems regulate the conditions under which those non-ownership proprietary interests which it recognizes may arise by operation of law, and the formalities which must be employed for their deliberate creation and transmission. All such matters are lawyers' law *par excellence*. They are enshrouded within juristic doctrine. The phenomenon of juristic doctrine and its putative justifications are considered later in this book.[45]

(iv) THE ALTERNATIVE CHARACTERIZATION OF PROPRIETARY INTERESTS

The outworks erected upon the minimal structure of a property institution considered in this Chapter suggest the following provisional conclusion. For an item to be fully comprehended within a property institution—that is, a specific point of reference for the rules which constitute the institution—it

---

[43] *Taddy and Co.* v. *Sterious and Co.* [1904] 1 Ch. 354.

[44] Bernard Rudden, 'Economic Theory versus Property Law: The *Numerus Clausus* Problem', in J. Eekelaar and J. Bell (eds.), *Oxford Essays in Jurisprudence* (3rd series, Clarendon Press, 1987).   [45] See Ch. 16, sect. (ii)(c) below.

must either be the subject of direct trespassory protection, or else be separately assignable, or, of course, both. An interest is 'proprietary' if either characteristic may be predicated of it. Both characteristics are true of most ownership interests recognized in modern English law, whether in land, goods, ideational entities, money, or cashable rights. But an ownership interest could receive general trespassory protection at the same time that exploitation of it is limited to the exercise of control-powers without powers of transmission, as was the case with statutory tenancies under the English Rent Acts, and as was universally true of the mere-property interests in the imaginary Wood Land and Pink Land societies. Some non-ownership proprietary interests are the subject of general trespassory protection but are not separately transmissible. There could be hived-off elements of wealth-potential which are not directly protected by trespassory rules but may be freely traded as part of a person's private wealth.

(a) Property Talk

This alternative characterization of proprietary interests reflects the duality of functions of property institutions, as mechanisms for controlling use and for allocating some items of social wealth. It also roughly tracks a whole style of property talk common to lawyers and non-lawyers. Resources are your 'property' if others are not supposed to interfere with them without your leave or if you are free to spend them or give them away as you please. Lawyers' technical vocabulary of 'choses in action' and the distinction between 'rights *in rem*' and 'rights *in personam*' merely builds on these shared assumptions.

Nevertheless, property talk is fluid and fluctuating. One cause is the variety of ownership interests along the ownership spectrum. As we shall point out in the next chapter, there is no settled convention according to which any particular point on this spectrum receives the description 'ownership'.

Another cause of fluidity is variability in the degree of trespassory protection. For example, rights conferred on bailees of chattels by contracts of bailment are not, in English law, usually protected against successors of the bailor.[46] At the same time, protection is afforded against other third-party

---

[46] Some degree of protection might arise, in special circumstances, from application of the law relating to *in personam* constructive trusts (invoked *obiter* by the CA in relation to land in *Ashburn Anstalt* v. *Arnold* [1989] Ch. 1, but applicable also, presumably, to chattels); the tort of inducing breach of contract (*Manchester Ship Canal Co.* v. *Manchester Racecourse Co.* [1901] 2 Ch. 37, *Esso Petroleum Co. Ltd* v. *Kingswood Motors (Adelston) Ltd* [1974] QB 141 (a remedy which does not avail against a second transferee —*Law Debenture Trust Corp. Plc* v. *Ural Caspian Oil Corp. Ltd* [1995] 1 All ER 157)); or the principle stated by Knight Bruce LJ in *De Mattos* v. *Gibson* (1858) 4 de G. and J. 276 at 282: 'Reason and justice seem to prescribe that at least as a general rule where a man by gift or purchase acquires property from another, with knowledge of a previous contract lawfully and for valuable consideration made by him with a third person to use and employ the property for a particular purpose in a specified manner, the acquirer shall not, to the material damage of the third person, in opposition to the contract and

intermeddlers. The right to sue for chattel torts is vested both in the bailor and in the bailee on a first-come basis. If the chattel is destroyed by a third party's tortious act, the bailee may sue for its full value. As against the wrongdoer it is 'deemed to be the chattel of the possessor and of no other'.[47] Once a claim has been brought by either bailor or bailee which is then settled as between claimant and the wrongdoer, the latter is altogether discharged. Bailor and bailee must thereafter share damages according to their respective interests in the chattel *inter se*.[48] The modern law of theft has been extended to protect persons who have 'possession' or 'control' of chattels.[49] Not surprisingly, therefore, even though bailments are not technically 'rights *in rem*' they are sometimes referred to as involving a 'special property' in goods.

Cashable rights (when assignable) are within the core of property institutions even if they are not protected by trespassory rules because they figure within expropriation and appropriation rules. 'Property' terminology may, however, be extended to reflect mere cashability. We have seen that business goodwill, even though it is not separately assignable, is nevertheless considered to be 'property' in some legal contexts. A court may go so far as to treat any cashable opportunity as 'property' if doing so would, in its view, forward the underlying purpose of some legal provision. We shall see later that divorce courts are sometimes authorized to redistribute spouses' property by reference, *inter alia*, to considerations of labour-desert.[50] A New York court has ruled that, in exercising such a jurisdiction, the career and celebrity status of an opera singer should be considered 'marital property' subject to equitable distribution, because her husband had, by his services, assisted in their growth.[51] The court recognized, however, that, for the purpose of the provision in hand, it was applying property terminology to earning opportunities 'even though they may fall outside the scope of traditional property concepts'.[52]

inconsistently with it, use and employ the property in a manner not allowable to the giver or seller.' The principle was applied to ship time charters in the *De Mattos* case itself and in *Lord Strathcona Steamship Co. Ltd* v. *Dominion Coal Co. Ltd* [1926] AC 108 (a decision of the Privy Council which was disapproved by Diplock J in *Port Line Ltd* v. *Ben Line Steamer Ltd* [1958] 2 QB 146.) It was not applied to purchasers of stock subject to resale price agreements (*Taddy and Co.* v. *Sterious and Co.* [1904] 1 Ch. 354, *McGrowther* v. *Pitcher* [1904] 2 Ch. 306), nor to the assignee of a copyright who takes with notice a royalty payment contract (*Barker* v. *Stickney* [1919] 1 KB 121), nor to a chargee of the assets of a company who takes with notice that the company has an unfulfilled contractual obligation to set aside a fund to meet specific liabilities (*MacJordan Construction Ltd* v. *Brookmount Erostin Ltd* [1992] BCLB 350. Recent authority suggests that the principle is valid but that it can at best only provide the basis for a negative injunction, not a mandatory order—*Swiss Bank Corporation* v. *Lloyds Bank Ltd* [1979] Ch. 458, at 571–5, *per* Browne Wilkinson J.

[47] *The Winkfield* [1902] P 42, at 60, *per* Collins MR.
[48] *O'Sullivan* v. *Williams* [1992] 3 All ER 385.
[49] Theft Act 1968, s. 5(1).
[50] See Ch. 11, sect. (iv)(c) below.
[51] *Elkus* v. *Elkus*, 572 NYS 2d 901 (1991), New York High Court, Appellate Division.
[52] Ibid. 902.

(b) Specifically Enforceable Contracts

In English law, contractual rights have sometimes been treated as proprietary interests, even if non-assignable, solely on the ground that they are specifically enforceable.

Consider two developments in the law relating to contractual licences over land. In the last century the view was accepted that, if a licensor sought to evict a licensee in breach of contract, the licensee had to vacate the land and had only a remedy in damages.[53] That view is now completely discredited. Equity will specifically enforce the contractual rights of the licensee against the licensor, either by injunction against breach if the contract has been partially executed,[54] or by specific performance if the contract is still executory.[55]

The other development concerns the question whether contractual licences bind successors of the licensor to the same extent that other equitable rights *in rem* bind transferees of legal estates in land. The traditional view was that they did not. A decade ago, the contrary assumption appeared to have taken root.[56] The traditional answer has now been reinstated.[57] (In Part II of this book we discuss the kinds of reasons which are relevant to such an issue.[58]).

The second development and its overturning are, in the authorities and in academic commentaries thereon, associated with the question whether contractual licences are or are not 'interests in land'. That reflects the assumption that general trespassory protection entails proprietary status, within the first limb of our alternative characterization.

Nevertheless, on occasion, the first development was also said to involve the question whether contractual licences gave rise merely to rights to damages or were instead 'interests in land'. That terminology has been criticized as an unnecessary 'torturing' of the term 'interest in land'.[59] However, for the purposes of interpreting specific expropriation rules, as opposed to the general question of demarcating the bounds of a property institution, it may be appropriate to describe such a contract as an 'interest in land' simply on the ground that it is specifically enforceable against the other contracting party.

In one case, the Court of Appeal has held that a contractual licensee had an 'interest in land' for the purpose of legislation which made compensation payable, upon the revocation of planning permission, to any person 'interested in the land'.[60] In another case the Court of Appeal held that a specifically

---

[53] *Wood* v. *Leadbitter* (1845) 13 M. & W. 638.

[54] *Hounslow London Borough Council* v. *Twickenham Garden Developments Ltd* [1971] Ch. 233.

[55] *Verrall* v. *Great Yarmouth Borough Council* [1981] QB 202.

[56] *Midland Bank Ltd* v. *Farm Pride Hatcheries Ltd* [1981] 260 EG 493.

[57] *Ashburn Anstalt* v. *Arnold* [1989] Ch. 1.   [58] See Ch. 16, sect. (ii)(c) below.

[59] *Hounslow London Borough Council* v. *Twickenham Garden Developments Ltd* [1971] Ch. 223, at 254, *per* Megarry J.

[60] *Pennine Raceway Ltd* v. *Kirklees Metropolitan Council* [1983] QB 382.

enforceable contract for the lease of an aircraft is an 'interest in property' for the purposes of insolvency law.[61]

These decisions would not carry the implication that all specifically enforceable contracts are, *prima facie*, to be regarded as conferring proprietary interests for the purpose of certain classes of rules. They both related to contracts over tangible entities and, as was pointed out in Chapter 1, objects of proprietary rights are in current English usage, lay and legal, spoken of as themselves being 'property'. One could not, for example, by analogy with these decisions infer that specifically enforceable contracts of service would be held to be 'interests in land' or 'interests in property' within rules of these types. Yet such a holding, in an appropriate context, might be open. It would all depend on the court's *ad hoc* assessment of the appropriate statutory purpose and context. Indeed, as we shall see in Chapter 9, any right, liberty, or opportunity, contractual or otherwise, might be held to come within some statutory or constitutional provision relating to 'property'.

For all that, some terminology is required in order to distinguish specifically enforceable contractual rights from those contractual rights which are also either assignable as part of private wealth or, as 'rights *in rem*', are granted specific trespassory protection. In the ordinary run of property talk, that distinction is expressed in terms of a vague and fluctuating line between rights comprised within the institution of property and those subject only to the institution of contract.

Much more important than such approximate reflection of property-talk distinctions is the question to which we return in Chapter 9. We need to draw some stipulative boundary around the items comprised within a property institution for that notion to be confronted with those property-specific justice reasons which, purportedly, support the existence of such institutions and, at an abstract level, justify various features of property-institutional design. As we shall see, expansive extensions of 'property' terminology, based on generalizations from *ad hoc* interpretations, yield only theoretical obfuscation.

[61] *Bristol Airport Plc* v. *Powdrill* [1990] 2 All ER 493.

5

Ownership as an Organizing Idea

When people confront the world with their claims, desires, projects, and plans, the world they perceive does not consist of a mass of value-free (brute) facts. We all begin situated within a network of social relations and interactions. Our perceptions are coloured by a host of value-laden assumptions. Some of these assumptions are local and passing, others are more pervasive and permanent facets of human association. Any of them may, one way or another, be raised to the level of conscious apprehension and then, perhaps, challenged. The bulk of them, however, provide a taken-for-granted background for all that we think and say. The latter are the organizing ideas of daily life.

At the beginning of Chapter 1 we said that a property institution may function as a complex organizing idea. Later we observed that, in most concrete situations, people are concerned with the bearing of a property institution upon some particular resource, and that it is usually 'ownership' which is the organizing idea.[1] Socialization of the individual carves grooves in the human psyche shaped by conceptions of ownership interests. That prosaic phenomenon is something which political philosophy cannot ignore. It is, as we shall see, a feature of social evolution which Hegel sought to clothe in metaphysical dress.[2]

What was so singular about the imaginary propertyless societies surveyed in Chapter 2 was that their use of resources was never guided by assumptions about ownership. They deployed other organizing ideas, such as the role-terms in Status Land. If property institutions can never be justified, all the value-laden assumptions about ownership which pervade real-world societies must be exposed and we must aspire to a community in which they have been eliminated, such as the world of *Nowhere* envisaged by William Morris.[3]

For the moment we are concerned with the world we know. Each of us encounters daily innumerable (seemingly uncontroversial) assumptions about what may be done to or with items of social wealth for the obvious reason that someone is their owner. This is a social phenomenon which we should have to regard as baleful, or even mysterious, were we to fall in with the kind of ownership-scepticism we shall discuss in Chapter 8.

Set against the fact that people take ownership for granted in daily life and in legal practice, is the failure of philosophy to discover a single concept of ownership.[4] The answer to this puzzle is to be found in what we have called the

---

[1] See Ch. 1, sect. (iii) above.   [2] See Ch. 13 below.
[3] See Ch. 18 below.   [4] See Ch. 1, sect. (i) above.

'ownership spectrum'. People's value-laden assumptions refer to a spectrum of ownership interests, from 'mere property'[5] to 'full-blooded ownership'.[6]

We employ the phrase 'ownership as an organizing idea' to encompass the entire social phenomenon—all those occasions on which unchallenged assumptions about the normative significance of ownership interests provide a background for discourse. In the next chapter we shall turn to situations in which invocations of ownership are explicitly confronted, in legal reasoning, with other values—'ownership as a principle'.

Ownership is everywhere, and has always been so far as written records of human association go, a pervasive organizing idea—however much there has been variation in the subject matters to which it has been applied, the place on the spectrum of various kinds of ownership interests, and the content of property-limitation, expropriation, and appropriation rules. Having described the basic structural features of property institutions in the last two chapters, we are now in a position to demonstrate how this social phenomenon fits into the working of such institutions.

Lawyers share the background assumptions about ownership interests which are prevalent in their societies and they build upon them when they construct other features of property institutions. With illustrations from English law, we shall see how taken-for-granted assumptions about ownership conceptions may be submerged within sophisticated lawyerly constructs.

We shall demonstrate that trespassory rules evolve or are enacted in parallel with these assumptions, so that conceptions of ownership interests are not reducible to the trespassory rules which protect them. Juristic construction makes bricks out of the straw of shared ownership assumptions. We shall examine this process in the special common law contexts of estates in land and the division between law and equity, since learning in these fields has produced much of the fuel for ownership-scepticism. We shall emphasize the plurality and mutability of ownership interests, and examine the sense in which ownership conceptions may be 'contested'.

(i) IRREDUCIBILITY OF OWNERSHIP CONCEPTIONS

The scope of a person's property domain is bounded by the trespassory rules which create it, the property-limitation rules which curtail it and the expropriation rules which may lead to its partial or total demise. Such rules, however, do not spell out its content. The content of ownership interests, anywhere along the spectrum from mere property to full-blooded ownership, is an imprecise and fluctuating product of cultural assumptions and, as such, is presupposed by legal regulation.

As will appear from our discussion of ownership as a principle in the next

---

[5] See Ch. 3, sect. (v) above.   [6] See Ch. 3, sect. (vi) above.

chapter, the rules themselves may be open-textured and their content fleshed out through interaction between conceptions of ownership interests and other values. But even if all the relevant rules could be spelled out with precision, no statement of their import, however exhaustive, could, within any legal or social system, fully convey the significance of property. Ownership acts as an irreducible organizing idea in the daily, non-contested functioning of a property institution. No inferential move from the content of all these rules can give us a list of the privileges and powers which ownership entails.

Brown may have rights against all other citizens that they do not enter or intentionally or recklessly damage his house. He may be prohibited from using it for business purposes without planning permission. He may be liable to have it taken from him by compulsory purchase as part of a road-widening scheme. And so on. Nothing, however, follows from these rules, one way or the other, as to whether he is free to paint the bedrooms a luminous green, or to keep coals in the bath, or to inscribe graffiti on the walls, or to breed spiders in the kitchen. Similarly, nothing in these rules tells us whether Brown can share his house with others on condition that they sing him to sleep at night, or may sell his house at half its cost to the first person to guess his weight. If he may use, abuse, exploit, or transmit in these and countless other less eccentric ways, it is because he is owner.

Eccentricity is merely an example of the legitimized self-seekingness which is the normative import of unreflective invocations of ownership interests. That is why we shall refer to property holdings vested in public agencies as conferring upon them 'quasi-ownership interests'[7] for, in their case, ultimate self-seekingness is absent. If Brown had been a public authority or a charitable trustee ('owning' the house in that capacity), his doings would have conflicted with his role.

Not every kind of self-regarding activity is open to every kind of owner. For one thing, the relevant ownership conception may fall below full-blooded ownership; and even if it does not, property-limitation rules may be in place. Within the parameters, however, it is taken to be obvious that an owner is entitled to suit himself. Whether his reasons for exercising use-privileges, control-powers, or powers of transmission are cogent or not, it is enough that they are his reasons. At the point at which ownership conceptions operate as organizing ideas, controversy is not joined.

Whether the world should be like that is another matter. If none of the property-specific justice reasons later to be investigated is sufficient support for ownership interests in anything at all, countless day-to-day unquestioned assumptions about people being free to do what they like with their own things and their own money would turn out to be morally suspect. Ownership interests are certainly imaginatively dispensable, as we saw (in Chapter 2) in Forest Land, Status Land, Red Land, and Contract Land.

---

[7] See Ch. 7, sect. (iii)(b) below.

Let it not be supposed, however, that there is anything especially modern or western about unreflective invocation of ownership interests. Starting-points along the ownership spectrum, and the kinds of things which it is taken for granted may be owned, change; but *en passant* assumptions about the obvious-ness of ownership implications are as old as written records go. In the parable of the labourers in the vineyard in St Matthew's Gospel, those workers who had toiled all day complained when those who had worked for only an hour received the same wages as had been paid to them. The land owner was speak-ing merely rhetorically when he answered them: '[i]s it not lawful for me to do what I will with mine own?'[8]

Ownership as an organizing idea, in matters small and great, is at work in social life everywhere and all the time. Ownership assumptions are among the trivia of daily life, from childhood up. 'I'll swap you my green marble for your red one!' 'Excuse me, I think that's my handbag actually!' 'Make yourself at home! Treat the place as your own!' And sometimes the matter is more serious. When Lady Churchill, the widow of Sir Winston, died, it was dis-covered that she had destroyed the portrait of her husband painted by Graham Sutherland and given to Sir Winston by an admiring nation. That was a pity, no doubt. But, so the popular reaction went, the picture was her property after all.[9]

(ii) MOVING UP THE SPECTRUM

No one could list the acts that are privileged or empowered by the prevailing conception of ownership, even if it stands near the bottom of the ownership spectrum. The Woodlanders and the Pinklanders would not be able to do that in respect of their mere-property interests. However, there are matters which are off-side lower down the spectrum, which come within the scope of owner-ship interests as one moves up. Privileges of use and abuse may, towards the lower end, not extend to destruction or waste. In modern legal systems, they do reach this far, at least so far as chattels are concerned. In English law, an owner's power of alienation over some works of art is curtailed by a property-limitation rule which requires an export licence to be obtained should they be sold to an overseas buyer. Yet he may destroy the same object and commit no legal wrong.

For chattels of small value, full-blooded ownership holds sway in law, though it may not, in the case of animals, so far as the social dimension of the property institution is concerned. Cruelty to animals is a property-independent prohibition. It makes no difference to the offence whether the perpetrator owned the animal or not. Short of cruelty, mistreatment of an animal may be

---

[8] The Gospel According to St Matthew, A.V., ch. 20, v. 15.
[9] See *The Times,* 17 Jan. 1978, correspondence.

no legal wrong in an owner because it is his, whilst that justification would not be acceptable to societal opinion. It will be recalled that property is a social as well as a legal institution and that the content of the one is not necessarily coterminous with that of the other. 'You left the dog shut up in the car in the sun?' 'Well, it's my dog!' 'So what!'

Ownership powers of control and transmission all involve capacity to create relations with others by virtue of a person's ownership of something. Powers to control uses by others are as open-ended a class as are ownership use-privileges. Powers of transmission are typically subject to legal regulation as to the formalities required for their valid exercise. For that reason they are the subject of generalized legal categorization—gift, sale, bequest, and so on. Nevertheless, the range of concrete exercises of transmission powers—what to give and to whom, and so forth—is indeterminate and is premised upon a prevailing conception of ownership as an organizing idea. A person may give what she likes to whom she pleases because she is owner. She is not owner because the law specifies useful formalities for demarcating valid from ineffective gifts.

Like use and abuse privileges, ownership powers widen as we move up the spectrum, there being, however, that point of discontinuity in the transition to which we have already referred—*viz.*, where transmission of the owner's entire bundle of privileges and powers is allowed.[10] At the mere-property lower end of the spectrum, as we saw in Wood Land and Pink Land, there is no power in an 'owner' to transmit that entirety to others, either *inter vivos* or on death. He is restricted to such exploitation as flows from mere control-powers—that is, to transactions in which he confers, gratuitously or for returned favours, some limited share in his use-privileges. Further up the spectrum, the owner may be empowered to transmit his whole bundle of privileges and powers over the thing, *inter vivos*, by way of gift or exchange and, once a monetary medium appears, by way of sale. Finally, ownership-powers may encompass qualified or absolute freedom of testation.

A property institution may also include a variety of sub-institutions which facilitate diversity in an owner's transactional freedom. It may empower him to create ownership interests lower on the spectrum than the plenitude vested in him, through leases, settlements, or trusts. Or it may empower him to create non-ownership proprietary interests by the grant of easements, profits, and other 'incorporeal' hereditaments.

The more sophisticated the transaction, the less likely it is that the social and legal aspects of a property institution coincide. Ownership, as a lay organizing idea, encompasses the notion, in England, that if a person owns something it follows that he can sell it or give it away or leave it by will. But it is implausible to suppose that the layman would also infer that, as owner, a person can invoke that fearsome anachronism, the 'strict settlement' of land.[11]

---

[10] See Ch. 3, sect. (vi) above.　　[11] Discussed in sect. (iv) below.

For all that, 'ownership' is not a term of art in English law. It has no legally defined content at all.[12] Lay and legal practice draw on the same well of imprecise and fluctuating cultural assumptions about ownership interests, divergence occurring only where legal regulation has fallen out of line with societal opinion or where technical invention has outrun lay concerns.

This shared (legal and lay) employment of the same organizing idea is clear enough in the case of chattels. For example, the Theft Act 1968 defines theft as the dishonest appropriation of property belonging to another with an intention permanently to deprive, and it defines appropriation as 'any assumption by a person of the rights of an owner'.[13] What those rights are, however, is not defined by the Act. The courts have wrestled with the question whether an appropriation should be understood to occur if someone assumes any right which an owner has over his goods, or whether it requires an assumption of all of those rights, or some middle position between these extremes. In particular, the House of Lords has changed its mind twice on the question whether someone who makes use of chattels or money with the owner's permission—that is, who exercises a use-privilege but not the concomitant control-power—thereby assumes an ownership 'right'.[14] As the law now stands, if I invite you to take a seat and you do so, you 'appropriate' my chair—although, of course, you will lack the *mens rea* requisite for theft.

Throughout these controversies it has been taken for granted that what ownership rights actually are is to be inferred from the extra-legal conception of ownership. In the case of most chattels, they are therefore those of full-blooded ownership. Since the 'rights' of an owner of ordinary chattels include, *prima facie*, unlimited privileges of use and abuse and unlimited powers of control and transmission, it is hardly surprising that the definition of an offence, which builds this conception into the *actus reus*, has produced problems.

In contrast with chattels, ownership interests in land are, in common law systems, shrouded in obscurity as a consequence of the doctrine of estates.

(iii) ESTATES IN LAND

The significance of ownership interests as an every-day organizing idea is commonly obscured for lawyers in common law systems, and for theorists who seek to build upon the insights of the common law, by the doctrine of estates in land. Land-transfer transactions in common law systems convey or create estates, freehold or leasehold, never *dominium* or ownership. This is a consequence of the feudal origins of English real property law.

[12] Cf. J. W. C. Turner, 'Some Reflections on Ownership in English Law' (1941) 19 *Can. BR* 342.

[13] Theft Act 1968, s. 3(1).

[14] *Lawrence* v. *M.P.C.* [1972] AC 626; *R.* v. *Morris* [1984] AC 329; *R.* v. *Gomez* [1993] AC 442.

In Early English feudal law, that interest which was to develop into the fee simple estate was a grant of seisin by a superior lord to be held by the grantee and his heirs subject to one or other variant of free tenure. It seems that the consent of both the lord and the heir were necessary before the grantee could alienate his land.[15] Free alienability *inter vivos* of this estate evolved at common law, and free testamentary disposition of it was conferred by statute in the sixteenth century. There were as well lesser estates of freehold: estates for life; estates *pur autre vie*; and the estate tail which emerged as the result of judicial interpretation of the Statute *de donis conditionalibus* of 1285. There were also a variety of copyhold estates, the outcome of the progressive emancipation of land held on non-free tenure.

The leasehold estate was unknown to feudal law, but evolved from the end of the Middle Ages as common law actions were adapted to confer trespassory protection on a leaseholder, eventually, against all-comers to the land.[16] Like the fee simple, the leasehold estate became freely transmissible *inter vivos* or on death. A covenant in a lease may prohibit assignment of the estate. Its effect is not, technically, to make the estate inalienable but to give rise to a ground for forfeiture should the estate be assigned in breach of covenant.[17]

The terminology and conceptual structures elaborated in works on English real property law have reflected the technical concerns of conveyancers. Since what is conveyed is always an estate in the land, it has been widely assumed that 'ownership' of land, as such, is not a conception internal to English land law.[18] A. D. Hargreaves gave robust expression to this view:

English land law has made no contribution to the legal theory of ownership more striking, more brilliant and of more permanent value than the separation of the land from the estate in the land. . . . By distinguishing the land from the estate, English land law has shown conclusively that even within a society as individualistic and as legalistic as England in the nineteenth century, ownership is not a necessary legal concept. The problem of ownership remains, but it is not a legal problem; it is the concern of the politician, the economist, the sociologist, the moralist, the psychologist—of any and every specialist who can contribute his grain to the common heap. Ultimately the philosopher will try to unify this shifting mass into a coherent whole.[19]

The story of the evolution of the doctrine of estates is one of complex elaboration based on the writ system, ancient statutes, and the conveyancing cunning of legal practitioners. If asked what was the content of the interests which

[15] W. S. Holdsworth, *A History of English Law* (3rd edn., Methuen & Co. Ltd, 1923) iii, 73–87; S. F. C. Milsom, *The Legal Framework of English Feudalism* (CUP, 1976), ch. 5; A. W. B. Simpson, *A History of the Land Law* (2nd edn., Clarendon Press, 1986) 51–4.
[16] F. W. Maitland, *The Forms of Action at Common Law* (CUP, 1936), lecture V.
[17] *Governors of the Peabody Donation Fund* v. *Higgins* [1983] 3 All ER 122 (CA).
[18] See, e.g, Bernard Rudden, 'Notes Towards a Grammar of Property' [1980] *Conv.* 325.
[19] A. D. Hargreaves, 'Modern Real Property' (1956) 19 *MLR* 14, at 17.

came thus to be freely disposable by their holders, the traditional real property lawyer will answer that it consisted of a right to seisin or possession of the land. But if a man was the beneficiary of seisin or possession, what use-privileges over the land did that entail, and what powers to control uses by others? No general answer to that question is usually to be found in land law textbooks, although the case law on nuisance summarized in works on tort is replete with partial answers to it.

The answer to the general question about the normative content of a right to seisin or a right to possession is glaringly obvious. Perhaps it is so manifest as to be trite, and so beneath the notice of a technical lawyer who seeks to expound only that which is obscure and arcane. The truth is that ownership interests in land, of various magnitudes, are and always have been incidents of legal estates in land.[20] The jurists of the early medieval period took it for granted that the tenant who holds land in demesne is as much *dominus rei* as is the owner of a chattel.[21] As Pollock and Maitland point out, Bracton and his contemporaries (rightly in their view) 'ascribed to the tenant in demesne ownership and nothing less than ownership'.[22]

All the activities of the eccentric Brown (set out in section (i) of this Chapter) were open to him because the freehold or leasehold estate which had been conveyed to him carried an ownership interest. That notion must be interposed between the fact of conveyance and the questioned activity as an organizing idea.

This truth, however trite, makes claims such as those contained in the above citation from Hargreaves patently absurd. Ownership of land is not a conveyancer's problem, but it is a conception—or rather a battery of conceptions—internal to the law. An indefinitely large set of use-privileges and control-powers over the land follow from the fact that, as an incident to the estate, a person has an ownership interest in the land itself.

Real property lawyers, like everyone else, have always known that this was so. It was simply not worth dwelling on since, unlike the estates and title conditions themselves, the ownership interests carried by estates are not technical terms of art. Their content is imprecise, mutable, and a reflection of non-technical prevailing social assumptions. Challis, in a classic work on real property law, mentions almost as an aside that:

[A fee simple] confers, and since the beginning of legal history it has always conferred, the lawful right to exercise over, upon, and in respect to, the land, every act of ownership which can enter into the imagination, including the right to commit unlimited waste; and, for all practical purposes of ownership, it differs

---

[20] Cf. J. W. Harris, 'Ownership of Land in English Law', in N. MacCormick and P. Birks (eds.): *The Legal Mind* (Clarendon Press, 1986).

[21] See Sir Frederick Pollock and F. W. Maitland, *History of English Law* (CUP, 1911), ii, 2–6.

[22] *Ibid.* 6.

from the absolute dominion of a chattel, in nothing except the physical indestructibility of its subject.[23]

This statement is somewhat of an exaggeration. As we have seen, in the early
stages of its historical development transmission powers were restricted. As to
use and abuse privileges and powers of control over the land, some inherent
limitations may once have derived from particular species of tenure, and
some minerals have always been vested in the Crown. Apart from 'physical
indestructibility', buildings differ from chattels in that some uses of them,
especially æsthetic uses, cannot in practice be policed by trespassory rules.
The outer boundary of the control-powers entailed by ownership interests is
always reciprocally related to the trespassory rules which protect them.[24]

Nevertheless, Challis's point is basically correct. The ownership interest
which came to be the adjunct of a fee-simple-estate-in-possession in common
law systems approaches closely to full-blooded ownership. It must always be
borne in mind, however, that rights to exercise 'every act of ownership which
can enter into the imagination' are only *prima facie* privileges and powers.
There are many more property-limitation rules restricting ownership of land
than those which curtail ownership of chattels.

Conveyancing practice normally need take no account of the ownership
interest which is the taken-for-granted incident of a legal estate. Exceptionally,
however, it may surface even in this context. An example concerns the concept
of sham. A document is a sham, and hence without legal effect, if it is intended
'to give to third parties or to the court the appearance of creating between the
parties legal rights and obligations different from the actual rights and obligations (if any) which the parties intend to create'.[25] When is a conveyance of a
legal estate a sham? When the parties' true intention is that the conveyee is
not, in reality, to receive the legal estate. But by what test do we decide the
quality of such an intention? It turns on whether the parties envisaged that the
conveyee would carry out 'acts of ownership', for that is the ordinary attribute
of a legal estate.[26]

[23] H. W. Challis, *Law of Real Property* (3rd edn. by Charles Sweet, Butterworth, 1911),
218.   [24] See Ch. 3, sect. (vi) above.

[25] *Snook* v. *London & West Riding Investments Ltd* [1967] 2 QB 786 at 802, *per* Diplock
LJ.

[26] In *Ferris* v. *Weaven* [1952] 2 All ER 233, a husband purported to convey a house in
consideration of a payment of £30 to a collaborator, merely so that the husband himself
could dispose of it freed from his wife's residential rights. The parties' true intention was that
the husband should continue to act as owner, so the purported conveyance was held to be a
sham. (So the decision was interpreted in *National Provincial Bank Ltd* v. *Ainsworth* [1965]
AC 1175 at 1223, *per* Lord Hodson and at 1257, 1258, *per* Lord Wilberforce.) In *Miles* v.
Bull [1969] 1 QB 258, a comparable manœuvre was successful. A conveyance was rushed
through to frustrate any attempt by the wife to register her occupation rights. Nevertheless,
since the purchaser's intention to enjoy an ownership interest over the land was genuine, the
conveyance was not a sham. Megarry J said: 'if in *Ferris* v. *Weaven* the purchaser had sought
to exercise acts of ownership, and the husband had ceased to do them, . . . it would, in my
judgment, be very difficult to contend that the low price and the failure to pay it made the
transaction a sham' (*ibid.* 265).

According to the doctrine of estates, he who has a legal estate in land has the right to possess the land, either for a time or indefinitely. He has that right either presently or, if the estate is reversionary, in the future. What he is privileged or empowered to do to or with the land by virtue of that right to possession is, however, referred to conceptions of land-ownership as organizing ideas. In that sense, land-ownership is internal to the concept of an estate.

Every legal estate, including a short tenancy, carries an ownership interest of some kind—that is, an open-ended set of use-privileges and control-powers. That conceptual truth may or may not be reflected in lay and legal terminology. The privileges and powers of the holder of a short tenancy are of limited duration and hence of incomparably less economic and social significance than those of a freeholder or long leaseholder. So if one poses the question, who is *the* owner of this house or flat?, answers will refer only to those with leases of a substantial duration, although usage points to no particular cut-off point. In some contexts, reasoning proceeds on the assumption that the freeholder is an 'absolute owner' in a sense in which even a long leaseholder is not.[27] On the other hand, even in the case of a short tenancy, the house or flat is the tenant's to use and control as he pleases, subject to agreement to the contrary and to property-limitation rules. For the time being it is 'her' house or flat. She is its (temporary) owner.

The words 'owner' or 'ownership' need not be employed to express the essential organizing idea, for one can speak of 'possession' or 'occupation' instead.[28] From time to time, however, when the open-ended character of the organizing idea is actually in point, tenants, of all kinds, are spoken of as 'owners'. For example, a conspiracy to trespass on land was an offence at common law, whether an occupier was a freeholder or a tenant, 'where the intention is to occupy the premises to the exclusion of the owner's rights'.[29]

In English law a wide range of statutory protection turns on the distinction between tenancy and licence to occupy. In *Street* v. *Mountford*,[30] the House of Lords laid it down that the distinction must be applied by reference to the common law concept of an estate. If parties agree to confer and receive 'exclusive possession' for a term at a rent, they thereby automatically create a leasehold estate. Of course, exclusivity of possession is a matter of degree. The crucial question was whether the occupier was granted the limited rights of a lodger, in which case he had a licence, or whether he was accorded

---

[27] *Stokes (Inspector of Taxes)* v. *Costain Property Investments Ltd* [1984] 1 All ER 849 (CA): installations in a building did not 'belong to' the leaseholder, whatever the length of his lease, for purposes of capital allowances against tax, since only the freeholder was 'absolute owner'.

[28] See sect. (vii)(c) below.

[29] *Kamara* v. *DPP* [1974] AC 104 at 130, *per* Lord Hailsham LC. The offence has been abolished in England by the Criminal Law Act 1977.

[30] [1985] AC 809.

the open-ended set of use-privileges and control-powers characteristic of an ownership interest. In Lord Templeman's words:

The tenant possessing exclusive possession is able to exercise the rights of an owner of land which is in the real sense his land, albeit temporarily and subject to certain restrictions. A tenant armed with exclusive possession can keep out strangers and keep out the landlord unless the landlord is exercising limited rights reserved to him by the tenancy agreement to enter and view and repair. A licensee, lacking exclusive possession, can in no sense call the land his own and cannot be said to own any estate in the land.[31]

The common law deploys different conceptions of ownership along the ownership spectrum depending on the relationship, within the doctrine of estates, of the occupier to the land. If he is a freeholder vested with a fee simple estate his *prima facie* use and abuse privileges and his *prima facie* powers of control and transmission are almost unlimited. Subject to the very significant property-limitation rules contained in the law of nuisance, planning law, and so forth, he can do what he pleases to or with the land; and he can freely transmit his bundle of ownership privileges and powers as an adjunct to a conveyance of the estate.

The occupier vested with a long leasehold estate has no *prima facie* privileges of waste, but subject to that his *prima facie* use-privileges and powers of control and transmission are similar to those of the freeholder, although in practice he will have contracted not to exercise many of them by virtue of covenants in the lease. The short leaseholder or periodic tenant has such restrictions on his *prima facie* bundle of use-privileges and powers as flow from the tenuous nature of the particular possessory interest he holds; and his transmission powers will usually in substance be taken away by covenants against assignment, subletting, or parting with possession. A statutory tenancy created under the Rent Acts conferred security of tenure but was not assign-able *inter vivos*, did not vest in a trustee in bankruptcy, and could pass on death only to members of the tenant's family residing with him at his death. It was consequently described in the authorities as a merely personal right, as distinct from estates in land known to the common law. The same is true of the non-assignable secure periodic tenancy which now arises under Part 4 of the Housing Act 1985.[32] Yet even such a right carries an ownership interest in the dwelling, in the sense that the tenant has open-ended use-privileges and control-powers over it.[33]

The position of all such persons—long leaseholders, short leaseholders, and statutory tenants—ranks higher on the ownership spectrum than does that of the imaginary Pink Land licensees. Yet even the 'mere property' of the latter

---

[31] [1985] AC 816.
[32] *London City Corporation* v. *Brown*, *The Times*, 11 Oct. 1989.
[33] See Catherine Hand, 'The Statutory Tenancy: An Unrecognised Proprietary Interest?' [1980] *Conv.* 351.

constituted an ownership interest for, within severe limits, they enjoy an open-ended set of use-privileges and control-powers. The limiting case is that of someone whose occupation is protected by trespassory rules but who lacks any power to allow others to share his or her residual use-privileges. Such (as we saw) was the nature of a spousal half-property occupational right protected by registration under the Matrimonial Homes Act.[34] A mere lodger or guest is without even a half-property interest. His use-privileges are inferred from the terms of his contractual or bare licence without the mediation of any species of ownership interest as an organizing idea.

(iv) LAW AND EQUITY

The role of ownership interests as organizing ideas has been obscured by the common law doctrine of estates. The institution of trusts has added to such perplexities. How can something be owned if there is simultaneously a legal and an equitable owner?

The answer is that both law and equity presuppose the same bundle of ownership privileges and powers over the land as an incident of the legal estate. Where that legal estate is held on trust for private individuals, it is of the essence of what is traditionally termed the 'equitable estate'[35] that the beneficiaries may insist that the trustee exercise all the rights incident to the legal estate, including ownership privileges and powers over the land, not for his own benefit, but in the interests of the beneficiaries—so that, as we have seen, trusts constitute one mechanism for separating wealth from use.[36]

Equitable rules have instantiated this basic principle by imposing a variety of more concrete trustee duties. Equity created no trustee powers since such powers were already implicit in the common law ownership interest vested in the trustee as an incident of the estate. It is the province of equity to control the exercise of such powers in the service of the basic principle. Particular powers are conferred upon trustees by trust-creating instruments and by statute for two reasons. If a trustee exercises his inherent ownership powers entirely within the terms of such particular powers, then, first, he is protected against any allegation that the basic principle has been infringed and, secondly, those transacting with him are guaranteed against the exercise of a power being subsequently set aside.

The basic principle that ownership privileges and powers must be exercised in the interests of the beneficiaries is now overlaid with a wealth of statutory and case law detail, but it surfaces raw from time to time. For example, one of the exceptional circumstances in which a landlord could recover possession of

---

[34] See Ch. 3, sect. (iv) above.

[35] The 1925 English property legislation prefers the expression 'equitable interests'.

[36] See Ch. 4, sect. (ii)(b)(3) above.

a dwelling which was subject to a protected tenancy under the Rent Acts was where the dwelling was reasonably required by the landlord as a residence for himself. Landlords who were trustees were not normally able to take advantage of this exception, because such personal residence by them would necessarily involve exercising ownership privileges for their own benefit and hence amount to a breach of trust. It was otherwise if the reason for the trustees wishing to reside in the premises was that they proposed to occupy them together with infant beneficiaries in their guardianship, for then ownership privileges were being exercised in the interest of the beneficiaries.[37]

English law currently imposes elaborate statutory regimes on trusts of land. If the land is not held for a single adult beneficiary, then either the land is subjected to a notional trust for sale, or there is no duty to sell and successive beneficiaries take their interests under a 'strict settlement'. In the latter case extensive powers of disposition are conferred on the beneficiary presently entitled to an ownership interest (the 'tenant for life'). The Settled Land Act 1925 also insists that the tenant for life must be given the legal estate in the land for no better reason, it seems, than this: ownership privileges and powers are the incidents of legal estates; statute confers most such privileges and powers on the tenant for life; therefore, it is 'logical' that he should receive the legal estate.[38] The Law Commission has wisely suggested that all this statutory complexity should be swept away by straightforwardly invoking ownership as an organizing idea. The ramshackle dual system of trust for sale and strict settlement should be replaced by a simple land trust. The legal estate would be vested in the trustees and they would then have all the privileges and powers which are the incident of that concept. Statutory elaboration of powers can be scrapped. Of course, the trustees would be obliged to use every one of their privileges and powers in the interests of the beneficiaries.[39]

(v) THE PLURALITY AND MUTABILITY OF OWNERSHIP INTERESTS

Property institutions, of one kind or another, are ubiquitous. Everywhere 'ownership' acts as an organizing idea between desire and authorized choice. However, any attempt to articulate a single conception of ownership by reference to these invocations would be hopeless. Nothing unites them except their

[37] *Patel* v. *Patel* [1982] 1 All ER 65 (CA).

[38] It is sometimes suggested that the reason for vesting the legal estate in a tenant for life is to enable him to confer a clear title upon purchasers of the land. In fact, this objective is forwarded under the Act by requiring a vesting deed conveying the legal estate to be executed as a separate document, distinct from the trust instrument declaring the trusts. This two-document procedure could have been instituted whether the legal estate was vested in the trustees or the tenant for life. As things are, both trustees and tenant for life are involved when the tenant for life decides to exercise his power of sale, since a clear title will only be passed if the purchaser pays 'capital money' to the trustees.

[39] Law Com. no. 181: *Trusts of Land* (1989).

open-ended character, authorized self-seekingness, and the fact that they are
relations between persons and assets. They witness to a multiplicity of ownership interests along the ownership spectrum.

The common law doctrine of estates in land is merely one illustration of
the multiplicity of ownership interests. Full-blooded ownership may not be
presupposed even of all chattels, as our discussion of animals in section (ii)
suggests. When slavery existed, it was not necessarily the case that the ownership interests which property institutions recognized over human beings were
at the top of the spectrum. As we have seen, ownership interests over ideational
entities protected by modern systems of intellectual property fall short of this
point too.[40] Open-ended ownership interests in hived-off items of wealth-
potential—cashable rights—do not, by their nature, entail use-privileges.[41]

Furthermore, ownership interests, deriving as they do from societal assumptions, fluctuate over time even in relation to the same subject matters. We have
spoken of 'moving up the ownership spectrum'. It should not be supposed that
such movement coincides with any historical, uniform, and unilinear process.
On the contrary, the prevailing conception of ownership from which *prima
facie* privileges and powers flow may shrink as well as expand.

It was once part of legal doctrine that ownership privileges and powers over
land extended into the upper atmosphere. English lawyers for centuries
parroted the medieval maxim: *cujus est solum ejus est usque ad coelum et ad
inferos*. Needless to say, there was no social counterpart to this lawyerly flight
of fancy, so far as it purported to extend ownership upwards as well as
downwards. When aircraft were invented, it became necessary to determine
whether trespassory rules should actually be recognized extending protection
to the upper air. In England, the matter was initially dealt with by statute, but
eventually English common law fell into line with what were perceived to be
social assumptions about the extent of ownership interest in this respect. The
suggestion that an owner of land could maintain an action in trespass against
over-flying aircraft was rejected. A landowners' control-powers were held to
extend upwards only so far as was needed for protection of his enjoyment of
the surface and buildings.[42]

The problem is to balance the rights of an owner to enjoy the use of his land
against the rights of the general public to take advantage of all that science now
offers in the use of air space. This balance is in my judgement best struck in our
present society by restricting the rights of an owner in the air space above his
land to such height as is necessary for the ordinary use and enjoyment of his
land and the structures on it, and declaring that above that height he has no
greater rights in the air space than any other member of the public.[43]

[40] See Ch. 4, sect. (i) above.
[41] See Ch. 4, sect. (ii)(b) above.
[42] *Bernstein* v. *Skyviews and General Ltd* [1977] 2 All ER 902.
[43] [1977] 2 All ER 902 at 907, *per* Griffiths J.

However, even if over-flying itself does not constitute a trespass (in municipal as distinct from international law), it may, in particular contexts, interfere with a landowner's 'use and enjoyment of his land'. For example, the United States Supreme Court has ruled that government over-flights which caused chickens scared by the noise to fly into the walls of a coop and kill themselves constituted a taking of private property and required compensation.[44]

If conceptions of ownership interests mutate in the face of technological developments even in the case of land, how much more so is that likely to occur with the multitude of novel ownable entities thrown up by advances in electronic communication and the information industry. We shall not here speculate about the resources which may be brought within the scope of property institutions in the next century. Whatever they are, it may plausibly be predicted that the law will build upon shared cultural assumptions. The ingrained social phenomenon of ownership as an organizing idea is unlikely to disappear.

(vi) THE CONTESTABILITY OF OWNERSHIP CONCEPTIONS

Property-limitation rules presuppose ownership interests. If a particular privilege or power were not already taken to be part of an ownership interest, it would not be necessary to remove it. However, change in the base-line presupposed by a particular conception of an ownership interest may come about, either through long-term internalization of property-limitation rules, or for any other cause affecting cultural assumptions. In addition, the part played in social and legal practice by ownership interests, as taken-for-granted organizing ideas, may itself be contested. That is obviously the case where the range of privileges and powers is indeterminate—like the example of the man who leaves his dog shut in his car in the sun. More importantly, it is fortunately an attribute of human spirituality that it can stand back from the settled assumptions of its social context and challenge them on the grounds of justice.

Some theorists deny the existence of this human attribute, for the curious reason that to suppose it to exist is to envisage an individual human subject devoid of beliefs.[45] There is no need to whistle up straw men of this sort. Beliefs about justice are among the beliefs that we have and, exceptionally, deliberative reflection may give them priority over the other baggage of normative and factual assumptions which we also all carry.

Such moral distancing from settled practices of ownership-invocation is the province of the practising reformer or revolutionary. It may be beyond the

---

[44] *United States* v. *Causby*, 328 US 256 (1946).
[45] See, e.g., Stanley Fish, *Doing What Comes Naturally: Change, Rhetoric and the Practice of Theory in Literary and Legal Studies* (Clarendon Press, 1989), especially chs. 14 and 15.

power of the unsophisticated. Recall the poignant dilemma of Huckleberry Finn in Mark Twain's novel, who comes within an ace of betraying his runaway slave companion, but whose heart prevails over what he knows to be his duty:

Conscience says to me, 'What had poor Miss Watson done to you, that you could see her nigger go off right under your eyes and never say one word?' . . . Then I . . . says to myself, hold on,—s'pose you'd a done right and given Jim up; would you felt better than what you do now? No, says I, I'd feel bad—I'd feel just the same way I do now. Well, then, says I, what's the use you learning to do right, when it's troublesome to do right and ain't no trouble to do wrong, and the wages is just the same?[46]

We, removed as we are from the monstrous notion of ownership as an organizing idea applicable to human beings, can only enter empathetically into Huck's dilemma. Happily, there were in his day reformers who were able to challenge taken-for-granted assumptions even within cultures which shared them.

Prevailing ownership conceptions may be challenged in ways far less dramatic than those mounted by slavery abolitionists. Reformers may insist that settled ownership conceptions ought to be altered, not merely restricted by particular property-limitation rules. Environmental protection in an overcrowded world is accorded universal lip-service. The predominant approach seems to be that environmental harms override ownership use-privileges and control-powers which therefore need to be restricted. A more radical stance would be to claim that, whatever may have been assumed in the past, we should now persuade people to accept that ownership itself confers no *prima facie* privileges to engage in, or *prima facie* powers to permit, uses of resources which are environmentally deleterious.[47]

Perhaps the pay-off from such a shift in the way which ownership functions as an organizing idea would be that constraints could not then be viewed as taking anything away from owners. Supposing, for example, it were to be discovered that the use of a certain kind of pesticide in agriculture had intolerable side-effects on the human food chain and it was therefore agreed on all hands that its use should be completely banned. Now—so the radical critic might argue—conceived of as a property-limitation rule the new measure will raise questions of compensation for farmers, whereas that would not be the case if we had educated people to accept that decisions about what (if any) pesticides should be employed is exclusively a public matter and not something reached by use-privileges and control-powers inherent in ownership. He

---

[46] Mark Twain, *The Adventures of Huckleberry Finn* (Chatto and Windus, 1912 edn.), ch. xvi.

[47] That is the strategy recommended by Linton K. Caldwell, 'Rights of Ownership or Rights of Use: The Need for a New Conceptual Basis for Land Use Policy' (1974) 15 *William & Mary LR* 759.

might encounter responses of either of the two following kinds. First, the proposal has unwelcome implications. Are inhabitants of the developed world to instruct their brethren in poorer countries that, not only should they cease to destroy rainforests, but that no question of compensation for complying with such strictures can arise because the fact that the forests were theirs carried no rights to engage in or permit deforestation in the first place? Secondly, as we shall see, there are in any case many kinds of property-limitation rules which escape the compensation principle notwithstanding that they are recognized to be property-limitation rules.[48]

(vii) SOME RED HERRINGS

As we shall see in Chapter 8, juristic puzzles have been spawned by attempts to encompass different ownership interests along the ownership spectrum within a unitary concept of ownership. These puzzles have been worse confounded by admixtures of resource-ownership with other notions in which ownership terminology is deployed. Some of these refer to other features of property institutions, and some to matters outside the purview of property altogether. The most misleading of the latter concerns the notion of 'self-ownership'.[49] A few minor red herrings will be dealt with at this stage.

(a) Ownership and Owning

In analyses of the concept of ownership by English-speaking jurists, unnecessary complexities have sometimes been introduced as a result of the dual transitivity of the verb 'to own'. The object of the verb may be a resource, or it may be a right or collection of rights. Thus non-ownership proprietary interests, such as easements and mortgages, can be 'owned'. The latter sense of the verb is equivalent to being vested with, having title to, being entitled to, or simply 'having'.

A relationship to a right (or collection of rights) is one thing. What the right or rights to which one is related amount to is something else. It is unnecessary and mystifying to suppose, as some have done,[50] that both are somehow comprehended within the same concept merely because 'own' can, in correct English, be used in both contexts.

X is or he is not entitled to a particular right of way—he does or he does

---

[48] See Ch. 6, sect. (iii)(c) below.   [49] See Ch. 11, sect. (ii) below.

[50] See, e.g., Sir John Salmond, *Salmond on Jurisprudence* (7th edn., Sweet & Maxwell, 1924), 279: 'Ownership in its most comprehensive signification denotes the relation between a person and any right that is vested in him. That which a man owns in this sense is in all cases a right.' Editors of subsequent editions of Salmond's book retain this claim up to the 11th edn. (Glanville Williams (ed.), 1957), 300. It is repudiated in the 12th edn. (P. J. Fitzgerald (ed.), 1966), 250–1.

not 'own' it. If he is so entitled, what he may do in relation to the subject-matter of the right of way is fixed by the terms of the transaction or the application of the expropriation rule under which he became vested with it, not by reference to an open-ended set of privileges and powers along the ownership spectrum. What one may 'own' (be entitled to) may be an owner-ship interest, or a lesser proprietary, or other, right. Only if the entitlement is to an ownership interest does 'ownership' function as an organizing idea from which concrete privileges and powers may be inferred. As we shall see, this red herring has spawned baleful progeny in the modern literature on the economic analysis of law.[51]

(b) Relativity of Title

We have seen that property institutions necessarily contain title conditions.[52] If ownership interests are to function as organizing ideas, there must be means for determining in whom they are vested. Sometimes, these conditions are relative only, that is to say, certain facts may be sufficient, within the institu-tion, to enable X to claim the protection of trespassory rules as against Y, whilst not excluding the possibility that some other person, W, may be entitled to their protection as against X. In such contexts, W is commonly spoken of as 'the true owner'. Some commentators have gone on to infer that ownership means absolute title, so that if a property institution's rules make no provision for the establishment of absolute title it follows that they are indifferent to the concept of ownership.

One of the grounds upon which, at common law, X can establish that his title is superior to Y's, is by showing that he or his predecessors in title were in possession before Y or Y's predecessors in title. This applies both to chattels[53] and to land.[54] However, it was never settled at common law whether prior possession by itself, in the absence of proof of ouster, would suffice in the event that Y, as a defence to an action in conversion or ejectment, was able to point to some specific W who would have a better title than X—a defence of *jus tertii*.[55] The position as to land was the subject of a famous debate be-tween W. S. Holdsworth and A. D. Hargreaves.[56] Holdsworth maintained that

[51] See Ch. 9, sect. (iii)(a) below.
[52] See Ch. 3, sect. (xii) above.
[53] *Armory* v. *Delamirie* (1722) 1 Str. 505.
[54] *Asher* v. *Whitlock* [1865] 1 QB 1.
[55] In English law, the matter has now been settled for chattels by s. 8(1) of the Torts (Interference with Goods) Act 1977, which expressly allows such a defence. The issue is unlikely to arise for land, since once a proprietor has been registered with 'absolute title' to an estate in registered land, he is usually shielded from rectification claims based only on the fact of prior possession—see Land Registration Act 1925, s. 82(3), as interpreted in *Epps* v. *Esso Petroleum Ltd* [1973] 2 All ER 465.
[56] W. S. Holdsworth, *A History of English Law* (3rd edn., Methuen and Co. Ltd. 1923), vii, 57–81; A. D. Hargreaves, 'Terminology and Title in Ejectment' (1940) 56 *LQR* 376; W. S. Holdsworth, 'Terminology and Title in Ejectment—A Reply' (1940) 56 *LQR* 479.

a defence of *jus tertii* had evolved and that therefore the concept of 'ownership of land' had been introduced into the common law. Hargreaves supposed that, by refuting the availability of the defence, he had shown that no such concept had been introduced.

It is manifest that the debate had nothing to do with ownership interests. It posited the contrast between being 'the owner', in the sense of a person entitled to an estate, and being 'the true owner', in the sense of someone who could establish an absolute title to an estate. In either case, the content of the ownership interest which is the incident of the estate is the same. If a person has satisfied the conditions of title relative to anyone else with whom he is in dispute, he has, as against that person, the protection afforded by the relevant trespassory rules. If what those rules afford to him is an open-ended set of privileges and powers at some point along the ownership spectrum (technically as an adjunct to an estate in the case of land), what he is free to do or achieve has no inferential connection with title conditions. Ownership, as an organizing idea, is an independent variable.

(c) Ownership and Possession

We have from time to time spoken of interests along the ownership spectrum as open-ended 'possessive' relationships between persons and things. In what sense, then, are 'ownership' and 'possession' different concepts?

This question has presented a seemingly intractable puzzle for analytic jurists for this reason. On the one hand, ownership is eminently a normative concept. Once it is conceded that X is the owner of something, an open-ended set of conclusions follows, as to what he, and no one else, is permitted to do to or with it. Can we not then distinguish possession as a factual concept? It refers to some relationship which, as a matter of fact, holds between a person and a thing and in itself provides the basis for no normative judgements. It is merely a fact which rules of law deploy amongst the conditioning facts of some legal consequences.

However, it is notorious that whether or not a person is in possession may itself be decided as a question of law. It is not simply that 'possession' is a matter of degree, a factual concept which is fuzzy at the perimeter. Different rules of law employ it in different ways, and its interpretation is often related to the supposed purpose of particular rules and so involves normative judgement.[57]

The first step out of this quagmire is to recognize the plurality and mutability of ownership interests along the ownership spectrum. Property institutions deploy open-ended normative relations between persons and things along

For a comprehensive review of the literature relevant to this and related issues, see Kent McNeil, *Common Law Aboriginal Title* (Clarendon Press, 1989), ch. 2.

[57] See D. R. Harris, 'The Concept of Possession in English Law', in A. G. Guest (ed.), *Oxford Essays in Jurisprudence* (OUP, 1961).

this spectrum. In any system in which something approaching full-blooded ownership is sometimes invoked, it is to be expected that lawyers and laymen will make use of some other term to stand for open-ended ownership interests lower down the spectrum by way of contrast with the full-blooded paradigm. Modern lawyers, confronted with our imaginary Pink Land, would, no doubt, assert that what the licensees of dwellings were accorded in that society was, not ownership, but 'possession' or 'occupation'. Similarly, Wood Land tool-makers, since they had no right to sell or will away their rights, might be said to be merely protected possessors.

Short leaseholders and long-term hirers of chattels are not called 'owners', by lawyers or laymen, because there is someone else in the background with a much more extensive bundle of rights for whom the label is appropriately reserved. Yet all these people have, by virtue of their relationship to an asset, an open-ended set of use-privileges and control-powers. The cut-off point, at the foot of the ownership spectrum, is where they do not, where a contract specifically defines what may be done—for example, where a boat is hired out for half an hour's row, or a licensee of a flat is admitted merely to take care of it while the 'owner' is on holiday.

Once an open-ended 'possessive' relationship is deployed, we are on the spectrum of ownership interests whether we usefully employ the term 'owner-ship' or 'possession'; and if the interest is also protected by trespassory rules, it comes within the purview of a property institution. (In the case of chattels, as we have seen, the interest of a bailee may be protected against third-party wrongdoers, but is generally not enforceable against successors of the owner and hence such bailees are described as having a 'special property' in the goods.[58]) There is no advantage in stipulating a midway cut-off point. How long does a person's lease have to be before we do or do not speak of a house as 'his', or of him as its 'owner'?

Various rules of English property law deploy qualified conceptions of pos-session. Dig into the factual matrices envisaged by such ascriptions, and you will find that they include the notion of 'acting as owner' as a taken-for-granted organizing idea. We have seen that this is true of the conception of 'exclusive possession' which is crucial to the distinction between a lease and a licence.[59] Other examples are to be found in the contexts of relative title and the law of limitation.

As has been said, prior possession of land is, at common law, a basis for claiming relative title to an estate in the land. Squatter 1, and those claiming through him, could bring action against squatter 2 so long as he (squatter 1) was seised of the land (for no matter how short a period) prior to squatter 2. But not every instance of fleeting occupation would suffice for this purpose. What was the test for determining whether the first squatter's entry was suf-ficient to give him this relative title? This question was fully ventilated in the

---

[58] See Ch. 4, sect. (iv)(a) above.   [59] See sect. (iii) above.

judgments of the High Court of Australia in *Allen* v. *Roughley*.[60] It emerged, in effect, that the first squatter must have been openly acting as owner of the land before he could make out a claim to be owner of (that is, to have title to) the estate. 'There is abundant authority for the proposition that evidence of acts of ownership in relation to land is receivable as a *prima facie* case of ownership.'[61]

Under the Limitation Act 1980, twelve years' 'adverse possession' destroys the title of the former owner of an estate. Two of the conditions which must be satisfied before possession counts as 'adverse' are relatively straightforward. First, an action must have accrued in favour of the person whose title is being barred. Secondly, occupation must not be attributable to express or implied permission. There is, however, a third condition. The alleged adverse possessor must have been acting in such a way as to demonstrate that he had an *animus possidendi*. But what does this latinity amount to? In substance, it emerges that the adverse possessor must have been acting in relation to the land in the same sort of way as anyone else who supposed that he, and no other, was at liberty to exercise ownership-privileges and control-powers over it. In the words of Lord MacNaughten delivering the judgment of the Privy Council in *Perry* v. *Clissold*:

It cannot be disputed that a person in possession of land in the assumed character of owner and exercising peaceably the ordinary rights of ownership has a perfectly good title against all the world but the rightful owner. And if the rightful owner does not come forward and assert his title by process of law within the period prescribed by the provisions of the statute of limitations applicable to the case, his right is forever extinguished.[62]

In connection with the ownership spectrum, 'ownership' and 'possession' are overlapping and sometimes interchangeable normative conceptions. For this reason, property-limitation, expropriation, and appropriation rules may employ either term or, more commonly in the case of land, the term ' occupation', to pick out relevant ownership interests.

Rules of tort law may restrict the freedom of persons who have ownership interests by imposing duties on owners, possessors, or occupiers. The Occupiers Liability Acts of 1957 and 1984 impose duties of care upon occupiers of premises without defining 'occupier'. It is taken for granted that an occupier is someone exercising ownership powers of control. Rules of tax law may extract part of the wealth-potential of ownership interests by a similar variation in conceptual labels. English rating law was, for example, imposed on 'occupiers' of premises. A husband who left a matrimonial home was deemed to remain in rateable occupation where he retained an ownership interest which he was using in order partially to discharge his obligations to maintain his family; but if the house belonged entirely to the wife, the departed husband was no longer

---

[60] (1955) 94 CLR 98.   [61] *Ibid.* 144, *per* Taylor J.   [62] [1907] AC 73 at 79.

in rateable occupation since he did not derive any beneficial use from it.[63] English legislation empowers a business tenant to compel his landlord to grant him a new lease of premises which are 'occupied' by the tenant for the purposes of his business.[64] It has been held that a tenant does not 'occupy' land if he has sublet it in such a way as not to retain open-ended use-privileges and control-powers over it.[65]

In such contexts, 'possession' (or 'occupation') is as integral to property institutions as is ownership, since it is just another term for some kinds of ownership interests. But 'possession' may also figure in property-independent prohibitions. In that case the interpretation of the concept owes nothing to ownership as an organizing idea. It is, in English law, an offence to be in possession of prohibited drugs or unlicensed firearms. What precisely amounts to 'possession' in the context of these rules is a matter of interpretative judgement, weighing the general requirements of *mens rea* against the social policy supposed to be served by the prohibition.[66] The concept is open-textured, but absolutely nothing turns on whether the accused did, or did not, have an ownership interest in the drugs or the weapons.

[63] *Brown* v. *Oxford City Council* [1978] 3 All ER 1113.
[64] Landlord and Tenant Act 1954, Pt. 2.
[65] *Graysim Holdings Ltd* v. *P & O Property Holdings Ltd* [1995] 4 All ER 769 (HL).
[66] *Warner* v. *Metropolitan Police Commissioner* [1969] 2 AC 56; *R.* v. *Hussain* [1981] 2 All ER 287.

6

Ownership as a Principle

In the last chapter we considered that feature of property institutions which is exhibited when ownership is deployed, unreflectively, as an organizing idea. That is a pervasive day-to-day social phenomenon. Its manifestations are legion in ordinary discourse. It is also taken for granted in legal and judicial reasoning as a background assumption when the question at issue does not directly involve the cogency of normative claims based on ownership interests. Some examples of lawyerly and judicial presuppositions of ownership as an organizing idea were given.

The present Chapter seeks to bring to light a phenomenon peculiar to legal reasoning. When prevailing conceptions of ownership interests interact with the rules of a property institution, ownership operates as a 'principle' in the sense which Ronald Dworkin once gave to that word.[1] Depending on the 'weight' of invocations of ownership—that is, the normative force they are taken to derive from supporting property-specific justice reasons—rules may be more or less broadly or restrictively interpreted; or remedial relief, by way of damages or injunctions, may vary. An alleged trespass may be serious or *de minimis*. A neighbour's right to bring an action in nuisance, or the remedy he may obtain, for breach of a property-limitation rule may turn on the valuation given to the owner's freedom to act as he has done. The interpretation of expropriation rules reflects the perceived normative cogency of the ownership interest in question.

The property-specific justice reasons which allegedly justify property institutions are considered in Part II of this book. The reciprocal interaction of prevailing conceptions of ownership interests, on the one hand, and the concrete application of trespassory rules, property-limitation rules, and expropriation and appropriation rules, on the other, turns, ultimately, on how strongly, in terms of such justice reasons, ownership interests are valued. Their scope may be restricted, or their *prima facie* privileges and powers overridden, more readily, for example, if they are valued merely instrumentally as a relatively

[1] R. M. Dworkin, *Taking Rights Seriously* (Duckworth, 1978), ch. 2. In a later essay, *ibid*. ch. 4, Dworkin elaborates a distinction between 'principles' and 'policies', a distinction briefly foreshadowed in the earlier essay, *ibid*. 22–3. That distinction is not material to the discussion in the text. It would be difficult to differentiate invocations of ownership as a normative ideal affecting the interpretation and application of rules into appeals to the background rights of individuals, on the one hand, or appeals to a community goal, on the other hand.

effective marketing device than if they are viewed as the subject of natural rights or as essential attributes of human freedom.

The characteristic difference between invocations of ownership as an organizing idea and invocations of ownership as a principle is that in the latter, but not in the former, the values supposedly underlying ownership are confronted with other values in the interpretation and development of the law. Contrast 'since X is owner, it is obviously he who may . . .' with 'since ownership is a good thing, this rule should be read as . . .'. Both sorts of invocation presuppose property-specific justice reasons as the foundations for normative conclusions. But when ownership is appealed to as a principle, those reasons are nearer the surface, although, in the examples we shall consider, they are seldom articulated with clarity. The assumed justness of property institutions infuses all property talk. The assumption is totally submerged when ownership is deployed, as it is everywhere and all the time, as an organizing idea. It presses intermittently on to the moral and political agenda when a ruling is required over some controverted legal proposition.

As a legal institution, property is fashioned and adapted through the filter of juristic doctrine. Everyone knows that lawyers and courts have added a battery of specialist concepts to the central core of the ownership spectrum and trespassory rules—that property law is peculiarly technical and inbred. We have sketched some of those sophistications in Chapter 4. We shall consider the justifiability of juristic doctrine later on.[2] For the moment, it should be stressed that invocations of ownership as a principle differ from other aspects of juristic doctrine (to be met in the operation of property institutions) in that 'ownership', in common law systems, is not a term of art. The lawyer or judge who settles a disputed issue of rule-interpretation by appeal to the values of 'ownership' gives to that concept no meaning peculiar to the lawyerly caste. On the contrary, ownership interests derive their imprecise and fluctuating import from the wider culture of the community in which the property institution is situated.

'Ownership as a principle' is a portmanteau category. It covers appeals to a range of ownership interests along the ownership spectrum, and a variety of supposedly supporting justice reasons. Since the underlying reasons are often only obliquely indicated, if indicated at all, and since the relevant ownership-interest conception is seldom spelled out, no more discriminating classification is practical in the context of the examples we shall consider.

(i) OWNERSHIP AND TRESPASSORY RULES

We have seen that the outer boundary of the control-powers entailed by ownership interests is reciprocally related to the trespassory rules which protect

---

[2] See Ch. 16, sect. (ii)(c) below.

them.[3] Trespassory rules are established by legislation or, in common law jurisdictions, by rulings of the higher courts in accordance with the local version of the doctrine of binding precedents. Like any other rules, trespassory rules are, in H. L. A. Hart's terminology, 'open-textured'.[4] Some instances of conduct come clearly within their scope, but often it will be a disputed question whether what was done was prohibited. In the latter situation, the issue may be settled in favour of a wider rather than a narrower interpretation of the rule by appeal to the inherent value of protecting the ownership interest in question, even though some other value would have been served by a narrower construction. The judge who settles an open question in this way does so by affirming or assuming that the ownership interest is supported by one or more property-specific justice reasons. This process can be illustrated by examples taken successively from the fields of intellectual property, ownership of chattels, and ownership of land.

Prince Albert v. *Strange*[5] is the celebrated case in which Lord Cottenham LC had to decide whether an injunction would lie against a printer to restrain him from publishing a catalogue listing private etchings made by Queen Victoria and the Prince Consort. The defendant asserted no liberty to publish copies of the etchings. He wished merely to produce a catalogue communicating information that would show that the etchings existed. There was no authority directly in point. Was his freedom to communicate this information outweighed by the ownership interests in these artistic works? The Lord Chancellor was sure that it was. There is some hint in the judgment that extending protection this far was justified by appeal to the right of privacy, but the principal reason appears to have been broader. He who creates an ideational entity ought (merely because he is the creator) to be vested with exclusive powers to control all uses of it at least prior to publication, including mere dissemination of knowledge that it exists. We consider later the general topics of privacy[6] and creation-without-wrong[7] as property-specific justice reasons, and the arguments for bringing information within the scope of property institutions.[8] The Lord Chancellor said:

[T]he matter or thing of which the party has obtained knowledge, being the exclusive property of the owner, he has a right to the interposition of this Court to prevent any use being made of it, that is to say, he is entitled to be protected in the exclusive use and enjoyment of that which is exclusively his.[9]

In *Howard E. Perry and Co. Ltd* v. *British Railways Board*,[10] the defendants were refusing to allow the plaintiffs to collect a quantity of steel owned by the plaintiffs which was lying on the defendants' premises. They did this because there was a strike by workers in the steel industry and their own employees had

---

[3] See Ch. 3, sect. (vi) above.
[4] H. L. A. Hart, *The Concept of Law* (2nd edn., Clarendon Press, 1994), 124–36.
[5] (1849) 1 Mac. and G. 25.   [6] See Ch. 12, sect. (iii) below.
[7] See Ch. 11, sect. (iii) below.   [8] See Ch. 17, sect. (iii) below.
[9] N. 5 above, at 46.   [10] [1980] 2 All ER 579.

threatened to take industrial action if the Board frustrated efforts by the strikers to 'black' steel deliveries. The plaintiffs claimed that the defendants' refusal to let them collect their steel was tortious within the terms of the Torts (Interference with Goods) Act 1977 and, secondly, that the Court ought to exercise its discretion under that statute by ordering specific delivery rather than merely awarding damages. Megarry V-C found for the plaintiffs on both issues.

The relevant statutory trespassory rule was open to more than one interpretation. The statute had abolished the common law tort of detinue, so it had to be determined whether what the defendants were doing constituted the tort of conversion (the substance of the latter wrong having been preserved by the Act). Counsel and the judge rehearsed several judicial definitions of conversion, none of which was decisive. In particular, attention was drawn to the definition advanced by Bramwell B in *Hiort* v. *Bott*:[11] conversion includes a situation where a man does an unauthorized act which deprives another of his property 'permanently or for an indefinite time'. Counsel for the defendants submitted that this description did not fit the defendants' conduct since they had no intention of damaging or disposing of the steel and would not retain it once the strike was over. He suggested that 'indefinite time' should be understood as meaning a period of substantial duration. Megarry V-C rejected that interpretation by simply invoking ownership as a principle: '[l]ooking at the matter as one of principle, I would conclude that this is a clear case of conversion. The defendants are denying the plaintiffs most of the rights of ownership, including the right to possession, for a period which plainly is indefinite.'[12] Megarry V-C gave no more specific reason why the open-textured definition of conversion should be broadly rather than narrowly construed. What was it about the plaintiffs' ownership rights which made them more deserving of recognition than the defendants' desire to placate their employees? Some indication of an answer may be gleaned from the judge's comments on the second question he had to decide: whether, in the exercise of his discretion, he should grant a remedy by way of an order for specific delivery of the goods rather than damages. He opted for the former remedy because, in the circumstances of the strike, the plaintiffs would not be able to purchase alternative supplies of steel. Their business operations would be impaired. They would have to disappoint customers and might be required to lay off workers. Damages were consequently an inadequate remedy. As against that, the defendants were only reluctant to let the plaintiffs collect their property because of threats of industrial action from their own employees, and such threats should not be allowed to impede commerce.[13] In other words, the ownership rights of the plaintiffs were something to be prized because they subserved a commercial market. The market-instrumental argument for property institutions is one we shall consider.[14]

[11] (1874) LR 9 ch. 86, at 89.   [12] N. 10 above, at 583.
[13] *Ibid.* 585–8.   [14] See Ch. 15, sect. (iii) below.

The application of trespassory rules may be open to question because an ownership principle pulls in one direction while some other specifically legal principle pulls the other way. The Court must then make a decision as to which has the greater normative force. In some exceptional circumstances, common law courts have held ownership to be outweighed by necessity. A person who throws another's goods into the sea in an emergency to lighten a ship, or destroys another's property to forestall the spread of fire, or shoots another's dog to prevent sheep-worrying commits no civil wrong or criminal offence.[15] On the other hand, Blackstone asserted that a starving man who takes food would have no defence to a charge of larceny.[16]

In the early 1970s the plight of the homeless led to a movement of organized squatting in empty houses and a spate of litigation. In *Southwark London Borough Council* v. *Williams*,[17] two homeless families, with the assistance of a squatters' association, had entered houses owned by a local authority which the council was keeping empty with a view to redevelopment. They claimed the right to stay there and invoked the common law doctrine of necessity. The trial judge ordered them to vacate the premises on a summary application by the council, on the ground that they had no arguable case in law. Their appeal was unanimously dismissed by the Court of Appeal.

One of the judgments in the Court of Appeal was delivered by Lord Denning MR. Lord Denning, as all English lawyers are aware, has, in many contexts, interpreted or manufactured legal principles so as to give effect to his assessment of the just outcome, including situations in which ownership interests have been drastically qualified for the sake of spouses and dependants. In so doing, he has provoked the ire of traditional property lawyers.[18] But even Lord Denning was not prepared to develop the principle of necessity in favour of squatters, nor to question the view that starvation does not excuse theft:

If homelessness were once admitted as a defence to trespass no-one's house could be safe. Necessity would open a door which no man could shut. It would not only be those in extreme need who would enter. There would be others who would imagine that they were in need or would invent a need so as to gain entry. Each man would say his need was greater than the next man's and the plea would be an excuse for all sorts of wrongdoing. So the courts must, for the sake of law and order, take a firm stand. They must refuse to admit the plea of necessity to the hungry and the homeless and trust that their distress will be relieved by the charitable and the good.[19]

[15] *Mouse's Case* (1609) 12 Co. Rep. 63; *Cope* v. *Sharpe* [1912] 1 KB 496; *Creswell* v. *Sirl* [1948] 1 KB 241.
[16] Sir William Blackstone, *Commentaries on the Laws of England* (16th edn., J. Butterworth and Son, 1825), book 4, 30–2.
[17] [1971] 1 Ch. 734.
[18] See, e.g., D. J. Hayton, 'Equity and Trusts', in G. G. Jowell and J. P. W. McAuslan, *Lord Denning: The Judge and the Law* (Sweet and Maxwell, 1984), 79–108.
[19] N. 17 above, 744.

Another argument was advanced on behalf of homeless squatters in subsequent cases. Ever since the fifteenth century a person with title to a fee simple or leasehold estate in possession has, at common law, been able, as of right, to claim possession of land as against a mere trespasser. It was urged that the common law rule could be modified by equity. The court should assume an equitable discretion to postpone an order for possession for some weeks or days if the justice of the case, in broad social and human terms, demanded it. This novel suggestion was rejected out of hand. The person or body vested with the freehold or leasehold estate could, at his or her say-so, insist that the bailiffs be sent in at once.[20]

It is to be noted that, in rejecting the extension of the principle of necessity and the proposed equitable defence, the courts drew no distinction between plaintiffs who were private owners and organs of the state vested with what we shall call 'quasi-ownership interests'.[21] A bright line must be drawn favouring all those vested with legal estates in land against all intruders lest any tincture of flexibility should be exploited by the undeserving.[22] We shall later consider whether the community can justly impose trespassory obligations whilst leaving the satisfaction of the basic needs of those upon whom the obligations are imposed to 'the charitable and the good' and the merits of bright-line rules in such a context.[23]

(ii) OWNERSHIP AND PROPERTY-LIMITATION RULES

Property-limitation rules, subtracting *prima facie* privileges and powers from ownership interests, bulk largest in relation to land. In modern states, the most important ones are statutory in origin. The common law, however, has never lacked them. They have evolved through the law of nuisance and the rule in *Rylands* v. *Fletcher* and in the recognition and demarcation of various kinds of easements.[24]

Where novel questions arise as to the extent of such rules, the values taken to be inherent in ownership are set against other values, individual or social. In the following examples, freedom to act, self-seekingly, in relation to that which is one's own has served as a powerful normative lodestone. Economic justifications for such an attitude might be invoked.[25] On the face of it,

---

[20] *Department of the Environment* v. *James* [1972] 3 All ER 629; *McPhail* v. *Persons Unknown* [1973] Ch. 447.

[21] See Ch. 7, sect. (iii)(b) below.

[22] Megaw LJ, in *Southwark London Borough Council* v. *Williams*, did refer to the functions of a Council as a housing authority, concluding that their discharge would be impeded were any leeway granted to squatters. But he stressed that these observations were entirely superfluous to the conclusion that the defendants lacked any arguable case—n. 17 above, 747.

[23] See Ch.15, sect. (ii) below.

[24] See Ch. 3, sect. (viii) above.   [25] See Ch. 15, sect. (iii) below.

however, the judges in these cases were not making consequentialist calcula-
tions as to which of the alternative rulings open to them would result in the
most efficient use of resources. The surface appeal, at any rate, is to ownership
freedoms simply as freedoms. It will be argued in Part II of this book that,
whilst all ownership freedoms are *prima facie* valuable, none are sacrosanct.[26]
The following examples also add further support (if any is needed) to the
rejection in the last chapter of the curious notion that ownership of land, as
distinct from ownership of estates in land, is a conception unknown to the
common law.

In *Taplin* v. *Jones*,[27] the House of Lords was called on to resolve the following question. If a landowner had acquired a right to light over his neighbour's
land by prescription (an 'ancient light') so far as a particular window in his
premises was concerned, did he forfeit that right by opening other adjoining
windows the light to which could not be obstructed by his neighbour without
obstructing light to the original window? The answer was no, and the reason
was couched in terms of appeal to ownership freedoms. Opening windows was
a use-privilege inherent in the ownership of a building. It could not affect the
legal relations of the parties. Building to obstruct light to a neighbour's windows was also such a use-privilege unless it had been abrogated by the prescription of an ancient light. In the words of Lord Chelmsford:

It is not correct to say that the plaintiff by putting new windows into his house or
altering the dimensions of the old ones 'exceeded the limits of his rights' because
the owner of a house has a right at all times, apart of course from any agreement
to the contrary, to open as many windows in his own house as he pleases. By
exercise of the right he may materially interfere with the comfort and enjoyment
of his neighbour, but of this species of injury the law takes no cognizance. It leaves
everyone to his self-defence against an annoyance of this description and the
only remedy in the power of the adjoining owner is to build on his own ground
and so to shut out the offensive windows.[28]

A more flagrant invocation of the sacrosanctness of ownership freedoms
occurred in *Mayor and Corporation of Bradford* v. *Pickles*.[29] The defendant
sank a well on his own land to interfere with percolating water flowing to the
plaintiffs' waterworks. He did this in order to force the plaintiffs to buy his
land at a high price. The House of Lords upheld the refusal of an injunction to
prevent Pickles from acting in this way. It had already been laid down in an
earlier decision of the House that interfering with percolating water was not
an actionable nuisance.[30] The plaintiffs argued that there should be an exception to this rule where the defendant was acting, not to improve his own land,
but simply to damnify his neighbour. They invoked as warrant for introducing
this exception the principle of the law of nuisance that conduct otherwise
permitted to a landowner is not so permitted if motivated by malice. The

---

[26] See Ch. 14, sect. (v) below. [27] (1865) 11 HLC 290. [28] *Ibid.* 329.
[29] [1895] AC 587. [30] *Chasemore* v. *Richards* (1859) 7 HLC 349.

House regarded this argument as manifestly unsound. The privileges comprised within the concept of ownership of land clearly extended to economically self-seeking conduct. Lord MacNaughten said:

[The corporation] say that under the circumstances the operation which Mr Pickles threatens to carry out is something in excess of his rights as a landowner. ... The position of the appellants is one which it is not very easy to understand. ... They say that Mr Pickles' action in the matter is malicious, and that because his motive is a bad one, he is not at liberty to do a thing which every landowner in the country may do with impunity if his motives are good. ... Well, he has something to sell, or, at any rate, he has something he can prevent other people from enjoying unless he is paid for it. ... He prefers his own interest to the public good. He may be churlish, selfish, and grasping. His conduct may seem shocking to a moral philosopher. But where is the malice?[31]

In *Phipps* v. *Pears*,[32] the question was raised for the first time whether there was known to the law any such easement as an easement to be protected from the weather. The defendant had pulled down a house which was built up against the plaintiff's house, and recognition of the easement would have meant that he was not legally at liberty to do this. The plaintiff argued that such an easement should be admitted by analogy with the well established easement of support. This submission was, in the view of the Court of Appeal, clearly outweighed by the diminution in ownership privileges which such a novel ruling would entail. Lord Denning MR said: '[e]very man is entitled to pull down his own house if he likes. If it exposes your house to the weather, that is your misfortune. It is no wrong on his part.'[33]

In *United Steel Workers* v. *United States Steel Corporation*,[34] an American Federal Court of Appeals had to rule on a more unusual attempt to develop limitations on common law ownership interests. The defendant corporation owned industrial plants which had become technologically obsolete. Rather than invest the necessary funds to modernize them, they proposed to demolish them with the result that 3,500 workers employed at the plants would lose their jobs. The plaintiffs, a trade union representing the employees, wished to buy the plants at a fair market price so that they could be continued in operation. The corporation refused to sell to the union, apparently because they feared that continued working of the plants would be financed by government grants and would thus put them at a competitive disadvantage as far as their other steel-making operations were concerned. The plaintiffs sought an order that the defendants be required to sell to them. The court, with reluctance, rejected the plaintiffs' suit, holding that the corporation, as owners, were free to decide whether or not to sell and free to destroy the plants if they chose. Demolition of the plants was then carried out. The court took it for granted that the same justice reasons which support ownership freedoms in general

---

[31] N. 29 above, at 600–1.   [32] [1965] 1 QB 76.
[33] *Ibid*. 83.   [34] 631 F 2d 1264 (1980).

also apply to ownership of industrial enterprises. We shall consider later the powerful arguments against valuing ownership freedoms which flow from the consequent ability to exercise domination over the lives of workers.[35]

(iii) OWNERSHIP AND EXPROPRIATION RULES

It is widely assumed in liberal-democratic societies that property-holding features among the basic rights of persons. Whether that assumption is warranted and what precisely it entails remains to be seen. The present section is concerned with qualifications which uniformly accompany this assumption. Not only may ownership interests be properly restricted by property-limitation rules, but they may also be expropriated to enforce civil claims or punishment for wrongdoing, and to fund the discharge by the State of functions which it has rightly undertaken (what we shall call 'justice costs'[36]). Article 1 of the First Protocol to the 1950 European Convention for the Protection of Human Rights and Fundamental Freedoms (added in 1952) puts the matter as follows:

Every natural or legal person is entitled to the peaceful enjoyment of his possessions. No one shall be deprived of his possessions except in the public interest and subject to the conditions provided for by law and by the general principles of international law.

The preceding provisions shall not, however, in any way impair the right of a state to enforce such laws as it deems necessary to control the use of property in accordance with the general interest or to secure the payment of taxes or other contributions or penalties.

That governments are entitled to expropriate the property of citizens for the purpose of discharging some justice costs is hardly controversial. It could be disputed only by someone who is able to advance both of the following propositions: (1) property is sacred; (2) the community has no legitimate role in protecting either property or the person which requires the expenditure of resources. In practice disputes rage as to, first, what the community's other proper roles are and hence the extent of justice costs, and, secondly, the kind of tax regime which is appropriate for funding them.

In the development and interpretation of expropriation rules, English judges have invoked the *prima facie* normative status of private ownership by insisting that tax legislation be specific, by subjecting to judicial review discretionary powers which affect property, and by appeal to the no-expropriation-without-compensation principle.

---

[35] See Ch. 14, sect. (iv)(a) below.
[36] Ch.15, sects. (i) and (ii) below.

(a) Taxing Statutes must be Specific

Since the English revolutions of the seventeenth century, common law courts have taken it to be axiomatic that taxation must be governed by legislative rules rather than executive fiat. In *Vestey* v. *Inland Revenue Commissioners*,[37] for example, the House of Lords rejected the interpretation of a taxing statute argued for by the Revenue because it would have the following consequence: every potential beneficiary under a discretionary trust would be liable to pay tax on the entire income of the settled fund and hence, in practice, allocation of liability would be left to the discretion of the Commissioners.[38] Lord Wilberforce said:

Taxes are imposed upon subjects by Parliament. A citizen cannot be taxed unless he is designated in clear terms by a taxing Act as a taxpayer and the amount of his liability is clearly defined.

A proposition that whether a subject is to be taxed or not, or, if he is, the amount of his liability is to be decided (even though within a limit) by an administrative body represents a radical departure from constitutional principle. It may be that the revenue could persuade Parliament to enact such a proposition in such terms that the courts have to give effect to it: but, unless it has done so, the courts, acting on constitutional principles, not only should not, but cannot, validate it.[39]

In the recent decision of Woolwich Equitable Building Society v. Inland Revenue Commissioners,[40] the House of Lords has extended this principle by an admittedly novel ruling. The majority of the House laid down that at common law taxes paid under a demand by a public authority which later turns out to have been ultra vires are recoverable by the subject as of right. In both the *Vestey* and *Woolwich* cases appeal was made in the opinions to the provisions of the Bill of Rights of 1689, and also to what was perceived as the manifest injustice of allowing the property of the subject to be at the arbitrary disposal of the executive.

(b) Judicial Review

Under the modern public law doctrine of judicial review, English courts have developed a jurisdiction whereby the exercise of the discretion conferred on an official may be set aside if he failed to have regard to matters he ought to have taken into account or took into account matters which he should not have done, or if he otherwise arrived at a decision which no reasonable official

---

[37] [1980] AC 1148.
[38] They overrule an earlier decision of the House, *Congreve* v. *Inland Revenue Commissioners* [1948] 1 All ER 948, on the ground that the members of the House who decided that case had not foreseen that this would be the consequence of their ruling.
[39] N. 37 above, 1172.   [40] [1993] AC 70.

could have reached.[41] In deciding on what ought or ought not to be taken into account, or on the outer boundaries of reasonableness, the courts add to the wording of a statute which confers the discretion their own assessment of the proper constitutional basis for the exercise of the particular power. When the power is a ministerial discretion to confirm compulsory purchase, courts require to be satisfied that the minister acted on the basis that only a clear demonstration of the public interest can justify expropriation.

The taking of a person's land against his will is a serious invasion of his proprietary rights. The use of statutory authority for the destruction of those rights requires to be most carefully scrutinized. The courts must be vigilant to see to it that that authority is not abused.[42]

Given the obvious importance and value to land owners of their property rights, the abrogation of those rights in the exercise of his discretionary power to confirm a compulsory purchase order would, in the absence of what he perceived to be a sufficient justification on the merits, be a course which surely no reasonable Secretary of State would take.[43]

(c) No Expropriation without Compensation

The principle that private property should not be taken by the State without payment of compensation has emerged as a settled feature of legal doctrine in both common law and civilian systems since at least the seventeenth century. It is commonly enshrined in constitutional documents, most famously in the Fifth Amendment to the American constitution—'nor shall private property be taken for public use, without just compensation'. Even where the powers of a sovereign legislature are not subject to the constraints of a written constitution, as in the United Kingdom, the principle is operative as a common law constitutional principle.[44] The courts insist, as a maxim of statutory construction, that Parliament is presumed to intend that property should not be taken without compensation.[45] They also interpret the prerogative powers of the Crown, exercised by the executive branch of government, in such a way as not to infringe the principle.[46]

---

[41] *Associated Pictures Houses Ltd* v. *Wednesbury Corporation* [1948] 1 KB 223; *Ashbridge Investments Ltd* v. *Minister of Housing and Local Government* [1965] 3 All ER 371.

[42] *Prest* v. *Secretary of State for Wales* (1982) 81 LGR 193 at 211, *per* Watkins LJ.

[43] *R.* v. *Secretary of State for Transport, ex parte de Rothschild* [1989] 1 All ER 933 at 939, *per* Slade LJ.

[44] See Blackstone, *Commentaries*, n. 16 above, book 1, 135.

[45] *Aberdonian Ry. Co.* v. *Walters Trustees* (1882) 7 App. Cas. 259; *London and North-western Ry.* v. *Evans* [1893] 1 Ch. 16; *Central Control Board Liqr.* v. *Cannon Brewery Ltd* [1919] AC 744; *Newcastle Breweries Ltd* v. *R.* [1920] 1 KB 854.

[46] *Attorney-General* v. *De Keyser's Royal Hotel* [1920] AC 508; *Burma Oil Company (Burma Trading) Ltd* v. *Lord Advocate* [1965] AC 75.

Laws which authorize the taking of property without compensation 'are generally recognized as being repugnant to justice'.[47] 'It is plainly just and equitable that when the state takes or destroys a subject's property for the general good of the state it shall pay him compensation.'[48]

Such statements presuppose that ownership interests were justly held in the first place. The normative force of the no-taking-without-compensation principle is thus derivative from more basic property-specific justice reasons. Hence the principle has no application where fines are imposed as part of what is conceded to be just punishment, since (as we shall see) the policing of wrongs is a more fundamental feature of just political associations than is the maintenance of property.[49] So also (as we shall argue) the principle is not infringed by a system of taxation which constitutes a morally acceptable mechanism for discharging the community's obligation to meet the basic needs of citizens, since the moral bindingness of a property institution's trespassory rules depends on that obligation being discharged.[50]

Where the application of the principle is disputed, it is because a balancing exercise is required between the mix of property-specific justice reasons which purportedly underpin a package of property rules and some allegedly overriding governmental objective. There may be clear cases of 'taking' of property by public authorities which are so indisputably for the common good that they ought not to be inhibited by the requirement to pay compensation. The members of the House of Lords were divided over just such a question in *Burma Oil Company (Burma Trading) Ltd* v. *Lord Advocate*.[51] During the Second World War the British military authorities ordered installations belonging to Burma Oil in Rangoon to be destroyed to prevent them falling into the hands of the advancing Japanese army. Destruction was carried out one day before the city was occupied by the enemy. That this step was a proper exercise of executive power was not disputed. The question before their Lordships was whether Burma Oil were entitled to claim compensation. No English authority was directly in point. A decision of the Supreme Court of the United States had held that no compensation was payable in such circumstances within the Fifth Amendment 'takings' clause.[52] On the other hand, the writings of civilian jurists favoured the view that compensation was owed when the property of subjects was destroyed as part of a war effort, the only exception being 'battle damage'—destruction directly inflicted while hostilities raged. In the end the

---

[47] *Government of Malaysia* v. *Salangore Pilot Association* [1978] AC 337, 356, *per* Lord Salmon.
[48] *Burma Oil Company (Burma Trading) Ltd* v. *Lord Advocate* [1965] AC 75, 149, *per* Lord Pearce.
[49] See Ch. 10, sect. (iii)(c) below.
[50] See Ch. 15, sect. (ii) below.
[51] [1965] AC 75.
[52] *United States* v. *Caltex (Philippines) Inc.*, 344 US 149 (1952). For discussion of this ruling, see Jed Rubenfeld, 'On Using' (1993) 102 *YLJ* 1077 at 1126.

matter turned on their Lordships' perceptions of the just outcome. The dissenting opinions favoured the view that it was for the Legislature to decide how losses of this kind should be apportioned; whilst the majority could see no reason why the right to compensation, which applied when property was requisitioned for war purposes, should not also extend to property destroyed as a precautionary measure prior to engagement. Parliament then proceeded to reinstate the minority view by legislation in the War Damage Act 1965.

For the most part, controversial interpretations of the principle appear in contexts where it is disputed in terms of whether or not there has been a 'taking' of property. Property-limitation rules which impose modest restraints on one power for the sake of neighbouring owners are internal features of property institutions which do not implicate the principle at all. No advocate of private property would be heard to insist that every abstraction of a *prima facie* ownership privilege or power entails a right to compensation. John Locke, who expressed the principle as one which prohibited the arbitrary taking of property without the express or implied consent of the subject, recognized that the prince or senate 'may have power to make laws for the regulating of property between the subjects one amongst another.'[53] At the other extreme, a property-limitation rule which denied all ownership privileges and powers would be tantamount to expropriation.

The line between regulation and taking is notoriously difficult to draw, as the wealth of American constitutional case law and commentary reveals. So far as land-use regulation is concerned, the United States Supreme Court has evolved a two-pronged test for determining the proper scope of the 'police power'. Legislative restrictions constitute a 'taking' either if, in the court's view, the underlying legislative purpose was something other than the advancement of some legitimate public goal (such as a re-allocation of merely private interests), or if it denies to an owner any economically viable use of his property.[54] '[T]he general rule at least is, that while property may be regulated to a certain extent, if regulation goes too far it will be recognized as a taking.'[55]

A cautious approach has been adopted in England as far as concerns the application of the common law principle to the prerogative of the Crown[56] and in interpreting constitutional instruments in which the principle is embodied. In *Belfast Corporation* v. *O.D. Cars Ltd*,[57] the House of Lords held that

[53] John Locke, *The Second Treatise of Government* (J. W. Gough (ed.), Blackwell, 1976), ch. 11, 139.

[54] *Pennsylvania Coal Company* v. *Mahon*, 260 US 393 (1922); *Penn Central Transportation Company* v. *New York City*, 438 US 104 (1978); *Agins* v. *Tilburon*, 447 US 255 (1980); *Keystone Bituminous Coal Association* v. *Debenedictis*, 480 US 470 (1987).

[55] *Pennsylvania Coal Company* v. *Mahon*, n. 54 above, at 415, *per* Holmes J.

[56] 'A mere negative prohibition, though it involves interference with an owner's enjoyment of property, does not, I think, merely because it is obeyed, carry with it at common law any right to compensation': *France Fenwick and Co. Ltd* v. *The King* [1927] 1 KB 458, 467, *per* Wright J.

[57] [1960] AC 490.

the restraint imposed upon the parliament of Northern Ireland not to make laws whose direct or indirect effect was to 'take any property without compensation' was not infringed by planning legislation. The consequence was that a landowner who was denied permission to build factories and shops in an area which the planning authority had zoned off for residential development had no constitutional right to compensation. Lord Radcliffe suggested that the American term 'police power' was inadequate to describe the complex of property-limitation rules which had emerged in the United Kingdom in the interests of public health and amenity from the second half of the nineteenth century, most of which made no provision for compensation.[58]

Without entering into the constitutional doctrines of any particular jurisdiction, the underlying issues may be stated abstractly in the following way. To begin with, there are property-independent prohibitions addressed to everyone which may happen, incidentally, to deny certain uses of property to owners. In their case, no question of expropriation arises.[59] Either such prohibitions are justifiable restraints on the conduct of all persons (owners included) or they are not. It is a crime for anyone to drive a motor vehicle dangerously. It would be absurd to suggest that those who happen to own cars are thereby subjected to a compensable loss. Those who oppose a legal requirement that all drivers and passengers are to wear seat-belts do so on the ground of infringement of liberty, not as an attack on property.

As we contended when discussing the contestability of 'ownership', it is a necessary condition for the application of the compensation principle that the suspect provision purports to remove some *prima facie* privilege or power inherent in the prevailing conception of an ownership interest.[60] It must at least constitute a property-limitation rule. Granted that it does, the question then becomes one as to the proper boundary between private and social wealth.

Every property institution discharges the dual functions of controlling use and allocating social wealth.[61] When it delegates control over competing uses of a scarce resource, R, to X by recognizing an ownership interest, OI, in X over R, it simultaneously accords to X an item of private wealth associated with the exploitation of the privileges and powers inherent in OI. Suppose that, to further some public goal, an amalgam of privileges and powers, P, is abstracted from OI. The compensation principle is implicated if and only if the mix of property-specific justice reasons which supports X being vested with OI also requires that OI contain P. Compensation preserves X's allocated share of social wealth even though P has been taken from him.

In most cases of health and amenity regulation in England over the past

---

[58] [1960] AC 523–4.
[59] The contrary view has, however, been put foward by Bruce Ackerman—see Ch. 9, sect. (iii)(c) below.
[60] See Ch. 5, sect. (vi) above.   [61] See Ch. 3, sect. (iii) above.

century and a half it has been assumed that the privileges and powers taken from owners were not accorded to them as of right so that the uncompensated recapture of this aspect of their private wealth into undifferentiated social wealth was not unjust. In view of the conclusions reached in Part II of this book—that there are no natural rights to full-blooded ownership, that the *prima facie* value of all ownership freedoms is subject to the pervasive counter-consideration of domination-potential and that instrumental arguments from incentives are merely pragmatic and contextual—it is submitted that this assumption was eminently justified.

7

Private and Non-private Property

A common charge brought against the political philosophers of the seventeenth century who sought to justify property institutions is that they concentrated on individual private property, to the exclusion of many other conceptions of property. They ignored many varieties of collective or public property which had existed in the past, so that their accounts were ahistorical. They did not foresee the developments which have taken place in capitalist and state property, so that their accounts (if applied to modern property) are anachronistic.

There is certainly force in this kind of criticism. Yet critics have seldom attempted any analysis of modern property institutions which exhibits that which unites, and that which divides, these differing conceptions of property—in particular, what precisely is the difference between 'ownership' when ascribed to private persons or groups or to agencies discharging public functions. We attempt that task in this Chapter.[1] It will emerge that conceptions of private property are logically prior to conceptions of non-private property and that justifications for the latter are parasitic on justifications or disjustifications for the former.

(i) JOINT, GROUP, AND CORPORATE PROPERTY

Trespassory rules are a necessary feature of property institutions. They may reserve use-privileges and control-powers to an individual; or they may accord ownership interests to two or more individuals jointly, to a group, or to a corporation. Should that possibility affect our overall view of the structure of such institutions?

It is of the essence of joint property that no trespassory rules regarding the asset in question subsist between the joint owners. Rules prohibiting 'trespass to the person' will, of course, typically obtain. If two people jointly own a house and one sits on the other while she is taking a bath, there may be a battery. There can, however, be no question of one of the two enforcing permanent exclusion of the other from any part of the house so long as their joint property rights remain unmodified.

The same may be true of group property. In the imaginary Wood Land

[1] An earlier version of this Chapter appeared as 'Private and Non-Private Property: What is the Difference?' (1995) 111 *LQR* 421.

(described in Chapter 2), kinship groups with property in hunting lodges could exclude members of other groups, but the members of a group could not exclude each other. There can, however, be internal regulations allocating use-privileges and control-powers between members of a group, as will often be the case with associations like clubs or trade unions. These may amount to no more than social understandings, or they may be embodied in enforceable legal transactions. In either case, should such internal regulations encompass intra-group trespassory rules, then there will be individual property interests of one kind or another. Where regulation does not go that far, members are not vested with property which is independent of the group property. Each member differs from outsiders by virtue of enjoying, first, a share in the protection conferred on the group as a whole over some asset and in its wealth-potential and, secondly, a right not to be excluded by other members of the group.

In modern legal systems, personified corporations are, formally, the direct beneficiaries of trespassory rules protecting corporate property. The technical apparatus of corporate property extends to situations in which the personified entity holds what we shall call a 'quasi-ownership' interest in resources, as in the case of State, charitable, or public corporations. It is also employed, however, as a sophisticated variant of group property.

As with other forms of group property, there may be internal trespassory rules conferring limited ownership interests on particular members. However, the relationship between the rights which members, as distinct from non-members, have to the property vested in the corporation takes a special form. The technique of incorporation enables the use-control and wealth-allocation functions of property institutions to be prised apart. External trespassory rules vest use-privileges, control-powers, and powers of transmission in the corporation and hence, via its constitution, in particular office-holders. Individual members retain the right to share in the wealth-potential of this protection but not, usually, the right not to be excluded from corporate assets. It is this facet of corporate property to which attention is drawn in the classic work on the modern corporation by Berle and Means, described by them as the 'separation between control and ownership'.[2]

Joint, group, and (non-public) corporate property are all variations of private property. Joint, group, and corporate owners are free to make such uses of their assets as they jointly or collectively decide, in accordance with the prevailing conception of the ownership interest in question, within whatever property-limitation rules apply to all owners. It is taken for granted that, to the extent that an individual owner may insist, as of right, on the immediate return of his chattels which another is detaining, so may an owner-company.[3] If

---

[2] Adolf A. Berle, Jr., and Gardiner C. Means, *The Modern Corporation and Private Property* (Commerce Clearing House, 1932). Cf. J. W. Jones, 'Forms of Ownership' (1947) 22 *Tulane LR* 82 at 86–9, 93.

[3] *Howard E. Perry and Co. Ltd* v. *British Railways Board* [1980] 2 All ER 579. This case was discussed in Ch. 6, sect. (i) above.

an individual owner of a factory is free to demolish it and thereby deprive thousands of employment, so too, is a corporate owner.[4] The principle of no expropriation without compensation applies in the same way whether the property belongs to an individual or to a corporation.[5]

Of course, there are characteristic differences between these variations of private property and individual property, apart from the separation of ownership from control. Mechanisms exist for dissolving joint, group, and corporate property into individual property. Group and corporate ownership carry no power of testation. Traditionally, the transacting power of companies incorporated under statute has been limited, in English law, by the doctrine of *ultra vires*. In the interests both of subscribers and general creditors, transactions not permitted by the objects clause contained in the company's memorandum of association were void and unenforceable.[6] However, transaction powers inherent in private ownership interests constituted the background against which objects clauses were drafted and interpreted; and the entire doctrine has become more and more attenuated as corporate powers have become increasingly assimilated to ordinary ownership powers.

Joint, group, and private corporate property are of the greatest importance within modern property institutions. Corporate property, in particular, is a uniquely convenient mechanism for hiving off wealth-potential and thus an instrumentality for the creation of important cashable rights (shareholdings) as distinct items within property institutions. These forms of private property constitute sophisticated elaborations of the minimal structure of property institutions. They are outworks from the essential twinned notions of trespassory rules and the ownership spectrum. Whatever the internal mechanisms, those who exercise control are free, within the terms of the property institution, to justify their actions on the ground that they are in the self-seeking interests of their members or shareholders. In the case of these variants, as in that of individual private property, ownership interests serve as irreducible organizing ideas between desire and authorized choice.

(ii) COMMUNITARIAN PROPERTY

A vast swathe of the private wealth in modern western societies is held in the form of joint, group, or corporate property. In all variations, whatever latitude may be conferred on members to arrange their affairs at pleasure, internal regulation cannot exceed the tolerance accorded by the wider social or legal property institution. The general law lays down a framework within which

---

[4] *United Steel Workers* v. *United States Steel Corporation*, 631 F 2d 1264 (1980). This case was discussed in Ch. 6, sect. (ii) above.

[5] *Burma Oil Company (Burma Trading) Ltd* v. *Lord Advocate* [1965] AC 75. This case was discussed in Ch. 6, sect. (iii)(c) above.

[6] *Cotman* v. *Brougham* [1918] AC 514 at 520, *per* Lord Parker.

partnership or corporate property must subsist. With all these must be contrasted a spontaneously evolved category of property-holding which has been of the greatest historical significance but which, for better or for worse, has been largely eclipsed in modern societies. So long as it survives and receives external trespassory protection without intrusion on its internal regulation, the relationship of the participants to the resource is essentially different from the varieties of joint private property just discussed. Any label for this relationship which borrows on the technical terminology of modern property systems would be misleading. We shall call it 'communitarian property'.[7]

'Communitarian property' is a global term employed here to designate a wide range of land-holding arrangements which, in many parts of the world, used to subsist alongside conventional forms of private property.[8] The positive content would depend on social, economic, and spiritual variables. Nothing unites the category except its negative contrast with individual or joint private property. As a category it is, in this way, logically dependent on familiar conceptions of ownership interests. It is a relationship which the wider society depicts by differentiation. It is not, of itself, an organizing idea internal to the particular community, except by way of contrast with the otherness of individual or group private property.

Thus, 'communitarian property' refers to a situation in which a community of persons has the following relationship to a resource, usually land. They have the benefit of trespassory rules excluding outsiders from the resource—in that sense it is their private property. However, whatever powers of internal division or transmission they possess are referable, not to the wider institution which contains the trespassory rules that confer protection against outsiders, but to internal regulations arising from their mutual sense of community.

A surviving instance of communitarian property was recognized in the recent decision of the High Court of Australia in *Mabo* v. *Queensland*.[9] The court ruled that, according to the common law of Australia, the 'radical title' to land acquired by the Crown on settlement was burdened with the 'native title' of any aboriginal clan or group which was in occupation of any distinct portion of territory for so long as its descendants remained in occupation, unless and until native title was effectively extinguished by legislation or exercise of executive power, or surrendered to the Crown.[10] The Meriam people were vested with such a title to the Murray Islands in the Torres Strait. So long as it persisted, the community's native title was subject to appropriate legal protection against all the world. All questions as to the rights of individual

---

[7] The label should not be understood to imply that all such forms of property-holding would conform to the prescriptions of philosophic advocates of 'communitarianism', cited in Ch. 10, sect. (iii)(b) below.

[8] See P. Vinogradoff, *Outlines of Historical Jurisprudence* (OUP, 1920), i, 321–43.

[9] *Mabo* v. *State of Queensland (No. 2)* [1992] 175 CLR 1.

[10] For less sympathetic treatment by common law courts of land claims by native peoples, see Ch. 12, sect. (i)(b) below.

members of the community over their land were to be determined, as questions of fact, by reference to the particular evolving traditions of the group. It was not requisite to show that, internally, the members viewed their relationship to the land as an 'ownership' interest, in any way comparable to the range of ownership interests known to modern legal systems. It was not an institution of the common law, but a special defeasible interest which the common law ought in justice to (and therefore did) recognize. Like other instances of communitarian property, its 'proprietary' nature is defined negatively by comparison with more familiar conceptions of private property. Like ownership interests, it is accorded trespassory protection. But unlike them, it carries no connotation of open-ended self-regarding exploitation.

It is noteworthy that the High Court did not accept an alternative argument advanced on behalf of the Meriam people, that the group had acquired title to an ordinary fee simple estate by virtue of prior possession. That argument was founded on the ingenious suggestion put forward by Kent McNeil that, when English common law flowed into a territory upon settlement, any group occupying a portion of land became vested as individual joint tenants with a fee simple held of the Crown.[11] Adoption of McNeil's proposal would have meant that any group or tribe of native inhabitants would be as free to trade their land (if they all wished to do so) as are the members of any commercial partnership or other unincorporated association. They would have joint property within the institution, not communitarian property recognized by the institution. The court's ruling entailed, instead, that native title persisted only so long as a group retained some spontaneously evolving connection to the land, and could be disposed of to no-one but the Crown.

(iii) STATE AND PUBLIC PROPERTY

(a) Non-self-seekingness

The trespassory rules of modern property institutions typically include, amongst those to whom privileged uses and powers are afforded, agents of the State or of other public institutions. The assets to which they apply are commonly referred to as 'State' or 'public' property, as opposed to 'private' property. Access to State factories, farms, or offices may be prohibited to all except officials and those whom they authorize. Appropriation of State money

---

[11] Kent McNeil, *Common Law Aboriginal Title* (Clarendon Press, 1989). Only Toohey J, in the *Mabo* case, accepted that the plaintiffs' claim might be supportable by reference to prior possession as well as traditional title, but His Honour seems to have assumed that it would make no practical difference—n. 9 above at 206–14. All the members of the majority of the court were, however, influenced by McNeil's criticism of older views of the common law position, according to which the Crown, on settlement, acquired beneficial ownership of land along with sovereignty.

or chattels will be criminal unless it was done in performance of an official function.

However, the privileged domain thus afforded to officials falls nowhere along the ownership spectrum since it lacks the crucial feature of legitimate, self-seeking exploitation. Exploitation is governed by conceptions of social function which vary according to the public enterprise in question, but which uniformly do not include the idea that the officials, or any personified complex of them, may, *prima facie*, do what they like with 'their' assets.

It would be otherwise if 'the State' were identified with some personal sovereign with proper desires and appetites of his own; for then his 'State property' would be accurately equated to anyone else's private property.[12] Furthermore, within the arena of public international law, self-seeking exploitation is allowed. Its trespassory rules protect 'State territory' and 'State territorial sea', concepts which, in this respect, are frankly modelled on private property ownership interests; albeit the *imperium* of States over their territory encompasses governmental obligations as well as open-ended privileges and powers.[13]

Within the municipal law of modern States, some features of private property accompany State property. Managers of State farms and factories may be vested with powers of contracting (but seldom powers of giving) modelled on those inherent in the prevailing conception of private ownership. Functionaries may have open-ended powers of control over access to their office buildings resembling, to some degree, the control-powers of owners of private residences. But neither law nor social convention entitles a manager or a functionary to answer any disputed exercise of such a power by saying 'The thing is mine to do as I like with'.

The same is true of property dedicated to public use, but not vested in State organs. Charitable corporations and charitable trusts have emerged as mechanisms for discharging community-approved objectives with the co-operation of private initiatives. The powers of corporate managers and trustees are largely modelled on those inherent in ownership interests. However, they are not at liberty to exploit any such powers for their own benefit nor (unlike their counterparts in private corporations and trusts) to discharge them at the self-interested direction of any private class of citizens. It was suggested in a recent English case that, broadly speaking, the property held by charity trustees falls into two categories: property held for 'functional' purposes, such as historic houses, hostels for the destitute, or office premises; and property held as investments for the purpose of generating money needed for the charity's work. As to both kinds of property, ownership powers must be exercised solely to forward the particular purpose of the trust.[14]

---

[12] See Ian Brownlie, *Principles of Public International Law* (4th edn., Clarendon Press, 1990), 128.

[13] *Ibid.* 107–9, 123–4.

[14] *Harries* v. *Church Commissioners for England* [1993] 2 All ER 301, 304, *per* Sir Donald Nicholls V-C.

The fact that the same legal sub-institutions, corporations and trusts, feature both in the private and the semi-public arenas should not distract us from recognizing the essential difference between private and public property. Within the law of private corporations and trusts, as we saw in Chapter 4, devices exist for hiving off claims to wealth-potential from use-privileges and control-powers. Nevertheless, in the case of these private institutions, a company director or trustee can defend an allegedly socially deleterious use of property by pointing out that it was for the benefit of shareholders or beneficiaries and that shareholders or beneficiaries, as a collectivity, are free to do what they like with their own.

(b) Quasi-ownership Interests

The content of the domain conferred on an official (or trustee) over State (or public) property in his charge is a variable composed of elements borrowed from ownership interests and elements deriving from the particular social function which that relationship is supposed to serve. For want of any better label, we may call such relationships 'quasi-ownership interests'. At one extreme, a State corporation may be vested with 'ownership' of some industrial enterprise, have some of its powers and duties specified by statute in general terms, but for the rest be presumed to have virtually the same ownership privileges and powers as any private corporation would have—always bearing in mind the non-self-seeking limitation. At the other extreme, the majority of the rights, duties, privileges, and powers of such a corporation are laid down in detail in legislative codes, ownership privileges and powers being resorted to only, if necessary, to fill in the gaps.

Public parks fall towards the latter end of this spectrum. Some agency is vested with title to the park and is obliged, by statute or the terms of the vesting instrument, to allow access for recreation to members of the public. Nevertheless, juridical implications may be derived from its 'ownership'. In a recent case the Court of Appeal had to decide whether a medieval gold brooch, discovered buried in a park by a metal-detector enthusiast, should belong to the finder or to the local authority which 'owned' the park.[15] The matter was not addressed in any relevant bye-law, nor was the use of metal detectors in the park legally prohibited. However, there is an established principle of English common law that, whereas finders of chattels are normally entitled to them as against all the world except the original owner, that is not so if they are found in or attached to land; in the latter event, they belong to the person with a current ownership interest in the land. The court ruled that this exception applied in favour of the local authority, even though it was a trustee for the general public in the exercise of its powers and duties of management and control.

In English law, even public highways are the subject of quasi-ownership

---

[15] *Waverley Borough Council* v. *Fletcher* [1995] 4 All ER 756.

interests. Statutes vest in highway authorities the surface of the road and so much of the subsoil and superjacent airspace as is needed for the discharge of statutory functions.[16] Such an interest has been held to constitute an estate in the land.[17] The authority, notwithstanding its duty to allow passage to all members of the public, has nevertheless the protection of trespassory rules. Anyone deliberately digging up the road without the permission of the authority would commit criminal damage and be liable to civil injunctive relief. Most of the functions of highway authorities are laid down by statute. But it is taken for granted that the detailed implementation of these functions, for example, powers to enter into employment contracts or to bargain for repair contracts, are modelled on those which any other owner would have by virtue of his ownership.

When a court has to rule on the validity of the exercise of a power by a body vested with a quasi-ownership interest, it reaches a conclusion by some synthesis of legally defined, and residual, ownership, privileges, and powers. Take, for example, the decision of the Queen's Bench Divisional Court in *British Airports Authority* v. *Ashton*.[18] Ownership of Heathrow Aerodrome had been vested in an authority created by statute, with a statutory duty to provide facilities to the public and with defined powers ancillary to the discharge of that duty. The court had to decide whether its powers enabled it to make regulations under which it would be an offence for trade union members to carry out peaceful picketing on the airport after being asked to leave. It held that they did, as an incident to the authority's 'ownership' control-powers.

B.A.A.'s ownership, unlike that of the private landowner, is subject to the right of the public to have access for the purpose of taking advantage of the services and facilities provided by B.A.A. in pursuance of its statutory duty. However, access for the purposes of picketing is not a right to which B.A.A.'s ownership is subject.[19]

A private owner may refuse to permit hunting on his land for any reason that seems good to him. It has been held, however, that a local authority 'landowner' may not prohibit stag-hunting on its land merely because its members objected to it on ethical grounds. The prohibition did not come within the statutory function for which the land was held, *viz.*, the 'benefit, improvement, or development' of the area under the authority's control.[20]

In another case, the sensitive question of access by patients to their medical records has been dealt with in terms of a quasi-ownership interest. The Court of Appeal laid down that, although written medical records were 'owned' by a

---

[16] *Coverdale* v. *Charlton* (1878) 4 QBD 104; *Rolls* v. *St George the Martyr, Southwark (Vestry)* (1880) 14 Ch.D 785; *Tunbridge Wells Corp.* v. *Baird* [1896] AC 434.
[17] *Tithe Redemption Commission* v. *Runcorn UDC* [1954] Ch. 383.
[18] [1983] 3 All ER 6.
[19] *Ibid.* 14, *per* Mann J.
[20] *R.* v. *Somerset County Council, ex parte Fewings* [1995] 3 All ER 20.

health authority or by an individual medical practitioner, the position at common law was as follows. The 'owner' had no absolute right to deal with the records in any way it chose since its ownership was subject to its duty to act at all times in the best interests of the patient. Nevertheless, the doctor or the health authority could, as 'owner', refuse to disclose them to the patient on the ground that disclosure would be detrimental to the patient.[21]

Even money is the subject of merely quasi-ownership interests, comprised of an amalgam of ordinary ownership powers and powers derived from designated functions, when it is vested in a public authority. This was discovered to their dismay by several leading banks in the recent ruling of the House of Lords in *Hazell* v. *Hammersmith and Fulham LBC*.[22] The House held that interest-swap transactions, entered into by a local authority as a speculation, were *ultra vires* its statutory powers and so unenforceable. 'Individual trading corporations and others may speculate as much as they please or consider prudent. But a local authority . . . is a public authority dealing with public monies'.[23]

The ownership privileges and powers comprised within quasi-ownership interests may be docked by property-limitation rules applicable to ownership interests proper. Title conditions for State and public property are, for the most part, modelled on those applicable to private property. Non-ownership proprietary interests avail against successors in title in much the same way whether those successors have ownership or quasi-ownership interests, unless a legislative specification of the functions of a public agency is interpreted as an implicit abrogation of inconsistent private proprietary rights.[24] However, the difference between them is typically reflected by the drastically foreshortened application to quasi-ownership interests of expropriation rules and principles. Most State and public property is not subjected to bankruptcy law or the law of criminal forfeiture, and it typically features differently in taxation law. That principle of statutory construction which presumes that Parliament does not intend to expropriate private property without payment of compensation[25] has been held inapplicable to statutes which divest some public bodies of their property.[26]

Quasi-ownership interests, lacking legitimized self-seekingness, are not private wealth. Their varying contours none the less reflect, in part, prevailing conceptions of ownership interests proper. The concept of private property is thus logically prior to any conceptions of State or public property. All such

---

[21] *R.* v. *Mid Glamorgan Family Health Services Authority, ex parte Martin* [1995] 1 All ER 356. The matter is governed by the Access to Health Records Act 1990, in relation to records made after 31 Oct. 1991.   [22] [1992] 2 AC 1.

[23] *Ibid.* 31, *per* Lord Templeman.

[24] *Kirkby* v. *Schoolboard for Harrogate* [1896] 1 Ch. 437; *Re 6, 8, 10 and 12 Elm Avenue, New Milton, ex parte New Forest District Council* [1984] 3 All ER 632; *Brown* v. *Heathlands Mental Health National Health Service Trust* [1996] 1 All ER 133.

[25] See Ch. 6, sect. (iii)(c) above.

[26] *R.* v. *Secretary of State for the Environment, ex parte Newham LBC* (1987) 85 LGR 737; *Sheffield County Council* v. *Yorkshire Water Services Ltd* [1991] 2 All ER 280.

conceptions build upon the twinned notions of trespassory rules and owner-ship interests which constitute the core of all property institutions.

(iv) COMMON PROPERTY

Political philosophers, from Plato and Aristotle to the present day, have con-trasted both private and public property with 'common property'. Often enough, the term is used as a synonym for some form of group or communitarian property. It is also sometimes used to refer to an asset which is vested in a public authority with a quasi-ownership interest, where the discharge of the function for which it is so vested requires access to be afforded to members of the public on most occasions, such as a park or a highway.[27] In English law the expression 'common land' refers either to land which is subject to the rights of common (such as grazing rights) of a defined class of persons, or to land which is (or was) part of the waste land of a manor which is subject as well to public rights of access and recreation.[28] In either case there is an 'owner' of the land, often a public authority vested with a quasi-ownership interest, whose title to the fee simple estate requires to be registered.[29] The owner retains residual rights in the soil, subject to the rights of commoners or of the public, and is protected by trespassory rules against unlawful intereference with the land.[30]

In so far as 'common property' has a meaning distinct from these other forms of property, it designates a context in which no-one may, by virtue of an ownership or quasi-ownership interest, dispute the right of any other person to make use of a resource. Uses may be banned to all by property-independent prohibitions, as with the taboo rules protecting sacred animals in Forest Land. There may be positive resource-relevant duties imposed on all, like the repair obligations in regard to the Forest Land communal dwelling; or imposed on those occupying special roles, as in Status Land. None of these regulations, however, presuppose proprietary concepts. If property is 'common', no man may say you nay because the thing is his.[31]

---

[27] See C. M. Rose, 'The Comedy of the Commons: Custom, Commerce and Inherently Public Property' (1986) 53 *U. Chi. LR* 711. Rose encompasses within one concept—'inherently public property'—all assets as to which there is a public right of access, whether title is vested in private owners or public agencies, or whether trespassory rules are altogether absent. Rose employs this classification to make the point that property-institutional design should not be conceived of as limited to choosing between the alternatives of vesting exclusionary managerial control either in private individuals or in the State.

[28] *Mid Glamorgan County Council* v. *Ogwr Borough Council* [1995] EGCS 12 (HL).

[29] Commons Registration Act 1965.

[30] S. 9 of the Commons Registration Act 1965 provides that where no person is regis-tered as the owner of common land, 'any local authority in whose area the land or part of the land is situated may take such steps for the protection of the land against unlawful interference as could be taken by an owner in possession of the land and may . . . institute proceedings for any offence committed in respect of the land.'

[31] In Hohfeldian terminology, all use-privileges correlate with ownership 'no-rights'—see

In this sense the term 'common property' may be employed as a way of pointing out that a particular resource has not been subjected to a property institution. In the international arena, the open sea, the Antarctic continent, and the extraterrestrial universe may be described as 'common property'.[32] Within municipal legal systems, the term may be applied to some kinds of wild animals, sunlight, atmospheric oxygen, and airspace above a certain height. It is used judicially, on occasion, particularly in the context of ideas or information within the public domain.[33]

The same point can be made by asserting the absence of ownership or quasi-ownership interests. For example, the label 'common property' could have been applied, in English law, to subjacent percolating water. Anyone who can lawfully sink a well commits no wrong, in any circumstances, by the further act of drawing off percolating water from under his neighbour's ground.[34] To describe underground percolating water as 'common property' would signify no more than that trespassory rules conferring ownership interests could have been, but have not been, extended to that resource. In fact the term is not applied to it by the courts because all that need be said has been said in terms of articulating the absence of ownership rights.

'Common property' means no property. It would be a redundant (indeed meaningless) concept within a society, like Forest Land or Status Land, which knew nothing of property institutions. For such imaginary societies, the term can only serve as an external classificatory label—as it was employed by the visiting anthropologist in Chapter 2. In real societies, it is an optional way of referring to any corporeal or ideational entity as to which there are neither ownership or quasi-ownership interests nor trespassory rules.

(v) PROTECTED NON-PROPERTY HOLDINGS

'Common property', in the foregoing sense, is employed as a term to designate resources which are exempted, not merely from ownership and quasi-ownership

Wesley Newcomb Hohfeld, *Fundamental Legal Conceptions as Applied in Judicial Reasoning* (Yale UP, 1919), 38–50. Hohfeld's analysis is discussed in the next chapter.

[32] In customary public international law, the expression *res communis omnium* has traditionally been applied to the high seas and more recently to outer space and celestial bodies—Brownlie, n. 12 above, 178, 267–71. Technically, Antarctica has, in the past, been treated as *terra nullius*, that is, land subject to appropriation by States, and claims to sovereignty over sectors of it have been asserted: *ibid*. 151–2. However, a regime of co-operation has been established by the Antarctic Treaty of 1959 under which, in effect, claims to sovereignty have been frozen and the area kept open for scientific investigation by all-comers: *ibid*. 265–6. In substance, therefore, trespassory rules are not enforced in respect of the Antarctic continent.

[33] See, e.g., *International News Service* v. *Associated Press*, 284 US 215 (1918) at 219, *per* Pitney J. This case is discussed in Ch. 17, sect. (iii)(a) below.

[34] *Chasemore* v. *Richards* (1859) 7 HLC 349; *Bradford Corporation* v. *Pickles* [1895] AC 587; *Langbrook Properties Ltd* v. *Surrey County Council* [1969] 3 All ER 1424; *Stevens* v. *Anglian Water Authority* (1987) 137 NLJ 829.

interests, but also from trespassory rules. It would seem inapt in the case of any asset whose control is reserved to some official or agency discharging public functions by trespassory rules, whether or not that official or agency is vested with a quasi-ownership interest.

Trespassory protection alone is not sufficient to create a quasi-ownership interest. Exceptionally, use of a resource may be banned to all persons save X, but X's use-privileges and control-powers over the resource are enumerated in terms of role-duties which borrow nothing from ownership conceptions. Such resources are removed altogether from the property domain. We shall call them 'protected non-property holdings'.

Consider the regime instituted in the United Kingdom by the Human Fertilisation and Embryology Act 1990 for embryos and live gametes. The Act prohibits storage and use of these materials to anyone except the holder of a licence granted by the Human Fertilisation and Embryology Authority. Licensees are permitted to store these products and their duties are elaborated in the Act and in regulations made under it. There is no reservation to the Authority or to any licensee of a set of privileges or powers modelled on those inherent in an ownership interest anywhere along the ownership spectrum. (As we shall see later, separated bodily parts hover at the limits of property.[35])

Such items are not State or public property, since proprietary notions play no part whatever in determining how they must or may be used. It also seems unlikely that anyone would refer to these embryos and gametes as 'common property'. In any case, we need terms to distinguish two kinds of resources which fall outside the scope of property institutions: those as to which there are neither trespassory rules, nor ownership or quasi-ownership interests; and those where the first are present but the second are not. The former, borrowing on an existing usage, will be called 'common property'. For the latter we invent the term 'protected non-property holdings'.

As we saw in Chapter 2, societies are imaginable in which all resources under public control take the form of protected non-property holdings. That was the position in Red Land and Contract Land. State officials were protected in their exclusive control of factories and offices by trespassory rules; but every conceivable use was settled by reference to social function (or contract) without invoking, even as a residual organizing idea, the notion that these things were 'owned' by the State. In real societies, the analogy with private ownership is part of the background against which assumptions are made about what officials can do with or to 'State property' or 'public property'. Protected non-property holdings are, one suspects, rare.

(vi) THE LOGICAL PRIORITY OF PRIVATE PROPERTY

It is often claimed that property is a conception of which there are three parallel ideal types: private property, State (or collective) property, and common

---

[35] See Ch. 17, sect. (iv) below.

property. The first encompasses ownership relations; the second and third do not. Jeremy Waldron presents one example of this sub-categorization.[36] He defines the concept of property as that of 'the concept of a system of rules governing access to and control of material resources'.[37] He claims that in private property systems these rules are organized around the idea that particular material resources are owned by individuals; that in a system of collective property the organizing idea is that access and control is to be allocated by reference to the collective interests of the society as a whole; and that in a system of common property, the organizing idea is that such allocations are to be made on the basis that each resource is in principle for the use of every member alike.[38]

Parallel sub-categorizing of this sort should be rejected. Waldron demonstrates how 'ownership' plays an indispensable role as an internal organizing idea within a system of private property. He offers no examples to show how some non-ownership proprietary conception could fulfil a similar internal role within systems of collective or common property. Allocation of resources 'by reference to the collective interests of society as a whole', or allocation 'on the basis that each resource is in principle for the use of every member', merely negate the presence of private property. They say nothing about how rules are actually to be applied or interpreted. They are external classificatory labels for ideal-typical systems, not internal organizing ideas. Such systems might employ other organizing ideas, reflecting their goals of collective and fraternal social living but, as our imaginary Forest Land and Red Land demonstrate, notions of 'property' play no role whatsoever.

So long as the Forestlanders exist in splendid isolation from the rest of mankind, it is clear enough that 'property' notions play no part in their lives. Might contact with others force some conception of property upon them? Suppose they encountered other tribes and resented intrusion on the territory they occupy. Then, perhaps, inter-tribal trespassory rules would emerge. It would still be difficult to envisage the tribesmen grasping some such notion as group/tribal common or collective 'property', on our assumption that they had no

---

[36] Jeremy Waldron, *The Right to Private Property* (Clarendon Press, 1988), ch. 2. For a longer version of this chapter, see his 'What is Private Property?' [1985] 5 *OJLS* 313.

[37] *The Right to Private Property*, n. 36 above, 31.

[38] *Ibid.* 37–46. The term 'collective' property is a little misleading, since it is often used to stand for group or communitarian property as well as State property. Waldron uses it in a wide sense to meet the difficulty that there appear to be proprietary interests in incorporeal entities which, on his understanding, cannot constitute 'ownership' and therefore must be within the domain of collective rather than private property (*ibid.* 35–7). He overlooks expropriation and appropriation rules which, typically, presuppose ownership interests in tangible and intangible entities alike. On his view, the law of bankruptcy or succession would redistribute private property, so far as it applies to goods and land, but collective property so far as it applies to copyrights or bank accounts. He is also inconsistent since he assumes that enterprises like newspapers (44), or organs of production (46), can be the subject of private property. In such cases, ownership is not limited to material resources.

internal property institution. It might be suggested that they had acquired the germ of the notion of 'sovereignty', as that term is employed today in the international arena. Even that would not be entirely apt since public international law, as an external system, purports to regulate conditions for acquisition and cession of territory, as well as its protection.

If some outsider turned up with a proposal that the Forestlanders should vacate part of their territory and transfer it to his tribe or government, they might react with incredulity or indignation; or, perhaps, after reflection and deliberation, they might agree to the transaction in exchange for some benefit. The same variety of reactions might greet a suggestion from a returning tribesman that they should divide up their territory into plots protected by intra-tribal trespassory rules just as (he had discovered) some foreigners do.

Without embarking on far more invention about the mores and spiritual lives of the tribesmen, we cannot be privy to whatever internal organizing ideas would capture their sense that their territory was protected from outsiders and the possibility (or unthinkability) of its transfer or sub-division. So far as such ideas referred to 'property', they would reflect the accepted (or rejected) property notions introduced from outside—that is, notions of private property. All conceptions of group, tribal, or communitarian property are parasitic on conceptions of private property.

Consider the protected non-property holdings of Red Land. There are buildings to which everyone, except State officials, is forbidden access save with the leave of officials. Might the citizens employ some conception to draw a contrast between the privileges and powers these rules conferred on officials with the privileges and powers accorded to licensees of dwellings (which are also protected by trespassory rules)? Any such distinction would be articulated in terms of their fully-socialized goals of fraternal living. It could not be a distinction between 'State property' and 'private property', on our stipulation that the dwelling licences incorporated not even an exiguous notion of ownership.

It could be otherwise in Pink Land. Buildings reserved for officials might there be described as 'State property' in contradistinction to the (limited) private property conceded to licensees of scarce assets. The distinction would be that licensees, so far as their mere-property ownership interests go, may act properly in a self-seeking fashion. Officials, *qua* officials, cannot. They are vested with quasi-ownership interests modelled, in part, on ownership interests proper.

Thus in Red Land the notion of 'State property' has no internal role; in Pink Land it has meaning only in contrast with citizens' private property.

In all real societies, the internal utility of a distinctive concept of 'common property' is limited to ruling out one kind of reason which might be advanced for denying that X is privileged to make some use of an asset. It excludes the possibility that X's use conflicts with Y's ownership (or quasi-ownership) interest. In that negative sense, common property presupposes private property. In contrast, the concept of State (or public property) presupposes private property in a positive sense. Every quasi-ownership interest borrows some of its content, great or small, from the open-ended privileges and powers which belong to the prevailing private ownership conception. State (or public) property is thus parasitic on private property.

The twinned conceptions of trespassory rules and the ownership spectrum are indispensable features of what is meant by a property institution. That combination is presupposed by property-limitation rules, expropriation rules and appropriation rules; by devices for hiving off wealth potential as distinct property items; and by the recognition of non-ownership proprietary interests. A property institution will also typically include quasi-ownership interests vested in bodies discharging public functions; and will also allow for some features of the environment, and most ideational entities, to be altogether exempt from the scope of the institution. It may also acknowledge surviving instances of spontaneously-evolved communitarian property. However, unless some ownership interests are accorded to individuals or groups, there will be no property institution. All other institutional features take their meaning from, or in contrast to, ownership interests. It follows that 'private property' is logically prior to all non-private conceptions of property.

(vii) THE JUSTIFICATORY PRIORITY OF 'COMMON PROPERTY'

Influential political philosophers of the seventeenth century, like Grotius,[39] Pufendorf,[40] and Locke,[41] begin their arguments for individualist private property regimes by positing a starting-point of common ownership. Granted that God had given all things to men in common it was possible, so they thought, to support a just evolution of private property-holdings. The crucial step, in the view of Grotius and Pufendorf, was tacit agreement and, in Locke's view, creative labour. Sound or not, do these arguments contradict our claim about the logical priority of private property?

They do not. What has to be noticed is that the conception of 'common property' deployed by these theorists is not merely a situation in which there was no property. As Stephen Buckle has argued in his commentary on Pufendorf, 'negative community'—Pufendorf's term for original common property—is a complex normative conception. It entails a power in individuals, assuming

[39] Hugo Grotius, *De Jure Belli ac Pacis* (trans. F. W. Kelsey, Oceana Publications, 1964), book ii, ch. 2.

[40] Samuel Pufendorf, *De Jure Naturae et Gentium* (trans. C. H. and W. A. Oldfather, Oceana Publications, 1964), book iv, ch. 4.

[41] John Locke, *Second Treatise of Government* (G. W. Gough (ed.), Basil Blackwell, 1976), ch. v.

the proper steps, to appropriate part of what was before such appropriation the property of no-one.[42]

Thus, the whole idea of 'common property' is infused with the conceptual possibility of individual property. It would make no sense to speak of common property, in the sense of that to which no-one presently has any special claim but parts of which may at any time be rendered the private property of individuals, unless we already had some notion of what it is for something to be the private property of individuals. Of course, speculators about original common property always do come to that subject armed with such a conception.

When we come to assess some of the arguments for natural property rights, we shall adopt the traditional state-of-nature mode of theorizing: one imagines a situation in which there is no property (what an outsider might call 'common property') and considers what might justify a change. But it will be necessary to insert into the story the experience of a participant who goes away to some place where the inhabitants have property in order that he may return and propose introducing a property institution.

(viii) THE HISTORICAL PRIORITY OF COMMUNITARIAN PROPERTY

We have coined the term 'communitarian property' to stand for any situation in which the members of a group have mutual rights over a resource, referable exclusively to their own traditions, but are protected against the rest of mankind by trespassory rules. If it were historically the case that individual appropriations arose, not from enclosures of what was previously owned by no-one, but by encroachments on what had already been possessed in the form of communitarian property, how could arguments which presupposed mere 'negative community', even if abstractly sound, have any relevant application?

That problem came to the fore as a result of the researches of the historical school of jurists in the nineteenth century. They accumulated data suggesting that early Germanic and Slavic law had recognized communitarian property in land, and pointed to comparable surviving institutions in medieval Europe and contemporary instances in other parts of the world. Maine collated all this information and made it the basis of a scorching critique of natural rights theories of property.[43]

Many features of Maine's speculations have been disputed. Indeed, anthropological and ethnographic studies in the twentieth century reveal such a variety of property arrangements within primitive societies that any generalizations about historical priority must probably be rejected. Lawrence Becker,

---

[42] Stephen Buckle, *Natural Law and the Theory of Property: Grotius to Hume* (Clarendon Press, 1991), 95–6.
[43] Sir Henry Sumner Maine, *Ancient Law* (Pollock revised edn., John Murray, 1906), ch. 8.

having reviewed this literature, announces that, for his part, he will give up any attempt to draw useful generalizations:

Every attempt I have made is refuted by a counterexample actually observed in the field. The data indicate that, although property rights exist everywhere, what is necessary about them is just *that some exist*. It appears that many specific systems of ownership are compatible with any set of environmental conditions and social structures.[44]

Supposing, however, that, at least as to land, communitarian property did historically precede individual and group ownership interests. That would not affect our claim about the logical priority of private property. Communitarian property is a conception deployed by historians, comparativists, and anthropologists, under various labels, in order to distinguish the relationship of a community to a particular resource from individual or group full-blooded ownership. Nothing but contrast with private property unites this category of resource-holding. This is confirmed in a recent survey by Paolo Grossi of the debate sparked off among nineteenth-century continental theorists by the publication of Maine's *Ancient Law*, between the proponents and opponents of 'primitive communism'.[45] Whatever term the scholars employed, it is clear that what Grossi calls 'collective property' played no role, as a distinct organizing idea, within the societies in which it was found to have been present. It was an outsider's label.

Since it was historically just the historical and logical oppositum of ownership by a single proprietor, it is defined by a complex of alternative characteristics that emerge from that origin: the priority of the group and the subordination of individuals and their ends to the group; the priority of objective ends, of the economic nature, destination and use of things over subjective ends; the priority within the group of subjective situations of duty over those of power or right typical of the traditional *jura in re*.[46]

Grossi draws conservative implications from his survey. He commends the social values served by surviving instances of what I have called 'communitarian property'. He recognizes that the term 'collective property' is ambiguous since it might be confused with socialist proposals for deliberately created property-holding entitlements, from which he distances his enquiry.[47]

Socialist theorists of the nineteenth century drew on similar historical information to that used by Maine as a basis for condemning and reconstructing capitalist private property. Communitarian property had once existed and, in a new socialist guise, it could be re-instituted. There were many variants—utopian, syndicalist, and 'scientific'.

[44] Lawrence C. Becker, 'The Moral Basis of Property Rights', in J. Rowland Pennock and John W. Chapman (eds.), *Property: Nomos XXII* (NYUP, 1980), at 200.
[45] Paolo Grossi, *An Alternative to Private Property: Collective Property in the Juridical Consciousness of the Nineteenth Century* (trans. Lydia G. Cochrane, U Chi. P, 1981).
[46] *Ibid*. 24.   [47] *Ibid*. 22–3.

Marx contrasts all variations of private property with 'social' or 'collective' property.[48] According to Marx's theory of history, there was, at the dawn of history, universal communitarian property. Evolution in the forces of production resulted, inevitably but deplorably, in successive stages culminating with capitalist private property which will in turn, inevitably and triumphantly, be superseded by a new form of common ownership—'an association of free men, working with the means of production held in common, and expending their many different forms of labour-power in full self-awareness as one single social labour force.'[49]

It is notoriously unclear whether this 'joint ownership' entails literal common property—no-one who wishes to exert his labour-power on or with the means of production is to be excluded; or revived communitarian property—different associations jointly own assets from which members of other associations are excluded, and the owners arrange matters between themselves without reference to any external property institution; or, as those who have tried to implement the prophecy have generally assumed, the means of production are to be vested in State organs which will be endowed, by suitable trespassory rules, with quasi-ownership interests in them. All that need to be noted here is that the supposed primitive communism of the past, and the joint ownership of the future, are alike analysed by reference to, and in contrast with, various species of private property.

The social, ethical, and spiritual bonds which unite a spontaneously-evolved community to the resource it collectively claims for its own are infinitely variable. In the absence of private property institutions, that variable relationship has its normative force independently of any conception of property whatever. The collective assertion of 'ourness' need only be made as a defensive reaction to intrusion by outsiders or to unwelcome proposals for instituting private appropriation. If what commentators call by labels equivalent to communitarian property had been, and had remained, the universal basis on which resource-use was allocated, then that specific institution whose justification or disjustification looms large in the history of political philosophy—a property institution—would never have emerged.

Communitarian property, in a pure form, would entail that all internal decisions about resource-allocation are dictated by traditional notions internal to the group without any borrowing of proprietary conceptions from a wider society. Assuming that it ever existed in this pure form, it is unlikely that it has anywhere survived the intrusion of the modern State. As a conception, it arises as a contrast to self-seeking private property notions, and with contrast comes contamination. Individual members of the Meriam people, whose landholding communitarian property was recognized in the *Mabo* case, today own money and goods. In a sense, when communitarian property was pure it did

[48] Karl Marx, *Capital* (Penguin Classics trans. B. Fowkes, Penguin Books, 1990), i, 927–30.   [49] *Ibid*. 171.

not exist, for there was no-one around to point out the difference between it and property institutions.

Property-specific justice reasons are always addressed to private property. If their rejection yields the conclusion that, as to some resource, there ought to be no trespassory rules, then that resource is to be 'common property'. If they point to the desirability of some kind of trespassory protection, but also indicate, as to some resource, the injustice of individual self-seeking ownership, recommendations of various kinds may be put forward: group private property; group communitarian property, either modelled (so far as possible) on the communitarian property of the past, or invented *de novo* for a newly constructed society peopled with reclaimed human beings; a protected non-property holding; or some form of quasi-ownership vested in some public authority.

The logical priority of conceptions of private property over those of non-private property demonstrates that, if we discuss the justice of property at all, private property is our focus. There can be no question of speculating about, approving, or condemning public, common or communitarian property in isolation from private property.

8

Person–Thing and Person–Person Relations

Contemporary property theorists in the English-speaking world commonly pose a contrast between the lay and the legal view of property. The layman, it is said, conceives of ownership as a relationship of a person to a thing, whilst the lawyer knows that proprietary interests are always concerned with relationships between persons as to the use or exploitation of things (objects, resources, items of wealth).[1]

The contrast is a false one. Of course, property, as a social and legal institution, controls relations between persons. There would have been no point in Robinson Crusoe soliloquizing about his proprietary rights over the resources of his island if he was sure that no other human being would ever turn up. However, as we saw in Chapters 5 and 6, ownership interests in things play their roles in this process both as organizing ideas and as principles. Conclusions that certain relations obtain between persons follow, for laymen and lawyers alike, from conceptions of ownership interests in things.

The social conception of property embraces, simultaneously, some idea of trespassory rules—'thou shalt not steal!'—and some version of the idea that a man may do what he likes with that which is his—'is it not lawful for me to do what I will with mine own?' Legal property institutions build on the twin foundations of trespassory rules and the ownership spectrum in various ways. The lawyer is professionally aware of the details of trespassory rules and of relevant property-limitation, expropriation and appropriation rules, of the title conditions peculiar to her jurisdiction, of the multifarious instrumentalities for detaching the wealth-allocation function of property from its use-control function, of the historical and doctrinal elements entering into the *numerus clausus* of non-ownership proprietary interests and of the technical formality rules in which all these matters are shrouded. All these rules and juristic superstructures both yield relations between persons and presuppose relations between persons and things (tangible or ideational).

How has this false contrast—person–thing relations versus person–person relations—come about? In part it appears to be due to illegitimate inferences drawn from two seminal analytical treatments of the topic—those of

---

[1] See, e.g., Bruce A. Ackerman, *Private Property and the Constitution* (Yale UP, 1977), 26–7; Thomas C. Grey, 'The Disintegration of Property', in J. Rowland Pennock and John W. Chapman (eds.), *Property: Nomos XXII* (NYUP, 1980), at 69–71; Stephen R. Munzer, *A Theory of Property* (CUP, 1990), 15–17.

W. N. Hohfeld and A. M. Honoré. Those authors rightly argued that, for many purposes, proprietary interests must be unpacked into their constituent elements. It will be argued, however, that nothing in their analyses yields the conclusion that all thought of ownership interests over things is somehow misconceived.

Then there are varieties of scepticism about ownership. One source of this scepticism is psychological reductionism. The layman supposes he owns things, but scientific enquiry reveals this to be an illusion. A more important source of scepticism among English-speaking theorists is what may be called 'totality ownership'. Those who insist on it attribute to others the (misguided) notion that anyone who owns something is always free to do absolutely anything he pleases with and to the thing. Now it can easily be demonstrated that no such totality of use-privileges ever exists. Quite apart from property-limitation rules, there will always be universal property-independent prohibitions proscribing some uses. It follows that, contrary to the assumptions of the misguided, there never are 'owners' of things. It will be shown that this totality conception of ownership is a ridiculous Aunt Sally. It can easily be knocked down, but then it need never have been put up in the first place.

(i) UNPACKING PROPERTY

Property institutions deploy portmanteau conceptions everywhere and all the time. Ownership interests over tangible and ideational things, at various points along the ownership spectrum, entail both use-privileges and control-powers, and, usually, powers of transmission as well. Ownership interests over cashable rights entail varying powers of transmission, but normally no use-privileges. Non-ownership proprietary interests comprise different sorts of use-privileges, control-powers, or resort to wealth-potential. Quasi-ownership interests are comprised of assorted mixes of privileges and powers derived from their analogy to ordinary ownership interests and the particular social functions they serve. Unpacking, on demand, of these variable elements is inevitable. Could one posit some global unpacking of all these items such that person–thing conceptions could be made to disappear?

(a) Hohfeld's Analysis

In the early years of this century, W. N. Hohfeld offered an analysis of legal conceptions, in terms of paired relations, which has served as a starting-point for a wide range of analytical enterprises ever since.[2] He expounded the lowest

---

[2] The analysis has been applied to proprietary interests by, e.g., Lawrence C. Becker, *Property Rights: Philosophic Foundations* (Routledge and Kegan Paul, 1977), 11–14, 21–2; and Stephen R. Munzer, *A Theory of Property* (CUP, 1990), 17–27. For criticism of

common denominators of the law by reference to two squares of correlation and opposition.

Right	Privilege	Power	Immunity
Duty	No-right	Liability	Disability

Within these squares every vertical represents a correlation, and every diagonal an opposition. To say that X has a duty to Φ entails that he owes this duty to someone, Y, who has the correlative right; and also that he has no privilege not to Φ as against Y. To say that A has a power entails that he can by his voluntary act change the legal relations of some other person, B, who has the correlative liability; and that it is not true that A has a disability as against B, correlating with an immunity of B. Hohfeld argues that if all more complex legal conceptions were reduced to combinations of these various bi-party relations, legal reasoning would be clarified, fallacious conceptualization would be avoided, and genuine normative choices made apparent.[3]

The soundness and the utility of Hohfeld's analytical scheme have been the subject of prolonged juristic controversy, especially his implicit assumption that all the problems we have about the notion of legal rights can be dispelled so long as we distinguish four senses in which that term is commonly employed—claim-right, privilege, power, and immunity.[4] We are concerned here only with the application of the analysis to proprietary interests. Hohfeld maintained that 'rights *in rem*' should not be distinguished from 'rights *in personam*' by being thought of as rights over things. Every legal conception must be reduced to combinations of bilateral relations. Every such relation has three elements: X, X's act or omission so far as it affects Y or Y's legal relations, and Y. Once analysed in this way, the person–thing relation drops out of sight. How is this done?

We take one person, O (the so-called owner of Blackacre), and begin by examining his legal relations with a hypothetical member of his community, X. There are trespassory rules, civil or criminal, prohibiting X from acting in certain ways in relation to Blackacre without O's leave. In our earlier discussion we have spoken of such rules as protecting ownership interests in things. However, following Hohfeld, we may express the duties imposed by

'the bundle of rights analysis of property', see James Penner, *The Idea of Property in Law* (OUP, forthcoming).

[3] W. N. Hohfeld, *Fundamental Legal Conceptions as Applied in Judicial Reasoning* (Yale UP, 1919).

[4] For a summary of the debate, see J. W. Harris, *Legal Philosophies* (Butterworths, 1980), ch. 7.

the trespassory rules simply in terms of X's relations with O. X owes duties to O correlating with O's claim-rights that X shall not act in ways which infringe the rules. The rules empower O to waive the duties imposed by the trespassory rules in an indefinitely large number of ways. We have spoken of the open-ended set of control-powers inherent in an ownership interest. We could express the same legal content by saying that, by virtue of the rules, there is an indefinite set of relations between O and X whereby O has powers to change X's legal situation correlating, in each case, with X's liability to have his legal relations changed.

Various property-limitation rules—nuisance law, planning law, and the like —restrict what O may do in relation to Blackacre. We have described such rules as presupposing an open-ended set of use-privileges inherent in an owner-ship interest some of which they remove. Instead, we could say that, without the rules, O would be privileged to perform any number of actions in relation to Blackacre, each such action correlating with a no-right in X that O should not so act; but that, as regard the actions banned by the property-limitation rules, O has no such privileges and X no such no-rights. The law relating to gifts, wills, servitudes, contracts, conveyances, mortgages, settlements, and trusts empowers O to divest himself of all or parts of Blackacre. We have spoken of open-ended powers of transmission being inherent in ownership interests. But instead we could express all this law as powers in O to change X's legal relations, correlating with X's liabilities to have them changed.

To carry through the elimination of the person–thing relation from our analytical picture we cannot, of course, stop with X. Trespassory rules bind everyone. Hohfeld's solution was to suggest the label 'multital relation' for all the sets of relations between O and X, to indicate the fact that each of them would be duplicated, *prima facie*, by relations with the same content obtaining between O and Y, O and Z, and O and each and every other member of the community.[5] That way we can account, for example, for expropriation rules, not by saying (as we have) that they presuppose ownership interests, but by pointing out that they vest in certain categories of persons, such as trustees in bankruptcy, powers to change O's 'multital' legal relations.

What are we to make of this analytic endeavour? Eliminating the person–thing idea is, in principle, possible provided, first, that all the relevant legal provisions are known and determinate—no open texture; and, secondly, that we are seeking to convey information about the legal situation at a particular moment of time. Only within these two constraints is ownership dispensable both as an organizing idea and as a principle.

Beginning with the second constraint, we must notice the distinction between 'law' in the sense of a momentary legal system and 'law' as a historic congeries of conceptions, maxims, definitions, and classifications, forming part of the tradition of some body of officials.[6] 'Law' in the former sense refers to

[5] N. 3 above, 71 ff.

[6] I have discussed this distinction in J. W. Harris, *Law and Legal Science* (Clarendon Press, 1979), especially at 17–24, 41–3, 65–73, 97–103, 111–22.

that body of mutually consistent prescriptions in force at a particular time. That is the conception of law presupposed in the introduction to any textbook that announces that the law set forth is that in force at a certain date. 'The law' as a historic system is comprised, *inter alia*, of relatively timeless conceptions whose significations must be appealed to, on occasion, in order to comprehend the scope of the present law. Even supposing we have determinacy of content and can represent the present law in terms which eschew person–thing relations, we will only have arrived at that outcome by first employing conceptions drawn from the historic system. Within historic systems, ownership interests over things are indispensable organizing ideas.

Hohfeld was concerned to analyse momentary legal systems. This emerges clearly in the context of his controversy with Maitland about the relations between equity and common law. Maitland maintained that equity supplements the common law.[7] Hohfeld argued that, on the contrary, equity *pro tanto* replaces the common law. He said:

Since, in any sovereign state, there must, in the last analysis, be but a single system of *genuine law*, since the various principles and rules of that system must be consistent with one another, and since, accordingly, all *genuine* jural relations must be consistent with one another, two conflicting rules, the one 'legal' and the other 'equitable', cannot be valid at the same moment of time; one must be valid and determinative to the exclusion of the other.[8]

Given that our attention is focused on the present law, Hohfeld is right. Is O (who is vested with the fee simple in Blackacre) legally free at time T to cut down the trees, or is he not? The common law says he may because (as owner of the fee simple estate) he is privileged to act as 'owner' in relation to the land, and cutting down trees is one of the use-privileges incident in this ownership interest—assuming that he has not granted or contracted it away, and that no tree preservation order or other property-limitation rule has taken it from him. Equity says that he is not free to cut down the trees because he is a trustee, and such 'waste' would not be in the interest of the beneficiary. It follows that, as to the relevant situation at time T, equity has repealed the common law. On the other hand, we cannot dispense with the conceptions of legal estate, trust, equitable estate, and ownership of land in any generalized description of the law. For here, 'the law' means the battery of conceptions and other items which are called in aid in crystallizing the present law for any momentary fact-situation. We were only able to answer the question about the trees because we were equipped with these relatively timeless conceptions. In that sense, Maitland is right, and equity fulfils and does not take away the common law.

Having worked through our historically given conceptions, we are able to say, in Hohfeldian terms, that O had a duty not to cut down the trees correlating with the beneficiary's right in that he should not do that. We need not speak

---

[7] F. W. Maitland, *Equity* (J. Brunyate (ed.), CUP, 1936), especially lectures 9 and 12.
[8] W. N. Hohfeld, 'Relations between Equity and Law' (1913) 11 *Mich. LR* 537 at 557.

either of O's ownership of the estate or of his ownership interest in the land. But should we wish to convey information about the conceptions which we will need for any future such presentation of jural relations, we will need to talk of legal and equitable estates and trusts and also, as we saw in Chapter 5, of ownership of land as an incident of the legal estate. Thus for lawyers as for laymen, even when we are not confronted with open-textured rules, ownership interests are indispensable conceptions.

All the more is this the case when the content of the present law is the subject of controversy. Hohfeld's analysis is simply inapplicable to all those situations, as illustrated in Chapter 6, where judicial reasoning itself invokes ownership as a principle, and to those situations, illustrated in the last chapter, where quasi-ownership interests are constructed from a combination of ownership interests and social function.

For example, in *Bradford* v. *Pickles*[9] the issue before the House of Lords was whether or not the corporation had a right that Pickles should not deliberately seek to damage its water supply by removing percolating water under his land. The House having ruled as it did, the law as stated at any subsequent time includes a no-right/privilege relationship in such circumstances, and that will continue to be true unless the House of Lords overrules that decision or it is abolished by statute. But their Lordships reached their controversial conclusion by appealing to ownership values. Ownership as a principle was an indispensable feature of their reasoning, and noticing that fact precisely brings to light the highly questionable normative choice they made. The person–thing relation can only be dispensed with by representing the decision as a repetitious tautology—Pickles is privileged to do this and the Corporation has no right to stop him because Pickles is privileged to do this and the Corporation has no right to stop him. Apart from the perverseness of ignoring the reasons actually invoked in support of decisions, such tautological, Hohfeldian representation fails to expose questionable normative elements in judicial reasoning.

The same would be true were we to try to disguise the part played by person–thing relations in all the other examples given of ownership serving as a principle in common law adjudication—choosing broad interpretations of rules protecting intellectual property and chattels; rejecting defences for squatters; extending ancient rights; rejecting easements of shelter; denying employees' rights to prevent plant closures; restrictive interpretations of the powers of revenue and compulsory-purchase authorities.

Person–thing relations are similarly indispensable to the understanding of judicial reasoning in connection with quasi-ownership interests. For example, in *British Airports Authority* v. *Ashton*[10] the court invoked BAA's ownership of Heathrow Airport as a reason for concluding that it had power to make the

---

[9] [1895] AC 587. This case is discussed in Ch. 6, sect. (ii) above.
[10] [1983] 3 All ER 6. This case is discussed in Ch. 7, sect. (iii)(b) above.

regulations excluding picketers. The point may have been a bad one, but we cannot isolate the (bad) point at all if we try to eliminate the person–thing ownership relation altogether.

By all means let us attack the justice reasons underlying appeals to person–thing relations. But it would be foolish to wish them away in the service of some presupposed analytical scheme.

(b) Honoré's Analysis

Anglo-American property theorists writing in the past thirty years have often taken as the starting-point for their analysis of ownership the seminal essay of A. M. Honoré.[11] Honoré unpacks ownership, not into bi-party jural relations, but into the 'standard incidents' of 'the liberal concept of full individual ownership'.[12] He recognizes that actual deployments of 'owner' and 'owner-ship' within modern property institutions often exhibit usages in which some of these incidents are missing.[13] That being so, should we not, in the last resort, drop any enquiry into who is owner of any particular thing and instead con-centrate on the variable complex of relations established between persons as to the use and control of resources?

Such a conclusion does not follow from Honoré's analysis. In its terms, invocations of ownership involve assumptions about person–thing relations which, even if they do not match the full liberal concept, are nevertheless indebted to it. Honoré acknowledges that in primitive communities this full concept could be unknown and lesser conceptions of ownership interests may be invoked.[14]

It is suggested here that the work actually done by ownership conceptions is better brought to light if we speak in terms of an ownership spectrum, from mere property to full-blooded ownership. Modern property institutions pro-tect ownership interests well down the spectrum over some resources. Ancient and primitive societies recognize something approaching full-blooded owner-ship over some things. There is, as we have seen, a plurality of mutable owner-ship interests and moving up the spectrum is not to be identified with any unilinear historical process.[15] What is specifically 'liberal' about full-blooded ownership will be considered later.[16] No hostage should be offered to the

---

[11] A. M. Honoré, 'Ownership' originally published in A. G. Guest (ed.), *Oxford Essays in Jurisprudence* (OUP, 1961), reprinted in Tony Honoré, *Making Law Bind: Essays Legal and Philosophical* (Clarendon Press, 1987), 161–92. For application and modification of Honoré's analysis, see Lawrence C. Becker, *Property Rights: Philosophic Foundations* (Routledge and Kegan Paul, 1977), 20–1; 'The Moral Basis of Property Rights', in Pennock and Chapman (eds.), n. 1 above, 189–91; Jeremy Waldron, *The Right to Private Property* (Clarendon Press, 1988), 48–50; Stephen R. Munzer, *A Theory of Property* (CUP, 1990), 22–7; John Christman, *The Myth of Property* (OUP, 1994), 19–20.
[12] Honoré, *Making Law Bind*, n. 11 above, 161.
[13] *Ibid*. 164–5, 175–9, 181–4.   [14] *Ibid*. 162.
[15] See Ch. 5, sect. (v) above.   [16] See Ch. 13, sect. (i) below.

extraordinary notion which seems to pervade some commentaries on property —that the idea of there being things which some people can use as they like but which others may steal was invented by the contemporaries of John Locke.[17]

The analysis offered here is in some ways more complicated than Honoré's, in that it speaks of a spectrum rather than a unitary concept of ownership. Nothing unites the ownership interests on this spectrum except their open-ended character, the self-seekingness which they license, and the fact that they are person–thing relations. In other ways our analysis is less complex than Honoré's. Where he lists eleven incidents of 'the liberal concept of full individual ownership', we have defined 'full-blooded ownership' in terms only of privileges and powers. Full-blooded ownership of things entails a relationship between a person (or persons) and a thing such that he (or they) have, *prima facie*, unlimited privileges of use or abuse over the thing, and *prima facie*, unlimited powers of control and transmission, so far as such use or exercise of power does not infringe some property-independent prohibition.

Honoré's incidents have the effect of incorporating within the concept of individual ownership particular features of the rules standardly to be found in modern property institutions. We have opted for a simpler conception in order to bring to light the interactions between ownership and other features of property institutions.

Honoré's eleven incidents are as follows: (i) The right to possess; (ii) the right to use; (iii) the right to manage; (iv) the right to the income; (v) the right to the capital; (vi) the right to security; (vii) the incident of transmissibility; (viii) the incident of absence of term; (ix) the duty to prevent harm; (x) liability to execution; (xi) residuary character.[18]

The right to possess is, he says '[t]he foundation on which the whole superstructure of ownership rests'.[19] It is of the essence of this right that it is *in rem* in the sense of availing against persons generally.[20] It has two aspects: it entails both a claim that others should not interfere with the owner's possession and a claim that the owner should be put into possession.[21]

That is one way of characterizing the combined effect of ownership interests and trespassory rules. It is indeed the case that, without the *in rem* protection to which Honoré refers, there would be no property institution at all. However, the inter-personal claims which arise will depend on the particular interactions between ownership interests and specific trespassory rules. Any 'claim-rights' (in Hohfeld's sense) which accompany ownership interests have the same content as the duties which trespassory rules impose.

---

[17] See our discussion of the views of C. B. MacPherson at the end of the next chapter. For a corrective of this way of thinking, see Charles Donahue, jr., 'The Future of the Concept of Property Predicted from its Past', in Pennock and Chapman (eds.), n. 1 above, 35–40.

[18] N. 12 above, 165–79.

[19] *Ibid.* 166.

[20] *Ibid.*

[21] *Ibid.* 166–8.

The crime of theft and the tort of conversion would be meaningless unless it were presupposed that there was someone, the owner, who has specially privileged relations to chattels. The definitions of wrongs and sanctions do not, however, vest in the owner an unqualified set of claims correlating with duties on others not to interfere with, or to restore, his physical control. Open-ended possessory privileges are always in the background, but the specific duties (and hence the correlative claim-rights) depend on the terms of the particular criminal or civil trespassory rules. Under the English Theft Act 1968 an appropriation is not criminal unless it is dishonest so that, so far as that criminal prohibition goes, an owner has at best[22] only a claim that others do not take his goods dishonestly. The prohibition of tortious conversion confers no general right to be restored to possession, since damages are, at the court's discretion, an alternative remedy.

Honoré's incidents ii–v (rights to use, to manage, to the income, and to the capital) are all employed by him in the sense of privileges or powers, rather than as claims correlating with duties.[23] All these privileges and powers are encompassed by our notion of *prima facie* unlimited privileges of use or abuse and *prima facie* unlimited powers of control and transmission.

Honoré's incident vi, the right to security, is, he says, legally 'an immunity from expropriation'.[24] He acknowledges that the immunity is subject to exceptions, but insists that a general power to expropriate subject to compensation 'would be fatal to the institution of ownership as we know it'.[25] Then under incident viii, absence of term, he points out that so-called 'indeterminate' interests are really determinable, because rules always provide for some contingency, such as bankruptcy, sale in execution, or state expropriation, on which the holder of an interest may lose it.[26] In incident X, liability to execution, he gives separate treatment to the general liability for an owner's interest to be taken away from him for debt, without which 'the growth of credit would be impeded and ownership would be an instrument by which the owner could freely defraud his creditors'.[27]

These three overlapping 'incidents' exemplify the interrelationship between ownership interests and various kinds of expropriation rules. They are none of them analytic features of ownership interests as such. If a person has an

---

[22] We leave aside the contention that a 'right', in the sense of a claim-right, arises only where the correlative duty may be waived by the rightholder or is otherwise under his control, from which it follows that criminal prohibitions do not usually create rights—see H. L. A. Hart, *Essays on Bentham: Studies in Jurisprudence and Political Theory* (Clarendon Press, 1982), 174–88.

[23] In connection with the 'right' to use, he rightly points out that the permissible types of use inherent in ownership 'constitute an open list' (n. 11 above, 168). The right to manage includes clusters of powers of control and powers of contracting (168–9). The 'right' to income is the power to trade uses for money—'Income . . . may be thought of as a surrogate of use, a benefit derived from foregoing the personal use of a thing and allowing others to use it for reward' (169). 'The right to the capital consists in the power to alienate the thing and the liberty to consume, waste, or destroy the whole or part of it' (170).

[24] *Ibid.* 171.   [25] *Ibid.*   [26] *Ibid.* 173.   [27] *Ibid.* 175.

ownership interest in a thing it follows, analytically, that he has some *prima facie* privileges and powers over it. It does not follow, analytically, that he is liable to be expropriated by the State or in the process of civil execution. Nevertheless, all modern property institutions no doubt contain some expropriation rules and this important general truth Honoré seeks to bring to the fore by describing the impact of such rules as standard 'incidents' of ownership. However, he draws back from listing liability to tax and unlimited liability to expropriation by the State among standard incidents, the former because it might be thought to obliterate the 'useful contrast between taxes on what is owned and on what is earned',[28] and the latter because expropriation 'tends to be restricted to special classes of property'.[29]

It is certainly true that what we have termed collectively 'expropriation rules'[30] serve a wide variety of social functions. It is questionable, however, whether it is useful to discriminate amongst these different social functions by classifying the impact of some expropriation rules as 'standard incidents' of ownership whilst the impact of others is not. Income, once earned, is also owned and is, standardly, taxed. Some items of domestic use which are owned are, standardly, immune from civil execution. What ownership interests analytically are is one thing. Their socially significant interrelations with expropriation rules is another.

In a similar way, Honoré seeks to incorporate other kinds of rules to be met within property institutions into his standard incidents and thereby renders the conception of ownership more complex than it need be. He dockets various kinds of what we have called 'appropriation rules'[31] under his incidents vii (transmissibility)[32] and xi (residuary character).[33] He encompasses within incident ix (the duty to prevent harm)[34] both property-limitation rules and also what we have called 'property-independent prohibitions'. The latter (we have contended) are not features of property institutions at all, since their impact is entirely independent of ownership interests.[35]

Trespassory rules, property-limitation rules, expropriation rules, and appropriation rules presuppose ownership interests. So too do invocations of ownership as an organizing idea in daily life, or as a principle within legal reasoning. Privileges and powers are intrinsic elements of ownership interests. Claim-rights, duties, liabilities, and immunities are important concomitants of ownership interests but are not analytically intrinsic to ownership interests in resources (material or ideational). (Claim-rights are, of course, intrinsic to those cashable rights which are brought within the purview of property institutions; and various kinds of non-ownership proprietary interests will represent one, or a combination of, Hohfeldian jural relations with owners.)

---

[28] Ibid.   [29] *Ibid*.   [30] See Ch. 3, sect. (x) above.
[31] See Ch. 3, sect. (xi) above.   [32] N. 11 above, 171–3.   [33] *Ibid*. 175–9.
[34] *Ibid*. 174. The equivalent incident was described in the original version of the essay 'too narrowly' as the 'prohibition of harmful use': *ibid*. 174 n. 1.
[35] See Ch. 3, sects. (vii) and (xiii) above.

Ownership interests could not exist without trespassory rules. The outer boundary of the control-powers intrinsic to various kinds of ownership interests is reciprocally related to the trespassory rules which protect them.[36] Nevertheless, the internal content of the ownership interests and the internal content of the trespassory rules are mutually independent. These twin pillars of property institutions cannot be collapsed either one into the other. The *prima facie* privileges and powers intrinsic to an ownership interest cannot be spelled out from the trespassory rules which protect it.[37] The content of the trespassory rules is given by the social practices, legislation, or case law which create them. The content of claim-rights which accompany ownership interests is the same as that of the duties which the trespassory rules impose. They are the correlatives of such duties. It follows that claim-rights are not intrinsic to ownership interests.

Neither are duties intrinsic to ownership interest, although duties of many kinds are imposed upon owners. Property-limitation rules commonly restrict the *prima facie* use-privileges and control-powers inherent in ownership interests by imposing duties towards others, as well as by simply docking such privileges and powers.[38] There have also been 'property-duty rules' unconnected with ownership privileges and powers.[39]

In feudal law, as we have seen, the tenant in demesne was taken to have an ownership interest in the land.[40] The *feodum* of the tenant carried duties of some kind towards the superior lord in the form of tenurial services. The holding of the land, and hence the enjoyment of ownership privileges and powers, was conditional on performance of these services. However, in feudal theory, the ownership and the tenurial services were both incidents of the *feodum*.[41] When an estate became alienable it carried with it both an ownership interest over the land and tenurial obligations. The tenurial duties were not part of the ownership relation. Both were part of the estate.

A similar analysis can be applied to post-feudal leasehold estates. A person vested with such an estate has, in common law systems, an ownership interest in land as an attribute of the estate. For the duration of the lease, he is protected against the world by trespassory rules and his use-privileges and powers are, subject to the terms of the lease, open-ended (as we saw in Chapter 5). A lease arises always from contract and most of the contractual obligations of the tenant pass to successive holders of the lease by the doctrine of privity of estate. Both the ownership interest in the land and the tenant's obligations to the landlord are attributes of the estate. The duties do not inhere in the ownership privileges/powers bundle itself.

---

[36] See Ch. 3, sect. (vi) above.
[37] See Ch. 5, sect. (i) above.
[38] See Ch. 3, sect. (viii) above.
[39] See Ch. 3, sect. (ix) above.
[40] See Ch. 5, sect. (iii) above.
[41] See Sir Frederick Pollock and F. W. Maitland, *History of English Law* (CUP, 1911), ii, 2–6.

Liabilities and immunities of various sorts are imposed upon, or conceded to, owners by expropriation rules. Undoubtedly, as Honoré indicates, the institution of liberal societies would be very different from what they are if liability to execution for debt was not imposed on most ownership interests, or, conversely, if the State's power to expropriate such interests was not carefully circumscribed. In every case, however, we can detach the notion of a particular ownership interest from a description of the rules which lay down or delimit the circumstances in which it may be expropriated. Analytically, then, no liability or immunity is intrinsic to ownership interests.

When we speak of 'the rights of ownership' we may refer, compositely, to the privileges and powers intrinsic to ownership interests and also to particular sets of claim-rights and immunities. When an assertion about ownership is proffered as a premise from which some conclusion about claim-right or immunity follows, then the 'rights of ownership' so invoked cannot, without tautology, include the particular claim-right or immunity mentioned in the conclusion. In such contexts the 'rights of ownership', invoked as a premise, refer only to *prima facie* use-privileges, control-powers, and, in the case of ownership interests in the upper half of the ownership spectrum, powers of transmission.

(ii) SCEPTICISM ABOUT OWNERSHIP

(a) Psychological Reductionism

One way of being sceptical about ownership is as follows. Granted that we encounter countless unreflective invocations of ownership interests, in the way described in Chapter 5, that merely brings to the fore a prevalent feature of social psychology. It does not demonstrate that ownership has any genuine semantic reference—that it is a concept with 'real meaning'. People may have been culturalized to talk as if owning something referred to some feature of the external universe, but that only shows the pervasive power of illusions over the human psyche. The illusions should be exposed. Echoes of psychological reductionism crop up in any political controversy in which ownership-invocations are dismissed as mere 'ideology'.

The most consistent exponents of such psychological reductionism in the field of legal theory have been those followers of Axel Hagerström[42] to whom the collective label 'Scandinavian Legal Realists' has come to be applied.[43] The leading exponents of the school were Karl Olivecrona and Alf Ross.

Olivecrona argued that words standing for legal concepts were 'hollow' or

---

[42] A. Hagerström, *Enquiries into the Nature of Law and Morals* (trans. C. D. Broad, Almqvist and Wikfell, 1953).

[43] For a summary of their views, see Harris, n. 4 above, 98–102.

'empty', since they were without semantic reference.[44] They were none the less efficacious as a means of social control because of the way they ring in 'the common mind'[45] with directive or suggestive effect.

Legal language is not a descriptive language. It is a directive, influential language serving as an instrument of social control. The 'hollow' words are like sign-posts with which people have been taught to associate ideas concerning their own behaviour and that of others. . . . The ascription of a right of property to a person is, so to speak, an echo of the rules concerning the right of property.[46]

The entire enterprise is based on a theoretical assumption about the onto-logical status of conceptual entities: either they directly reflect brute reality, or they are metaphysical chimera and their employment must be explained away in psychological terms. It ignores the possibility that the human mind may create abstract entities which human institutions can then usefully employ for a variety of functions, without it having to be supposed that the entities belong to some mysterious supra-sensible realm. There is a case for investigating, as a facet of sociological enquiry, the extent to which rules of property institutions have been internalized in the psychological lives of individuals; but even to do that we will need to employ theoretical constructs—like Olivecrona's notion of 'the common mind'—which, by the canons of his ontological preconcep-tions, are as 'unreal' as any other abstract entities. Psychological reductionism of this sort is thus misconceived and inconsistent.[47]

Ross seeks to support the contention that it is 'nonsense' to attribute mean-ing to ownership by citing the practices of an island community where people believe in a magical form of contamination which they call 'tu-tu'.[48] If you eat the chief's food you become tu-tu. If you become tu-tu, you have to undergo a purification ceremony. Now, argues Ross, the rule could be rewritten: 'if you eat the chief's food, you must undergo a purification ceremony'. In the same way, one could rewrite all the rules of a property institution which employ ownership conceptions without using them. The law says: 'if X has completed a valid purchase, he is owner'; and 'if X is owner, he can sue for recovery'. One could rewrite the law: 'if X has completed a valid purchase, he can sue for recovery'. It is convenient to employ some middle term, but anything would do. The fact that it is in principle dispensable shows that ownership, like tu-tu, stands for nothing real.

The comparison ignores problems thrown up by the open texture of rules.

---

[44] Karl Olivecrona, 'Legal Language and Reality', in R. Newman (ed.), *Essays in Juris-prudence in Honor of Roscoe Pound* (The Bobbs-Merrill Co., 1962), 151; *Law as Fact* (2nd edn., Stevens, 1971), 245–59.

[45] *Law as Fact*, n. 44 above, 3–4.   [46] *Ibid*. 253, 259.

[47] See J. W. Harris, 'Olivecrona on Law and Language—The Search for Legal Culture' (1982) *Tidsskrift för Rettsvitenskap* 625.

[48] A. Ross, 'tu-tu' (1957) 70 *Harv. LR* 625.

Suppose a dispute arises when the person who has become tu-tu is the community witch doctor and the imposition upon him of the purification ceremony would prevent him from carrying out a crucial engagement for blessing the crops. Some contend that the purification ceremony must nevertheless proceed, others that it can be postponed, others that the witch doctor is exempt. The elders—or whoever else decides such disputes—will refer to what tu-tu actually means and weigh the values it serves against the competing values served by the crop-blessing. Their 'lawyers', understanding the magical metaphysic from the inside, would know what sorts of arguments were relevant. We can neither join in, nor properly understand, their debate unless, avoiding psychological reductionism, we accept that the meaning of tu-tu is their meaning for it.

A consistent psychological reductionist could express no view as to the soundness or unsoundness of the decisions mentioned in Chapter 6 in which ownership was invoked as a principle justifying certain interpretations of open-textured trespassory, property-limitation, and expropriation rules. Indeed, he must stand back from any debate about the justice of property or any other institutions. An inconsistent psychological reductionist is one who believes that, having exposed the set of psychological commitments (the 'ideology') implicit in a social practice, he has by that alone produced information supporting normative conclusions. Condemnation of an institution requires demonstration that the values underlying both the unreflective and self-conscious applications of its rules and principles fail the test of justice.

(b) Totality Ownership

There is a special reason why theorists trained against the background of the common law should be nudged in the direction of ownership scepticism. The feudal origins of English law have produced the conceptual categories in which Anglo-American law applies property institutions to the allocation of wealth in land. As a result, the concept of 'ownership' as such plays little part in the initiation of law students to property law, for land law is, within common law academies, still seen as the paradigm of property law. The doctrine of estates in land permits various bundles of rights to be allocated to different persons over the same resource as do trusts, corporate holdings, and non-ownership proprietary interests. All of this is commonly referred to as the 'splitting' of ownership.

We have seen in Chapters 5 and 6 how ownership conceptions operate as organizing ideas and principles within all these juristic constructs. The right conclusion to draw from them is that ownership is not a univocal concept because there is a spectrum of ownership interests. It is true that, in the history of continental legal dogmatics, scholars have struggled to advance a univocal meaning for 'ownership', such that it would denote a concept with the same content whenever the term is correctly applied. Nothing of the sort was attempted in classical Roman law[49] and the continental scholarly tradition has always found it difficult to square its invention with the complexities of real-life property institutions.[50] The difference between the juristic traditions yields only the conclusion that, whereas in civil law systems there may be a case for reserving the term 'ownership' (*dominium*) for one of the bundles of privileges and powers on the ownership spectrum, that is not so in common law systems (at least so far as land is concerned).

However, some theorists have moved from the idea of splitting ownership to a global scepticism about ownership in the following way. That totality which is split by the doctrine of estates and other juristic devices must comprise a complete set of privileges enabling a single individual to make any use that he pleases of that which he is said to own. No doubt the layman supposes that he does 'own' things in this sense. Yet any lawyer is aware that there are always divisions and limits. Since ownership (in the sense of this totality conception of ownership) can easily be disproved, no-one ever owns anything. Even with simple chattels, so-called 'owners' cannot do anything they like (if property-independent prohibitions are taken into account); and in the case of land it is laughably easy to put the layman in his place.

Here is a flat. The block of which it forms part is vested in a property development company, in which many people have shares. The company has mortgaged the block to another company, in which other people have shares. The flat is let on a ninety-nine-year lease to Jones. The lease contains many covenants restricting what Jones may do with the flat and requiring him to pay rent and contribute to a service fund to cover the cost of maintaining common parts of the block. Jones has assigned the lease, after ten years of the term have run, to Smith. Smith, as the lease permits, has sublet the flat for five years to Brown. Further, when purchasing the lease from Jones, Smith obtained a mortgage from a third company in which people have shares. Brown lives in the flat with his wife and children. 'Now, O benighted layman, tell us lawyers who is the owner and of what! What price your fuzzy notions of person–thing relations!'

The challenge need not be met. Nothing in law or in social life turns, in such a context, on a unique (all-encompassing) person–thing relationship. The bearing of particular rules separates out different person–thing relationships, whether or not it deploys 'ownership' terminology. Trespassory rules protect Brown, the five-year leaseholder. In English law, if someone moves into his flat while he and his family are on holiday, he will have a civil action for

[49] See W. W. Buckland and Arnold D. McNair, *Roman Law and Common Law* (2nd edn. revised by F. H. Lawson, CUP, 1952), ch. III; P. Birks, 'The Roman Concept of Dominium and the Idea of Absolute Ownership' (1986) *Acta Juridica* 1.

[50] See. J. W. Jones, 'Forms of Ownership' (1947) 22 Tulane LR 82, at 82–5; Boudewijn Bouckaert, 'What is Property?' (1990) 13 *Harvard Journal of Public Policy* 775 at 776–7, 784–9.

recovery and the interloper will commit an offence contrary to the Criminal Law Act 1977 if he refuses to go after being requested to leave by 'a displaced residential occupier'. If there is a planning restriction relating to the external appearance of the block, the freeholder property company will be restricted thereby. If there is a property tax on the block as a whole or on the flat, its terms will need to be looked at to see whether it applies to the freeholder, the leaseholder, or the sub-lessee. Rules may require interpretation and this may involve, among other things, interaction between the rules and open-ended conceptions along the ownership spectrum. If Brown wishes to exercise some use-privilege, say to engage in eccentric decoration, he will be free to do so unless public property-limitation rules or the terms of his sub-lease prohibit it, because, as an incident of his five-year sub-lease, the flat is open-endedly 'his'. If a share holder in one of the companies wishes to transmit his portion of the wealth-potential of the flat by making a gift of the shares to another, he will be free to do so unless some provision of the articles of association of the relevant company forbids it because, again, the shares are open-endedly 'his'. If Brown's wife, or Smith's wife, sues for divorce and the Court has a discretion to order transfers of 'property' the jurisdiction *prima facie* extends to the sub-lease or the leasehold interest because they are Brown's and Smith's to be taken away. No all-embracing person–thing ownership relationship exists, but a multitude of open-ended person–thing ownership relationships interact with trespassory, property-limitation, expropriation, and appropriation rules.

Where are we to find those unenlightened ones who believe that owning entails freedom to do anything one likes with a thing? Blackstone is often indicted as an exemplar but, as we saw in Chapter 3, even he will have to be discharged since (like any lawyer and most non-lawyers) he was well aware of the existence of property-limitation and expropriation rules.[51] Even full-blooded ownership carries no *prima facie* rights to contravene property-independent prohibitions. Has any civilian advocate of absolute dominion ever supposed that if I 'own' a chopper it follows that I am at liberty to use it to cut off my neighbour's head? Totality ownership is an invention of ownership-sceptics, an Aunt Sally erected to be knocked down.

Bruce Ackerman is a notable purveyor of lawyerly scepticism about ownership. In his *Private Property and the Constitution*,[52] Ackerman focuses on the takings clause of the Fifth Amendment to the United States constitution— '[n]or shall private property be taken for public use, without just compensation'. It is notorious, he says, that the voluminous case law on this topic is a frightful muddle. No progress is possible, he suggests, unless constitutional lawyers face up to a fundamental choice. Should the problem be approached from the stance of an 'ordinary observer', or from that of a 'Scientific Policy-maker'?[53] These are both ideal-typical positions. The former combines

---

[51] See Ch. 3, sect. (vi) above.

[52] Bruce A. Ackerman, *Private Property and the Constitution* (Yale UP, 1977).

[53] *Ibid.* 4 and *passim*.

(1) commitment to using only lay (and never technical) discourse with (2) the assumption that settled expectations are the sole ground on which normative choices can be supported.[54] The latter (1) aspires to solve all problems by attributing to the legal system a single 'comprehensive view' of the just society ('policy-making') and also (2) insists that everything must be addressed in a specialist technical ('scientific') vocabulary.[55]

Objection to bifurcation in terms of these paired attributes might be taken on many grounds. Why should it be supposed that a legal commentator who does not put forward a comprehensive view is bound to appeal only to expectations? Why should such a commentator also eschew legal-technical categories? Why should a critic who does advance a comprehensive view formulate all that he has to say in specialist (non-ordinary) language?[56]

However that may be, we are here only concerned with the ownership-scepticism with which Ackerman begins his enquiry. He says that there is a consensus so pervasive among property lawyers that even 'the dimmest law student' is brought to share it.[57] The law never assigns to any single person 'the right to use anything in absolutely *any* way he pleases'.[58] Hence 'it risks serious confusion to identify any single individual as *the* owner of any particular thing'.[59] It is one of the main points of a first-year property course to get this message across and so 'to disabuse entering law students of their primitive lay notions regarding ownership'.[60]

Thus, the unsophisticated suppose that people own things, while all lawyers know that nobody ever owns anything. (Of course, Ackerman is referring only to lawyers in common law jurisdictions. He recognizes that continental European lawyers, not having derived their land law from English feudal categories of estates, are still in the dark on the matter.[61])

If Ackerman is right, the rest of his book is witness to a startling paradox. He demonstrates that, in the vast majority of cases dealing with the takings clause, American judges have themselves taken the layman's view—that people do own things.[62] How did it come about that they so readily forgot what they had learned in the first year of their legal studies? How was it that Oliver Wendell Holmes no less[63]—a 'legal genius' as Ackerman describes him[64]— was unable to grasp something known to the dimmest law student?

Ackerman offers no explanation for the paradox and indeed seems unaware of it. The answer is, however, not far to seek. It is true that the law never

---

[54] *Ibid*. 12, 15 and *passim*.   [55] *Ibid*. 11, 15, 29 and *passim*.

[56] Ackerman appears to waver over the question whether policy-making is to be tied to 'scientific' terminology. On p. 20 he rejects as incoherent the view, which he attributes to Dworkin, that a comprehensive view can be expressed in terms of 'ordinary' concepts. Yet later we find him citing Dworkin on the policy-making, as opposed to the ordinary-observing, side of the divide (172–4).   [57] N. 52 above, 26.

[58] *Ibid*.   [59] *Ibid*. 26–7.   [60] *Ibid*. 26.

[61] *Ibid*. 27 n. 3.   [62] *Ibid*. 66, 86, 129–33 and *passim*.

[63] *Ibid*. 163–5.   [64] *Ibid*. 167.

assigns to anyone 'the right to use anything in absolutely any way he pleases', if one takes into account all those property-independent prohibitions which ban, for example, using one's chattels as instruments of aggression or destruction. Hence the sort of ownership which is put up, attributed to the unsophisticated layman, and then knocked down is the Aunt Sally of 'totality ownership'. In terms of such a conception, to 'own' something would entail that one could use it in any fashion, however anti-social or even lethal. There is indeed a consensus that no-one ever 'owns' anything in this sense, but that consensus is not limited to lawyers. As Ackerman himself recognizes, it is shared at least by all well-socialized middle-class Americans.[65] Even a child who supposed he could ride a bicycle over the neighbour's flowers provided he 'owned' the bicycle would be 'perverse'.[66]

Neither Ackerman's lay 'ordinary observer', nor the judges who (as he rightly contends) for the most part share the same ideas of ownership, actually believe in totality ownership. Everyone knows that you are not supposed to brain people with a paperweight, and that it is completely irrelevant whether or not you own it. What the laymen and the judges who have interpreted the takings clause assume is that people 'own' resources in the sense that they have, in relation to them, an open-ended set of *prima facie* use-privileges, control-powers, and powers of transmission. They also know—although lawyers' information is likely to be more exact—that property-limitation rules impinge specifically on ownership interests over some kinds of resources such as land and enterprises. The problem cases are those in which it is disputed whether the impact of some property-limitation rule on a particular owner ought, in justice, to carry compensation.[67]

It is possible to advance a comprehensive view about the just allocation of resources which yields the conclusion that no-one should be accorded an ownership interest in any resource (material, ideational, or financial[68]). In principle, it seems, that is the position of Ackerman's scientific policy-maker; for he is one who regards ordinary ownership talk (lay and judicial) as 'be-nighted'.[69] However, this self-denying ordinance is something Ackerman appears to find it impossible to maintain with consistency. For when he con-structs the view that the ideal scientific policy-maker would take of the takings clause, reference to 'property owners' crop up again and again.[70] As for law students, if we think that, merely by teaching them the technical vocabulary of land law, we have induced them (or ourselves) to believe that nobody ever owns a house, or a car, or a patent, or a £10 note, we err.

It is, in practice, very difficult for anyone advancing a proposal for reform of a property institution to adhere consistently to that form of scepticism which

---

[65] Bruce A. Ackerman, n. 52 above, at 98–101.   [66] *Ibid*. 101.
[67] See Ch. 6, sect. (iii)(c) above.   [68] See Ch. 18 below.
[69] N. 52 above, 64.   [70] See, e.g., *ibid*. 52, 53, 55, 56, 60.

is rooted in the conception of totality ownership. Take, for example, the criticism of the *United Steel Workers* case[71] advanced by Joseph Singer.[72] The Court ruled that, as owner of the plants, the corporation was free to demolish them and was not obliged to sell them to the union even at a fair market price. Singer argues that this decision was wrong as a question of common law. He cites a range of property rules, all of which (he maintains) give effect to 'reliance' interests.[73] Since reliance interests have been admitted in other areas of property law, it was open to the court to extend the underlying principle by recognizing, for the first time, the right of employees to purchase a factory which is threatened with closure. A step which was open at common law was one the court should have taken if the requirements of justice, all things considered, warranted it; and they did.

During the course of the argument, Singer inserts a bit of ownership-scepticism which serves only to obfuscate his brief. He repeats the hallowed sceptical observation about the first-year law student knowing something which Blackstone had overlooked; and he reminds us that property interests are often divided by virtue of estates, trusts, corporate holdings, and so forth.[74] It is time, he says, to 'deconstruct' the familiar assumption which 'we' make— that owners can 'control and use their property as they see fit'.[75] As to the particular decision, asking who was the owner of the plants is like asking 'how many angels can dance on the head of a pin. . . . To say the company can blow up the plant *because* it owns it states a conclusion rather than a premise.'[76]

This is an example of the perverse tautologizing to which we referred at the end of the discussion of Hohfeld's analysis. Manifestly ownership is not an empty premise from which to draw the conclusion reached by the court (any more than it was in all the other judicial instances of ownership operating as a principle mentioned in Chapter 6), although it may not carry the normative weight which the court accorded to it. An apologist for the court's ruling would argue as follows. There are sound reasons for conferring open-ended use-privileges and control-powers over industrial plants on individuals and groups—for example, the inherent-property-freedom argument and the market-instrumental argument considered later in this book. Those property-specific justice reasons support liberty to act in a self-seeking way. When the judges invoked ownership, they were keying into those reasons. They warrant the conclusion that the corporation could act for the benefit of the shareholders without regard to the effect of their decisions on others.

That this was the normative import of the invocation of ownership is recognized by Singer himself. Throughout the rest of his paper, he deploys the

---

[71] *United Steel Workers* v. *United States Steel Corporation*, 631 F2d 1264 (1980). This case is discussed in Ch. 6, sect. (ii) above.

[72] Joseph William Singer, 'The Reliance Interest in Property' (1988) 40 *Stan. LR* 611.

[73] Some of his illustrations (prescription and estoppel) are more plausible examples of 'reliance' than others (obligations to shelter the homeless).

[74] *Ibid.* 637–41.   [75] *Ibid.* 641.   [76] *Ibid.* 638.

angels-on-a-pin notion of ownership just as if it meant something after all. He reminds us, rightly, that there have been many cases in which 'owners' *prima facie* privileges and powers have been restricted for the sake of other values. He argues, forcefully, that what we shall call 'domination-potential' has to be taken as a serious counter to the freedom and market-instrumental arguments in such contexts.[77] None of this would have been necessary (or indeed would have made sense) if it were really the case that ownership could never serve as a premise because it refers to nothing.

Replace the chimera of totality ownership with the reality of the ownership spectrum and the grounds for scepticism disappear. Ownership interests, however labelled in law, are among the organizing ideas through which social wealth is filtered. Social wealth confronts citizens as lumps over which open-ended privileges and powers obtain, not as packages of specified rights. It would be possible to dispense with the ownership spectrum altogether, as was done in some of the imaginary societies discussed in Chapter 2. None of the societies we know are, however, structured in that way.

[77] See Ch. 14, sect. (iv)(a) below.

9

What Property Is

(i) A STIPULATION

'Property' designates those items which are points of reference within, and therefore presupposed by, the rules of a property institution, *viz.*, trespassory, property-limitation, expropriation, and appropriation rules. Such items are either the subject of direct trespassory protection or else separately assignable as parts of private wealth.

Therefore, 'property' comprises (1) ownership and quasi-ownership interests in things (tangible or ideational); (2) other rights over such things which are enforceable against all-comers (non-ownership proprietary interests); (3) money; and (4) cashable rights. That is what 'property' is.

The foregoing definition roughly tracks a wide range of conventional property talk, but it also contains a large element of stipulation. Why do we proffer it?

(a) No 'True' Property

There is no uniquely correct meaning of the word 'property' such that employment of the term in some other sense would be a misuse of language. As we saw in Chapter 1, the elusiveness of the concept can in no way be dispelled by mere reflection on terminology. Yet there is a range of usages of this and associated terms—'property' talk—which concerns itself with a certain kind of legal or social institution. We reflect those usages when we refer to those institutions as 'property' institutions. We wish to confront institutions of this kind with justice. For that purpose we stipulate that 'property' shall only be used according to this particular conventional range of usages. That this is a sensible stipulation will appear from our discussion of more expansive employments of the term 'property'.

There is no 'true' property in the sense of a uniquely correct use of terminology. We shall also eschew any search for 'true property' in another sense. We assume that 'property' does not refer to a morally contested concept in the way that 'justice' does. It would be a contradiction to affirm of a social institution both that it was perfectly just and also that it was devoid of moral status. We wish to preserve the sense of 'property' such that it is no contradiction to predicate of any particular property institution, or of all property institutions, that it or they flout the requirements of justice. We shall leave to one side that familiar jurisprudential controversy between those legal positivists who claim that the existence of a legal system is one thing, its moral merits another, and anti-positivists who deny this on the ground that moral goodness enters into the very concept of law. Someone committed to the latter view either denies the propriety of speaking about 'unjust laws', or at least affirms that the word 'law' in 'unjust law' points to a derivative or non-central instance of the true concept of law. It might be possible to take a similar tack with property, and to insist that a complex of rules which imposed unjust obligations or which distributed wealth unfairly was not a true system of 'property'. To adopt such a position one would have to have already established the basis in justice of true property. We leave it aside because it would befuddle our entire enterprise.

(b) Property as Things and Property as Wealth

Conventional property-talk (lay and legal) displays an ambivalence which reflects the dual function of property institutions, as instrumentalities for controlling the use of things and for the allocation of wealth. 'Property' may refer to the things in respect of which ownership or quasi-ownership interests subsist. Or it may refer to the monetary value of such interests. Crudely the contrast may be expressed as one between 'property as things' and 'property as wealth'. The ambivalence is manifested by the way in which money is sometimes contrasted with 'property' and sometimes spoken of as a species of property.[1]

For many reasons, a conception of property which builds on conventional property-talk must reflect both halves of this ambivalent usage. For one thing, the one slides into the other in many contexts. A person who envies or wishes to share in another's 'property' may perfectly well have in mind his land and his goods, or his money and his bank balance, or both. Secondly, although some kinds of property-limitation rules are focused only on the use of things, many property rules apply indifferently to things and to money. My chattels and my cash may be stolen. The 'property' which a person is free to dispose of at her death comprehends ownership interest in things and also her money and cashable rights. The 'property' which is taxed, allocated, or redistributed by a property institution may refer to property as things or to property as wealth.

Above all, justificatory or disjustificatory arguments about property should not deploy a concept which is limited either to property as things or to property as wealth, because the operation of any property institution fulfils both its functions simultaneously. Even in the imaginary Wood Land and Pink Land societies (described in Chapter 2), where there was no monetary exchange, according 'mere property' in things to persons enabled them to become modest accumulators of private wealth. In real societies, recognition of

[1] See Ch. 4, sect. (ii)(a) above.

anything approaching full-blooded ownership over scarce things inevitably leads to unequal holdings of private wealth, whether those holdings take the form at any particular moment of ownership interests in things or of bank balances. For all that, as we shall see, competing property theories may appear mutually disengaged precisely because their respective emphases are directed either to property as things or to property as wealth. A theorist who supposes that ownership interests in objects may be justified, say, by a natural-rights argument, but then ignores questions of wealth-distribution, tells only half the story. The same is true, in the opposite direction, of one who advocates a certain distribution of 'resources' but who neglects the question whether person–thing ownership relations are to form part of a property-institutional design.

A property institution is the social and legal institution which constitutes the background for conventional property-talk among both laymen and lawyers. We have endeavoured to bring out the salient features of such institutions and to show how they build upon the twinned and mutually irreducible notions of trespassory rules and the ownership spectrum. We have tried to steer a middle course between over-simplification and excessive detail. Nothing like a summary of English or of any other system of property law has been attempted. On the other hand, what has been included goes beyond the scope of traditional textbooks on property law. Such books usually omit discussion of much of what here has come under the headings of trespassory rules, property-limitation, expropriation, and appropriation rules. Such discussion appears in works on criminal law, the law of torts, bankruptcy law, revenue law, the law of succession, family law, and constitutional law. Some of the devices for hiving off wealth from use conventionally appear in works on contract or company law. These are matters of textbook convenience. Works without 'property' in the title none the less refer repeatedly to property. Lay talk naturally does not reflect textbook breakdowns.

The property talk of both laymen and lawyers has a lumpy focus. There are things (objects, resources, money, portions of wealth) which some may own, trade, or inherit, and which others may steal, appropriate, or bestow. Our object has been to provide a picture of what is essential to, and what is typical of, property institutions such that discussion of putative justifications of property may have a focus.

The following overview emerges from our discussion. A property institution typically comprises (1) trespassory rules; (2) property-limitation rules; (3) expropriation rules; (4) appropriation rules. (There may be as well property-duty rules and property-privilege rules.) Interests of individuals, groups, or agencies are proprietary in nature when they are protected or presupposed by the bulk of these rules. That is the case with ownership interests and quasi-ownership interests in land, chattels, ideas, money, and cashable rights, and with any rights over such things which are accorded general trespassory protection (non-ownership proprietary interests).

Other interests are marginal cases since, although they are brought within the scope of some of the property rules, the bulk of the rules neither protect them nor presuppose them. That is the case with business goodwill[2] and specifically enforceable contracts.[3] Any right or opportunity may be 'property' for the purpose of a particular legal rule.[4] For the purpose of a general overview, an interest must display characteristics which bring it within the general scope of the institution, that is, which entail that it is likely to constitute a point of reference for a wide variety of property rules. On that basis we now make firm the provisional stipulation mentioned at the end of Chapter 4, that for a right (or bundle of rights) to be proprietary it (or they) must either be the subject of specific trespassory protection or else be separately assignable as part of a person's private wealth. That alternative characterization enables us to capture the ambivalence in property-talk between property as things and property as wealth, as well as the lawyerly distinction between rights *in rem* and rights *in personam*.

We referred in Chapter 1 to the widespread, much criticized, tendency to speak of the material objects over which ownership interests subsist, rather than the ownership interests themselves, as 'property'. This usage is harmless enough when the ownership interests in question constitute something approaching full-blooded ownership. It might possibly obscure the fact that a range of different ownership interests, as well as non-ownership proprietary interests, may subsist in respect of the same object. Consequently, our stipulation refers to as 'property', not objects themselves, but ownership interests, quasi-ownership interests and non-ownership proprietary interests over the objects. It would, however, be unduly pedantic to insist on the same stipulation as regards money and cashable rights—to insist, that is, that 'property' refers to rights over money or rights over choses in action rather than to the money or choses themselves.

Thus, we eschew any 'true' semantic or conceptual essence of 'property'. We none the less build on conventional property-talk to arrive at the stipulated definition of property mentioned at the beginning of this Chapter. That stipulation will now be supported by arguments from social heuristics which prevail, for our purposes, over various arguments for more expansive definitions.

---

[2] See Ch. 4, sect. (ii)(b)(2) above.
[3] See Ch. 4, sect. (iv)(b) above.
[4] See Ch. 4, sect. (iv)(a) above.

(ii) SOCIAL HEURISTICS

Stipulations are never correct, only more or less serviceable. We have fashioned a stipulation for what property is by reference to a certain conventional range of property-talk. We left out of account more expansive uses of 'property' now familiar amongst some theorists, and also to some extent reflected within ordinary political controversies. The label 'property' may be applied, for example, to familial rights, welfare rights, jobs, and political rights. Why stipulate in such a way as to leave such things out?

Our answer appeals to social heuristics. Most things and services are scarce. Either they are, or they are not, or should be, or should not be, allocated via that institution which deploys at its core the twinned ideas of trespassory rules and the ownership spectrum. Let us reserve the label 'property institution' for that instrumentality, not merely because it tracks a range of linguistic usages, but because we need to isolate it and keep it distinct from other possible resource-allocating devices for the purposes of social evaluation.

Probably all human services should be considered as at least potentially scarce. There might at a particular place and time be more people willing to render some gratuitous amical or familial service than there are people anxious to avail themselves of it. But one cannot assume that to be universally true of any particular category of service. Thus, all categories of service are potentially constituents of social wealth, with demand outstripping supply. Allocation must then, somehow or other, be achieved.

Social institutions may allow or require scarce services to be allocated in accordance with the norms of family life, nepotistic preference, or hit-and-miss social intercourse. Or they may establish institutions of public law whereby such services as child-care, education, transport, health, police, and fire-prevention are provided according to perceived need. Alternatively, some or all of the services just mentioned may be allocated by virtue of what we have called a property institution. This may be done either by making the services themselves, or the human individuals who provide them, directly the subject of ownership interests protected by trespassory rules, as in feudal or slave-owning societies; or by making services available to the highest bidder, and thus locking into the ownership principles and trespassory rules which apply to money. In either of these ways a property institution allocates part of the scarce services comprised within social wealth to an individual as part of her private wealth. All such contrasts are blurred if we insist that rights to services, however allocated, are a species of 'property'.

Most things are scarce. They may be allocated via ownership interests or by way of rationed and defined use-rights. One requires some terminology to distinguish these two methods of allocation.

Consider the argument that free milk ought to be made available to school children, free medicine to patients, or free safety clothing to workers. These are, let us assume, entitlements. They have priority over any other deployment of the resources needed to produce and distribute these things. However, the milk, medicine, or clothing may only be used by the recipient in defined ways and may certainly not be given away to others, let alone traded. In terms of our discussion in Chapters 2 and 3, the recipients lack even 'mere property' in these items.

It might be contended that, rather than meet such needs *in specie*, parents or patients should be awarded monetary grants, and employees paid higher wages, to enable them to purchase these things if they wished and that, once purchased, the things should be theirs to dispose of as they wished. The latter arrangement may be inferior to the first because proprietary freedom is just what we do not want in the context of such important needs. If so, the welfare solution is better than the property solution. Just this contrast is lost if we insist that in both cases allocation of scarce resources is made through the medium of property rights.

The label of 'property' may be attached to welfare rights to buttress support for them as against mere discretionary payments.[5] The position of such right-holders is, however, importantly distinguishable from, for example, that of someone who has a claim on a pension fund which he can, if he chooses, encash and spend as he pleases. The former have acquired a claim on social wealth through an allocative decision made by whatever legislative or regulative body created the welfare right. The latter has a present power to make allocative choices. His claim on social wealth is already part of his private wealth. He can at any time choose to spend his money as he likes. This difference is captured by our stipulation. Cashable rights to money are property rights. Fixed rights to future payments, which the rightholder can neither assign nor in any other way anticipate, are not. Of course, once the money is paid over the recipient has property. Money is always property.

There have been epochs in which jobs were themselves a form of property, as distinct from a means of obtaining it, as when commissions in the army could be bought and sold. A reversion to such a state of affairs is not intended by those who claim that people ought to be regarded as having 'property' in jobs. The claim is, rather, that an employee should be accorded tenure, that his employment should not be terminable by an employer at will under the terms of a contract. The property label is not needed to make this point.

Furthermore, if 'property' is employed in an extended sense, it will still be necessary to employ some terminology or other to reflect the distinctions captured by conventional property-talk. Someone claiming that jobs are 'property' could not leave it at that. He would need to make it clear, for example, whether the right to the job was to endure until retirement merely against a particular employer, or whether it was conceived of as a right to work in, and

---

[5] See the discussion of Reich's 'new property' in sect. (iii)(b) below.

receive remuneration out of the assets of, a particular enterprise, no matter into whose ownership the enterprise might pass. In the former case, conventional terminology would speak of a 'right *in personam*'. In the latter case, the right would constitute a non-ownership proprietary interest burdening the enterprise within the bounds of a property institution as conventionally understood.[6]

In short, what is conventionally understood to be 'property' has to be called something. The burden rests with those who wish to expand the concept to show why this should be done.

(iii) EXPANSIVE DEFINITIONS

The foregoing argument does not establish that for all purposes 'property' should be limited to ownership, quasi-ownership, and non-ownership proprietary interests in things, money, and cashable rights. We shall in Chapter 11 explore a centuries-old philosophical tradition whereby people are said to have 'property' in their own persons—a notion which has been exploited, as we shall argue, to draw contradictory and illegitimate conclusions about 'property' in resources. In the present section we turn to a variety of recent theoretical projects which in effect recognize that 'property', as conventionally understood, matches our stipulated definition but go on to argue that the concept should be expanded. They concern economic analysis, Reich's 'new property', constitutional theory, and MacPherson's political property-rhetoric. We shall see that the proposed conceptual shifts serve only to obfuscate such projects.

(a) Economic Analysis

Throughout the history of theorizing about property, economic considerations have played an important role. We shall later discuss instrumental arguments based on creator-incentives and markets.[7] Such arguments purport to show that freely transferable ownership interests over resources ought to be instituted or maintained. They require no conceptual shift in our understanding of what property is.

However, in the last thirty years there has emerged a style of economic analysis of legal and social institutions which deploys the concept of 'property right' in an extended sense specifically adapted to the requirements of the analysis. In the preface to a recent book entitled *Economic Analysis of Property Rights*, Yoram Barzel writes:

The intellectual content of 'property rights,' a term that has enchanted and occasionally mesmerized economists, seems to lie within the jurisdiction of the legal

---

[6] See the discussion of labour as a commodity in Ch. 11, sect. (ii)(b)(3) below.
[7] See Ch. 15, sect. (iii) below.

profession. Consistent with their imperialist tendencies, however, economists have also attempted to appropriate it. Both disciplines can justify their claims, since the term is given different meanings on different occasions. Perhaps economists should initially have coined a term distinct from the one used for legal purposes, but by now the cost of doing so is too high.[8]

Nowhere in the rest of this book does Barzel offer a conceptual analysis which distinguishes the two senses of 'property rights'. Furthermore, his discussion appears often to be directed towards property in the legal-conventional, rather than in the supposed specialist-economic, sense.[9] These are failings commonly encountered in the modern genre of economic analysis of property rights.

At its widest, the extended property concept appears to be as follows. The term 'property right' includes any right—whether Hohfeldian claim-right, privilege, power, or immunity[10]—concerning the use of a resource, where 'resource' includes all bodily and mental capacities of the rightholder. In other words, all rights are property rights. Not all deployments of property-concept expansion go this far; but once conventional property-talk is explicitly disavowed, stopping-points tend to be *ad hoc* and unexplained.

How has the tendency to property-concept expansion come about? There is, as we shall see, an important argument for property institutions which derives from their use-channelling and use-policing advantages as compared with non-property allocations of resource-use.[11] That argument can be framed in the terminology of economic analysis as follows. The use which any person makes of a resource will often have effects (good or bad) on others. How should the problem of these 'externalities' be met in order that all resources are put to uses which all involved value most (that is, to achieve the 'efficient' or 'pareto-optimal' solution)? If there is a free-for-all the problem can only be solved by inter-personal transactions. They will need to involve all those affected, to avoid 'free-loader' problems. They will be difficult to achieve because of transaction costs and because of 'hold-outs'. They will be expensive to police. If, instead of a free-for-all, we substitute ownership interests over the resource—that is, open-ended use-privileges, control-powers, and powers of transmission—the efficient solution to the externalities problem is much easier to achieve. Anyone wishing to share in beneficial externalities must bargain with resource-owners. Owners themselves will do most of the policing. Owners can be called to account, by suitable property-limitation rules, for harmful externalities. In sum, property solutions are to be preferred to non-property solutions because they facilitate the internalization of externalities.

Nothing in the foregoing argument requires any departure from conventional notions of property. However, some economic analysts have supposed

---

[8] Yoram Barzel, *Economic Analysis of Property Rights* (CUP, 1989), xi.
[9] See his discussion of leases—*ibid*. ch. 3.
[10] Hohfeld's distinctions are set out in Ch. 8, sect. (i)(a) above.
[11] See Ch. 13, sect. (iii) below.

that similar considerations are in play in the case of each and every right to use a resource provided the right is one I might bargain not to exercise—and that proviso could, in principle, be fulfilled for any right. Hence, if society favours me with a right over any resource (including all my bodily and mental resources) then, so long as it has not prohibited me from agreeing with another not to exercise the right, it has already adopted a 'property' solution in relation to the right and the right therefore comes within the category of 'property rights'. Strictly speaking, we should not speak of ownership interests over resources at all, but only of a multiplicity of individuated property rights.

The drift from economic analysis of 'property' in the conventional sense to a specialist economic conception of 'property' may be illustrated from two papers written by Harold Demsetz. In 'Toward a Theory of Property Rights',[12] Demsetz advances the above-cited argument, in terms of internalizing externalities, for private ownership interests (property in the ordinary sense). He proffers it as an explanation for the historical emergence of 'ownership of land'. In passing, he suggests that a similar analysis could be applied to other possible rights. For example, if instead of there being a compulsory military draft, either the State had to buy citizens into (or citizens had to buy themselves out of) military service, in either case externalities would be internalized.[13] In a subsequent paper, written with Armen Alchian,[14] the same argument is rehearsed, but this time it is prefaced with a general conceptual claim: although in common speech we frequently refer to someone owning resources, we would do better to speak of owning rights to use resources, 'including one's body and mind'.[15] 'What are owned are socially recognized rights of action.'[16] 'Property' rights include, for example, 'the right to advocate particular political doctrines'.[17]

This conceptual shift relies, terminologically, on one of the red herrings we identified at the end of Chapter 5—the conflation of 'owning' and 'ownership'. As we saw there, it is one thing to say that a person is vested with ('owns') either a right or a bundle of rights; it is another to say that what he is vested with is that particular set of open-ended privileges and powers over a resource which counts as an ownership interest. (Alchian and Demsetz themselves speak of 'owners' of apartments,[18] and 'owners' of toll roads,[19] forgetful of their stricture against resource-ownership terminology.)

The terminological conflation is exploited here in the service of an obliquely indicated methodological assumption for economic analysis: just as considerations of transaction costs and the internalization of externalities are at play when ownership interests are substituted for communal use regimes, so too they can be invoked whenever any right—personal, political, familial, or

---

[12] (1967) 57 *American Economic Review* 347.   [13] *Ibid.* 348–9.
[14] Armen A. Alchian and Harold Demsetz, 'The Property Rights Paradigm' (1973) 33 *Journal of Economic History* 16.   [15] *Ibid.* 17.
[16] *Ibid.*   [17] *Ibid.* 18.
[18] *Ibid.* 20.   [19] *Ibid.* 21.

whatever—is granted rather than withheld. Therefore, let all rights be termed 'property rights'.

Another instance of this same tendency is to be found in a much-cited article written by Guido Calabresi and A. Douglas Mellamed.[20] They recommend that, for the purposes of economic analysis, all entitlements to resources (including bodily resources) should be subjected to a three-fold classification according to the rules which protect them. First, X may be prohibited from disposing of his entitlement, in which case it is an inalienable entitlement.[21] Secondly, X's entitlement may be protected only by a civil remedy for damages, a 'liability rule', which makes it a liability-entitlement.[22] Thirdly, X's entitlement may be protected by a 'property rule', that is, either by criminal sanctions or by civil injunctive relief. Only and always when either kind of sanction is available is the entitlement a 'property-entitlement'. Hence, should the invasion of 'what is generally called private property' be answerable only in damages, we should speak of a liability-entitlement, not a property-entitlement.[23] On the other hand, the right not to be raped, since it is protected by a criminal sanction, is (it seems) a property-entitlement.[24] We are to concern ourselves exclusively with individual resource-rights, taken one by one, and never with open-ended sets (such as those comprised in ownership interests); and we are to apply the 'property' label to all those, and only those, rights where the rightholder's own valuation of his entitlement is never to be gainsaid, whatever the externalities may be. If damages is the only sanction for invasion of a right, it can be taken from the rightholder at a price fixed by the State and so is not a 'property' right.

Calabaresi and Mellamed sometimes stray from their own conceptual prescription. For example, they speak of the 'owner' of an object as one who has property-entitlements rather than mere liability-entitlements because of the law of theft.[25] Yet it ought to follow from their analysis that, while an owner's entitlement not to have his chattel stolen is a property right, his entitlement not to have it converted is a liability right (the remedy for the tort of conversion being usually only damages). Quite how we should classify the owner's use-privileges which are protected both by the criminal law of theft and the civil law of conversion it is difficult to say. As we saw in the last chapter, conflation of the content of ownership interests with rights conferred on owners by specific trespassory rules breeds obscurity.[26]

[20] 'Property Rules, Liability Rules and Inalienability: One View of the Cathedral' (1972) 85 *Harv. LR* 1089.

[21] For an elaboration, in economic terms, of Calabresi and Mellamed's category of inalienability rules, see Susan Rose Ackerman, 'Inalienability and the Theory of Property Rights' (1985) 85 *Col. LR* 931. As with other essays in the genre under discussion, this article fluctuates between conventional conceptions of 'property' and expansive conceptions which view entitlements of all kinds as 'property'.

[22] This possibility, they claim, was overlooked by Demsetz, n. 20 above, 1089 note.

[23] *Ibid.* 1105.   [24] *Ibid.* 1125–7.

[25] *Ibid.* 1125.   [26] See Ch. 8, sect. (i)(b) above.

What we have called 'cashable rights' (bank accounts, shares, and so forth) are conventionally described as 'property' because expropriation and appropriation rules apply to them—they pass into a bankrupt's estate and they can be inherited. The same would not be true of the following rights: (1) X's claim that the State should provide his children with free education; (2) X's liberty to take a shower when it suits him; (3) X's power to enter into a contract to have his hair cut; (4) X's immunity from compulsory military service. Within the genre of economic analysis just discussed, all the foregoing would be 'property' rights provided, first, that X is free to contract not only to exercise any of them (Alchian and Demsetz), and, secondly, that infraction of them is not remediable only in damages (Calabresi and Mellamed). Cashable rights are the subject of real markets. These analysts seek an extended definition which will enable the effects of notional markets to be explored in terms of transaction costs, efficiency, and distribution considerations, and effects on externalities.

By all means let rights of all kinds be analysed in these terms. Calling all rights 'property rights' is, however, anything but an aid to clarity for the enterprises at hand since both the analyst and the reader must constantly remind themselves that they are not talking about 'property' as ordinarily understood. More importantly, if we wish to confront and contrast economic with non-economic justifications for property institutions, we cannot employ an extended definition fashioned solely for the use of economic analysis.[27]

(b) Reich's 'New Property'

When the boundaries of the concept of property are discussed in modern Anglo-American theory, reference is frequently made to an article written by Charles Reich, published in 1964, which is entitled 'The New Property'.[28] Reich seeks to show that the wealth-allocation function of property institutions is, in modern societies, of diminishing relative importance because of the growth of 'government largesse'. Wealth is increasingly allocated through welfare benefits, government jobs, occupational licences, State franchises, contracts, and subsidies, and access to State-owned resources and to governmental services.[29] Allocation takes place in accordance with the assessment by various governmental agencies of what would best serve the public interest.[30] In the past, Reich contends, holdings of wealth in the form of private property had the great merit of securing independence from the State.[31] However, it also had the great demerit that holders of wealth were increasingly able to dominate the lives of others, especially as wealth became consolidated in the form of large corporate holdings.[32] The 'public interest State' has evolved as a

---

[27] So much is recognized in the leading textbook on the subject—see Richard A. Posner, *Economic Analysis of Law* (4th edn., Little Brown and Co., 1992), 46–7.

[28] Charles A. Reich, 'The New Property' (1964) 73 *YLJ* 733.

[29] *Ibid*. 734–9.   [30] *Ibid*. 746–55.   [31] *Ibid*. 771.   [32] *Ibid*. 772.

counter to this domination-potential of private property holdings, as well as a vehicle for performing many functions which modern societies expect their governments to discharge. But with it has come the loss of independence which private property once secured.[33]

The discretionary power to award, withhold, or terminate largesse introduces new dangers of illegitimate domination.[34] A notable example of this, cited by Reich, is the decision of the majority of the Supreme Court in *Fleming* v. *Nestor*.[35] There an immigrant who had, throughout his working life, paid contributions entitling him to a statutory retirement pension was retrospectively deprived of this entitlement upon his deportation as a member of the Communist Party; and the Court ruled that this retrospective legislation was constitutional.

Reich disavows any suggestion that the remedy for the independence-threatening aspects of the public-interest State is to turn the clock back to a time when wealth was distributed via agglomerated private holdings.[36] Government largesse we must have. He advocates measures which will, so far as possible, ensure that the wealth which results from government largesse confers upon its recipients an independence equivalent to that which private property provides. Discretionary receipts should be replaced, where possible, with entitlements held as of right. Substantive restraints should be imposed so that discretion cannot be exercised on improper grounds—especially so as to prevent rights guaranteed by the constitution being indirectly infringed. All withholding or cancellation of government largesse should be subjected to procedural due process.[37]

That independence is one of the instrumental justifications for property institutions, and that domination-potential counts as an important disjustification, are matters considered later in this book.[38] For the moment we are only concerned with the question whether Reich's important diagnosis entails an expansion in the concept of property beyond the conventional understanding which the stipulation at the beginning of this Chapter seeks to capture. Some commentators have taken it for granted that it does: that, according to the diagnosis, welfare benefits, government jobs, subsidies, and other categories of largesse simply are, or should be thought of as being, 'property'.[39] Consider, however, the following three claims which emerge from Reich's article (1) property used to secure independence; (2) the terms on which government

[33] Charles A. Reich, 'The New Property', 773–4.
[34] *Ibid.* 756–71, 774–7.
[35] 363 US 603 (1960).
[36] *Ibid.* 778.
[37] *Ibid.* 779–86.
[38] See Ch. 15, sect. (iv) and Ch. 14, sect. (iv) below.
[39] See, e.g., Bruce A. Ackerman, *Private Property and the Constitution* (Yale UP, 1977), 165, n. 115. C. B. MacPherson, 'Capitalism and the Changing Concept of Property', in E. Kamenka and R. S. Neale, *Feudalism, Capitalism and Beyond* (Edward Arnold, 1975), 115.

largesse is available today threaten independence; (3) we ought to change the terms on which largesse is allocated so that it accords an independence similar to that which property once afforded. None of these claims warrants any shift in what property means. If the article had been entitled '[t]he need for a property substitute', and if it had not ended with the clarion call: '[w]e must create a new property', there would have been no doubt about it. No expansive definition would have been proposed. As it is, the article can be understood as calling for an extension in the concept of property beyond its conventional use in the service of a justificatory analogy. Property is justified by its instrumental advantages in securing citizen independence against the all-encroaching public-interest State. The recommended reforms in the way largesse is distributed are justified because they too would secure independence. Therefore, they should also be called 'property'.

Note, however, that it is the reformed largesse, not the present array of discretionary welfare benefits and the rest, to which the extended label is to be applied. As Reich says: '[g]overnment largesse is plainly "wealth", but it is not necessarily "property".'[40] Different concept-expansion arguments, not advanced by Reich, can be put forward for insisting that discretionary access to wealth already is property, namely, those considered under (c) and (d) of this section. It can be argued that if they are given the property label, then they can be subsumed under constitutional provisions which protect 'property'; or that announcing the label will serve as part of a political rhetoric which will induce people to accord them greater respect.

Reich's justificatory-analogy argument raises many problems. What if one disagrees with his contention that independence was a justification for property institutions whilst agreeing with his proposed reforms for largesse? What if one supposes that reformed largesse cannot or should not be modelled on property-substitutes? What if one considers that claims to largesse should indeed become entitlements as of right, but that, unlike cashable rights, they should not be freely tradable or fall within the purview of bankruptcy law? In all these cases, calling reformed largesse 'property' serves only to confuse. 'The New Property' was a catchy title for an article which highlighted important dangers of the modern wealth-allocating State. But it is possible to support any or all of Reich's remedial proposals without any expansion in the concept of property.

(c) Constitutional Theory

The doctrine of separation of powers, which is a cornerstone of constitutional theory in modern liberal-democratic societies, calls on lawyers and judges to answer the following questions (among others). In what circumstances, and by

---

[40] *Ibid*. 739.

reference to what criteria, should courts undertake the responsibility of deciding on the validity of measures adopted by legislators, deputy legislators, or
agents of the executive? In practice such theorizing is usually piecemeal rather
than holistic, but in either case it is likely to announce respect for individuated
citizen rights (whether political, welfarist, familial, or personal). By virtue
either of constitutional instruments or of principles emerging from case-law
doctrine, the constitutional theory may separate out property rights as one
species of constitutionally protected right. In the view of some commentators,
property rights can find their place within an acceptable constitutional theory
only if 'property' is understood in a sense wider than that suggested by the
stipulation at the beginning of this Chapter.

As we have seen, *ad hoc* reasons may always be advanced for giving references to 'property' or 'proprietary interest' a wide interpretation in the context
of particular rules.[41] Given the range of political considerations typically in
play, interpretative strategies directed towards 'property' rules in a constitutional context may be thought to license even greater flexibility. If a constitutional text protects 'property', and there is to hand a good case for saying that
some personal or political right merits that kind of protection, then perhaps
the concept of property should be extended, for that particular constitutional
context, to include the favoured right.

For example, the Fourteenth Amendment to the American Constitution
provides: 'nor shall any State deprive any person of life, liberty, or property,
without due process of law'. The Supreme Court has, on occasion, ruled that
the word 'property' in this provision should be given an expansive interpretation. It has been held to include welfare payments, with the consequence that a
recipient whose receipt of welfare is terminated without a proper hearing is
denied 'due process'.[42] It applies to the employment expectations of a
university teacher who has (by contract or settled understanding) a tenured
post,[43] but not where the post was from the outset only for a fixed term;[44] so
that the former, but not the latter, is entitled to a hearing before a decision not
to renew his appointment is implemented. However, as Willliam Van Alstyne
has forcefully argued, metaphorical expansions of the notion of 'property' cannot yield, and in practice have not yielded, a secure constitutional basis for
challenging the multifarious ways in which arbitrary decisions by governmental agencies may unfairly affect the lives of citizens.[45]

In jurisdictions lacking such a constitutional provision, holdings such as
these might be rendered on the basis of a common law constitutional power of
judicial review, without any extension of the concept of property. When the

[41] See Ch. 4, sect. (iv) above.
[42] *Goldberg* v. *Edwards*, 397 US 254 (1970).
[43] *Perry* v. *Sinderman*, 408 US 593 (1972).
[44] *Board of Regions of State Colleges* v. *Roth*, 408 US 564 (1972).
[45] William Van Alstyne, 'Cracks in the "New Property": Adjudicative Due Process in
the Administrative State' (1977) 62 *Cornell LR* 445.

Canadian Charter of Rights and Freedoms was introduced into the constitutional law of Canada in 1982, drawing on the experience of American and European bills of rights as well as the common law, no specific protection for 'property' was included, even though such a clause had been contained in the earlier Canadian Bill of Rights. The Charter mentions rights to 'life, liberty and security of the person', but not 'property'; and this omission appears to have caused the Canadian Supreme Court no difficulty in articulating a coherent view of constitutionally-protected basic rights.[46]

In the American cases mentioned above, the court asserted a judicial responsibility to impose some procedural restraints on the actions of governmental institutions as they affected some kinds of access to wealth (government 'largesse', as Reich has called it). Since they had the text of the Fourteenth Amendment before them, they understandably subsumed their conclusions within the terms of that provision.

Might not a much broader judicial power to uphold all rights against other branches of government be asserted on the basis of that principle which, in one form or another, appears in all liberal-democratic polities—that which prohibits expropriation without just compensation? We have argued that this principle is of limited scope. It applies to some kinds of expropriation rules and some kinds of property-limitation rules addressed to ownership interests, but has no bearing on property-independent prohibitions.[47] A contrary view would be that, for the purposes of constitutional theory, 'property' in this principle should be understood as encompassing rights of all kinds, so that the no-taking-without-compensation principle licenses judges to pass judgment on the justice of all executive and legislative measures.

Bruce Ackerman has argued that it is open to American lawyers to take just this view of the 'takings' clause of the Fifth Amendment—'nor shall private property be taken for public use, without just compensation'. As we saw in the last chapter, Ackerman acknowledges that, as things are, American judges do not give a wide interpretation to the term 'property' in this provision. They assume that it bears the same meaning as in ordinary, lay property talk. It would, however, Ackerman contends, be open to them to approach the matter from the point of view of a 'Scientific Policy-maker'.[48] Scientifically understood, the clause can only have 'an extraordinarily wide application'.[49]

Ackerman maintains that 'ordinary' conceptions of property lead to insuperable problems in applying the takings clause. In contrast, a 'scientific' conception of property would transform all difficulties as to the scope of the clause 'into the simplest of children's games'.[50] Although Ackerman is

---

[46] See E. R. Alexander, 'The Canadian Charter of Rights and Freedoms in the Supreme Court of Canada' (1989)105 *LQR* 561, 588–93.

[47] See Ch. 6, sect. (iii)(c) above.

[48] See Ch. 8, sect. (ii)(b) above.

[49] Bruce A. Ackerman, *Private Property and the Constitution* (Yale UP, 1977), 28.

[50] *Ibid*. 167.

nowhere explicit on the point, the drift of his argument appears to be that, from the stance of a scientific policy-maker, there are no limits at all. All enactments and all executive decisions take 'property' so that the Fifth Amendment empowers courts to pass judgment on the justice of any action of the other branches of government. He tells us that 'government largesse' of all kinds would be included.[51] He also says that a restriction of 'any user right' could be treated as a taking of 'property'.[52] Thus, takings law would reach far beyond property-limitation rules, such as those arising from environmental restrictions on ownership interests. It would encompass all property-independent prohibitions on anti-social uses of things. Ackerman instances speed limits.[53] Narcotics law, gun-control law, and any law bearing on conduct which could include 'the use of a thing' would, it seems, raise a *prima facie* takings problem. There must be very few crimes or civil wrongs which one cannot commit, *inter alia*, by using things. Indeed, the exemplars of scientific policy-making mentioned by Ackerman are precisely writers in the genre of the economic analysis of law who, as we have seen, include all rights over one's bodily and mental faculties as 'property' rights.

If the Fifth Amendment constitutes a blanket licence for judicial review of all legislative and executive measures, there is indeed no problem about its scope. But then Ackerman's scientific policy-maker would have to advance a constitutional theory which casts all the other amendments in the Bill of Rights as mere surplusage. If property means everything, why devote any separate consideration to freedom of expression, cruel and unusual punishments, or due process? Such a theory would pay scant respect to the constitutional document itself and to the wealth of case law and learning which supposes that basic rights can be individuated and so treated as separate and distinct. Personal and political rights of fundamental importance deserve a firmer basis than any which can be supplied by controversial extensions of provisions historically targeted on the protection of private wealth. There are more important things than property.

(d) MacPherson's Political Property-Rhetoric

An advocate of a particular right—political or personal—may invoke 'property' as part of a frankly rhetorical strategy. He may suppose that 'property', in the conventional sense, has a certain prestige in his society. He may not share the assumptions upon which this prestige has been built. Nevertheless, he may seek to cash in on it by proclaiming, for example, that welfare rights, or rights to jobs, or the right to participate in political decision-making, or the right to pursue a lifestyle reflecting personal sexual preferences, are (all or any of them) facets of a person's 'property'.

---

[51] Ackerman, *Private Property and the Constitution* 70, 165.
[52] *Op. cit.*. 28.   [53] *Ibid.* 124–5.

It is, in the end, to such a rhetorical strategy that appeal is made in the most sustained case for a change in the concept of property that has been advanced in recent years—that of C. B. MacPherson.[54] We have already noted that MacPherson considered that using 'property' to refer to things was a misusage peculiar to laymen and that it was unlikely to survive beyond this century.[55] He recognized, however, that the existing paradigm of a property right is the exclusive right to something (what has here been called an ownership, or quasi-ownership, interest). This, he maintained, should be changed. We should conceive of a property right as an enforceable claim to the use or benefit of something, of which the paradigm is a right not to be excluded whilst the right to exclude others is merely a special case. Armed with this conceptual shift, we will then be able to extend the idea of property to encompass, not merely rights to welfare payments and services, rights to jobs, and rights to a decent environment, but also rights of access to the means of production, equal rights to share in social produce, rights to share in political power, and, finally, rights to a truly free and democratic society. 'Property will . . . increasingly have to become a right to a set of social relations, a right to a kind of society.'[56]

MacPherson makes two background claims as the setting for his contention that the concept of property should be expanded in the way he proposes, one 'logical', and one historical. His 'logical'[57] point is that there is nothing in the concept of property which prevents its extension to a right not to be excluded since all that the concept of property entails is a right to the use or benefit of something. This argument he founds on a familiar sub-categorization of property into private property, State property, and common property, criticized earlier in this book.[58] Since the parent concept, 'property', encompasses the distinct notion of 'common property', and since common property prevails wherever resources have been set aside for common use, any 'enforceable claim' not to be excluded from a resource must be a property right.[59]

This analytical jump, from the idea of common property to the assertion that all universal rights to anything are property rights of individuals,[60] raises a number of problems. To begin with, the argument is supposed to yield the conclusion that the essence of a property right is an 'enforceable claim' to access. Yet if a resource is set aside as common property, the rights of use

---

[54] C. B. MacPherson, *Property: Mainstream and Critical Positions* (Basil Blackwell, 1978), chs. 1 and 12; 'Capitalism and the Changing Concept of Property', in E. Kamenka and R. S. Neale (eds.), *Feudalism, Capitalism and Beyond* (Edward Arnold, 1975).

[55] See Ch. 1, sect. (iii) above.

[56] 'Capitalism and the Changing Concept of Property', n. 54 above, 121.

[57] *Property: Mainstream and Critical Positions*, n. 54 above, 6.

[58] See Ch. 7, sect. (vi) above.

[59] *Property: Mainstream and Critical Positions*, n. 54 above, 4. 'Capitalism and the Changing Concept of Property', n. 54 above, 106, 117.

[60] MacPherson makes the juridically false claim that rights over common property are always enjoyed by natural, never by artificial (corporate), persons—*Property: Mainstream and Critical Positions*, n. 54 above, 6.

thereby reserved are strictly Hohfeldian privileges, in the sense discussed in the last chapter, rather than 'claim rights'. Such privileges are enforceable only in the sense that no other person has a correlative right that they be not exercised. Secondly, access rights may subsist over resources which are not common property. Consider, for example, the case of *British Airports Authority* v. *Ashton*.[61] The court held that since the airport was 'owned' by BAA, the authority could exclude picketers. But it was also said that, in view of the authority's statutory functions, any ordinary passenger would be entitled to make use of the airport.

There is no conceptual barrier to describing passengers' rights, or any access rights, as 'property' rights; but MacPherson's claim that the notion of common property supplies a 'logical' basis for such a move is misconceived. Use-privileges over common property are not enforceable claim-rights; and access open to all is compatible both with public quasi-ownership and with private ownership interests.[62]

MacPherson's historical background claim builds on his logical one. Since the emergence of capitalist market societies in the seventeenth century, writers have equated property with private property and hence they have (he contends) regarded 'common property' as a 'contradiction in terms'.[63] That explains why the right to exclude has come to be regarded as the paradigm of a property right.

It is not clear which writers MacPherson has in mind when he speaks of theorists who treat 'common property' as a contradiction in terms. As we have seen, seventeenth-century apologists for private property, like Grotius, Pufendorf, and Locke, took common property as their starting-point.[64] It appears that MacPherson supposes that any author who defines property as an exclusionary right is thereby denying the logical possibility of common property.[65] It follows, however, from the logical priority of private property over other forms of property[66] that such definitions carry no such implication. If property institutions centrally comprise, as we have argued, ownership and quasi-ownership interests protected by trespassory rules, the term 'common property' may be used, and has always been used, to designate resources in respect of which there are no ownership interests (or quasi-ownership interests), and hence no trespassory rules.[67] If ownership interests had never emerged, it is hard to see what anyone could have meant by describing the universal access

---

[61] [1983] 3 All ER 6. This case was discussed in Ch. 7, sect. (iii)(b) above.

[62] It has been held that a privately owned caravan park to which anyone is admitted is a 'public place' for the purposes of the offence of 'driving in a public place' whilst being over the alcohol limit—*DPP* v. *Vivier* [1991] 4 All ER 18 (DC). See also *Hickman* v. *Maisey* [1900] 1 QB 752, discussed in Ch. 3, sect. (vi) above (privately owned highway).

[63] *Property: Mainstream and Critical Positions*, n. 54 above, 10. 'Capitalism and the Changing Concept of Property', n. 54 above, 106.

[64] See Ch. 7, sect. (vii) above.

[65] MacPherson cites Hume in this connection—'Capitalism and the Changing Concept of Property', n. 54 above, 108.

[66] See Ch. 7, sect. (vi) above.   [67] See Ch. 7, sect. (iv) above.

rights of all mankind as 'property' rights. As it is, no-one has ever spoken of property being in common who was not familiar with the idea of exclusive private property.

It is true that when a resource is the subject of common property, everyone has identical use-privileges. The only point in terming such privileges 'property' rights would be to make the negative claim that no-one has a right to challenge them by virtue of an ownership (or quasi-ownership) interest. The content of the privilege is not given by the 'property' label. In contrast, if I own a book or a house, an open-ended set of privileges and powers follows from the designation of that (exclusive) property relationship.

MacPherson asserts that 'a right to clean air and water is coming to be regarded as a property'.[68] Now that there are increasingly insistent demands for everyone to be accorded rights to unpolluted air and water is certainly true. The implementation of such demands requires a complex of measures. It calls for property-independent prohibitions on pollution—no-one, whether he owns anything or not, should be permitted to dump noxious substances. It also calls for property-limitation rules—persons with ownership and quasi-ownership interests in agricultural land or industrial plants are to have docked from their bundles of ownership privileges such uses as have polluting side-effects. Such measures would give content to citizens' rights to clean air and water. What is added by terming such rights 'property' rights? Nothing—it seems—except the negative point that, because the atmosphere and open stretches of water are owned by nobody and for that reason can be described as 'common property', no-one can counter the demand for these measures by asserting ownership of the air and the water.

MacPherson's historical claim—that the notion of an exclusive right as the property paradigm emerged only with seventeenth-century capitalist market societies—confronts, as he recognizes, a formidable objection. The right to exclude appears to have been treated as the property paradigm throughout the history of writing on the topic, from classical times onwards. He advances an ingenious suggestion for down-playing this persistent 'misusage'.[69] In ancient and medieval times, only freemen could have property rights and it was therefore necessary to treat such rights as exclusive in order to protect them from slaves and serfs. Such exclusivity was 'very easily generalized' into an individual right to exclude all others.[70] He offers no evidence that the trespassory rules, which from ancient times have protected ownership interests, like the prohibition on theft, were initially thought of as directed only against slaves or serfs. That assumption follows merely from his dogmatic commitment to the belief that treating property primarily as a right to exclude *must* be the result of historical accident.

---

[68] *Property: Mainstream and Critical Positions*, n. 54 above, 11.
[69] *Ibid.* 2.   [70] *Ibid.* 203.

MacPherson's attempt to found his expansion of the concept of property on the idea of 'common property' clearly fails. However, since, as we have seen, there is no such thing as 'true' property, that failure need not (if there are other reasons) stand in the way of expanding the concept to include any and every right to the use or benefit of something—services, employment, political participation, the good life—including every right not to be excluded from any of these things. In the light of the Marxist critique of capitalist private property, and the circumstances of modern life which in all societies have called forth the regulatory state, the next step, MacPherson argues, is, not to limit or abrogate property rights, but to redefine the concept of property itself away from its time-honoured paradigm. We already, he says, regard rights to jobs and welfare benefits (in cash or kind) as property rights.[71] We should move on to regarding as universal 'property' rights the right to equal access to the means of labour (with a consequent right to the income from one's work); and a right to an income from the whole produce of society related to what is needed for a fully human life.[72] The achievement of these 'property' rights will be of provisional importance only. Ultimately, with the abolition of scarcity and the requirement to engage in productive labour, the basic property rights will consist of a right to share in political power, and a right to a kind of society or set of power relations which will enable the individual to live a fully human life.[73]

As we have seen, future property programmes inspired by a Marxist critique of capitalist production are notoriously imprecise,[74] and the same is true of MacPherson's proposals. Presumably, the right of equal access to the means of labour is not to entail that material factors of production or service-provision are to be literally 'common property', for that would mean that no-one had a right to prevent anyone else who wished to do so from going into a factory or a hospital and operating the equipment. If (given specialization of labour) there must be trespassory protection of some sort, are the trespassory rules to reserve group collective property, revived communitarian property, public quasi-ownership interests, or protected non-property holdings (along the lines of our imaginary Red Land)?

MacPherson allows that individual property rights, in the traditional sense of a right to exclude, should continue for goods used up in consumption.[75] He apparently envisages that there should be individual ownership of nothing else. Like many other property theorists (Marxist and non-Marxist) his property speculations leave out of account that most important subject of property rights—money. Would the right to share in net social income be discharged

---

[71] 'Capitalism and the Changing Concept of Property', n. 54 above, 114–15.

[72] *Property: Mainstream and Critical Positions*, n. 54 above, 205–6. 'Capitalism and the Changing Concept of Property', n. 54 above, 219–20.

[73] 'Capitalism and the Changing Concept of Property', n. 54 above, 120–2.

[74] See Ch. 7, sect. (viii) above.

[75] *Property: Mainstream and Critical Positions*, n. 54 above, 206.

entirely in kind, as in Red Land, or would citizens receive cash? If the latter, since the right is to be an 'enforceable claim', there will presumably be some paying-up agency bearing the correlative duty. Does that agency hold the money, pending payment, subject to a quasi-ownership interest, or does it retain no property-like discretion so that it is vested with a protected non-property holding?[76] More importantly, on what would MacPhersonians be free to expend their money? Ownership of money, as we have seen, necessarily involves powers of transmission.[77] You can do nothing with money (as distinct from monetary tokens) except spend it or give it away. MacPherson's egalitarian aspirations would be threatened unless citizens' powers to make gifts of their money (especially *post-mortem* gifts) were limited.[78] Further (it seems) they should not be at liberty to use their money to purchase the labour-power of others, since MacPherson is a staunch critic of what he called 'possessive individualism'—that is, any social arrangement which permits people to sell their labour for cash.[79]

What MacPherson proposes, were its basic structure at all fleshed out, might be entirely workable and just. The question for this Chapter is this. What is to be gained by calling the proposed new rights 'property' rights? Why should the entire programme be hitched to a conceptual shift?

MacPherson does not invoke arguments from constitutional theory, nor those employed in the genre of economic analysis of law. He nods in the direction of a justificatory-analogy argument similar to that used by Reich. He notes that justifications of private property have always appealed, at bottom, to what is required in order to enable people to live a fully human life.[80] Rights of access to the means of work, to share in net social income, to share in political power, and to a truly free and democratic society are required in order to enable people to live a fully human life. Therefore, such rights should be styled 'property' rights.[81]

However, unlike Reich, MacPherson cannot, in the end, take his stance on this argument because he supposes that those who appealed to such considerations as political independence as the justification for conventional private property were mistaken.[82] His concept-expansion strategy is as follows. Let us accept, arguendo, the prestige which attaches to the idea of 'property' and then manipulate the concept towards sound egalitarian ends. In other words, it reduces to a political-rhetorical argument. It is addressed to someone who

[76] See Ch. 7, sects. (iii) and (v) above.
[77] See Ch. 4, sect. (ii)(a) above.
[78] See Ch. 14, sect. (iii) and Ch. 16, sect. (i) below.
[79] C. B. MacPherson, *The Political Theory of Possessive Individualism: Hobbes to Locke* (OUP, 1962). MacPherson's conception of 'possessive individualism' is discussed in Ch. 11, sect. (ii)(b)(2) below.
[80] 'Capitalism and the Changing Concept of Property', n. 54 above, 118–20.
[81] *Ibid.* 120–1.
[82] *Property: Mainstream and Critical Positions*, n. 54 above, 177.

wrongly believes that conventional private property is justifiable. MacPherson writes:

> I am suggesting that the broader claims will not be firmly anchored unless they are seen as property, for in the liberal ethos which prevails in our liberal-democratic societies property has more prestige than has almost anything else; and if the new claims are not brought under the head of property the narrow idea of property will be used with all the prestige of property to combat them. In short, the new foreseeable and justifiable demands of the members of at least the most technologically advanced societies cannot now be met without a new concept of property.[83]

The plausibility of rhetorical expedients of this sort is difficult to assess. They depend on the way you suppose 'property' will ring in the ears of an addressee and on his willingness to fall in line with the terminological shift. Imagine the following dialogue:

Egalitarian: 'For reasons a, b and c, I maintain that everyone ought to have an enforceable right to work.'
Conservative: 'For reasons X, Y and Z, I disagree with you.'
Egalitarian: 'But you believe that property ought to be protected, don't you?'
Conservative: 'I do.'
Egalitarian: 'Well the right to work is property.'
Conservative response 1:   'No it isn't.'
Conservative response 2:   'Why didn't you say that before? Of course, I now change my view to yours.'

The rhetoric might be invoked in the 'wrong' direction:

Egalitarian: 'I favour financing local authority expenditure by a tax on premises rather than a poll tax, *inter alia*, because the former is a tax on property whereas the latter is a tax on people.'
Conservative: 'But if a poll tax is imposed on all those who receive local authority services it will be a tax on property, because rights to receive such services are property.'
Egalitarian response 1:   'No they're not.'
Egalitarian response 2:   'I had overlooked that. I now withdraw that objection to the poll tax.'

I suspect that response 1 is more likely than response 2 in both cases. Whether that is true or not, MacPherson's elevation of a conceptual programme on the back of political rhetoric should not deflect us from the philosophical problems which, as he recognizes, have always surrounded the moral justification of property. There are, and throughout history have always been, institutions which exhibit the twinned conceptions of trespassory rules and the ownership spectrum in relation to some resources. They are extremely malleable. Our enquiry will be whether they can, in any form, be justified.

---

[83] 'Capitalism and the Changing Concept of Property', n. 54 above, 122.

The concept-expanding arguments based on analogy, constitutions, and political rhetoric suffer from a common drawback as compared with those considerations of social heuristics which support the stipulation set out at the beginning of this Chapter. They concede, at least arguendo, that property as conventionally understood really deserves prestige and that the rights contended for have an importance which is merely parallel to conventional proprietary interests. One might wish to claim, instead, either that the complex property institutions typically to be found in modern States cannot be justified at all; or, at any rate, that some of the rights for whose promotion these expansive arguments are pressed into service are more fundamental to just human associations than are many (conventional) property rights. Property is an important institution, but it needs to be kept in its place. The justificatory-analogy arguments, the constitutional-theory arguments, and, above all, the political-rhetoric arguments make too much of property.

Part II

Is Property Just?

10

The Agenda

In Part I we sketched what property institutions are like and designated the items which are the reference-points of such institutions—what 'property' is. Justifications or disjustifications of property must, in the end, always be institution-focused. If there is any valid argument that a person or group ought, in justice, to be accorded an ownership interest in some resource, the argument must establish that there ought to be trespassory rules protecting that ownership interest. If it is supposed that the argument is strong enough to support full-blooded ownership, then it must establish that there ought to be trespassory rules protecting transferees from the owner and that all exploitation of the resource is justly a separate holding of private wealth to be taken into account by any property-limitation or expropriation rules. If, starting from the standpoint of society rather than that of the individual, it is contended that resources ought in justice to be distributed in a certain way, the argument must support whatever mix of property rules is needed to achieve that distribution.

Private property is controversial for the same reason that it is commonly prized. It emphasizes the individuality of the property-holder. A property institution at least confers some private domain over some scarce things, so that the separateness of persons is made evident in the face of collect-ive decision-making. But that domain necessarily confers some power over others and hence is distributionally problematic.

General justifications or disjustifications of property which have appeared in Western political philosophy have characteristically been addressed only to particular facets of the complex institution which, as we have seen, property represents in modern societies. It is often difficult to assess how an abstract argument addressed to a particular feature of the institution is supposed to carry over to other features. Supposing one hits on a sound justificatory argument for ownership of tangible things. Does it carry sufficient weight to justify full-blooded ownership and also the separation of wealth from use, not to mention extension of ownership into the sphere of ideas, quasi-ownership interests, and the panoply of non-ownership proprietary interests? Con-versely, supposing one has a sound argument, in justice, against unlimited ownership rights over items of social wealth, does it condemn full-blooded ownership of trivial chattels and limited ownership interests in more valuable things? Does it exclude money altogether from the just society?

(i) PROPERTY-SPECIFIC JUSTICE REASONS

There is no etymological or conceptual warrant for insisting that the term 'justice' must be deployed in only one sense. Justice is often perceived as a virtue of persons as well as of institutions; and, in the case of institutions, it may be contrasted with other virtues, such as liberty or fraternity.[1] We opt for a broader usage. As John Rawls puts it: '[j]ustice is the first virtue of social institutions, as truth is of systems of thought.'[2]

We are concerned only with the merits and demerits of social arrangements. We shall treat 'justice' as an inclusive term encompassing all qualities of institutions which make them of value to human beings. Any ground on which, it is alleged, that that particular legal and social institution which we have differentiated as a property institution should be valued will here be called a 'property-specific justice reason'.

The subject of our enquiry is the justifiability of property institutions, both in the abstract and in concrete situations. The variety and complexity of property institutions throw up an enormous range of questions about institutional design. A sound reason for holding that such a question should be answered one way rather than another is a 'property-specific justice reason'.

We shall investigate, one by one, a wide selection of alleged property-specific justice reasons, both to assess what normative merits they actually possess, and to explore their generalized implications for property institutions. This is a kind of middle-range theorizing about property. It eschews, on the one hand, the straightforward *ipse dixit* of one who says 'I happen to believe' that desert or privacy or need or whatever requires property institutions to encompass a particular feature. But it also eschews, on the other hand, that region of high abstraction where over-arching theories of justice compete and meta-ethical controversies are joined. The former cuts off normative debate about the substantive issues thrown up by property institutions too quickly; the latter postpones it too indefinitely.[3]

Many theories of justice contain explicit or implicit recommendations for particular features of property institutions. Some of these will be noted as we proceed. However, from the point of view of an over-arching theory, property is merely one facet of what is involved in political association. Sometimes, it is no more than a vaguely-conceived point of reference between some fundamental assumptions and concretized social life. Indeed, as

---

[1] J. R. Lucas, *On Justice* (Clarendon Press, 1980), ch. 1.

[2] John Rawls, *A Theory of Justice* (OUP, 1972), 3.

[3] For the view that excessive meta-ethical abstraction serves to distract attention from important normative questions, see Bernard Williams, *Ethics and the Limits of Philosophy* (3rd edn., Fontana, 1993). It is noteworthy that John Rawls insists that the basis of his celebrated theory of justice is political, not metaphysical—Rawls, *Political Liberalism* (Col. UP, 1993), pt. 1.

we shall see, the justness of any particular property institution cannot be assessed in isolation from other institutional practices with which it is associated. Nevertheless, important questions of moral, political, and legal philosophy are brought to light if we concentrate on property institutions as such. We would never get round to these questions if we first had to settle which over-arching theory of justice is correct.

The approach taken here may be termed, in technical philosophical parlance, 'intuitionistic'.[4] This is because, by examining justice reasons one by one, it both assumes that they are not referable to an underlying grand-scale theory and also that their implications are mutually incommensurable. That, of course, does not make it 'intuitionistic' in the more popular sense that what one 'happens to believe' carries normative force simply because one happens to believe it. If justice is worth debating at all, untutored intuitions must always be open to revision in the light of considered reflection.[5] Possible implications for property institutions are one source of information which may contribute to such reflections. The incommensurability of justice reasons is a problem for our enquiry only when, and to the extent that, it turns out that they yield incompatible implications for property institutions.

Property theorizing invariably comes burdened with assumptions about other aspects of society. Richard Schlatter has provided an excellent survey of theories of property appearing in the writings of Western political philosophers from classical Greece to the nineteenth century.[6] As he shows, the same theory is often employed by those who are opponents to some fundamental controversy about just social arrangements. St Augustin's contention that private property arises as a result of Man's fallen nature and is consequently merely a palliative for the human sinful condition was invoked, in medieval times, on either side of the controversy about Papal authority over worldly possessions. Since the seventeenth century, the Lockean contention that a man's labour gives a just title to individual ownership has been invoked both to support and to deny the legitimacy of capitalist accumulation of wealth.

As Schlatter's survey also makes clear, conclusions about the justice or injustice of property-holdings never stand alone as the blueprint for any version of the just society. How could it be otherwise? Access to portions of the environment needed to support human existence, and the appropriate allocation of wealth, are matters which no adequate political philosophy can ignore. However, they cannot constitute the whole story. Human beings interact in a myriad ways, not all of which arise directly from competition for resources. The springs of self-assertion and of sociability, of aggression and

---

[4] See Rawls, n. 2 above, 34–40.

[5] Compare our discussion of the contestability of ownership conceptions in Ch. 5, sect. (vi) above.

[6] Richard Schlatter, *Private Property: The History of an Idea* (George Allen and Unwin, 1951).

co-operation, are deeply rooted in the human psyche. Grabbing and giving are but part of their manifestations.

Even in the hands of classical liberal individualist philosophers, where 'property' apparently looms so large, it is manifestly not the sole consideration relevant to political obligation and justifiable authority. John Locke wrote that the great and chief end of men's uniting into commonwealths, and putting themselves under government, is 'the preservation of their property'.[7] But, as he explicitly states, by 'property' in this context he means, 'lives, liberties, and estates'.[8] Security from violence to the person and a host of freedoms of self-expression unconnected with use of resources must necessarily enter into the plan of the just society.

Nevertheless, justificatory and disjustificatory arguments about the proper use and distribution of resources commonly play an independent role in the tradition of political philosophy. At the level of grand theory they must be subsumed within some master vision. At the level of middle-range theorizing, however, they are detachable and we shall endeavour to detach them in what follows. They are the justice reasons directly associated with property institutions as such. Once detached, they can be reconstituted in many ways. We shall as we proceed examine a fourfold typology of property-specific justice reasons.

The first purport to show that, by virtue of an individual's interactions with the world and with others, he has a claim to an ownership interest over a resource. The reasons considered under this heading are self-ownership, creation-without-wrong, labour-desert, first occupancy, personhood-constituting, and privacy. These are alleged foundations for natural property rights. They centre around either productive labour or an analogy with physical assaults.

The second type of reason appeals to those freedoms which are the inherent concomitants of property institutions. We shall consider the varieties of autonomous choice which such institutions make possible, and the arguments for and against valuing such choices.

The third category of property-specific justice reasons relates to alleged instrumental merits of property institutions. They concern the discharge of justice costs and basic needs, incentives, markets, and independence.

Finally, we consider what, if any, dominating role over all other property-specific justice reasons should be accorded to arguments based on equality of resources or social convention.

---

[7] John Locke, *Second Treatise of Government* (G. W. Gough (ed.), Basil Blackwell, 1976), ch. IX, 124.

[8] *Ibid.*, chs. IX, 123; XV, 173.

(ii) PROPERTY RIGHTS

In Chapter 8, section (i), we considered that juristic tradition, largely inspired by Hohfeld, which seeks to unpack property conceptions. We concluded that references to the 'rights of ownership' might point either to the privileges and powers which are intrinsic to ownership interests, or to those privileges and powers together with particular sets of claim-rights and immunities conferred by the rules of a property institution to protect ownership interests. These are categories of rights internal to property institutions. If, however, arguments based on property-specific justice reasons yield the conclusion that people have moral rights to property, these are rights external to any particular property institution and, on the face of it, 'right' is being used in a different sense. Without entering into the philosophical and jurisprudential controversy which surrounds the concept of 'a right', some clarificatory distinctions are warranted.

A property right may signify:

(1) one of the open-ended set of privileges or powers entailed by a particular conception of an ownership or quasi-ownership interest;

(2) a claim-right, privilege, power, or immunity comprised by, or contained within, a non-ownership proprietary interest;

(3) a right correlative to the duty imposed by a trespassory rule;

(4) an immunity-right which is the resultant of exceptions to, or absence of, expropriation rules;

(5) a right conferred by an appropriation rule to be vested with an ownership or quasi-ownership interest or a non-ownership proprietary interest;

(6) the moral standing to claim that a person or group ought to be vested with an ownership or quasi-ownership interest or a non-ownership proprietary interest over some specific resource;

(7) the moral standing of a person or group to insist that a property institution (of some kind) be in place in a particular society.

The first five categories of property rights are (legal or conventional) institutional rights. The first four could be expressed in terms of Hohfeldian correlatives provided, as we saw in Chapter 8, we have in mind only a static representation of rules. The fifth category creates special problems for a Hohfeldian analysis. A person entitled to succeed to property under intestacy law might be said to be vested, as against the administrator of the deceased's estate, both with a liability correlative to the administrator's power to transfer the property to him and a right correlative to the administrator's duty to exercise that power. However, where an appropriation rule confers title to a chattel on a finder, there appears to be no power-liability jural relation and the rights/duties conferred by trespassory rules are the same as those which obtain for anyone else who has a valid title to an ownership interest (category 3).

Categories 6 and 7 escape the Hohfeldian analysis altogether. They constitute purported moral reasons for creating jural relations. It might be maintained, on the basis of the first and fourth types of property-specific justice reasons listed at the end of the last section (natural rights, equality of resources, or the moral significance of social conventions), that someone ought, in justice, to be allocated a concrete ownership interest (property right category 6). That would entail both that trespassory rules should be in place in respect of the particular resource and that the person should be vested with privileges and powers over it. Or it might be claimed that, by virtue of the second and third types of property-specific justice reason (inherent property freedoms or the instrumental merits of property), everyone has a right that a property institution (of some kind) should be introduced or maintained (property right category 7). It would then follow that the requisite complex of trespassory rules, property-limitation rules, expropriation and appropriation rules should be in force with all resulting jural relations.

Justified property rights in categories 6 and 7 are necessarily moral rights, although they might be proclaimed in legal texts. In practice, constitutional formulations of property rights are usually limited to immunity-rights (category 4). However, the first paragraph of Article 1 of the first protocol to the European Convention on Human Rights[9] contains two sentences, the second of which asserts an immunity, but the first of which could be understood as a proclamation of rights within category 7: '[e]very natural or legal person is entitled to the peaceful enjoyment of his possessions.'

Moral property rights (categories 6 and 7) allegedly follow from some feature of a person's or group's 'well-being', if we use that term broadly to encompass both activities an agent may wish to engage in and states of affairs which are of value to the agent. It would therefore appear that these categories should be understood according to what is called the 'interest' conception of rights. In their case we may adopt, with one slight modification, Joseph Raz's abstract definition of the concept of a right: ' "X has a right" if and only if X can have rights, and, other things being equal, an aspect of X's well-being (his interest) is a sufficient reason for holding some other person(s) to be under a duty.'[10] The modification concerns the adequacy of

[9] Set out at the beginning of Ch. 6, sect. (iii) above.

[10] Joseph Raz, *The Morality of Freedom* (Clarendon Press, 1986), 166. We shall not consider whether 'right' is a univocal concept so that, as Raz maintains, legal rights must also be understood in the same sense—Raz, *Ethics in the Public Domain* (Clarendon Press, 1994), ch. 11; nor the question whether, if legal rights may be analysed separately from moral rights, they should be understood according to a 'choice' conception (see H. L. A. Hart, *Essays on Bentham* (Clarendon Press, 1982), 174–88), or an 'interest' conception (see Neil MacCor-

this abstract characterization of rights for the purposes of moral property rights. Certainly, successful arguments for category 6 or 7 provide reasons for the imposition of duties by trespassory rules. However, they also provide reasons for conferring further rights of various kinds—either concrete privileges and powers, or generalized 'rights' resulting from a property institution (of a particular kind) being in place. Raz's definition would fit the bill for the two categories of moral property rights if we insert the words 'at least'. 'X has a right if and only if . . . an aspect of X's well-being (his interest) is a sufficient reason for at least holding some other person(s) to be under a duty.'

(iii) A MINIMALIST CONCEPTION OF JUSTICE

We aim to test the normative force of the justice reasons to be surveyed, as well as to explore their scope and implications for property institutions. No property-specific justice reason will be taken to be axiomatic. Nevertheless, on the score of justice, we shall not begin with a clean slate. We start with a minimalist conception of just human association, comprised of three elements only: natural equality; the value of autonomous choice; and the banning of unprovoked invasions of bodily integrity. It is a conception designed for public debate about social and political institutions. It is not intended as a guide to any individual who may be perplexed as to whether, and in what way, considerations of justice should enter into his reasons for action.

(a) Natural Equality

Some such maxim as 'treat like cases alike' is integral to any abstract conception of justice.[11] However else maxims of this kind should be substantively encashed, it is common to humanist opinion (liberal, socialist, or theocratic) that it entails the following negative implication. If treatment of a certain kind is due to one human being, X, nothing less is due to another person, Y, merely because Y is an inferior type of human being to X. If treatment of citizens varies according to age, disability, or gender, the differentiation has to be justified on some ground other than that the young or the old, the disabled, or the disfavoured gender are inherently inferior kinds of human beings. That is all that we mean by 'natural equality'.

This negative implication of 'treat like cases alike' is sometimes combined, under the designation of 'neutrality', with the further postulate that no exercise of power over others is warranted if it presupposes any priority

mick, 'Rights in Legislation', in P. M. S. Hacker and Joseph Raz (eds.), *Law, Morality and Society* (Clarendon Press, 1977).

[11] H. L. A. Hart, *The Concept of Law* (2nd edn., Clarendon Press, 1994), 157–67.

among conceptions of the good.[12] That further claim is not built into our minimalist conception of justice. A government which treats all its human subjects alike in the light of its own conception of what is the best life for everyone to lead does not violate natural equality. But we shall assume that its dispositions are unjust if they are supported only on the ground that some kinds of human beings are inherently inferior to others.

Aristotle thought otherwise because he supposed that some people were naturally slaves.[13] There have been so many racists and xenophobics over the millennia of human history that if one took a notional opinion poll of all those who have ever lived it is very likely that this minimal negative implication of justice would receive a resounding thumbs-down.

For all that, we must proceed on the assumption that Aristotle and the trans-historical racist and xenophobic majority are mistaken on this matter and that the common core of humanist opinion is correct. Whether or not it has a metaphysical basis in the self-evidence of a special faculty known as human reason, or in divine ordination, need not detain us. The assumption of natural equality must go hand-in-hand with any discursive enterprise which puts the agenda of justice in the public domain. Such an enterprise has no limits on potential addressees. It necessarily excludes the possibility that some addressees are naturally inferior to fellow humans. If we are to join in a debate about the true implications of justice, we must all take it as axiomatic that we stand in the same relationship of mutual humanity to one another.

Why labour the point any further? No reader of this book is likely to go on record as proclaiming that he or she is, intrinsically, of a genus superior to other people.

(b) Autonomous Choice

The second element of the minimalist conception of justice is the assumption that autonomous choice, over some range of actions open to individuals, is of value to all human beings. Intricate questions concerning the pre-conditions for authentic choice or the conceptual connections between autonomy and rationality will not be investigated here.[14] Such questions would not be asked unless it was taken to be axiomatic that 'choice', in some sense, is a valued feature of human agency.

Human agency is a logically primitive element amongst the describable features of the world. 'He did it' is not reducible to any set of assertions that

[12] See, e.g., Bruce A. Ackerman, *Social Justice in the Liberal State* (Yale UP, 1980), 10–12.
[13] Aristotle, *The Politics* (Stephen Everson (ed.), trans. Jonathan Barnes, CUP, 1988), bk. I, 2, 3–10.
[14] For a recent collection of essays on such matters, see John Christman (ed.), *The Inner Citadel: Essays on Individual Autonomy* (OUP, 1989).

'X happened'. That this must be true, at least of any discourse in which moral concepts are critically deployed and hence of any debate which invokes the agenda of justice, is adequately demonstrated in Kantian ethics.[15]

Human agents are, ultimately, all the 'persons' whose interactions are potentially controlled by institutions. That is true whether we take an extreme ('Kantian') monadic conception of individuality, in which the person is conceived of as fully subsisting independently of any contingent relations with others, or the more plausible ('communitarian') position that part of personhood consists in such relations.[16] There would only be a complete divorce between human agency and human personality if the latter were conceived as constituted exclusively in relationships, on which assumption agency would have to be explained away as somehow epiphenomenal. What institutions would be like under the latter assumption it is hard to conceive, but at any rate they would not be the domain of justice; for that concept concerns the relations between persons whose identity is not entirely obliterated within such relations.

Public agencies of the modern world uniformly announce that they respect the dignity of human personhood. If institutions presuppose that persons are also agents, and that any description of their acting cannot be reduced to other descriptions of the world, it follows that institutions presuppose the idea of autonomous choice as an aspect of personhood. Given that respecting personhood is intrinsic to just treatment, it follows that, other things being equal, it counts in favour of the justice of an institution if it accords a wider rather than a narrower scope for autonomous choice. In that sense, 'freedom' is a consideration of justice. Furthermore, other things being equal, the wider the range of autonomous choice the better. Wherever one comes down, if come down one should, between the contestants over the issue of 'negative' or 'positive' liberty,[17] or between the proponents of 'communitarianism' and 'individualism',[18] 'freedom' of any kind presupposes choice and, at the abstract level, more choices must entail more freedom. All liberals and most non-liberals would, it is thought, assent to the bald assertion that autonomous choice is to be valued, differ though they do as to the kinds of social arrangement which make genuine choices possible.

---

[15] See Kant, *Critique of Practical Reason and Other Works on the Theory of Ethics* (trans. Thomas Kingsmill Abbott, Longmans Green and Co., 1879), especially *Fundamental Principles of the Metaphysic of Morals*, 3rd Sect.; *Critique of Practical Reason* Pt. I, Bk. I, ch. III.

[16] See Michael J. Sandel, *Liberalism and the Limits of Justice* (CUP, 1982); Alasdair MacIntyre, *After Virtue: a Study in Moral Theory* (Duckworth, 1981); Charles Taylor, *Sources of the Self: the Making of the Modern Identity* (Harv. UP, 1989).

[17] For a collection of essays on this theme, see Alan Ryan (ed.), *The Idea of Freedom: Essays in Honour of Isaiah Berlin* (OUP, 1979).

[18] For discussion of this theme, see Shlomo Avineri and Avner De-Shalit (eds.), *Communitarianism and Individualism* (OUP, 1992); S. Gardbaum, 'Law, Politics, and the Claims of Community' (1992) 90 *Mich. LR* 685.

(c) Bodily Integrity

The third element of the minimalist conception of justice with which we begin concerns the prima facie banning of unprovoked invasions of bodily integrity. Without some such justification as medical treatment, promotion of public health, self-defence, just punishment, the maintenance of order or legitimate struggle, homicides, assaults, and forceable detention are natural wrongs (whether committed by private individuals or State officials) and their correlatives are natural rights. Whether self-preservation is an adequate exculpatory excuse for persons who would otherwise fall under these bans is a notoriously difficult issue. Students of the common law are familiar with the nineteenth-century English case in which it was ruled that starving mariners, adrift on the ocean in an open boat, could not plead the defence of necessity to a charge of murder when they killed and ate one of their number.[19] The House of Lords has, in recent years, first ruled that life-threatening duress may be a defence to murder[20] and subsequently that it never is.[21] Such questions would not be difficult if it were not taken for granted that, in all normal circumstances, acts of unprovoked violence to other human beings are *mala in se*.

It is probable that a trans-historical majority opinion would dissent from this claim, as it would deny natural equality. Societies of the past have regarded the killing or enslavement of strangers as something requiring no special justification. Indeed, such acts may have been looked on as peculiarly virtuous. For centuries, heads of families have considered violent treatment of dependants as entirely their own business, and may have supposed it to require no justification. A thousand years of Graeco-Roman civilization took it for granted that infanticide was an entirely optional means of disposing of unwanted children. Attitudes associated with all such practices may still be prevalent, but public culture does not concede that they may be frankly avowed.

This third element of the minimalist conception of justice is a corollary of the first on the assumption that any potential wrongdoer has an interest in not himself being the subject of such violent intrusions. The only notable dissenter from this corollary in the past four centuries of Western political philosophy is Thomas Hobbes. He conceded natural equality, but denied that, in a state of nature, there were any just restraints on the violence which any man might offer to his neighbour. His reason for this denial needs careful attention.

State-of-nature theorists commonly argue that, as well as primary rights not to be assaulted, human beings also have secondary rights to resist and

---

[19] *R. v. Dudley and Stephens* [1884] 14 QBD 273.
[20] *DPP for Northern Ireland v. Lynch* [1975] AC 653.
[21] *R. v. Howe* [1987] AC 417.

punish transgressions of their primary rights by others.[22] In Hobbes's view the primary rights were drowned by the secondary rights. Without government, the danger of invasion of one's primary rights by others was so pressing that one was always entitled to a pre-emptive strike.

And from this diffidence of one another there is no way for any man to secure himself so reasonable as anticipation, that is, by force or wiles to master the persons of all men he can so long till he see no other power great enough to endanger him. And this is no more than his own conservation requireth and is generally allowed.[23]

Once governments are installed, subjects lay down this right of pre-emptive strike. The sovereign alone retains it, to use 'as he should think fit for the preservation of them all'.[24]

The precepts of natural law were available for the sovereign or his representatives to consult if they so chose. However, nothing the sovereign did to any of his subjects could be stigmatized as unjust, since, via the social contract, the subjects had conceded him arbitrary power. Nothing can be reputed unjust 'that is not contrary to some law'.[25] The sovereign and those whom he deputes are the only authentic interpreters of both positive enactments and unwritten natural law precepts. 'The authority of writers without the authority of the commonwealth maketh not their opinions law be they never so true.'[26]

Subjects once having submitted to a sovereign authority thereby tacitly agree to the authority's unlimited right to dispose of them. If a sovereign prince puts to death an innocent subject, 'though the action be against the law of nature as being contrary to equity as was the killing of Uriah by David, yet it was not an injury to Uriah but to God—not to Uriah because the right to do what he pleased was given him by Uriah himself'.[27]

The subordination of primary to secondary rights is, in Hobbes's view, an instrumental necessity following from the insecurity of human life. To dissent from Hobbes's conclusions we need not take issue with his pessimistic assessment of human passions. It is enough that we can envisage political institutions in which the primary rights not to be killed, assaulted, or kidnapped can be policed and enforced, albeit imperfectly, without conceding to State officials exemption from the correlative obligations. Notwithstanding the dark history of State oppressions, there is enough evidence on the credit side to suggest that this aspiration is not chimerical.

So Hobbes was wrong. There will always be a tension between the primary rights which all human beings have, *prima facie*, not to be subjected to personal violence by others and legitimate policing and punishing functions

[22] See, e.g., Locke, n. 7 above, ch. II, 7; ch. VII, 87; Robert Nozick, *Anarchy, State and Utopia* (Basil Blackwell, 1974), 10–12, 88–90, 137–42.
[23] Thomas Hobbes, *Leviathan* (C. B. MacPherson (ed.), Penguin Books, 1968), 184.
[24] *Ibid.* 354.   [25] *Ibid.* 312.
[26] *Ibid.* 322.   [27] *Ibid.* 265.

of the State. But there is no sound reason for supposing that the former must necessarily be overwhelmed by the latter.

(iv) SCEPTICISM

The property-specific justice reasons which we shall survey play a part, either centrally or peripherally, in a variety of theories of justice and are also part of the familiar vocabulary of political debate and legal justification. A sceptic might claim that the questions about property to which such reasons purport to contribute solutions cannot be answered at all in terms of reasons which transcend self-interest. Alf Ross, for example, asserts that the words 'just' and 'unjust' make sense only when employed to characterize a decision that conforms to objective criteria laid down by a given set of rules.[28] When applied to characterize the rules themselves, these words are 'entirely devoid of meaning'.[29]

> To invoke justice is the same thing as banging on the table: an emotional expression which turns one's demand into an absolute postulate. That is no proper way to mutual understanding. It is impossible to have a rational discussion with a man who mobilises 'justice', because he says nothing that can be argued for or against. His words are persuasion, not argument. The ideology of justice leads to implacability and conflict, since on the one hand it incites to the belief that one's demand is not merely the expression of a certain interest in conflict with opposing interests, but that it possesses a higher, absolute validity; and on the other hand it precludes all rational argument and discussion of a settlement. The ideology of justice is a militant attitude of a biological–emotional kind, to which one incites oneself for the implacable and blind defence of certain interests.[30]

In accordance with such scepticism, you can describe the rules of a particular property institution and assess who benefits and who loses from their implementation; but any further rational reflection on their interpretation or alteration is spurious. Politicians who appeal to the self-interest of their constituents are the honest fellows. Those who invoke conceptions of inter-personal justice are deluded or rogues. For the consistent sceptic, it is literally not possible to give a 'reason' for any facet of a property institution which tells against the self-interest of an addressee. Ross claims that invocations of justice impede rational discussion. But if he is right, once interests have been accurately identified there is nothing to discuss or to reason about.

The sceptical view, though widely shared, cannot be rigorously incorporated into a theory of property. It assumes an atomistic view of the human individual which is incompatible with the very idea of a property institution. As we have seen, such an institution requires, at least, trespassory rules. For

---

[28] Alf Ross, *On Law and Justice* (Stevens, 1958), 273–4.
[29] *Ibid.* 274.   [30] *Ibid.* 274–5.

such rules to impose intelligible obligations, it must be the case that those to whom they are addressed have the capacity to recognize interests of others as factors relevant to their practical deliberations. They may choose to break the rules whenever they can 'get away with it'. (Indeed, we shall argue that they are entitled to take this attitude if the property institution fails 'the justice threshold'.[31]) However, to understand what the rules require of them they must be capable of internalizing the provisional claims of others. As Kant contended, it does not follow from the fact that a man decides to flout moral obligations that he is incapable of understanding what they require. When a sceptic is proffered justice reasons for a property institution, he may respond: 'I don't wish to know!' But if he seeks to take issue with the contention that the reasons have the normative force claimed for them he must needs adopt, arguendo, the same stance as a non-sceptic would.

If the members of a society could not understand trespassory obligations, there would be no property institution. If there is such an institution, it follows that when further property issues emerge the human population to which they apply is comprised of individuals who are at least sufficiently involved in inter-personal interaction to make rational appeals to 'the common good' intelligible. Such appeals may be couched in terms of brute (or speculatively tutored) intuitions about human worth, human deserts, human needs, or the conventional understanding of these things, or whatever. These are reasons for institutional design which purport to transcend the interests of an addressee. They are 'justice reasons'; and if they relate to property institutions, they are property-specific justice reasons.

(v) REALISM AND CONVENTIONALISM

We have espoused a minimalist conception of justice in the conscious recognition that, in some respects, it flies in the face of the moral convictions which, over the centuries, have been held by most people. We have spoken of 'natural' equality and 'natural' wrongs and rights. It may be objected that we are thereby committed to a moral-realist conception of justice: the view that judgements about just human association, like other ethical claims, have a truth value in the same way that ordinary assertions about the facts of the world are thought of as true or false. (That position may also be termed 'objectivist' or 'absolutist', although some would insist that these labels implicate significant differences from 'realist'. These are meta-ethical complexities which we shall not explore.)

It may further be urged that moral realism is unacceptable. We should, rather, understand justice in terms of an ethical position often styled 'moral conventionalism'. According to a moral conventionalist, no ethical claim can

---

[31] See Ch. 18, sect. (ii) below.

be regarded as straightforwardly true or false. On the other hand, it is certainly possible to proffer information about what most people in a particular society at a particular time believe (or say they believe) about the rightness or wrongness of conduct or about the value or disvalue of practices. Information of the latter kind (it might be contended) should be the only base-line from which we proceed to assess such an institution as property. (Moral conventionalism may be combined with a variety of anti-realist analyses of the nature of moral judgements: 'relativism', the view that a judgement expresses only the speaker's (or his group's) opinion; 'emotivism', the claim that such judgements evince the speaker's emotions; or 'prescriptivism', the analysis of moral judgements as commitments to universalizable prescriptions. True conventionalist claims would accurately record moral judgements shared by most members of a social group, in whichever of these ways the internality of such judgements is explained.)

One argument for preferring a moral-conventionalist to a moral-realist conception of justice is anthropological. It is the fact that societies, past and present, differ widely on many normative issues. It follows that we should deploy variable conceptions of justice, tailored to each particular social context.[32] That fact, however, does not preclude the possibility that there could be, as well, a cross-cultural conception of justice with some such content as that we have given to the minimalist conception. Furthermore, alongside the phenomenon of cultural diversity over questions of rightness and value is the phenomenon of intra-cultural controversy and agitation for reform. It might be the case that a particular society witnesses to settled convictions about many things together with a higher-order conviction, espoused by most but denied by some, that settled practices are 'really' just. If so, we cannot dissipate questions about what such higher-order convictions amount to merely by proffering further anthropological information. It is over such facets of ethical discourse that meta-ethical controversies are joined.

A meta-ethical argument which might seem to undermine all moral-realist positions is the following. Alleged moral qualities of actions and moral values ascribed to practices are not part of the furniture of the world 'out there'. There is something manifestly 'queer' in supposing that they are and that they can, in and of themselves, furnish belief-independent reasons for action.[33] Moral realists ask us to believe in the existence of something (moral truth) which is supra-temporal and convention-independent. Why on earth should we?

Moral realists respond to such attacks by appealing directly to the phe-

---

[32] See Michael Walzer, *Spheres of Justice: A Defence of Pluralism and Equality* (Basic Books, 1982).
[33] See J. L. Mackie, *Ethics: Inventing Right and Wrong* (Penguin Books, 1977).

nomenon of ethical discourse.[34] They maintain that all engaged in moral controversy are, by the nature of their disputatious claims, committed to the view that there is a normative reality. Just as in the natural sciences we do not say that exploded theories were correct (as distinct from being believed to be correct) in their day, but that we now know that they mistook the truth; so too, over disputed questions of morals, we engage in discourse which supposes that there is a truth to be sought. We are all of us engaged on the same quest for that which is, really, right or just. Crudely put, the argument is: since we talk as though justice really exists, justice really exists.

Moral realists deny that they are committed to spooky metaphysics—to assumptions about supra-natural goings-on. There is no need to posit an ontological discontinuity or parallelism between moral facts and any other facts. To the contrary, they purport to up-end anti-realists in their own metaphysical wheelbarrow: '[i]f you maintain that there can be no moral truth because there is nothing out there, it is you anti-realists who have invented the out-thereness in which nothing is. We realists take discourse as we find it, and the reality presupposed in discourse is the only ontology we need.'

Anti-realists answer that the moral realists have misrepresented ethical discourse or, even if they have not, they are not entitled to found upon such discourse their special claims about ontology or rationality. We shall not consider further the complexities and subtle variations thrown up at an abstract level by these meta-ethical controversies.[35] Instead we shall ask: supposing conventionalism rather than realism to be correct, does that disable us from adopting the minimalist conception of justice set out in this Chapter as a foundation from which to assess the justice of property institutions?

How might it do so? It might be contended, for example, that the third element (the *prima facie* prohibition of unprovoked invasions of bodily integrity) lacks the appropriate standing from a conventionalist point of view. Gilbert Harman suggests the example of a successful professional criminal. He has no reason to refrain from killing or injuring his victims arising from the possibility of punishment because, by assumption, he knows

---

[34] Michael Moore, 'Moral Reality' (1982) *Wisconsin LR* 1061; 'A Natural Law Theory of Interpretation' (1985) 58 *S Cali. LR* 277; Thomas Nagel, *The View From Nowhere* (OUP, 1985); William G. Lycan, *Judgment and Justification* (CUP, 1988); David O. Brink, *Moral Realism and the Foundation of Ethics* (CUP, 1989). For criticism of such claims in relation to legal interpretation, see Stephen R. Munzer, 'Realistic Limits on Realist Interpretation' (1985) 58 *S Cali. LR* 459; Larry Alexander, 'All or Nothing At All: The Intentions of Authorities and the Authority of Intentions', in Andrei Marmor (ed.), *Law and Interpretation* (OUP, 1995).

[35] For essays debating the meta-ethical credentials of 'moral realism', 'moral foundationalism', 'moral cognitivism', 'moral objectivism', or 'moral absolutism', see Philippa Foot, 'Moral Realism and Moral Dilemma' (1983) 80 *J. Phil.* 379; David Copp and David Zimmerman (eds.), *Morality, Reason and Truth* (Rowman and Allen Held, 1985), pt. 1; Ted Honderich (ed.), *Morality and Objectivity* (Routledge and Kegan Paul, 1985); Geoffrey Sayre-McCord (ed.), *Essays on Moral Realism* (Cornell UP, 1988); Robert P. George (ed.), *Natural Law Theory* (Clarendon Press, 1992), chs. 4 and 7.

that he can always successfully avoid detection or capture. He does not share the conventional view that acting in these ways is morally wrong. From a relativist stance, he has no reason to desist.[36] Similarly, it might be claimed, the pædophiliac sadist who does not subscribe to social conventions against torturing children, or the rapist whose personal moral code includes the assumption that women have value only as objects for male sexual gratification, have no moral reasons to refrain from child-torture or rape.

Suppose this anti-realist conception of rationality is correct. It is nevertheless the case that social agencies have buckets of reasons for enforcing majoritarian moral opinion as though the majority's conventions represented moral truth. They may wish, not merely to incapacitate these 'deviants' (should they be detected) by incarcerating them but also, if possible, to 'reform' them. They may aim to convince the children of such people that their parents' examples are not ones to follow because, quite apart from adverse reactions, such conduct is 'cruel' or 'wicked'. They may aspire to bring about a social climate in which no-one shares the moral convictions of the criminal, the pædophiliac, or the rapist.

A thorough-going conventionalist need dissent from none of these objectives. He may, for his part, hold passionately to the view that such activities are appallingly evil. He can welcome the fact that most people agree with him. If public agencies implement conventional opinion in the ways suggested, he is scarcely likely to quibble if condemnation and education are not persistently coupled with qualifications of the form: '[w]hen we say that such conduct is deplorable and inhuman, we are, of course, only voicing majority opinion.'

It is here claimed that the very modest elements of our minimalist conception of justice are, in fact, assented to by the public culture of the modern world. It is, of course, the case that attitudes and actions which flout that conception are rife. Governmental agencies do not, however, defend the measures they adopt by proclaiming that human beings are divided into inherently superior and inherently inferior kinds, or that they reject completely the notion of autonomous human dignity, or that killing, assaulting, or detaining people requires no justification. The minimalist conception is also taken for granted by most participants in public, critical debate. It is unlikely that any reader of this book is going to go on record as a dissenter from any of its conclusions on the ground that, since he is a Mafioso, or a child-torturer, or a rapist, it can have nothing to say to him.

A conventionalist might concede all this but nevertheless object to the minimalist-justice foundation on the ground that it ignores the time-frame of conventionalist moralities. Supposing that public culture does, in our day, incorporate the minimalist conception, it has been conceded that that was

---

[36] Gilbert Harman, 'Is There a Single True Morality?', in Copp and Zimmerman (eds.), n. 35 above, 27 at 36–41.

not so in past societies. Surely, then, we ought not, as realists might, conceive of our three elements as eternal verities.

In answer to this it is submitted that modern public culture is not, internally, imprisoned within any strict time frame. Genocide—a practice which flouts the minimalist conception—is not spoken of as nowadays wrong, but unobjectionable when it occurred—especially if it was perpetrated within living memory, but even if it took place centuries ago. Certainly the Nazis believed that their practices were morally legitimate, as did the European slavers who captured people from the African continent. Our conventional attitudes and practices presuppose that both groups were morally mistaken.

Thus, even if moral conventionalism is, according to sound meta-ethical theory, to be preferred to moral realism, we may proceed. Without committing ourselves to any special ontological claims, we may deploy the minimalist conception of justice as though moral realism were sound.

A much more important objection to the minimalist conception of justice is that, by expounding it in terms sufficiently abstract and imprecise that it escapes the conventionalist challenge of partisanship, it approaches vacuity. How could something so skimpy be the starting-point for assessing the justice of property institutions? We shall see that it can, although much else that is challengeable will be taken into account along the way.

11

Natural Property Rights and Labour

In this Chapter and the next we are going to consider whether there are moral property rights to ownership falling within the sixth of the seven categories of property rights set out in section (ii) of the last chapter—that is, moral standing to claim that a person or group ought to be vested with an ownership interest over some specific resource.

(i) NATURAL PROPERTY RIGHTS

'Natural rights' are such rights as follow from the interaction between the formal and substantive requirements of just treatment and the facts of the world. 'Human rights' are such rights as are claimed, for whatever reason, to be due to all human beings, or to all humans who participate in a particular culture.[1] Human rights are potentially a much more extensive category than natural rights since their avowed basis may be nothing more than their explicit articulation within particular conventions. Natural rights might be more extensive than human rights if, for example, it were supposed that the interaction of just treatment and the facts of the world led to the conclusion that non-humans, such as animals or alien visitors to this planet if there ever were any, had rights. If it can be demonstrated that any human being is, by virtue of his or her interactions with the world and with others, entitled, in justice, to claim ownership privileges and powers over some resource, then there are both natural and human property rights.

Can a relationship arise between a person and a thing such that, independently of social convention or positive legal provision, that person ought to be conceded by others' ownership use-privileges and control-powers over that thing? If there are any such natural rights, society should institute or maintain trespassory rules to protect them and should accord them such recognition along the ownership spectrum as is entailed by the kinds of arguments upon which they rest. Supposing such a right can be established, the extent of the right is always a separable question. Does it involve an open-ended, but yet

[1] See E. Kamenka and A. E. S. Tay (eds.), *Human Rights* (Edward Arnold, 1979); C. S. Nino, *The Ethics of Human Rights* (Clarendon Press, 1991); R. P. Claude and B. H. Weston (eds.), *Human Rights in the World Community* (2nd edn., U Pa. P, 1992); R. Beddard, *Human Rights and Europe* (3rd edn., CUP, 1993).

circumscribed, bundle of use-privileges and control-powers—what we have called 'mere property'?[2] Does it rise to the level of unlimited use-privileges and control-powers together with unlimited powers of transmission ('full-blooded ownership')?[3] Or does it fall somewhere between these extremes?

If there are any natural property rights, the moral background for the operation of property institutions is radically different from what it is if there are none. For example, if it could be shown that there are natural rights to full-blooded ownership in respect of those resources which the modern regulatory State subjects to property-limitation rules in the interests of public health or amenity, then the common assumption that compensation is not called for in such cases[4] would be mistaken. Even if some community goal requires that an owner be stripped of use-privileges or control-powers, that could not justly be done unless the wealth-potential of the privilege or power was preserved—on the assumption that it was something to which the individual was entitled in his or her own right against the rest of mankind.

In the last chapter we claimed that, contrary to Hobbes' opinion, there are natural rights not to be subjected to unprovoked invasions of bodily integrity (the third element of our minimalist conception of justice). However, if Hobbes was mistaken in arguing that human beings carry into political communities no rights to bodily integrity which entail negative obligations on the part of the State, he may have been correct in maintaining that they carry no such rights to property—that distribution of social wealth is at the uncontrolled discretion of the sovereign authority, there being annexed to sovereignty 'the whole power of prescribing the rules whereby every man may know what goods he may enjoy'.[5]

Other state-of-nature theorists, from the seventeenth century onwards, have assumed that individuals have a domain that others must not infringe which comprises portions of the physical environment as well as bodily integrity. Locke asserted that in the state of nature all enjoy 'perfect freedom to order their actions and dispose of their possessions and persons as they think fit';[6] and that by the law of nature 'no one ought to harm another in his life, health, liberty, or possessions'.[7] Robert Nozick similarly begins his analysis of the proper limits of the minimal State by envisaging a state of nature in which independent persons have equal rights to a private domain which includes portions of the external environment.[8]

We argued in the last chapter that bans on unprovoked invasions of bodily integrity were a corollary of natural equality (the first element of our

---

[2] See Ch. 3, sect. (v) above.   [3] See Ch. 3, sect. (vi) above.

[4] See Ch. 6, sect. (iii)(c) above.

[5] Thomas Hobbes, *Leviathan* (C. B. MacPherson (ed.), Penguin Books, 1968), 237.

[6] John Locke, *Second Treatise of Government* (G. W. Gough (ed.), Basil Blackwell, 1976), ch. II, 4.

[7] *Ibid.*, Ch. II, 6.

[8] Robert Nozick, *Anarchy, State and Utopia* (Basil Blackwell, 1974), 10–12, 150–3.

minimalist conception of justice).[9] The same can hardly be said of the assumptions made by these state-of-nature theorists. Everyone has a body capable of being killed or violated so that, given natural equality and the individual's interest in surviving intact, he cannot deny the universalizability of primary rights against physical assault. But no-one enters the world naturally endowed with a private domain over some divisible portion of the earth or anything it contains. Merely by insisting that no person should be treated differently from any other on the ground that he is less than fully human, one is not committed to the view that anybody owns any particular resource. On the face of it, indeed, natural equality might suggest that everyone has an equal natural right to everything.[10]

Some feature of the interaction between just treatment and the facts of the world must be supplied to unlock the key to natural property rights. In this Chapter we consider productive labour, which appears (either in our philosophical traditions or in day-to-day political or legal controversies) in the dress of three arguments—those from self-ownership, creation-without-wrong and labour-desert. In the next Chapter we turn to more modest claims to natural property rights in special cases, centring on analogical extensions of the ban on assaults.

(ii) SELF-OWNERSHIP

(a) Body Ownership Rhetoric

'Remember your body is your own private property. Your body's nobody's body but your own.'[11] These lines are taken from a cassette produced for the entertainment and instruction of young children. The author warns her child audience about not crossing roads without looking for traffic, not playing on their own near deep water, and not allowing adults 'to interfere with you privately'. She accompanies each piece of advice with a catchy jingle. In the case of the warning against adults who might sexually abuse her young addressees, she sings the above-quoted two lines about your body being your own private property.

Property rhetoric is a pervasive phenomenon of both ordinary and literary discourse. Property is a familiar and deeply ingrained notion in the consciousness of everyone, including children. It is regularly invoked, analogically, to confer heightened force on claims which, in themselves, have nothing to do with any of the structural elements of property institutions discussed in the first part of this book. 'You don't own me!' says the teenager

---

[9] See Ch. 10, sect. (iii)(c) above.
[10] See Alan Gibbard, 'Natural Property Rights' (1976) 10 *Nous* 77.
[11] Rochelle Brader, *Rochelle's Place* (Kiwi Pacific Records Ltd, 1986).

in rebellion against what she considers to be excessive parental restraints. 'My life belongs to me!' insists the suffering patient in protest against the prohibition of euthanasia.

Body ownership rhetoric may seem particularly apt for this reason. Just as there are trespassory rules against meddling with other people's chattels, so too there are rules prohibiting homicide, assault, rape, and false imprisonment. Furthermore, the second element of our minimalist conception of justice is today widely assumed to encompass what we may call the 'bodily-use freedom principle': a person is free to use his body as he pleases, and, at his say-so, to permit or refuse bodily (and especially sexual) contacts with others. Since there is this open-ended set of use-privileges and control-powers over one's body, it seems natural enough to speak of 'owning' one's body. Just as no-one should steal your books, but you can do what you like with them and authorize others to do what they like with them, so too no-one should invade your bodily integrity, but you yourself can do what you like to your body and permit others to do so.

Rhetorical invocations, in this context, of body-ownership are an optional extra. We do not need to appeal to the analogy with property in resources in order to make points which follow from the bodily-use freedom principle . For example, English courts now accept that an adult person of sound mind may refuse medical treatment needed to save his life, provided he is in a position to make a fully-informed and uncoerced decision; but they do not employ the terminology of self-ownership.[12]

Nevertheless, invocations of body-ownership may add pithiness and force to what would otherwise seem laboured and tame. They are not intended to be taken literally, for, if they were, they would prove too much. The ownership interest recognized both by law and by societal norms in ordinary chattels lies at the upper end of the ownership spectrum—full-blooded ownership. If I own a book it follows that I may scribble in it, use it to prop up the leg of a rickety table, burn it, lend or sell it to whom I please, or give it away *inter vivos* or by will. Someone invoking body-ownership, rhetorically, is not committed to claiming the same panoply of use-privileges, control-powers, and transmission powers over each person's body.

It is to be hoped that the addressees of the children's cassette are not too wickedly sophisticated. The author warns her audience against sexual molestation by adults. She invokes the property analogy on the assumption—a correct one—that children acquire a sense of ownership from a very young age. It is clearly not part of her message, however, that children may choose to accord sexual favours to adults if they please, just as they are free to share their toys. 'Samantha, how dare you let Uncle Joe do these things to you!' 'But the lady said "your body is your own private property"!'

---

[12] *In Re T (Adult: Refusal of Treatment)* [1993] Fam. 95; *Secretary of State for the Home Department* v. *Robb, The Times*, 21 Oct. 1994.

In other contexts, body-ownership rhetoric might be positively misleading or even double-edged. Sometimes those who appeal to the bodily-use free-dom principle in support of the contention that there should be no restraints on a woman's right to abortion seek to reinforce their argument by announ-cing that a woman's body is her own property.[13] Those who take this line, however, might not necessarily wish to commit themselves to the view that women are also morally free to sell their bodies for any use, however demeaning or even life-threatening. Rhetoric, including property-rhetoric, is not supposed to be confined by nice considerations of analogical accuracy.

The proper limits of the bodily-use freedom principle are controversial, especially when other contested values are in play. When this is so, body-ownership rhetoric settles nothing. It can be no more than a device for recasting in vivid form a conclusion already reached without it. In the United Kingdom, legislation criminalizes commercial promotion of surrogate motherhood;[14] and the committee chaired by Lady Warnock recommended that non-profit-making organizations involved in surrogacy should also be out-lawed.[15] These are controversial measures; but no critic could sensibly suppose that their injustice can be proved merely by announcing that, since potential surrogate mothers own their bodies, they ought to be as free to deal with them as they are with anything else they own.

The limits of the bodily-use freedom principle were the subject of a three–two division in the House of Lords in the recent case of *R.* v. *Brown*.[16] The issue was whether legislation which criminalizes unlawful wounding and assaults occasioning actual bodily harm[17] should be applied to masochistic practices engaged in between consenting adult men. The accused had, for their mutual sexual gratification and with the willing co-operation of all concerned, indulged in conduct which included sticking pins through parts of their genitals. The majority of the House found for the prosecution on the ground that all harms to the person, going beyond the merely transient and trifling, are, in English law, the proper subject of legal intervention, and doing it for sexual kicks was not an appropriate exception. The minority (especially Lord Mustill) argued forcefully that, however bizarre or disgust-ing the activities might seem to most people, the bodily-use freedom prin-ciple of a liberal society required that criminal law should not intrude. The minority said nothing whatever about persons' bodies being their own private property. Property-invocation would have proved far too much. You can smash up your own chattels if you have a mind to do so. The minority

---

[13] See Jeffrey D. Goldberg, 'Involuntary Servitudes: a Property-Based Notion of Abortion Choice' (1991) 38 *UCLA LR* 1597.
[14] Surrogacy Arrangements Act 1985.
[15] *Report on Human Fertilisation and Embryology*, Cmnd. 9314, 1984, para. 8.18.
[16] [1994] 1 AC 212.
[17] Offences against the Person Act 1861, ss. 20 and 47.

took it to be indisputable that people are not at liberty to consent to serious or permanent maiming of their bodies, let alone to take part in duels.

Property-rhetoric is occasionally invoked by judges as a top-up to appeals to the bodily-use freedom principle. The House of Lords recently abolished the marital exemption for rape. Ever since the days of Sir Matthew Hale in the seventeenth century it had been taken to be an axiom of the common law that husbands could not be guilty of raping their wives. The House of Lords unanimously declared that no such exemption now exists as part of English common law.[18] In delivering the only speech, Lord Keith said: 'marriage is in modern times regarded as a partnership of equals, and no longer one in which the wife must be the subservient chattel of her husband'.[19]

But did Hale and his contemporaries suppose that husbands were empowered to deal as freely with the bodies of their wives as they were with their chattels? Clearly not. Even in their day wife-murder or mutilation was criminal and—Thomas Hardy's Mayor of Casterbridge notwithstanding—the common law made no provision for selling or giving away wives. There may have been societies in which all these things were allowed, but they would be ones in which women were genuinely subjected to a property institution, like other slaves.

Hale had another argument. He maintained that women, upon marriage, must be taken to have given an irretractable consent to sexual intercourse. Lord Keith was well aware of this. He expressly deals with it and demolishes it as entirely fictional and out of touch with modern notions of personal freedom. It seems unlikely that anyone who was not convinced by that argument would be brought to modify his reactionary opinions by the force of the reference to 'chattels'. Lord Keith's 'chattel' aside was merely a bit of unnecessary, but harmless, rhetoric.

Property notions are so deeply ingrained as to be readily susceptible to rhetorical or literary use. John Galsworthy wrote a novel which is entitled 'A Man of Property'. One is to infer, it seems, that the principal character viewed both his possessions and his wife with an equivalent sense of egocentric self-assertion—indeed, he commits marital rape and sees no reason why he should not. But even Soames Forsyte did not suppose that he was at liberty to engage in jovial wife-swapping, or to leave his wife by will to the next generation.

The ordinary run of property-rhetoric is clearly not intended to be taken literally—as though some feature of a property institution were actually being invoked. It might be argued, however, that the case of owning one's own body is special—that people really do think that their bodies are among the things they own. It would have to be conceded that the relevant ownership interest was well down the ownership spectrum, far below the full-blooded ownership which applies to other chattels. It would need to be a

[18] *R. v. R* [1992] 1 AC 599.   [19] *Ibid.* 616.

unique kind of 'ownership', specially tailored for bodies, so that there was no danger of proving too much. (The fact that people deploy possessive pronouns in relation to their bodies is, in itself, no indication of ownership assumptions; for, as we have seen, such pronouns may signify a host of relationships which have nothing to do with owning.[20])

How then might it be established that people regard their bodies as among the things they own—albeit that they take 'owning' here to have specially circumscribed implications? We could only do that by showing that men and women make certain claims about what they are, or are not, free to do (or to permit to be done) to their bodies. In other words, the supposed body-ownership conception is the product of the bodily-use freedom principle and other relevant values—paternalism, self-esteem, intrinsic human dignity, and so forth. Ownership, in the case of ordinary chattels, is a primitive organizing idea from which innumerable conclusions are derived in daily life.[21] Ownership of one's body is not.

Societies which lack property institutions altogether might nevertheless be committed to the bodily-use freedom principle. Consider two of the imaginary societies described in Chapter 2. In Forest Land and Red Land there are rules protecting bodily integrity—prohibiting homicide, assault, rape, or false imprisonment. There are also rules requiring some positive services. Beyond these rules, and in interpreting and applying the rules, the tribesmen/citizens are (let us suppose) committed to a principle of personal freedom. Everyone is at liberty to do what he or she likes with, and to, his or her own body. It is at the individual's say-so whether he or she allows others physical or sexual contact, and whether he or she will perform physical services. Perhaps there are limits. Self-mutilation might be prohibited; and violent or demeaning treatment of another person's body might not be allowed, even with consent. It emerges that individuals have an open-ended (albeit circumscribed) set of use-privileges and control-powers over their bodies. Presumably, the tribesmen/citizens would react with incomprehension or incredulity to any visitor to their societies who insisted that it must therefore be the case that each of them 'has property in' his body or in his labouring or other bodily activities.

The bodily-use freedom principle has whatever normative force it has without benefit of self-ownership notions. Property rhetoric in this context is unnecessary, usually harmless, but always potentially proves too much.

(b) The Fruits of Labour

Body-ownership rhetoric presupposes a background in which a property institution reigns over various material, ideational, and monetary resources and applies the terminology of that institution to the human body. Its point

----

[20] See Ch. 1, sect. (iii) above.   [21] See Ch. 5 above.

is to provide dramatic support for the bodily-use freedom principle. The history of Western political philosophy includes a tradition of self-ownership invocations which have another object and which employ a different strategy. They seek to provide one kind of justificatory argument for property institutions, or for particular features of property-institutional design. Beginning with the premise of self-ownership, they move to the conclusion that every individual has a natural right to own the fruits of his or her labour.

(1) Self-Ownership—the Liberal Version

1. If I am not a slave, nobody else owns my body. Therefore
2. I must own myself. Therefore
3. I must own all my actions, including those which create or improve resources. Therefore
4. I own the resources, or the improvements, I produce.

The foregoing four steps purport to supply an argument for a natural property right beginning with premises no richer than those contained in the minimalist conception of justice set out in the last chapter. Conferring ownership interests over some persons in favour of other persons would be incompatible with applying rules protecting bodily integrity (the third element) and fostering some degree of autonomous choice (the second element) in a way which observes the constraint that no-one is to be treated differently from others on the ground that he is a different kind of human being (the first element). It follows that slavery is an unjustifiable feature of a property institution. As John Stuart Mill put it: '[i]t is almost superfluous to observe, that this institution [slavery] can have no place in any society even pretending to be founded on justice, or on fellowship between human creatures.'[22]

The crucial move in the liberal version of the self-ownership argument for a natural property right—one which, as we shall see, Mill himself does not make—is that from step 1 to step 2: if I am not a slave I must own myself. Granted self-ownership, ownership of the fruits of my labour follows automatically. My body is the tree; my actions are the branches; and the product of my labouring activities is the fruit.

This is one of the two principal arguments entwined in John Locke's celebrated defence of private property in the fifth chapter of his *Second Treatise of Government*—the other being, as we shall see, creation-without-wrong. By introducing the notion of self-ownership, Locke believed that he had hit on an argument for private property whose metaphysical simplicity avoided the need for appeal to tacit consent. He envisaged a natural State in which there was no enslavement, prohibitions on invasions of bodily integrity

---

[22] John Stuart Mill, *Principles of Political Economy: With Some of their Applications to Social Philosophy*, in J. M. Robson (ed.), *Collected Works of John Stuart Mill* (U Tor. P, Routledge and Kegan Paul, 1965), 233.

were universalized, and every man had access on equal terms to the bounties of nature which God had supplied—that is, there were trespassory rules protecting people's bodies, but none obtained, to begin with, so far as resources were concerned. What followed?

Though the earth and all inferior creatures be common to all men, yet every man has a property in his own person; this nobody has any right to but himself. The labour of his body and the work of his hands we may say are properly his. Whatsoever, then, he removes out of the state that nature hath provided and left it in, he hath mixed his labour with, and joined to it something that is his own, and thereby makes it his property.[23]

The literature spawned by the above passage is enormous. In particular, the 'mixing labour' metaphor has been subjected to minute analysis.[24] We are here concerned only with the self-ownership premise of the argument and, in particular, the problematic move between steps 1 and 2 in the four steps set out above.

Robert Nozick is the best known Lockean apologist of our day. He too criticizes the 'mixing' metaphor.[25] Nevertheless, he appeals to the self-ownership argument for a natural property right as part of his critique of measures aimed at redistributing wealth. He claims that redistributive taxation is 'on a par' with forced labour.[26] On the face of it, that looks like a very odd contention. There may be many objections to redistributive taxation, but surely it is very different from lining people up on a chain gang and whipping them to work. How could the two operations be on a par?

Nozick seeks to demonstrate the similarity by running the four steps in the self-ownership argument backwards. If the State expropriates any of the fruits of my labour, it is denying my moral ownership of them (contrary to step 4). Therefore, it is implicitly denying step 3, that I own all my labouring activities; and hence also step 2, that I own myself. Now since the only alternative to my owning myself is that someone else owns me, the redistributive state is implicitly denying even step 1, that I am not a slave. Thus, redistributive taxation turns me, at least partially, into the slave of the community and so is on a par with forced labour. 'Seizing the results of someone's labour is equivalent to seizing hours from him and directing him to carry on various activities. . . . This process whereby they take the decision from you makes them a *part-owner* of you.'[27] All measures of wealth redistribution represents a 'shift from the classical liberal's notion of self-ownership'.[28] The inegalitarian implications of Nozick's argument have been challenged on many grounds, but usually not by a simple denial of the self-ownership premise. G. A. Cohen, for example, in his response to Nozick,

---

[23] *Second Treatise of Government*, ch. V, 27.
[24] See, e.g., Jeremy Waldron, *The Right to Private Property* (Clarendon Press, 1988), 184–8.
[25] Nozick, n. 8 above, 174–5.   [26] *Ibid.* 169–70.
[27] *Ibid.* 172.   [28] *Ibid.*

makes heavy weather of self-ownership.[29] He suggests that Nozickian self-ownership, contrary to Nozick's own opinion, must be merely 'formal'—that is, it entails no right to use resources. That must be so because proletarians have no such right, and Nozick must suppose that they, like everyone else, own themselves. It follows that Nozickian self-ownership could be combined with 'joint ownership' of all external resources.[30] (Cohen's concept of joint ownership is invented *ad hoc*. It covers everything external to the human body, and it entails that no joint owner may make any use of the world—not so much as take water from a superabundant stream[31] or, presumably, breathe the air—without the prior consent of every other joint owner.[32]) Cohen conceives this manœuvre to be necessary because 'self-ownership' has plenty of initial appeal.[33] It is, nevertheless, a notion which he concludes socialists must reject.[34]

Cannot Nozick's claims be far more straightforwardly contested by questioning the move from step 1 to step 2 (or backwards from 2 to 1) in the liberal version of the self-ownership argument? If I am not a slave, must I own myself? If anyone denies that I own myself, must he be implying that I am a slave?

(2) Self-Ownership—the Marxist Version

1. If I am not a slave, nobody else owns my body. Therefore
2. I must own myself. Therefore
3. I must own all my actions, including those which produce a use value of any kind. Therefore
4. Every service contract into which I enter constitutes a conveyance of my labour power.

The self-ownership argument for a natural property right is not the exclusive province of the political right. Karl Marx deploys it in volume 1 of *Capital* as part of his immanent critique of capitalist production.

Marx takes over the first three steps in the liberal version of the self-ownership argument. When feudalism was superseded by capitalism the worker ceased to be a slave or a serf and consequently owned both himself and his labour-power (*arbeitskraft*). Self-ownership was a necessary precondition for labour-power's appearance on the market as a commodity. 'In order that its possessor may sell it as a commodity, he must have it at his disposal, he must be the free proprietor of his own labour-capacity, hence of his person.'[35]

One of the characteristic phenomena of the capitalist mode of production

---

[29] G. A. Cohen, *Self-Ownership, Freedom, and Equality* (CUP, 1995), chs. 3 and 4.
[30] *Ibid.* 94–102.   [31] *Ibid.* 98.
[32] Cohen does not relate his notion of 'joint ownership' to any conception of joint or group property to be found in the real world—see Ch. 7 above.
[33] Cohen, n. 29 above, 70.   [34] *Ibid.* ch. 10.
[35] Karl Marx, *Capital I* (Penguin Classics, trans. B. Fowkes, Penguin Books, 1990), 271.

is that 'the product is the property of the capitalist and not that of the worker, its immediate producer'.[36] To explain this phenomenon, Marx substitutes a new fourth step in the classic self-ownership argument. Within the circulation of commodities, every service contract is necessarily a conveyance of the ownership of labour-power from employee to employer. The worker places his labour-power at the disposal of a buyer for a definite period of time by 'handing it over to the buyer for him to consume'.[37]

'Labour-power' denotes 'the aggregate of those mental and physical capabilities existing in the physical form, the living personality, of a human being, capabilities which he sets in motion whenever he produces a use-value of any kind'.[38] Whenever one person contracts to sell his services to another it must be the case that, in legal form, there is an exchange of equivalents. The buyer has transferred money and the seller has transferred ownership, for a certain time, of his labour-power. Just as the purchaser of any other commodity acquires an ownership interest in it which confers on him exclusive use-privileges and control-powers over the thing he has bought, so too the purchaser of labour-power is, under bourgeois law, free to make any use, or control any use by others, of the aggregate mental and physical capabilities of the worker during the time for which it was sold. 'He then did what is done by every purchaser of commodities: he consumed their use-value.'[39]

In discussions of Marx's labour theory of value, scant attention has been paid to the use he makes of specifically proprietary concepts. His notions of conveyance and ownership of labour-power are, however, crucial planks in his analysis of the creation and 'expropriation' of 'surplus-value'.

Of course, Marx did not himself subscribe to the self-ownership fruits-of-labour argument as an eternal verity governing the just distribution of wealth. In the higher phase of communist society, it seems, the maxim would be: 'from each according to his ability, to each according to his needs!'; and, even in the primary stage which would replace capitalism, the maxim '[a]n equal amount of products for an equal amount of labour' may be intended to reflect the labour-desert argument rather than to assume that there is a distinct portion of social wealth which somehow accrues from the separate labour-power of each worker.[40] Nevertheless, the first three steps of the self-ownership argument are essential to Marx's immanent critique of capitalist production because they enable the fourth step to be added, and thereby to show both how surplus-value arises and in what sense it is expropriated.

The worker conveys a particular commodity, his labour-power, to the capitalist. Having thus become its owner, the capitalist uses this commodity to create other commodities. The purchase price of the labour-power is

[36] N. 35 above, 292.   [37] *Ibid.* 271.
[38] *Ibid.* 270.   [39] *Ibid.* 302.
[40] See V. I. Lenin, *The State and Revolution* (Progress Publishers, 1949), ch. v, 3–4.

limited to whatever minimum expenditure is needed to enable workers to survive and reproduce. Whatever exchange-value the new commodities have beyond this minimum is 'surplus-value'.

Expropriation occurs when property is taken away from its owner. Marx uses the term in this sense when he describes the historical circumstances of the primitive accumulation of capital. By violence, conducted within or outside forms of legality, capitalists expropriated the means of production and the basis of subsistence of peasant and handicraft owners.[41] 'And this history, the history of their expropriation, is written in the annals of mankind in letters of blood and fire.'[42]

In contrast, 'expropriation' of surplus-value is a continuing and inherent concomitant of capitalist production. Given the liberal version of the self-ownership argument, everything that results from the worker's labour ought, naturally, to belong to him. That is why the laws of capitalist expropriation constitute an 'inversion' or 'negation' of the property laws of commodity production.[43] It is the conveyance of his labour-power which robs the worker of surplus-value. However, since the worker is coerced by dire need into a transaction which results in the degradation of his humanity, and since all that he receives in exchange is nothing other than the embodiment of value already expropriated from him, this exchange of labour-power for money 'becomes a mere form, which is alien to the content of the transaction itself, and merely mystifies it'.[44]

Originally the rights of property seemed to us to be grounded in a man's own labour. . . . Now, however, property turns out to be the right, on the part of the capitalist, to appropriate the unpaid labour of others or its product, and the impossibility, on the part of the worker, of appropriating his own product.[45]

In this analysis, commodification is (grace of the self-ownership premise) identified with propertization. Although Marx has employment contracts primarily in mind, it seems that the analysis would apply, by the same logic, to all service contracts. There is no question of making the distinction familiar to lawyers between contracts of service (those between master and servant or employer and employee) and contracts for services (those between a principal and an independent contractor). If you buy a commodity of any kind, there *must* be an exchange of property for property. You pay money; he conveys ownership of his aggregate mental and physical capabilities.

C. B. MacPherson plays the Marxist version of the self-ownership argument backwards as the basis for distinguishing ideal-typical societies. All societies in which people are regarded as free to sell their services to others are different from all other kinds of society in the following way. Since every service contract is a conveyance of labour-power (step 4), such people must

---

[41] *Capital*, I, chs. 26–30. [42] *Ibid.* 875.
[43] *Ibid.* ch. 24. [44] *Ibid.* 729–30. [45] *Ibid.* 730.

think that they own all their use-producing actions (step 3), and therefore they must suppose that they own themselves (step 2). They are 'possessive individualists'.[46] MacPherson argued that Thomas Hobbes—who (as we saw in the last chapter) said that without an absolute and unlimited sovereign authority men would exist in a state of savage barbarism—was right about societies composed of possessive individualists, but wrong about all other kinds of society.[47] A community which tolerates service contracts is peopled by citizens who suppose they own themselves; and the mentality of that sort of person is such that, were a centralized and unlimited coercive power removed, they would become Hobbesian savages. In contrast, a society composed of men and women who are not thought of as free to sell their services and therefore do not suppose that they own themselves (such as a feudal society or, presumably, one subjected to a thorough-going command economy) is peopled by individuals who would not revert to savagery if sovereign coercive power were removed. Marx surrounded his analysis with a wealth of documented historical detail about industrial practice. MacPherson evidently saw no need for that. Everything followed from the Marxist version of the self-ownership argument, played backwards.

(3) Labour as a Commodity

As we have seen, a crucial plank in Marx's claim that capitalist production results in the expropriation of surplus-value is that bourgeois law, as a matter of form, does indeed conceive of service contracts as conveyances of labour-power. This form, he maintains, serves only to mystify the true reality of exploitation. But in adding this step to the self-ownership argument, it is Marx himself who is mystifying bourgeois law. The conveyance is a straw creation he puts up, and then exposes.

Picture the bafflement which would be provoked if a law teacher were to inform her students that every service contract is a conveyance. Commodification is not the same thing as propertization. If people disagree on whether a woman should be free to sell her charms for a beauty contest, they

[46] C. B. MacPherson, *The Political Theory of Possessive Individualism: Hobbes to Locke* (OUP, 1962).

[47] It is doubtful whether one can find any theory of self-ownership in Hobbes. In a footnote, Marx makes a passing reference to the following sentence from Leviathan: '[t]he *value*, or WORTH of a man, is as of all other things, his Price; that is to say, so much as would be given for the use of his Power:'—Hobbes, *Leviathan*, 151 (cited by Marx in *Capital*, i, 274, n. 5). That sentence appears in the 10th chapter of *Leviathan* in which Hobbes makes cynical observations about men vouchsafing honour, not by virtue of intrinsic merit, but according to people's 'power' to achieve their ends by any means, however brutal. In his introduction to *Leviathan*, MacPherson fastens on this sentence in support of his contention that Hobbes' analysis applies only to societies in which service contracts are allowed—*Leviathan*, 35, 38. Hobbes does indeed make passing references to labour as a 'commodity' (*ibid.* 294); and, following 17th century usage, he employs the term 'propriety' to cover interests people have in life and limb and conjugal affections (382). However, unlike Locke, he espouses no version of the liberal self-ownership argument for a natural property right.

differ on whether that kind of service ought to be a commodity. They might invoke body-ownership rhetorically on either side of the question— '[w]omen's bodies are their property to dispose of as they please!' '[w]omen's bodies are not chattels to be traded!'—neither side to such a dispute supposes that the organizer of the beauty contest would acquire an ownership interest over the totality of the woman's mental and physical capabilities.

Labour is a commodity but, outside slave-owning or feudal societies, it is not an entity in which ownership interests are transferred. Marx had before his mind's eye the down-trodden spinning hand or the skivvy servant of the Victorian household. No doubt the tyrannical employer of such people could, in practice, order them to make any use whatever of the totality of their capabilities so that property rhetoric would be in order. They were little better than slaves! But that is hardly a necessary feature of all service contracts. Only the self-ownership (and hence labour-ownership conveyance) premises could lend colour to the suggestion that it is.

If I hire a plumber or a gardener, or if I take on a job as university teacher, I buy or sell services. I receive or transfer ownership of nothing. The organizing idea in all service contracts is their express or implied terms. It is not an ownership interest. Property passes from one side only, *viz.* the money that is paid for the services. As we saw in Chapter 2, it is possible to imagine a society, Contract Land, in which service contracts exist in the entire absence of any property institution. Service contracts may or may not be harsh or exploitative; but, whatever else they are, they are not conveyances of a special ownable entity known as 'labour-power'.

We have argued that for a right (or bundle of rights) to be proprietary it (or they) must either be the subject of specific trespassory protection or else be separately assignable as part of a person's private wealth.[48] On that basis, employment contracts might be brought within the purview of property institutions in one of three ways. The employee might be accorded a right to attend certain premises to carry out his work and to receive remuneration from the owner of the premises, which rights would be enforceable against any successor in title to the premises. Then he would be vested with a non-ownership proprietary interest over the land in question, a special kind of personal servitude. Secondly, the employee might be empowered to sell all the rights granted to him by his employment contract on the open market, without any kind of veto by the employer. That would vest him with cashable rights, which could be made the subject of expropriation rules for the benefit of his creditors. Thirdly, the employer could be empowered to trade for money all his rights against the employee irrespective of the employee's consent, so that the employer would be vested with cashable rights which could again be the subject of expropriation rules. Whether any such rules are feasible or desirable is, as we saw in Chapter 9, smothered with

[48] See Ch. 9, sect. (i) above.

obfuscation if we insist that jobs are already necessarily a species of 'property'; and the obfuscation is worse confounded if, following the Marxist version of the self-ownership argument, labour-power itself is deemed to be property.

(4) The Spectacular Non Sequitur

The reader has probably already noticed the spectacular *non sequitur* between the first and the second steps of both the liberal and the Marxist versions of the self-ownership argument. From the fact that nobody owns me if I am not a slave, it simply does not follow that I must own myself. Nobody at all owns me, not even me.

It is one thing to invoke self-ownership in the context of the bodily-use freedom principle by borrowing, for rhetorical purposes, upon the familiar vocabulary of property institutions. It is another to place self-ownership inside a property institution and to go on to draw conclusions from it about ownership of resources as Locke, Nozick, and Marx do. Since the abolition of slavery, human beings have (so far as the actual working of property institutions is concerned) been removed from the property agenda. Only the speculations of philosophers and (as we saw in Chapter 9) some devotees of the economic analysis of law[49] have sought to keep them there.

By no means all philosophers who have addressed themselves to property have succumbed to the *non sequitur* and the self-ownership myth. They are not to be found in David Hume's social-conventional property theory.[50] Mill (as we saw) regarded it as 'almost superfluous to observe' that slavery can have no place in a just society. It followed from that, in Mill's view, not that human beings own themselves, but that they head the list of those things that are beyond the scope of property.[51] Mill, the arch apostle of liberty, did not find it necessary to invoke body ownership, even rhetorically.

Metaphorical employments of 'owning' one's body are frequently encountered, and we shall later discuss the special case of property in separated bodily parts.[52] As a thoroughgoing argument for a natural right to own resources, however, the self-ownership argument has received scant recognition in practical life. It has less plausibility than the other labour-arguments

---

[49] Yoram Barzel commits the spectacular *non sequitur* explicitly. 'The current prohibition of slavery implies that each individual is the owner of the capital asset embedded in her or him'—Barzel, *Economic Analysis of Property Rights* (CUP, 1989), 84.

[50] Hume distinguishes three species of 'goods': 'the internal satisfaction of our minds'; 'the external advantages of our body'; and 'the enjoyment of such possessions as we have acquired by our industry and good fortune'. Only the latter 'external goods', which are the subject of scarcity and which may be transferred without suffering any loss or alteration, are controlled by property institutions—David Hume, *A Treatise of Human Nature* (T. H. Green and T. H. Grose (eds.), Longmans, Green and Co., 1874), ii, 261–2. Hume specifically rejects the fruits-of-labour argument—*ibid.* 266, note. Hume's theory is discussed in Ch. 16, sect. (ii) of this book.

[51] N. 22 above, bk. 2, 2, 7.   [52] See Ch. 17, sect. (iv) below.

to be considered in this Chapter. The inhabitants of the imaginary property-less societies discussed in Chapter 2 would, one may conjecture, react with incredulity to a visitor who informed them: 'because you don't have slavery here, you are compelled, not merely to reinterpret your prohibitions on personal violence as property rules protecting body-ownership, but also, in justice, to introduce new trespassory rules protecting full-blooded individual ownership over the fruits of anyone's labour.' The spectacular *non sequitur* robs the self-ownership argument of all normative force.

(iii) CREATION-WITHOUT-WRONG

If a person (1) creates a new item of social wealth, and (2) wrongs no-one in doing so, it follows that (3) he ought to be accorded ownership of that new item.

The foregoing three steps summarize what we shall call the 'creation-without-wrong' argument for a natural property right. It is part of the traditional armoury invoked in support of private property. Both Locke and Mill have resort to it. It has a broader intuitive appeal than does the self-ownership argument since it does not require the infusion of a philosophically-manufactured technical conception; and, unlike the even more popular labour-desert argument to be considered in the next section, it is not hostage to convention. It relies on rhetorical questions of the following form: '[i]f some genius invents a wonderful new game using only his imagination and a few bits of plastic and a notebook, no-one is the worse for what he does; so, if he wants to own it, why should he not?'

(a) Locke's Version

The self-ownership argument and its concomitant mixing-labour metaphor is the more renowned of the arguments for private property contained in Locke's fifth chapter of the *Second Treatise of Government*. It will be contended that the chapter contains also a quite distinct argument based on creation-without-wrong.

Lockean critics have debated the significance of the two limitations[53] to which Locke makes repeated reference throughout the chapter: first, that the property right arises 'at least where there is enough and as good left in common for others';[54] and secondly, that it applies only to '[a]s much as any one can make use of to any advantage of life before it spoils'.[55] If ownership of what is created did follow automatically from self-ownership as ownership

---

[53] See Clark Wolf, 'Contemporary Property Rights: Lockean Provisos and the Interests of Future Generations' (1995) 105 *Ethics* 791.

[54] N. 6 above, ch. V, 27.

[55] *Ibid.*, ch. V, 31.

of fruit follows from ownership of a tree, why should it matter that there might not be enough and as good for others? If mixing labour leads to full-blooded ownership, why should the owner be answerable to others if he chooses to spoil what is his? The answer to these questions emerges if we recognize the independent role of the creation-without-wrong argument.

The background is a supposed state of nature in which the natural produce of the earth makes abundant provision for all the necessities of life. Nothing is scarce. Consequently, there is at this stage no property institution. No resource is the subject of trespassory rules. This negative state of affairs is all that is entailed by the earth's being 'given to mankind in common'.[56] The relationship of men *vis-à-vis* one another as respects the earth is—in terms of the distinctions we discussed in Chapter 7—one of 'negative community' rather than joint ownership or communitarian property.

Along comes a labourer who gathers acorns or apples, or draws water in a pitcher, or encloses and cultivates a parcel of land. Why should anyone, in this abundant world, want to take the gathering, or the pitcher, or the enclosed parcel, away from him, such that there may be a case for trespassory rules banning them from doing so? The answer is that the labourer has now created something which is scarce, something which more people may want to make use of than they simultaneously can. That is, the labourer has created an item of social wealth which he may wish to claim as his private wealth by the institution of trespassory rules. Such creative acts 'put a distinction' between the product and what remains in common,[57] precisely to the extent that labour augments both use-value and exchange-value.[58]

In creating this new item of social wealth and claiming it as his own, did the labourer wrong anybody? 'Was it a robbery thus to assume to himself what belonged to all in common?'[59] Locke's answer is no, provided the two limitations were observed. If there is 'enough and as good' left, no-one is harmed by the labourer's creative activity. The argument applies even to the enclosure of land, supposing there to be an abundance. 'Nor was this appropriation of any parcel of land, by improving it, any prejudice to any other man, since there was still enough and as good left.'[60]

The no-spoliation limitation serves, primarily, as a guarantee underpinning the enough-and-as-good limitation. So long as in the state of nature (before the invention of money) labourers only engross what they can themselves use without spoiling, there will, given natural abundance, always be enough and as good for others. 'The measure of property nature has well set by the extent of men's labour and the convenience of life. . . . This measure did confine every man's possession to a very moderate proportion, and such as he might appropriate to himself without injury to anybody.'[61]

No-spoliation seems to have served a secondary role, as a kind of natural

[56] N. 6 above, ch. V, 25.   [57] *Ibid.*, ch. V, 28.   [58] *Ibid.*, ch. V, 41–4.
[59] *Ibid.*, ch. V, 28.   [60] *Ibid.*, ch. V, 33.   [61] *Ibid.*, ch. V, 36.

property-limitation rule (derived, perhaps, from a divine ordination about good stewardship). The interest acquired by the Lockean creator lies well up the ownership spectrum. It comprises control-powers over uses made by his dependants and others together with powers of transmission by way of gift or barter and, once money is introduced, sale.[62] However, his use-privileges are not unlimited. Since the new item is of value to others, he is not to allow it to go to waste on pain of forfeiture.[63]

(b) Mill's Version

John Stuart Mill, as we have seen, made no use of the self-ownership argument. He did, however, suppose that what we have called the 'creation-without-wrong' argument is applicable to all items which could justly be the subject of private property, except land. Not that Mill argued for a natural property right as such. A property institution was a historically-evolved social arrangement. It could be justified only if, properly reformed, it would lead to a greater amount of human liberty and spontaneity than would a system under which all resources were subjected to a regime of communal use. On that question, Mill said, the jury of history was still out.[64]

Nevertheless, if one did opt for a system of private property, there was a difference between land and all other resources. The fundamental justification for the institution was 'the right of producers to what they themselves have produced'.[65] That foundation principle was inapplicable to 'the raw material of the earth'.[66] No man made the land, and appropriation of it by some necessarily left others bereft of what was 'the original inheritance of the whole species'.[67]

Locke also believed that the land had been given to mankind in common. He nevertheless takes the creation-without-wrong argument to apply to land because he treats an improved parcel of land as a new item of social wealth and because he locates the argument against the background of natural abundance. A parcel of land which someone had enclosed and improved was something which 'another had no title to, nor could without injury take from him'.[68]

Mill supposed that the creation-without-wrong argument applied, not in some notional state of abundance, but in the real world of scarcity. That being so, it could not hold for land. Ownership-interests in land, according to Mill, were justifiable only on the basis of the creator-incentive instrumental argument to which we turn later.[69] 'When private property in land is not expedient, it is unjust.'[70]

Why is the position different with every other item of social wealth?

---

[62] *Ibid.*, ch. V, 46–8.   [63] *Ibid.*, ch. V, 36–7.   [64] N. 22 above, bk. 2, ch. 1, sect. 3.
[65] *Ibid.*, 215.   [66] *Ibid.*, 227.   [67] *Ibid.*, 230.   [68] N. 6 above, ch. V, 32.
[69] See Ch. 15, sect. (iii)(c) below.   [70] N. 22 above, 230.

Should not Mill, an avowed adherent of utilitarianism, have required private ownership of all resources to be justified on the same instrumental basis? He does not. He supposes that, provided one adopts the institution of private property at all, producers have what amounts to a natural right to what they produce. His reason is the creation-without-wrong argument. He writes of all resources other than land: 'It is no hardship to any one, to be excluded from what others have produced: they were not bound to produce it for his use, and he loses nothing by not sharing in what otherwise would not have existed at all.'[71]

(c) Scope of the Argument

The creation-without-wrong argument might be dismissed out of hand on the ground that, in real life, there is no scope for it. Even granted that it would be abstractly sound in a Lockean state of nature, what possible application could it have today in an over-populated and under-resourced world? Should Locke not be dismissed as an irrelevant acorns-under-the-tree speculator?

Locke seems to have assumed that there would be scope for the argument in the context of European colonization of America.[72] We shall question that assumption when we come to consider first occupancy.[73]

There is one important context in which the argument (if sound) would apply, even if abundance is a necessary pre-condition. It concerns intellectual property, like the newly invented game posited in the rhetorical question at the beginning of this section. The ideas available for appropriation are potentially infinite.[74] In their case we are in what amounts to a Lockean state of nature. One who seeks to appropriate a copyright or patent for himself does leave 'enough and as good' for others.

In any case, is it necessary to tie the creation-without-wrong argument to conditions of abundance? The crucial point is that the creator of a new item of social wealth must, in creating it, have committed no wrong to others. Locke purported to demonstrate absence of wrong in his notional state of nature with the enough-and-as-good and no-spoliation limitations. May it not be demonstrated in other ways?

If an artist creates a sculpture out of the sand and shells on the seashore, he wrongs no-one because these things are abundant. If he does the same out of materials which are not literally abundant but which he has purchased from a willing seller, is it not also the case that, in creating, he has done no-one any wrong? Mill seems to have assumed that manufacture in general

---

[71] N. 22 above, 230.   [72] N. 6 above, ch. V, 36, 46, 48, 50.
[73] See Ch. 12, sect. (i)(b) below.
[74] See Justin Hughes, 'The Philosophy of Intellectual Property' (1988) 77 *Geo. LJ* 287, at 297–330.

could be looked on in the same light, so that the creation-without-wrong argument held for all resources except 'the raw material of the earth'.[75]

Various kinds of objection may be taken to so wide an application of the argument. For one thing, how is one to be sure that a particular holding of produced and transmitted wealth did not entail, at some stage of its creation, the appropriation of some part of 'the raw material of the earth'? Manufacture requires minerals or the vegetable products of the soil. Hence, the categorical contrast between land and everything else does not fit the terms of the argument. More importantly, some 'wrong' or other may have interposed itself in the production and transmission process. Mill himself is obliged to concede that the institution of private property cannot dispense with titles by prescription where that which was once produced by A was wrongfully taken by B.[76]

We have seen that Nozick invokes the liberal version of the self-ownership argument, backwards, as a critique of redistributive taxation. However, in advancing his own 'entitlement' theory of justice, Nozick appeals to the creation-without-wrong argument. His theory comprises three elements: original just acquisition; just transfers; and rectification, should any holdings be unjust.[77] The justice in holdings to which the theory gives rise is, he says, *historical*.[78] Hence he has to show how a natural right to ownership, carrying unlimited powers of transmission, might have arisen. If there were no such natural right, his theory would reduce to the purely social-conventional basis for property institutions discussed in Chapter 16 of this book; and rectification would come about only if title had been acquired in some way contrary to the particular conventions of a society. If original acquisition by natural right is possible, then rectification ought, in principle, to be available wherever historical titles do not conform to the natural-right argument. (Murray Rothbard argues that there can only be rectification if the heirs of the victims of unjust expropriation are identifiable so that, whereas in South America land ought to be handed over to the peasantry without compensation being paid to the successors of the *conquistadores*, land titles in North America are secure. That is (it seems) because, in North America, the colonial expropriators committed genocide so efficiently that no heirs of the original just owners can be identified.[79])

Nozick contends that Locke's enough-and-as-good proviso may be stated in such a way as to yield what he is looking for: original just acquisition. So long as the appropriation did not (and continues not to) make other people worse off, all things considered, than they would have been had it not

---

[75] N. 22 above, 227. [76] *Ibid.* bk. 2, ch. 2, sect. 2.
[77] Nozick, n. 8 above, 150–2 [78] *Ibid.*, 153.
[79] Murray N. Rothbard, 'Justice and Property Rights', in Samuel L. Blumenfeld (ed.), *Property in a Humane Economy* (Open Court, 1974), 101, at 115–20. Rothbard adopts the liberal version of the self-ownership argument and commits the 'if I am not a slave I must own myself' *non sequitur* discussed in the last section—*ibid.*, 106–15.

occurred (or were it not still insisted on), then the appropriation is just; and in making this comparison one may take into account all the familiar incentive and market-instrumental advantages of private property institutions.[80]

Locke, Mill, and Nozick all posit individual appropriators. Perhaps the scope of the creation-without-wrong argument is drastically reduced by the social character of labour. Lockean critics have suggested that, even in his notional state of nature, we are not confronted by isolated individuals toiling on their own. Six words in the fifth chapter of his *Second Treatise* are said to give the game away. That which, when removed from the common, becomes my property includes 'the turfs my servant has cut'.[81] In fact, the context of this observation refers, not to the state of nature, but to 'commons which remain so by compact'; and the point seems merely to be that even joint ownership of land must contemplate individual consumption and therefore some kinds of individual appropriation. One cannot deduce that in the state of nature, where original titles are supposed to have emerged, Locke was envisaging master/servant relationships or any other social basis of productive labour.

However that may be, in the real world productive labour is (and doubtless always has been) social, for the most part, in two respects. Most productive work is not carried on by isolated individuals; and, even when it is, the materials upon which it operates are not the spontaneous gift of nature, but rather the product of other people's labour. It was upon the social character of labour that, as we shall see, Proudhon founded his argument that all men are entitled to arithmetically equal shares in all accretions to social wealth.[82]

Thus, even if the creation-without-wrong argument is sound at root, we would have to examine details of institutional design in order, for example, to identify some corporate entity as the creator of something, and all the conditions of labouring and supply transactions to ensure that creation is not accompanied by 'wrong'.

(d) The Fatal Flaw

Creation-without-wrong, as an abstract argument for a natural property right, suffers from the following fatal flaw. It presupposes a unilateral power to create new trespassory obligations. It asks us to accept that if a person (1) creates a new item of social wealth, and (2) wrongs no-one in doing so, it follows that (3) he ought to be accorded ownership of that new item. However, he can only be owner if new trespassory obligations are brought into existence protecting his ownership interest. If the interest were full-blooded

---

[80] Nozick, n. 8 above, 175–82.
[81] N. 6 above, ch. V, 28. For reflections on these words, see C. B. MacPherson, n. 46 above, ch. 5.
[82] See Ch. 16, sect. (i)(a) below.

ownership there would need to be a set of timeless trespassory obligations sufficient to enable the owner and his successors in title to exercise transmission powers for the indefinite future. If the item is really new, there would need to be novel trespassory obligations even if (3) entailed only mere property. How can one man's acting non-wrongfully, of itself, create new potential wrongs in others? (3) simply does not follow from (1) and (2).

The flaw can be demonstrated by the following scenario set in one of the imaginary societies discussed in Chapter 2. In Forest Land there were no trespassory rules and consequently no property institution. In Wood Land mere property, something at the bottom of the ownership spectrum, was accorded to a tool-maker and it was protected by trespassory rules. Let us now imagine a traveller from Forest Land to Wood Land, who returns to his own society having learned two things which he communicates to his fellow tribesmen. First, that it is possible to make tools, with scarcity value, out of stones which have none. Secondly, that there is such a thing as a property institution. He now proposes to the others that, if any member of Forest Land does succeed in making a tool, its use and exploitation ought, in justice, to be protected by trespassory rules.

Let us suppose that he makes no appeal to desert or incentive, but deploys only the following argument: '[s]tones are abundant. We neither have, nor should have, trespassory rules prohibiting any use of them. If I make a tool out of a stone, I do no wrong to anyone; therefore, trespassory rules ought to be instituted granting me privileged use and exploitation of the tool.'

The Forest Land tribesmen may answer their returning member: '[o]f course, no-one can complain if you turn a worthless stone into a useful tool. But it does not follow from that alone that you are entitled to stop any of the rest of us using it.'

Granted that a product would not have existed at all if X had not created it, it does not follow, as Mill supposed it did, that '[i]t is no hardship to anyone to be excluded' from the product. It must be of potential use to others, or trespassory obligations protecting X's use-privileges and con-trolled-powers would not be needed.

Creation-without-wrong cannot serve as an original condition of title even for ideational entities. Intellectual property, as we have seen, requires the initiation of artificial scarcity in ideas introduced into the public domain through the imposition of new trespassory rules.[83] Its justification must be sought elsewhere.[84]

(e) The Fruits Doctrine

The creation-without-wrong argument for a natural property right, standing alone, fails as completely as does that from self-ownership. Unlike the latter,

---

[83] See Ch. 4, sect. (i) above.   [84] See Ch. 15, sect. (iii)(c)(2) below.

however, it can be combined with other arguments to yield property rights in special cases. Systems of property law embody, in one way or another, what we may call the 'fruits doctrine'. It assumes that if X owns R, he ought to be recognized as owner of any accretion to R or of anything into which R is transmuted. Creation-without-wrong serves as a partial justification for the fruits doctrine.

If justifiable trespassory rules are already in place protecting X's ownership of a resource and if X's creative activity consists in changing that resource into some new item, then by claiming that the ownership interest persists over what is created he does not purport to impose novel trespassory obligations. At most he concretizes, in a new form, trespassory obligations which already exist. Thus a painter who, for whatever reason, is regarded as justly owning his canvas and paints can, by virtue of the creation-without-wrong argument, claim to be the owner of the picture he paints. He who already rightly owns the seed and the ground in which he plants and tends it also owns the crop—provided always that management of the growing process itself involves no wrong to others.

Creation-without-wrong is insufficient to underpin all the ramifications of the fruits doctrine. Property institutions standardly confer upon owners any accretion in value, whether it arises from the owner's labour or not. Furthermore, one whose ownership of a resource is taken to be unquestioned will be recognized as owner of anything for which it is sold or exchanged, even, as we shall see, when the transaction was initially unauthorized.[85] The justification for such facets of the doctrine involves aspects of the property-freedom and incentive and market-instrumental arguments discussed in subsequent chapters of this book.

Creation-without-wrong, as a partial justification of the fruits doctrine, constitutes an important property-specific justice reason internal to the operation of property institutions. It nevertheless fails as a generalized argument for natural property rights because it entails a unilateral power in one person to impose new trespassory obligations on all other members of society. Such a power cannot flow from the mere non-wrongfulness of what the actor has done. It might be otherwise if we focus on the worthiness or worthwhileness of his creative labour. These matters we shall consider under the headings of Labour-desert[86] and Creator-incentives.[87]

(iv) LABOUR-DESERT

If a person by his labour confers benefit on others, he deserves to be rewarded with property.

---

[85] See Ch. 17, sect. (ii) below.   [86] See sect. (iv) below.
[87] See Ch. 15, sect. (iii)(c) below.

This is a statement, in its crudest form, of the labour-desert argument for a natural property right. Traces of it are to be found in both Locke and Mill. Locke adds to his other arguments the observation that 'he who appropriates land to himself by his labour does not lessen but increase the common stock of mankind'.[88] Mill, when proffering a general critique of contemporary property institutions rather than addressing himself specifically to the basis on which property rights should arise in different resources, makes passing references to the mismatch between meritorious work and reward.[89] In contrast, for some modern property theorists labour-desert is the core argument for founding just property claims on labour. Lawrence Becker contends that when a person produces something with the purpose of acquiring property in it and thereby confers benefit upon others, he deserves to receive property rights over the thing produced, provided that such rights are the only fitting reward for his labour and that they are not disproportionate to the benefit conferred.[90] Stephen Munzer maintains that those who engage in useful work have, *prima facie*, a just claim to property, based on desert, either in the form of ownership interests over what they produce, or in the form of monetary remuneration commensurate with their effort.[91]

Labour-desert arguments are natural rights arguments in the sense discussed at the beginning of this Chapter, since they focus on the actions of individuals and produce conclusions about what, in justice, is due to individuals. Can any version of the argument succeed, beginning only with the minimalist conception of justice set out in the last chapter? If so, what kind of property interest would it entail?

(a) Desert and Justice

Conceptions of desert are deployed within human interactions to invoke either beneficial or detrimental treatment on the basis of either human qualities or behaviour.[92] We are concerned only with rewards, and only with their alleged basis in labour. There have been cultures in which it has been supposed that a person ought to be accorded property merely by virtue of his intrinsic meritorious qualities or social position. Such a view is incompatible with natural equality (the first element of our minimalist conception of justice), since it assumes that preferential treatment is due to some merely on the ground that they are different kinds of human beings. It is doubtful whether anyone today would maintain that the intelligent or the beautiful ought to receive more simply because they are intelligent or beautiful.

---

[88] N. 6 above, ch. V, 37. [89] N. 22 above, bk. 2, ch. 1, sect. 3.

[90] Lawrence C. Becker, *Property Rights: Philosophic Foundations* (Routledge and Kegan Paul, 1977), 45–56.

[91] Stephen R. Munzer, *A Theory of Property* (CUP, 1990), 266–84.

[92] See generally Joel Feinberg, *Doing and Deserving* (Princeton UP, 1970), ch. 1; George Sherr, *Desert* (Princeton UP, 1987).

Conventional conceptions of justice witness to a widely shared consensus that desert is a distinct basis on which someone may found a claim to a special share in social wealth.[93] Such assumptions about desert relate, however, not to what talents people have, but to the use to which they put them. Desert is thus tied to labour.

It does not follow that talents are irrelevant. There are two reasons for alleging that a person who works deserves a reward. The first is that he has chosen to be industrious, whereas he might have been idle or less industrious. The second is that, through his work, he has achieved something which is worthy of admiration. The first ground is talent-independent—all who do their best have like desert claims. The second is not, since the talented are able, if they choose to make use of their talents, to produce achievements which the less talented cannot.

Both arguments appeal, on the one hand, to the moral relevance of autonomous choice and, on the other hand, to a conception of morally appropriate human intereaction. If people choose to engage in tasks which are of any value within the human scheme of things, they are in a morally-relevant different relationship *vis-à-vis* others from that which they would have been in had they chosen not to work. The morally appropriate reaction on the part of their fellows is 'reward'.

Three anti-desert arguments should be considered. The first derives from thoroughgoing determinism.[94] Just as being endowed with talents is a consequence of the genetic lottery, so too human endeavour is the product of forces which dictate so-called 'choice'. Therefore, neither talent nor the choice to labour should be the basis for moral differentiation. We are already committed to rejecting this argument by our espousal of the second element of our minimalist conception of justice—that autonomous choice, over some range of actions open to individuals, is of value to all human beings. The thorough-going determinist position excludes human agency from the moral agenda, but (as Kant argued) at the cost of putting an end to that agenda altogether. We cannot enter into any discussion about how people ought, in justice, to treat one another unless this position is put aside. If we engage in debates about the justice of institutions at all, determinism is irrelevant even were it true. We appear to make choices and we appear to debate.

The second anti-desert argument claims that every person ought to engage in valuable work to the best of his ability, so that 'reward' is inappropriate. A person may well see his own case in just this light. But for the rest of us, to withhold any kind of commendation on the ground that '[y]ou merely acted as you ought' would be an unattractive mode of human interaction. It would

---

[93] See Tony Honoré, *Making Law Bind* (Clarendon Press, 1987), 202–6; David Miller, *Social Justice* (Clarendon Press, 1976), 114–21.
[94] See Miller, n. 93 above, 95–102.

obliterate the moral difference between obligatory and supererogatory action. More importantly, it would presuppose a complete subservience of the individual's work-potential to the requirements of others. Only the most extreme form of communitarianism would accept such an ant-like denuding of individuality. The argument fails if we reject, as a moral starting-point for judging interaction, the view that the individual should employ his energies in all and only the ways which the community deems most valuable.

The third anti-desert argument claims that all desert considerations can be encompassed, without remainder, in the idea of a free market. Work has value only in the sense that, and to the extent that, others will pay for it to be done. There is no claim to merit beyond the claim to fulfilment of contractual undertakings. No further 'reward' is appropriate.[95]

We shall consider later the instrumental advantages of markets.[96] It will emerge that markets presuppose a distribution of wealth which, taken on their own, they cannot justify. It follows that the market-based anti-desert argument is entirely arbitrary in its insistence that the only choices governing labouring activities which ought to be valued are those which, by the happenstance of prior wealth-distribution, results in saleable commodities. It would have the consequence, for example, that a person who works selflessly to improve the lot of the disadvantaged deserves nothing if they are unable to pay for what he does.

The three anti-desert arguments are incompatible with the second element of our minimalist conception of justice, on the assumption that the individual's working activities come within the range of valued autonomous choice and that that range is not coterminous with marketable outcomes. Their rejection does not by itself, however, establish the soundness of desert claims in general, let alone of any particular desert claim. The second element holds only that autonomous choice is a value to those who make the choices. Whether choices over working activities are meritorious and whether, if they are, the appropriate response from fellow citizens is 'reward' cannot be settled independently of social convention. The conventional scale of values may accord merit to anything from the arduous intercessory prayers of a hermit to the discovery of a wonder drug. It may 'reward' merit with expressions of gratitude or acclaim, with honorific titles, or with property.

All desert claims are hostage to convention. Nevertheless, if the conventions are in place, they serve the purpose of marking society's recognition of the value of autonomous choice. They concretize that aspect of justice in relation to the labouring activities singled out as meritorious and reward-worthy. In that sense, desert claims constitute a derivative, but none the less important and distinct, facet of justice.

[95] See F. A. Hayek, *Law, Legislation and Liberty vol. 2: The Mirage of Social Justice* (Routledge and Kegan Paul, 1976), 70–3.　　　　　　　　[96] See Ch. 15, sect. (iii) below.

(b) Desert and Property

The labour-desert argument for property does not succeed in the abstract. It must invoke contingent convention. It cannot serve as the basis for a concrete natural property right. Even if it is accepted that some 'reward' is appropriate for labour, social convention may or may not include money or other property as the fitting recompense for the kind of work in question. If it does not, the abstract argument from desert is insufficient to establish that it should. Conversely, if it does, the abstract argument carries enough force to require that the convention be respected. If workers exert themselves to such effect that their work deserves recognition, and if convention dictates that appropriate recognition in such a context consists in more pay, it is no answer to suggest that we should give them a clap instead. In such a context pay, not applause, is the just reward for meritorious labour.

Where the matter is not settled by convention so that it is open to argument how desert should be rewarded, property is a particularly problematic candidate because of its distributional implications. There are no limits to the applause or titles of honour we might hand out. If one assumes a fixed quantum of social wealth—that is, of things and services which are scarce relative to global demands (or the monetary means of access to such things and services)—then allocating some portion of this totality to one person as his private wealth necessarily depletes the total available for allocation to others. Property, as a reward for meritorious labour, competes with other justice claims, such as need. Furthermore, desert claims compete with other desert claims, and no extra-conventional yardstick of comparison exists. Does a nurse deserve more pay than a dustman?

Problems of incommensurability may, at first sight, appear to be absent where what is at stake is not a claim to an allocation out of a fixed quantum of social wealth, but a claim to property arising from the labourer's own addition to social wealth. The Forest Land tool-making innovator might say: '[b]ut for me, this tool whose use is of value to all would not exist. As my fellow tribesmen you ought therefore, in justice, to reward me for my work in inventing and making it; and the only appropriate reward is that you should create trespassory rules according me ownership privileges and exploitation powers in respect of it.' His fellows might respond: '[a]s you are well aware, we have a conventional system of formal congratulations for meritorious work. That is a sufficient reward in this case.' In Wood Land, tool-makers are accorded mere property. Let us suppose that one of the reasons why this is done is because there the tribesmen regard property as a fitting reward for invention. Now a Woodlander who invents a new waterproof garment or creates an artistic artefact may be able to argue for new trespassory rules giving him property over these things because '[b]y our conventions, property is the appropriate reward for deserving labour.'

Conventional crystallization of the abstract desert argument is essential if desert through labour is to justify property; but, at least in these cases, it appears that distributional problems are out of the way.

The appearance is misleading. So soon as an item has been added to social wealth, competing demands arise. The tool would not be there but for the tool-maker's work. But it is there now. Others need to use it. Others, whose work has been valuable but not wealth-creating, have desert claims which might be satisfied by allocation of tool-use.

Similar distributional problems arise in real societies. If we suppose, for example, that the workers in a manufacturing industry have a desert claim to property in the product or its monetary equivalent, it does not follow that workers in a service industry do not have competing desert claims to the same product or monetary equivalent. More generally, as we shall see, all social wealth, however it arises, is the potential subject of 'justice costs', including the discharge of basic needs.

(c) The Shell of a Natural Property Right

The self-ownership and creation-without-wrong arguments, if they were sound, would have the advantage over labour-desert in that they would stand independently of social convention. However, as we have seen, the self-ownership argument is devoid of all normative force because of the spectacular *non sequitur* on which it depends and the creation-without-wrong argument can serve only in special cases where it would not have the effect of arming the creator with a unilateral power to impose novel obligations. Claims to property based on labour-desert are dependent on social convention both as determinative of when work is specially meritorious and also as determinative of the appropriate reward. Nevertheless, since it is the case that social conventions fulfilling both these functions are commonly to be found, labour-desert is, in practice, an important property-specific justice reason. Thus, labour-desert may be said to provide the shell of a natural right to property—a shell which, however, convention must fill.

Labour-desert could stand alone as the basis for distribution of social wealth only if two things were true. First, that there were in place conventions so specific and limited that one could say of every item of wealth that it was deserved by X and by no-one else (or by X and Y in certain proportions and by no-one else); and, secondly, that those same conventions denied all claims to share in social wealth other than those which arose from labour-desert. It is implausible to suppose that these conditions ever have been, or ever will be, met. Consequently, so far as large-scale questions of property-institutional design are concerned, labour-desert takes its place—an important place—among the 'mix' of property-specific justice reasons.

The upshot is that labour-desert serves better as a micro, rather than a macro, justification for property-allocation. If an enterprise has produced an accretion to social wealth and we confine our enquiry to the question of how, as between the members of the enterprise, the product should be distributed, convention may direct that reward is deserved proportionately to work and/or to achievement.[97] Such micro determinations are appealed to, for example, where wage-bargainers debate the just reward for higher productivity.

Labour-desert claims are sometimes invoked in the exercise by English courts of the jurisdiction to re-allocate property on divorce or death. Legislation empowers a divorce court to order periodical or lump sum payments and transfers of 'property'.[98] The factors to which the court is to have regard include: 'the contributions which each of the parties has made or is likely in the foreseeable future to make to the welfare of the family, including any contribution by looking after the home or caring for the family'.[99] Legislation requires the same factor to be taken into account when a court is deciding whether to override testamentary dispositions which fail to make 'reasonable financial provision' for spouses, former spouses, or (since 1996) persons who have been living for two years in the same household as the deceased 'as the husband or wife of the deceased'.[100]

In exercising these jurisdictions, courts are usually preoccupied with quantifying maintenance obligations. However, in the case of rich husbands, a court may award something going beyond that which is required to meet the housing and other needs of his divorced wife or his widow. In one case, for example, a childless couple had, through their joint efforts, built up a successful hotel business, ownership of which was vested in the husband. It was held in divorce proceedings that the share to be expropriated in favour of the wife should not be limited to that which she might need in order to make a fresh start, but should be measured by what she had earned through her exceptional contribution to the creation of the family assets.[101] In another case, a separated widow, who had worked towards the creation of her late husband's business, was awarded one half of his net estate (which the husband had sought to bequeath to Cambridge University), even though she already owned property (derived from her husband) sufficient to meet her present needs.[102]

It is open to question whether the courts have paid sufficient regard to desert claims arising merely from labour expended within the family home.

[97] Munzer appeals to the labour-desert argument in the context of the distribution of resources and control within a corporate enterprise—n. 91 above, 346–50.

[98] Matrimonial Causes Act 1973, ss. 23 and 24.

[99] Matrimonial Causes Act 1973, s. 25 (as substituted by s. 3 of the Matrimonial and Family Proceedings Act 1984).

[100] Inheritance (Provision for Family and Dependants) Act 1975, ss. 1(1) and 3(2) and (2A) (as amended by the Law Reform (Succession) Act 1995, s. 2).

[101] *Gojkovic v. Gojkovic* [1990] 2 All ER 84.

[102] *Re Bunning (decd.)* [1984] Ch. 480.

There may now be a settled social convention that a wife who has devoted her time to family care deserves, for that reason alone, a share in her divorced or deceased husband's property even if she already has enough resources of her own to meet all her needs. If so, the language of the statutes would provide ample warrant for the courts to take judicial notice of it.

In the case of unmarried cohabitees, there was before 1996 no legislative basis in English law for recognizing labour-desert claims.[103] Nor in current English law does any equitable doctrine enable the court to give effect to labour-desert claims as such.[104] Thus a female cohabitee has no standing to claim a share in her lover's property even if she has for many years devoted herself to domestic care of him or of their children.[105] Nevertheless, if there is evidence that the parties agreed to share beneficial ownership of a house and, in reliance on that understanding, the party in whom legal title is not vested performed services which the court deems to be out of the ordinary, the court will impose a constructive trust under which that party receives a share of the property to reflect that labour input. In one case, it was held that a woman who worked to improve a dilapidated dwelling, including wielding a fourteen-pound sledge hammer to break up concrete, was entitled to one quarter of the ownership.[106] In another case, a woman was held to be entitled to a half share of a bungalow purchased in her cohabitee's name because, following an understanding that beneficial ownership would be shared, she had lent her full support to business ventures carried out from the premises.[107]

The necessity for conventional crystallization and the significance of distributional implications entail that there can be no straightforward argument from labour-desert to full-blooded ownership, even where what is under consideration is an item of social wealth which someone has created. Never-

---

[103] The divorce jurisdiction did not apply. The Inheritance (Provision for Family and Dependants) Act 1975 empowered the court to expropriate part of a deceased's estate in favour of 'any person . . . who immediately before the death of the deceased was being maintained' by the deceased (s. 1(1)(e)). However, a person was to be treated as being maintained if the deceased was making a substantial contribution towards the reasonable needs of that person 'otherwise than for full valuable consideration' (s. 1(3)). Literally understood, the consequence was that the more an applicant does the less likely is his maintenance to have been provided otherwise than for full valuable consideration so that he is debarred from applying—*Re Wilkinson (decd.)* [1978] Fam. 22, *Re Beaumont (decd.)* [1980] Ch. 444, *Jelley* v. *Iliffe* [1981] Fam. 128. The CA eventually balked at this interpretation and refused to deny the claim of a woman who had lived with the deceased for several years and rendered him every loving care—*Bishop* v. *Plumley* [1991] 1 All ER 336. The law was amended by s. 2 of the Law Reform (Succession) Act 1995 to enable persons living in the same household as the deceased for two years as husband or wife to apply.

[104] *Pettitt* v. *Pettitt* [1970] AC 777; *Gissing* v. *Gissing* [1971] AC 886; *Lloyds Bank PLC* v. *Rossett* [1991] 1 AC 108.

[105] *Burns* v. *Burns* [1984] Ch. 317; *Combes* v. *Smith* [1986] 1 WLR 808; *Windeler* v. *Whitehall* [1990] FCR 268.

[106] *Eves* v. *Eves* [1975] 3 All ER 768.

[107] *Hammond* v. *Mitchell* [1992] 2 All ER 109.

theless, since desert claims constitute the shell of a natural property right, labour-desert has a proper place among the *pot pourri* of property-specific justice reasons. Its importance increases where what is at stake is the distribution among a limited class of persons of some asset—it being assumed that other claims have already been fully discharged, for example, by the imposition of appropriate property-limitation or tax-expropriation rules.

Labour-desert is the most significant survivor of this Chapter's analysis of natural property rights arising from labour. No one is ever entitled to an ownership interest in any resource simply upon the ground that he 'owns' himself. Only in very special circumstances are persons entitled to ownership interests in resources on the ground that those resources were created by them without wrongdoing anyone. But a person has a just claim to some portion of social wealth where, by convention, his work is valuable to others and where, by convention, he deserves a reward of that kind. We shall consider later whether, quite apart from natural right, there are instrumental reasons, in the form of creator-incentives, for rewarding labour with property.

12

Natural Property Rights and the Assault Analogy

We suggested at the beginning of the last chapter that natural rights are such rights as follow from the interaction between the requirements of just treatment and the facts of the world. The third element of our minimalist conception of justice, set out in Chapter 10, is the prohibition of unprovoked invasions of bodily integrity. Assaults on a human being are natural wrongs. Could it be the case that, by virtue of a relationship which has arisen between an individual or a group and some physical or ideational resource, any inter-meddling with that resource would, in practice, amount to an assault (or, at any rate, to a wrong of equivalent gravity)? If so, would it follow that, as regards that resource, the individual or group ought, in justice, to be accorded an ownership interest? Is it admissible to build, analogically, on the prohibition of invasions of bodily integrity to the point at which one has reached a natural property right? We shall consider that possibility in the context of three kinds of relationship to resources—first occupancy, personhood-constituting, and privacy.

(i) FIRST OCCUPANCY

The first occupant of a tangible resource ought to be regarded as its owner.

We mentioned in Chapter 5 (section vii) that English law recognizes prior possession as an original condition of title in the case of both chattels and land. If I find a chattel and no-one comes forward with a title subsisting prior to my finding, I may claim full-blooded ownership of it. If I enter on to land in the assumed character of owner and no-one can show a prior title, I may assert against all subsequent comers to the land a fee simple estate (which carries with it something close to full-blooded ownership). Similar provisions are to be found in most systems of positive law; and, in public international law, prior effective and continuous display of State authority over territory has been accepted as a sufficient basis for a claim to sovereignty.[1]

Do such provisions serve to concretize a requirement of just treatment, such

---

[1] Ian Brownlie, *Principles of Public International Law* (4th edn., Clarendon Press, 1990), 141–4.

as that set out at the beginning of this section? We shall see that they do not, at least in the case of individuals—the position with communitarian groups is more complicated. Justification for such provisions of positive law has to be sought elsewhere

(a) Individuals

From classical times there has been a juristic tendency to clothe the law's reliance on first occupancy as a root of title with the dress of natural right.[2] The (generally unarticulated) driving force of the argument is the analogy with assault. If I am there already, it is a manifest wrong for some stranger to come along and push me out just as would be any other attack on my person; so I have a just claim to remain in possession of that which I have first occupied.

Much-cited in the literature on first occupancy are references by Cicero and Seneca to the situation where seats at a theatre are allocated on a first-come basis.[3] Contrast with these citations the following anonymous anecdote. A visitor from the South of England to a cricket match in Yorkshire takes an unoccupied seat and leaves his top hat on it while he goes in search of refreshments. On his return he finds the seat occupied by a local spectator. To his protest that he has taken the seat, the local man responds: 'Nay, lad, up here it's bums that keep seats, not hats!'

Bodily turfing someone out of the place or the home which he has occupied, or snatching from him a chattel which he has taken up, is an assault and hence, *prima facie*, a natural wrong. He has a correlative right that such things be not done to him. Whether he has any further claim-rights against intermeddling with assets which he has occupied, where such intermeddling does not literally involve attacks on his person, depends entirely on the applicable legal and social conventions. They must stipulate both what conduct is sufficient to constitute first occupancy and also what perimeter of trespassory rules in respect of the thing occupied, going beyond prohibition of personal violence, is to be accepted.

It is manifest that a first occupant cannot, by extension of the assault analogy, assert full-blooded ownership, for that would entail the imposition on the rest of the world of trespassory rules subsisting in favour of anyone to whom he chose to transmit what he had occupied. Blackstone, for example, argued that, in the state of nature, someone who first occupied a determined spot, for rest, shade, or the like.

acquired therein a kind of transient property, that lasted so long as he was using it, and no longer: . . . a sort of ownership, from which it would have been unjust, and

---

[2] See Lawrence C. Becker, *Property Rights: Philosophic Foundations* (Routledge and Kegan Paul, 1977), ch. 3.

[3] Cicero, *De Finibus*, iii., xx., 67. Seneca, *De Beneficiis*, vii., xii., 3–4.

contrary to the law of nature, to have driven him by force: but the instant that he quitted the use or occupation of it, another might seize it, without injustice.[4]

The attributes of full-blooded ownership derived (Blackstone insisted) from positive law, not from natural justice. Peace and order required that most things should be in someone's ownership, and that the present owner should be free to alienate at his pleasure either *inter vivos* or on death. All particular questions of title and transmission could be settled only by convention—in the case of England, by those universal customs embodied in the common law. Title on the basis of mere occupancy was incorporated into the common law and other systems only as a last resort.[5]

Blackstone appears to concede that first occupancy might entail what we have called 'mere property'. Even this is questionable. As we saw in Chapter 8 (section i) claim-rights are not intrinsic to ownership interests. To the extent that a first occupant has a right correlating with a duty imposed by some trespassory rule, nothing follows as to the use-privileges and control-powers which the occupant ought to be conceded over the thing occupied. No-one may evict him where eviction cannot be accomplished without attacking his body. It is a distinct question whether his permitted exploitation of the thing occupied should be mediated through an organizing idea which confers on him an open-ended set of privileges and powers—an ownership interest. In the hallowed theatre-seats analogy, the first occupant may have a just claim that he should not be turned out; but it is implausible to suppose that he can defend uses made of the seat, or concessions of uses granted to others, on the basis that, even for a time, the seat is open-endedly his thing.

The social or legal conventions which confer ownership interests on first occupants may be supportable in terms of property-specific justice reasons which have nothing to do with natural right. If, for example, the property-freedom and market-instrumental arguments yet to be discussed require that someone be accorded full-blooded ownership of some resource, and if (as occupant) X has at least the right that he be not evicted from the resource, and if no other just basis of title is forthcoming, then X should be granted full-blooded ownership *faute de mieux*. In the upshot, X is the recipient of a distributional windfall.

A passenger who found a lost gold bracelet in the executive lounge at an airport has been held entitled to keep the proceeds of its sale.[6] The rule that finders are entitled against all the world if the true owner is unknown was said to be obviously right as a general proposition 'for otherwise lost property would be subject to a free-for-all in which the physically weakest would go to the wall'.[7] Similarly, a person may show no other title to a parcel of land than

[4] Sir William Blackstone, *Commentaries on the Laws of England* (16th edn., J. Butterworth and Son, 1825), bk. 2, 3.
[5] *Ibid*. bk. 3, 168.   [6] *Parker* v. *British Airways Board* [1982] QB 1004.
[7] *Ibid*. 1009, *per* Donaldson LJ.

that he and his forebears have been farming it. That may be enough to make him rich if it turns out that planning permission over the plot will be granted for housing development. In such a context, far from property-limitation rules impinging on natural right (in the way envisaged at the beginning of the last chapter), their absence confers windfall wealth. (The windfall element is even more blatant where, for the sake of achieving orderly title conditions, property institutions accord ownership to someone who has acted as owner for a pre-scribed period even though it is established that there was someone else who could have asserted a prior title. In English law, six years is enough for chattels, twelve years' 'adverse possession' for land.)[8]

(b) Communities

The assault analogy for a natural property right based on first occupancy carries more force where the occupant is a community rather than an indi-vidual. It may be argued that artefacts closely identified with the cultural identity of a particular community, which were taken from it in the past, ought now to be restored and vested in some agency representing the community, on the ground that, whether or not the taking was warranted by positive law, it constituted a natural wrong to the community. The analogy is much stronger in the case of land. If a community is in occupation of a territory the use of which is an essential part of its economic survival, incompatible uses by new-comers constitute an attack upon its collective integrity. The community may not be able to survive at all if the intrusion goes unchecked. Such a community is as entitled to insist upon trespassory rules prohibiting such incompatible uses as is an individual to call for bans on life-threatening attacks. It is not the accident of earlier arrival which makes intrusion a wrong, but the rupture in present usage. Occupancy must be continuous as well as prior to warrant protection.

As we saw in the last chapter, Locke appears to have assumed that the creation-without-wrong argument applied to European colonization in Amer-ica. If a settler turned a tract of the abundant American wilderness into a cultivated plot, he ought to be accorded property in it. Where, however, an aboriginal population was, prior to colonization, making such collective use of a territory as would be incompatible with the use to which a colonizer wished to put it, colonization constituted a 'wrong' so that Locke's assumption was unwarranted. It is unclear whether, according to the rules of public inter-national law accepted at the time when European colonization began, mere 'discovery', as distinct from the exercise of effective State jurisdiction, con-ferred sovereignty.[9] In any event, acquisition of sovereignty in accordance with

---

[8] Limitation Act 1980, ss. 3, 15(1), 17.

[9] See F. A. F. Von Der Heydte, 'Discovery, Symbolic Annexation and Virtual Effective-ness in International Law' (1935) 29 *Am. J. of Int. Law* 448; I. Brownlie, n. 1 above, 146–9.

those rules merely establishes that the colonizers were not infringing the conventions of other European States. It does not affect the argument that disruptive colonization was, by analogy with assault, trespassory as a matter of justice. As between the aboriginal groups and the colonizers, there was no 'abundant' wilderness.

If it is granted that primitive peoples could justly demand that they be left in peace, does it follow that their first occupancy entailed a natural right to ownership of their territory or any part of it? In so far as colonists have invoked considerations of justice at all, they have done so by postulating a negative answer to this question. In whatever terms they conceived of their relationship to the land they occupied, primitive peoples deployed no 'ownership' notions comparable to those to be found in modern property institutions. Consequently, so it has been maintained, ouster could not amount to 'expropriation'.

The question of the relationship between European colonizers and native Americans as to ownership of land was tackled in 1823 by the Supreme Court of the United States in the celebrated case of *Johnson* v. *M'Intosh*.[10] In that case the plaintiffs claimed title to land by virtue of private sales made by Indian tribes. It was not disputed that the tribes had been in exclusive occupation of the land at the time of sale. Subsequently, certain portions of the land in dispute had been sold by the United States Government to the defendant.

The court held that the plaintiffs could not succeed in any event because colonial law in force at the relevant time prohibited purchases of Indian land by private individuals. Two more far-reaching arguments were advanced on behalf of the defendant. First, by the established custom of European nations, absolute title to land in America vested in the various colonizing governments by right of discovery and conquest. Secondly, by natural law, the land was open to appropriation by individual colonists because the native peoples merely roamed over it without appropriating it, so that the land, just like the sea, was common property (as writers such as Grotius and Locke had demonstrated[11]).

Chief Justice Marshall, delivering the judgment of the court, found for the defendant on the first ground. The uniform practice of European States had indeed been to allocate title to land in America amongst themselves according to the principle of discovery and conquest. This principle had been adopted into British colonial law and subsequently into American law. The effect of the principle was that, first the Crown and then the governments of the various American states and of the United States, had acquired absolute title to the soil and could by grant transfer that title to individuals. Native tribes had but a mere 'right of occupancy' which the colonizing government and its successors could terminate at any time. He was much more dubious about the defendant's alternative natural-law argument.

We will not enter into the controversy, wheher agriculturalist, merchants, and manufacturers, have a right, on abstract principles, to expel hunters from the

---

[10] 21 US 8 Wheat 543 (1823).   [11] *Ibid.* 569–70.

territory they possess, or to contract their limits. Conquest gives a title which the courts of the conqueror cannot deny, whatever the private and speculative opinions of individuals may be, respecting the original justice of the claim which has been successfully asserted.[12]

The most that could be said, in his view, on behalf of the colonizers in terms of justice was that the only alternative to expelling the natives from their lands was not to colonize at all. In the case of conquests achieved over civilized populations, sovereignty could be asserted while their property rights were respected. That was not possible in the case of native Americans, owing to their warlike dispositions.

To leave them in possession of their country was to leave the country a wilderness; to govern them as a distinct people was impossible, because they were as brave and as high spirited as they were fierce, and were ready to repel by arms every attempt on their independence.[13]

As late as 1955, the Supreme Court of the United States has held that rights of native peoples to the land they inhabit do not amount to 'property' protected by the Fifth Amendment to the Constitution, which prohibits the taking of property except for public purposes.[14] In other jurisdictions where the common law has been introduced following upon colonization, the principle of acquisition of title by discovery and conquest has been combined with the doctrine of tenure, whereby all estates in land are held of the Crown, to justify the Crown's exclusive right to confer title.[15] Aboriginal land rights have received varying degrees of recognition, whether by virtue of customary law, treaty, legislation, Crown proclamation, or the Crown's fiduciary duty towards aboriginal peoples.[16]

The recent decision of the High Court of Australia in *Mabo* v. *Queensland*,[17] to which reference was made in Chapter 7 (section ii), has gone furthest in this respect. By a six to one majority the court rejected the view (embodied in Australian case law for the past 150 years) that the Crown had acquired beneficial ownership of all land in Australia when it obtained sovereignty. Such an understanding of the common law failed to recognize the fact that, prior to the arrival of Europeans, the territory of the Australian continent was occupied by distinct aboriginal tribes; and it failed to draw the conclusions which, as a matter of justice, flowed from that fact. The court ruled that the radical title acquired by the Crown on settlement was burdened with what has here been called the 'communitarian property' of any group which was already in

---

[12] 21 US 8 Wheat 543 (1823), n. 10 above, 588.   [13] *Ibid.* 590.

[14] *Tee-Hit-Ton Indians* v. *United States*, 348 US 272 (1955).

[15] *The Queen* v. *Symonds* (1847) [1840–1932] NZPC 387; *Milirrpum* v. *Nabalco Pty* (1971) 17 FLR 141; *Re Paulette* (1975) 63 DLR (3d) 1.

[16] *St Catherine's Mill Co.* v. *The Queen* (1888) 14 App. Cas. 46; *Re Ninety-Mile Beach* [1963] NZLR 461; *Calder* v. *A.-G. of B.C.* [1973] SCR 313; *Guerin* v. *The Queen* [1984] 2 SCR 335.

[17] *Mabo* v. *State of Queensland (No 2)* (1992) 175 CLR 1.

occupation for so long as it remained in occupation.[18] As we noted in Chapter 7, the Mabo court did not accept the contention that first occupancy conferred an ordinary transferable fee simple estate on the members of an aboriginal tribe as individual joint tenants. Should they have done so? The answer to that question would clearly be yes, if one accepted as universally applicable the market-instrumental argument for full-blooded ownership. On that assumption, aboriginal first occupants ought to be introduced into the system of private property by conferring (or indeed imposing) on them, as a group of individuals, full-blooded ownership of the land they occupy.[19] There would be a windfall element in that, for example, a group of individuals would be able to cash in on mineral rights, by virtue of the fact that their ancestors had once hunted and gathered on the ground. But it would be a windfall of the same kind that accrues whenever a person has occupied land for some limited purpose and thereby acquires a title which enables him to reap the development value of the land.

If, however, one supposes that preservation of a traditional way of life is a goal to be fostered at the expense of such economic consequentialist considerations, then justice is done by protection of existing community-occupancy with the details of individual privileges and powers reflecting, so far as may be in the modern world, their traditional significance for the group —that is, by recognizing communitarian property. Thus first occupancy, as such, carries (even in the case of communities) a natural right to protection, not to exploitative ownership.

Supposing, by a flight of historical fancy, one imagines these competing arguments being pressed at the commencement of European colonization before a court empowered to render all that justice required. It would have been obliged to gaze into its crystal ball and decide whether the future welfare of the inhabitants would be best served by merely throwing trespassory protection around their communitarian property, or whether, instead, they should be told that they were full owners, free to sell their birthright at whatever price the market would bear. In fact, economic progress was invoked, along with the other benefits of 'civilization', as a ploy for justifying denial of any protection. Consider the second, natural-law argument advanced for the defendant in

---

[18] The majority of the Court were divided on one important question of defeasibility. Mason CJ and Brennan and McHugh JJ held that, as an incident of its radical title, the Crown could extinguish native title unilaterally by an inconsistent grant of an estate to a third party. Deane, Gaudron, and Toohey JJ, on the other hand, held that such grants by the Crown would be wrongful and in principle compensable unless clearly authorized by legislation. They nevertheless accepted that such 'wrongful' exercises of power by the Crown had been effective to create individual estates throughout the continent, and that claims to compensation would, in the vast majority of cases, have long since been barred by limitation. Legislation has since been enacted establishing a tribunal for the resolution of native title issues—Native Title Act 1993.

[19] We leave aside technical problems that might be encountered concerning the devolution of joint tenancy interests in the case of an unincorporated association constituted by the entire membership of a tribe.

Johnson v. *M'Intosh*. It amounted to claiming that, since the native inhabitants were too uncivilized to put a territory over which they roamed to good
economic use, it was open for grabs by those colonists who could. The
retrospective judgment on the colonization process must be the same as that
implicit in Chief Justice Marshall's response to this argument. The process
inevitably constituted a wrong to the natives since settlement could not but
disrupt existing uses. This injustice has, nevertheless, been incorporated into
the positive law of the jurisdictions established by the colonizers and their
successors as the foundation of title to property in land. Hobbes, rather than
Locke, presents a truer picture of the basis of title in this context.

(ii) PERSONHOOD-CONSTITUTING

Where someone constitutes his personhood, in part, by incorporating a thing
into himself, he ought to be regarded as owner of that thing.

The above-stated basis for a natural property right has acquired some prov-
enance in the history of speculative metaphysical thought,[20] although it has
very little counterpart in the day-to-day operation of modern property institutions. It builds on the assault analogy in the following way. Respect for individual personhood must underlie the universal ban on invasions of bodily
integrity (the third element of our minimalist conception of justice). If a
person has incorporated something into himself, such respect will be fully
manifested only if comparable trespassory obligations are recognized as to
the thing incorporated. Furthermore, the incorporator should be accorded an
ownership interest over the thing by analogy to the use-privileges and control-
powers over a person's body which, as we saw in the last chapter, follow from
the bodily-use freedom principle.[21]

The present topic must be distinguished from two other arguments yet to be
considered. One appeals to the inherent qualities of property institutions in
making available a range of autonomous choices which would not exist without them.[22] Another appeals to the instrumental value of property in securing
independence.[23] Either type can be described as connected with a conception
of human fulfilment and thus as a 'personhood' argument. (The Hegelian
property-freedom argument discussed in the next chapter is frequently so
termed.) However, it has to be independently established that intrinsic property freedoms, or the independence which the possession of wealth can bring,
are, all things considered, a desirable feature of human flourishing. The present argument, in contrast, takes personhood-constituting incorporation as a

---

[20] It has even been suggested that Locke's theory can be understood in this way—see
Karl Olivecrona, 'Locke's Theory of Appropriation' (1974) 24 *Philosophical Quarterly* 222.
[21] See Samuel C. Wheeler III, 'Natural Property Rights as Body Rights' (1980) 14 *Nous*
171.
[22] See Ch. 13 below.   [23] See Ch. 15, sect. (iv) below.

datum of experience, interaction with which of the formal and substantive requirements of just treatment yields a property right. As Margaret Radin puts it:

once we admit that a person can be bound up with an external 'thing' in some constitutive sense, we can argue that by virtue of this connection the person should be accorded broad liberty with respect to control over that thing. . . . Personhood is the basic concept, not liberty.[24]

T. H. Green begins his discussion of the rationale of property with just such an invocation of a natural property right, based on personhood-constituting.[25] He says that historical enquiry about the circumstances in which appropriation of different things in different societies has arisen '. . . cannot take the place of a metaphysical or psychological analysis of the conditions on the part of the appropriating subject implied in the fact that he does such a thing as appropriate'.[26] Appropriation

implies the conception of himself on the part of the appropriator as a permanent subject for whose use, as instruments of satisfaction and expression, he takes and fashions certain external things, certain things external to his bodily members. These things, so taken and fashioned, cease to be external as they were before. They become a sort of extension of the man's organs, the constant apparatus through which he gives reality to his ideas and wishes.[27]

Recognition of such self-constituting appropriation is then accorded by society on the same basis that it accords recognition of personal integrity. All have a mutual interest in each being secured by appropriate restraints in the exercise of a free life, and the same applies as to what each has incorporated into himself.

And just as the recognized interest of a society constitutes for each member of it a right to free life, just as it makes each conceive of such life on the part of himself and his neighbour as what should be, and thus forms the basis of a restraining custom which secures it for each, so it constitutes the right to the instruments of such life, making each regard the possession of them by the other as for the common good, and thus through the medium first of custom, then of law, securing them to each.[28]

A successful invocation of the personhood-constituting argument would not yield full-blooded ownership. In particular, it appears incompatible with freedom to transmit. Such a power entails that the owner places the transferee within the same protecting perimeter of trespassory rules which applied to him. If I suppose that my intimate chattels or my home are part of me, that

[24] Margaret Jane Radin, 'Property and Personhood' (1982) 34 *Stan. LR* 957, 960.
[25] Thomas Hill Green, *Lectures on the Principles of Political Obligation*, reprinted from *Green's Philosophical Works* (Longman, Greens and Co., 1931), ii, sect. N.
[26] *Ibid.* 211–12.   [27] *Ibid.* 213–14.   [28] *Ibid.* 216–17.

may support my claim that I alone should say who is to use the chattels or enter the home, just as only I can authorize anyone to make use of my body. But it would surely be paradoxical if, because these things are part of me, I assert that they would also be part of him to whom I sell them or give them away.

Yet Green proceeds to argue for a right to full-blooded ownership, applicable to all items of wealth and carrying an unlimited power of accumulation and unfettered transmission powers. His theory, he says, 'logically necessitates freedom both in trading and in the disposition of his property by the owner'.[29] How can that be true of things which became 'a sort of extension of the man's organs, the constant apparatus through which he gives reality to his ideas and wishes'? The truth is that Green has moved—unwittingly as it seems—from an argument based on personhood-constituting (what I have taken into myself deserves the same universal recognition as does my person), to an instrumental argument (full-blooded ownership is required for moral independence). The latter argument is discussed later in this book.[30]

What scope might the personhood-constituting argument for a natural property right have in modern societies? To answer that question we must descend from Green's metaphysics to psychological generalizations and, at that level, distinguish between self-constitution and self-expression. A person may express his distinct individuality by his actions *vis-à-vis* some tangible or ideational entity. He may decorate a house in a way peculiar to his taste, or create a poem peculiar to his vision. He may then view the thing as imprinted with his personality, as constituted by an out-pouring of himself. Such phenomena may be cited in support of property-freedom or privacy arguments.

Personhood-constituting goes much further. We are asked to understand that someone conceives of some object as incorporated into himself so as to lose its moral identity as a mere thing. Samuel Wheeler, for example, contends that, in principle, 'nothing morally distinguishes my mansion from an artificial arm', so that my mansion is, morally speaking, 'a part of me. (The physical and emotional damage to me at its removal may be as intense as that I feel when I've lost a finger.)'[31] Even ownership of money, Wheeler maintains, may be justified in terms of personhood-constituting since 'the morally relevant description of money is it is just a kind of social artificial body-part construction material'.[32]

The phenomenon of personhood-constituting through incorporation of external resources does exist. If an artificial organ is implanted into someone's body, it becomes part of him. A wider psychological application of the phenomenon is imaginable. There may have been caste societies in which a warrior did indeed conceive of his sword in just this way. He would treat any unauthorized meddling with the sword in the same light as an assault on his

[29] Thomas Hill Green, n. 25 above, at 222.   [30] See Ch. 15, sect. (iv) below.
[31] Samuel C. Wheeler III, n. 21 above, at 181.   [32] *Ibid.*

body. He would not part with the sword for any price, any more than he would part with an arm or a leg; and he would expect it to be interred with him at his death.

A claim to ownership based on personhood-constituting must be psychologically plausible if it is to deserve respect, and its plausibility diminishes to the extent that it is idiosyncratic. For this reason cultural assumptions must, in practice, play a role in delimiting possible self-constituting relationships. We would hardly take seriously a manufacturer of boots who asserted that his ownership of them should be respected because 'these boots are part of me'.

Margaret Radin contends that we can register the presence of the phenomenon in modern societies, intuitively, at least if we regard it as a matter of degree. 'Most people', she says, possess certain objects they feel are 'almost part of themselves'.[33] She instances wedding rings, portraits, heirlooms, and houses.[34] Now it is true that a person's home may be the locus for psychologically significant instances of individual self-expression, but it seems far-fetched to suppose that most people incorporate their dwellings into themselves.[35] Since personhood itself is non-transferable,[36] it must be a *sine qua non* of any claim that a person has incorporated an external object into himself that it is something he could never envisage as belonging to anyone else; and that is hardly the light in which most people view even their much-loved houses or flats. Perhaps wedding rings, sacred mementoes, or even never-to-be-seen diaries are instances of the personhood-constituting phenomenon. If so, the argument now under consideration could stand alone as a property-specific justice reason for recognizing an ownership interest over such things (even if ownership could be justified on no other grounds); and the argument would support some features of property-institutional design— for example, that such things should be exempt from bankruptcy or tax-expropriation rules.

Thus, the personhood-constituting argument for a natural property right, when it can be plausibly invoked, does support a just claim to a limited, non-transferable ownership interest. Its authentic scope is, however, extremely limited. Furthermore, when it applies the privacy argument (to which we now turn and which has a potentially much wider scope) will invariably apply as well. Personhood-constituting is hence in practice a redundant as well as a rare phenomenon.

---

[33] Margaret Jane Radin, n. 24 above, at 959.

[34] *Ibid.* For expansion of her views, see Margaret Jane Radin, *Reinterpreting Property* (UChi. P, 1993).

[35] Radin claims that personhood-constituting assumptions underlie the view which courts have taken to the inviolability of dwellings (*ibid.* 91–101). All the examples she cites, however, are ones in which privacy, not personhood, was invoked.

[36] See P. F. Strawson, *Individuals* (Methuen & Co. Ltd, 1959), 97–8.

(iii) PRIVACY

Where a person's privacy can be effectively guaranteed only if he is granted an open-ended set of use-privileges and control-powers over some resources with which he is intimately connected, he ought to be regarded as owner of that resource.

As we saw in Chapter 6, when ownership is appealed to as a principle it is sometimes the case that the justificatory force stems from assumptions about privacy. There is a widespread, but by no means universally shared, consensus that respect for privacy represents a valuable facet of human association. Its ramifications range far beyond the agenda of property-specific justice reasons. Nevertheless, it may be invoked to support a natural property right, in the way set out at the beginning of this section. The intimate relationship which has arisen between a person and a thing may be such that, granted that privacy is intrinsically worthy of respect, just treatment entails recognition of an ownership interest.

The argument builds on the assault analogy in the following way. Invasions of bodily integrity are natural wrongs. Invasions of a person's privacy, whether by other citizens or by agents of the community, should be regarded as equivalent wrongs since people do (and ought to) regard them as equivalent affronts to their self-worth. Prohibition of privacy-infringing wrongs may, in appropriate contexts, entail trespassory rules relating to resources. Where that is so, the relevant property institution should be so designed as to make the individual the owner of the resource. Only if it does can he be furnished with the privileges and powers which his status as a private person requires.

The foregoing argument is not to be found, as a distinct argument, in general theoretical discussions of the justifications of property institutions. It is, rather, an implicit spin-off from more general contentions in support of respect for privacy as a value. If I can rightly demand, on privacy grounds, that my telephone conversations should not be intercepted and published to the world, that means that interceptive equipment should not be used either outside or within my home. Conferring on me ownership control-powers in respect of my dwelling is only a part, but nevertheless a necessary part, of what is required.

In the English-speaking world, the articulation of an alleged right to be designated 'the right to privacy' has been the product of legal culture rather than philosophical speculation; and it is of comparatively recent date. No such right was included in the English Bill of Rights of 1689 or in the Bill of Rights appended to the Constitution of the United States in 1791. Only at the end of the last century was there published a path-breaking article in the *Harvard Law Review* by Warren and Brandeis purporting to extrapolate a 'right to privacy' from such legal rules as those against defamation and those protecting literary and artistic property.[37] Such a right was eventually incorporated into the common law of American states. English common law does not admit of a generalized right to privacy even to this day, so that no action lies against press photographers who barge into a hospital ward to take photographs of a celebrity without his consent, although the Court of Appeal expressed regret that that should be the position and called on Parliament to remedy the omission.[38] In the United States, the Fourth Amendment to the Constitution—'[t]he right of the people to be secured in their persons, houses, papers, and effects, against unreasonable searches and seizures, shall not be violated'—is nowadays viewed as an instantiation of a general right to privacy. Accordingly, for example, statutes which restrict access to contraceptives have been held unconstitutional for violating privacy.[39]

In English law, privacy continues to be an attribute of property. Long before anyone spoke in terms of a 'right to privacy', English judges were taking privacy considerations into account in developing details of property-institutional design. In Chapter 4 we cited the view of Yates J to the effect that the courts should recognize and protect an author's property in an unpublished manuscript because '[i]t is certain every man has a right to keep his own sentiments, if he pleases: he has certainly a right to judge whether he will make them public, or commit them only to the sight of his friends.'[40] In the landmark case of *Entick* v. *Carrington*[41] the Court of King's Bench laid down that no-one could enter another's land against his will unless he was specifically empowered to do so by some provision of positive law; and it ruled that damages for trespass should be awarded against government officials who seized and pried into a subject's personal papers 'for papers are often the dearest property a man can have'.[42]

As is usually the case with constitutional rights in English law, the right to privacy-in-property takes the form of a common law presumption that Parliament does not intend to authorize what would otherwise be a trespass. It has been held, for example, that a statute empowering a police constable to require a motorist (suspected of being involved in a road accident) to take a breath test did not authorize the officer to enter into or remain in the motorist's dwelling without his consent.[43] On the other hand, legislation empowering the revenue to enter premises, by force if necessary, and to remove any documents which they reasonably suspected might contain evidence of illegal tax-evasion was held to contain language sufficiently explicit to permit such intrusions.[44]

---

[37] Samuel Warren and Louis Brandeis, 'The Right to Privacy' (1890) 4 *Harv. LR* 193.

[38] *Kaye* v. *Robertson* [1991] FSR 62.

[39] *Griswold* v. *Connecticut*, 85 S Ct. 1678 (1965); *Eisenstadt* v. *Baird*, 92 SCt. 1029 (1972).

[40] *Millard* v. *Taylor* (1769) 4 Burr. 2303 at 2379.   [41] (1765) 2 Wils. KB 275.

[42] *Ibid.* at 291.

[43] *Morris* v. *Beardmore* [1981]   AC 446.

[44] *R.* v. *Inland Revenue Commissioners, ex parte Rossminster* [1980] AC 952.

That resentment against infringements of privacy is a widespread psychological phenomenon in contemporary western societies cannot be doubted. It may be that those culturally-relative basic needs which, as will be argued in a later chapter, ought to be catered for in a just society should take account of this phenomenon by affording, *inter alia*, ownership interests over resources. For the moment we are concerned with the argument that, irrespective of the psychology of individuals, it is possible, at an abstract level, to move to a natural (albeit contingent) property right by analogy with the prohibition on unprovoked invasions of bodily integrity. The analogical move is greater than that invoked in the context of first occupancy or personhood-constituting. Some kinds of eviction of a first occupant literally involve assaults on the person. In so far as someone really has constituted himself, in part, by the incorporation of some external thing, meddling with that thing is an attack on his person. Placing a concealed camera in a couple's bedroom or rifling someone's private papers may be resented by the individuals concerned, but it is not, literally, an invasion of bodily integrity.

If we are to found a natural property right on the fact of intimate relationship between a person and a thing, we must invoke the second, as well as the third, element of our minimalist conception of justice. It must be shown that the ranges of autonomous choices associated with a right to privacy (1) are to be valued and (2) warrant special protection. There is a widespread consensus that this is the case, but there are powerful dissents. For example, one strand of feminist opinion condemns the view that sexual and familial relations are pre-eminently the domain of privacy as a belief which serves only to preserve male dominance and which entails no interference with wife-beating, incest, and child abuse.[45]

Privacy arguments contend that, as to a range of activities open to the individual, his decision to engage in them should not be second-guessed either by official agencies of the community or by journalists purporting to act in the public interest. They further contend that information about such activities should be kept in the private domain so that no possibility of second-guessing will arise. The controversiality of such claims depends, in part, on indeterminacy about the justice of inter-personal relations, and, in part, on generalizations as to the trustworthiness of community agents and of citizens, respectively, each to carry out their just roles. If we knew precisely what policing and contribution-raising activities on the part of agents of the community justice requires, and if they could be relied on never to overstep the limits, why should privacy be valued? Intrusions into residences and interception of mail would only take place, say, where that was necessary to prevent sexual exploitation of dependants or to prevent unjust tax-evasion. In such a scenario,

[45] See Lorenne M. F. Clark, 'Privacy, Property, Freedom, and the Family', in Richard Bronaugh (ed.), *Philosophical Law* (Greenwood Press, 1978), 166, at 182–3.

it could not be claimed that privacy (for child-abusers, wife-beaters, or tax-evaders) was a value worthy of respect. Conversely, if we knew precisely what amounted to unjust inter-personal conduct and to just contributions to social expenditure, and if we were blessed with citizens who automatically discharged their just obligations, no coercive societal powers would be required and a distinct domain of privacy would be irrelevant.

There are, however, a host of situations in which there can be no determinate answer as to what is the right thing to be done. In what order should Jill arrange the contents of her handbag? Should Jane furnish her house this way or that? Ought Peter to publish his diary? In such contexts as these, it is implausible to suggest that possibilities of abuse require the community to be armed with a power to second-guess the choice of her or him who is most intimately connected with the decision in question. The policing of alleged improper uses of such resources should not be entrusted to agents of the community, for they cannot be expected to deploy sufficient sympathetic imagination so as to appreciate the full significance of such intimate person–thing relations.

There is thus a legitimate domain of privacy. So far as it extends, outsiders have no standing to demand reasons for what is done and hence may rightly be denied information about what is done. There are resources in the world as to which particular individuals have, without wronging anyone else, assumed a relationship of intimacy. Where that is so, and where the intimately-connected individual should not be second-guessed as to the uses to which the resource should be put, he should be accorded an open-ended set of use-privileges and control-powers over the resource—that is, an ownership interest. The author of a manuscript should have the say-so as to whether it is published or not. The painter who chooses to destroy his picture is not to be second-guessed by the community as to whether this was the right thing to do. To return to the imaginary societies discussed in Chapter 2, the dwelling-licensees in Pink Land are more justly treated than their counterparts in Red Land, because their licences confer open-ended ownership privileges and powers over their residences. They (and not the agents of the community) determine whether bathrooms should be painted a luminous green and whether lodgers should be introduced.

Privacy, like labour-desert, constitutes the basis for a shell of a natural property right. Unlike labour-desert, however, it is hostage, not to social convention, but to the problematic balance between the requirement of a range of specially protected autonomous choice and necessary intervention by the community to prevent abuse. So much is apparent in day-to-day controversies which set privacy against the public's right to be informed. It surfaces also in legal formulations of privacy. For example, Article 8 of the European Convention for the Protection of Human Rights and Fundamental Freedoms proclaims, in paragraph (1), that: '[e]veryone has the right to respect for his private and family life, his home and his correspondence.' Paragraph (2) of that Article, however, goes on to provide that interference with this right is permitted where it is necessary 'in the interests of national security, public safety or the economic well-being of the country, for the prevention of disorder or crime, for the protection of health or morals, or for the protection of the rights and freedoms of others'.

The dependence of privacy-claims over resources on this balancing exercise entails that privacy, standing alone, may not yield a natural right to full-blooded ownership. Privacy may be fully respected without according unlimited use-privileges, control-powers, and powers of transmission. Recall that the Pink Land licensees had no power to assign their licences and that their *prima facie* privileges and powers did not extend to destruction or serious damage. Nothing can be established, in advance of a balancing between justifiably protected autonomous choice against safeguards from abuse, about how the shell of the natural right is to be filled.

Privacy is an important property-specific justice reason to be taken into account in property-institutional design. Its importance drowns any significance which might be attached to metaphysical notions of personhood-constituting. Nevertheless, it can in no way support the enormous range of ownership interests over holdings of private wealth recognized in modern property institutions. Justification of the latter must be sought in terms of the property-freedom and instrumental arguments to be considered in the succeeding chapters of this book.

(iv) NO NATURAL RIGHTS TO FULL-BLOODED OWNERSHIP

We said at the beginning of the last chapter that if there are any natural property rights that would radically affect the moral background against which property institutions operate. It emerges from our investigation in this and the last chapter that there are no natural rights to full-blooded ownership. Given our minimalist conception of justice, no relationship between an individual and a resource arises such that just treatment of the individual requires that a property institution both surround the resource with trespassory rules availing the individual and anyone to whom he chooses to transfer the resource and also conferring on the individual unlimited use-privileges, control-powers, and powers of transmission over the resource.

Of the six putative bases for natural property rights we have discussed, one (self-ownership) has sunk without trace; and the same is virtually true of another (personhood-constituting). Notwithstanding the role it occupies in the history of Western political philosophy, self-ownership is devoid of normative force. It builds, illegitimately, upon body-ownership rhetoric connected with the bodily-use freedom principle; and it is founded upon a no-slavery *non-sequitur*. Person-constituting through incorporation of resources is a possible, but extremely rare, psychological phenomenon. Where it does occur it supports a natural right to a limited, non-transferrable ownership interest. In practice its scope is rendered redundant by the right based on privacy.

Creation-without-wrong and first occupancy constitute important property-specific justice reasons internal to the operation of property institutions, but neither supports original conditions of title. Creation-without-wrong can be invoked in special contexts (notably, in relation to the 'fruits' doctrine) where the actions of the creator of a new item of social wealth serve merely to concretize existing obligations. It does not warrant a unilateral power in the creator to institute a novel set of trespassory obligations. First occupancy may serve as a basis of title, *faute de mieux*, granted that someone must be accorded ownership of some resource. When this happens a windfall is conferred since, of itself, first occupancy entails no just claim to an ownership interest in the case of individuals—although it does support communitarian property.

We are left with the shells of two natural rights based on labour-desert and privacy. No-one is so situated that he can, in defiance of established convention, insist that he deserves to be accorded full-blooded ownership of any resource. Nevertheless, social conventions commonly incorporate, and are shaped by reference to, the assumption that meritorious work should receive a reward in the form of property. Entitlement to 'the fruits of one's labour' (when it is not reducible to an incentive-instrumental argument) should be understood in terms of labour-desert, and not as encapsulating philosophers' contentions about self-ownership or creation-without-wrong.

Privacy-claims to an ownership interest over resources may, in principle, stand in the face of convention. They are, however, dependent on arguments sufficient to establish that, in a particular context, a range of protected autonomous choice ought (all things considered) to be valued and to show that this cannot be achieved without recognizing the ownership interest.

These largely negative conclusions about natural property rights will later be taken into account in our overall conclusions about property theory and specific questions of distribution and property-institutional design. We must first turn to other varieties of property-specific justice reasons.

13

Property and Freedom

In this and the next two chapters we are going to consider whether there are moral property rights falling within the last of the seven categories set out in section (ii) of Chapter 10—that is, the moral standing of a person or group to insist that a property institution (of some kind) be in place in a particular society.

We have seen that, starting with our minimalist conception of justice, there is nothing about the facts of human interaction with the world from which a natural right to full-blooded ownership over anything can be derived. We have yet to consider instrumental justifications for property institutions. Might it not be the case, however, that one can found a 'right to property' on a combination of the second element of the minimalist conception of justice —autonomous choice is of value to all human beings—and the inherent qualities of property institutions? The claim would be that, quite apart from instrumental considerations, property institutions, by their very nature, confer freedoms (ranges of autonomous choice) which would not exist without them; and for this reason no citizen is treated justly by his community unless it institutes or maintains a property institution.

(i) THE LIBERAL CONCEPTION OF OWNERSHIP

We referred in Chapter 8 to what A. M. Honoré has called 'the liberal concept of full individual ownership'.[1] We were there concerned only with the question of how such a concept might be unpacked. Our present concern is with the putative justificatory force of the attribute 'liberal'.

For some commentators property is straightforwardly justifiable because of its enhancement of the freedoms of those who are vested with property rights.[2] This is a blinkered approach since it ignores the effect of owners' freedoms on others; and it also leads commonly to the obfuscating expansion in the concept of property discussed in Chapter 9, whereby every freedom of an agent is treated as a 'property' right. Property institutions must be distinguished from other social institutions, the ranges of autonomous choice

---

[1] Tony Honoré, *Making Law Bind* (Clarendon Press, 1987), 161.
[2] See S. Coval, J. C. Smith, and Simon Coval, 'The Foundations of Property and Property Law' (1986) 45 *CLJ* 457.

which they inherently confer must be identified, and those choices must be assigned (or denied) a value (all things considered).

As we have seen, the core idea of a property institution consists in the twinned conceptions of trespassory rules and the ownership spectrum. These conceptions focus on resources (material, ideational, and monetary). Property institutions both regulate use and allocate wealth. 'Owners' are necessarily authorized, not merely to act as they please in relation to resources, but to control uses by others and to arrogate to themselves and to accumulate items of social wealth as part of their private wealth—the more so to the extent that the prevailing conception of ownership rises up the ownership spectrum. Must it be the case that a 'liberal' conception of ownership is one which calls for full-blooded individual ownership of all resources? Clearly not. Everything will depend on the interpretation which a particular liberal theory gives to the first element of the minimalist conception—natural equality. Autonomous choice is to be valued, the wider the range of it the better. Full-blooded ownership entails a wider range of choice than any lesser conception of property right. But it may be the case that universal allocation of resource-holdings in the form of full-blooded ownership will have the practical consequence that some people are treated differently from others on the ground that they are different kinds (less well-born, less talented, less canny) of human beings. Since we are not here concerned with the essence of 'liberalism' we shall drop the adjective 'liberal' altogether. Our enquiry is whether inherent property freedoms are a necessary feature of the just society.

We shall consider, first, Hegel's defence of private property since he, more clearly than any other writer on the subject, distinguishes the inherent choice-facilitating functions of property institutions at the level of what he calls 'abstract right' from their ultimate evaluation in 'ethical life'. Then, discarding the complexities of Hegel's metaphysics, we shall ask whether the ranges of freedoms inherent to property institutions are, all things considered, of value to human beings. Not surprisingly, the answer will depend on possible alternatives to property as instrumentalities for use-control and wealth-allocation and on the social setting in which a particular property institution is situated. In particular, does that setting embody institutional structures designed to mitigate the domination-potential of ownership powers?

Our conclusion will be that ownership freedoms do indeed contribute to autonomous choice and in that sense provide a *prima facie* justification for property institutions which appeals merely to their inherent qualities. This justification is overwhelming, however, only in relation to some assets. In all other cases its force is heavily context-dependent.

(ii) HEGEL AND PROPERTY FREEDOMS

(a) The Complexities of Hegel's Theory

It has become fashionable in recent theoretical discussions of property to appeal to Hegel's analysis of private property, in terms of abstract right, set out in the first section of part 1 of *The Philosophy of Right*.[3] Hegel's idealist metaphysics has a subtle and elusive internal structure. Abstract right appears only as the first 'moment' in the unfolding of the implications of the concept of abstract freedom. It is later to be taken up within other moments, those of morality, and then of ethical life. Ethical life itself resides in the institutions of the family, civil society, and, supremely, the State. Concrete conclusions about freedom and property, in the end, reflect all these moments. Hence, anything that is said about the relations between freedom and property at the level of abstract right are not to be interpreted as definitive justifications for property institutions.

Some Hegelian apologists regard it as an impertinence to seek to quarry justice reasons at all from Hegel's writings. Hegel's aim was to reveal the working out of the World Spirit through the march of history. Steps in this process should be analysed only from within his metaphysical structure. It is not warranted to regard his analysis as supporting the justice of property institutions or of any feature of property-institutional design.[4] That hands-off stance should be rejected. As we shall see, Hegel himself draws from his analysis important conclusions about perceived defects in the property institutions of his day. He argues that limitations on full-blooded ownership contradict the very concept of property as revealed at the level of abstract right.

However, it is important to identify the kind of justice reason which is enmeshed within Hegel's metaphysics. He eschews instrumentalism. 'The rational aspect of property is to be found not in the satisfaction of needs but in the superseding of mere subjectivity of personality.'[5] Nor, on the other hand, does Hegel appeal to any natural right which concrete flesh-and-blood human beings might have by virtue of their interaction with the world and with each other: original modes of acquisition of ownership, such as first occupancy, are mere inferences from the embodiment of abstract personality in things;[6] and are, in any case, largely discarded in civil society.[7]

Hegel has been commonly understood to advance an argument from

[3] G. W. F. Hegel, *Elements of the Philosophy of Right* (trans. H. B. Nisbet, CUP, 1991) 73–103.

[4] See, e.g., Alan Ryan, *Property and Political Theory* (Basil Blackwell, 1986), ch. 5; Alain Pottage, 'Property: Re-appropriating Hegel' (1990) 53 *MLR* 259.

[5] N. 3 above, 73 (para. 41 addition).

[6] *Ibid.* 81 (para. 50 and addition).   [7] *Ibid.* 249 (para. 217).

personhood-constituting. He refers frequently to the 'embodiment' of personality in property; and the philosophy of right contains the following much-cited claims: '[n]ot until he has property does the person exist as reason';[8] and 'everyone ought to have property'.[9] (Both claims are contained in additions compiled from notes on Hegel's lectures made by pupils, and it has been suggested that all such additions should be treated with caution.[10] We shall follow the conventional assumption that they represent an accurate rendering of Hegel's views.) From such remarks the conclusion has been drawn that Hegel is putting forward the following justification of private property. Unless people extend their personalities into the sphere of external resources, they do not exist as authentic persons either in their own eyes or for others. Therefore the psychological well-being of the human individual requires that he become a property-owner.[11]

If that were Hegel's position, it would have egalitarian implications for abstract right which he should have taken into account when he comes to ethical life within civil society and there announces the inevitability of a class of propertyless 'rabble'.[12] It would also give to the theory a highly truncated scope since (as we saw in the last chapter) personhood-constituting via incorporation of external resources is a highly unusual psychological phenomenon. Whatever affective relationships people may have towards the clothes in their wardrobes, the books on their shelves, their registered trade marks, the coins in their pockets, or any bank accounts or company shares which stand in their names, it beggars credulity to suppose that they regard all such things as parts of themselves. If embodiment of will is given a psychological interpretation, Hegel's theory deserves none of the acclaim it commonly receives among property theorists.

For example, Jeremy Waldron advances an interpretation of Hegel's theory which appeals to the developmental psychological needs of individuals.[13] Private property allows an object to register the effects of willing at one point of time and so forces an individual's willing to become consistent and stable.[14] In working on an object, using it, and having control over it, an individual confers on his will a stability and a maturity that would not otherwise be possible.[15] Waldron recognizes that, on this interpretation, Hegel failed to see that the argument requires everyone to be given significant holdings of property.[16] He points out that it is, on this interpretation, difficult to derive the free alienability of property dialectically from the notion of

---

[8] *Ibid.* 73 (para. 41 addition).   [9] *Ibid.* 81 (para. 49 addition).

[10] See H. B. Nisbet, n. 3 above, translator's preface, pp. xxxv ff.

[11] See, e.g., Margaret Jane Radin, 'Property and Personhood' (1982) 34 *Stan. LR* 957, at 971–8; Dudley Knowles, 'Hegel on Property and Personality' (1983) *Phil. Q.* 45; Justin Hughes, 'The Philosophy of Intellectual Property' (1988) 77 *Geo. LJ* 287, at 330–9; Jeremy Waldron, *The Right to Private Property* (Clarendon Press, 1988), ch. 10.

[12] N. 3 above, 266–7 (para. 244 and addition, para. 245).

[13] Waldron, n. 11 above, 347–59.   [14] *Ibid.* 373–4.

[15] *Ibid.* 378.   [16] *Ibid.* 389.

will-embodiment, as Hegel purported to do;[17] and he considers that the argument applies rather to the stage of bourgeois production than to the conditions of modern industry.[18] For all that, Waldron considers Hegel's justification of property to be 'deep, plausible and attractive'.[19] Why that should be, given the limitations to which he points, Waldron does not explain. (There is further the problem of Waldron's ambivalence about money-as-property discussed in section iv of this Chapter.)

It will here be contended that Hegel was not making this kind of person-hood argument for property, but rather a freedom argument. His appeal is to the choice-facilitating functions which are inherent to historically-evolved property institutions. For all this talk of wills being embodied in things, he does not invoke the assault analogy as the foundation of trespassory rules protecting property. On the contrary, he draws a clear distinction between violence to the person and injury or damage to 'external' property. 'Because I feel, contact with or violence to my body touches me immediately as *actual* and *present*. This constitutes the difference between personal injury and infringement of my external property; for in the latter, my will does not have this immediate presence and actuality.'[20] It is only that will which is implicit in the concept of *abstract* personality which is embodied in things. It is not an attribute of personhood in any psychological conception of personality. Consequently, alienation is possible by the withdrawal of the will from a thing 'in so far as the thing [*Sache*] is *external in nature*'.[21]

Hegel's starting-point for the analysis of abstract right is not the natural human entity but '[t]he will which is free in and for itself, as it is in its *abstract* concept'.[22] 'Any discussion of freedom must begin not with the individuality [*Einzelheit*] or the individual self-consciousness, but only with the essence of self-consciousness'.[23] It is then for philosophic science to work out the necessary implications of this concept, its manifestations as 'Idea'. They include property.

The argument from freedom to property runs as follows. If we take seriously the concept of the free individual, the person capable of bearing rights, we must necessarily recognize a sphere of *meum* and *tuum*, for in no other way can the abstract person differentiate himself from the world and from other persons. 'The person must give himself an external *sphere of freedom* in order to have being as Idea.'[24] We confront this philosophical truth with a historically-evolved institution, property. That institution, in its modern guise of individual private property, precisely matches the necessity for abstract freedom to be concretized in an external sphere. It enables the abstractly free will to become actualized through asserting exclusive pos-session over things, through making unlimited use of things, and through

[17] N. 11 above, 367–9.   [18] *Ibid.* 373–4,   [19] *Ibid.* 389.
[20] N. 3 above, 79 (para. 48).   [21] *Ibid.* 95 (para. 65).   [22] *Ibid.* 67 (para. 34).
[23] *Ibid.* 279 (para. 258).   [24] *Ibid.* 73 (para. 41).

alienating things to others. Its inherent choice-facilitating role is thus *the* rationale of a property institution. 'In relation to needs—if these are taken as primary—the possession of property appears as a means; but the true position is that, from the point of view of freedom, property, as the first *existence* [*Dasein*] of freedom, is an essential end for itself.'[25]

Hence, when Hegel says that everyone ought to have property, he is to be understood as meaning only that the opportunity of owning property should be denied to none. One of the 'substantial determinations' which constitutes personality is that one 'be capable of owning property'.[26] In other words, although no-one has a natural right to any particular property-holding, everyone has a right that his society afford him the facilities of a property institution.

But it must be the right kind of property institution, the one to which the progress of World Spirit has only recently attained, and that not perfectly. The true concept of property, as the embodiment of freedom, must discard those old feudal notions which conceived of different and limited ownership interests subsisting in the same subject-matter through the doctrine of estates, and it must reject those limitations on alienability inherent in the Roman law of *Fideicommissa*.[27] Only what we have called full-blooded ownership fits the freedom bill. For the abstractly free will to be capable of appearing on the world stage as a fully rational will it must be presented with an institution that makes possible exclusive, unlimited, and transferable ownership.

That is Hegel's diagnosis of the inherent freedom-conferring qualities of property institutions at the level of abstract right. But it is far from representing his final conclusions about the justifiability of individual private property. Features of concretely just property institutions need not reflect precisely the implications of full-blooded ownership, once the 'moment' of abstract right is subsumed within those of morality and ethical life. So far as morality is concerned, 'the good' may require that starving individuals be licensed to commit what would, at the level of abstract right, amount to theft.[28] Within ethical life, family property may take precedence over individual private property so that, for example, the right of free testation is appropriately restricted.[29] Within the State, political considerations warrant the permanent maintenance of an independent class of landed proprietors and that justifies restraints on alienation of land which, in terms of abstract right, would not be permissible.[30] Although individual private property is 'more rational' than any other form of property, the higher sphere of right embodied in the State may justify corporate property and mortmain.[31]

[25] *Ibid.* 77 (para. 45).   [26] *Ibid.* 95 (para. 66).
[27] *Ibid.* 90–3 (paras. 61, 62, 63, and addition).
[28] *Ibid.* 153–8 (para. 126 and addition, para. 127 and addition, paras. 128–30).
[29] *Ibid.* 208–9 (paras. 169–71), 214–15 (paras. 178–9), 218 (para. 180 addition).
[30] *Ibid.* 345 (para. 306).   [31] *Ibid.* 77–8 (para. 46 and addition).

(b) Hegel's Argument Summarized

Hegel's argument from freedom to individual private property may be summarized in the following propositions:

1. The concept of freedom presupposes the idea of a choosing agent.
2. The wider the range of choices open to an agent, the freer he is.
3. Property institutions provide agents with a range of choices which would not exist without property institutions.
4. Furthermore, an agent could make no rational choices at all without property institutions.
5. The choices which property institutions make possible are *prima facie* valuable, although they may in the end be rightly overridden by considerations independent of abstract human agency. Therefore
6. irrespective of any alleged natural rights to property and independently of any instrumental values property may serve, property institutions are inherently justifiable.

Proposition 4 should be rejected for reasons to be considered below. However, even if 4 is crossed out, we still have an argument for property institutions which, on the face of it, seems convincing. Propositions 1 and 2 instantiate the second element of our minimal conception of justice with the approbative label 'freedom'. That 3 is true follows from our entire analysis of property institutions in terms of protected ownership use-privileges, control-powers, and powers of transmission. Whether the choices which property institutions inherently confer upon owners ought to be valued in the human scale of things depends, first, on a comparison with alternative mechanisms for the control and distribution of resources. To that matter we turn in the succeeding sections of this Chapter.

Even if property freedoms are to be preferred to regimes of communal use, propositions 5 and 6 suggest that Hegel's freedom argument is to be viewed only as a *prima facie* property-specific justice reason. In the next chapter we shall discuss certain familiar objections to property freedoms. In pursuing that enquiry we need not follow Hegel in his typology of 'moments', nor accept any of his particular views as to which features of 'morality' or 'ethical life' supersede the freedoms which property institutions inherently confer.

Proposition 4—an agent could make no rational choices at all without property institutions—grossly over-states the case. 'Not until he has property does the person exist as reason'[32] is, on the face of it, an extraordinary claim. Cannot individuality be rationally manifested otherwise than through ownership? Are the tribesmen/citizens of our imaginary Forest Land and Red Land incapable of concretizing their abstractly free wills because their societies lack property institutions?

---

[32] N. 3 above, 73 (para. 41 addition).

It is true that, in this context, Hegel is only speaking of the domain of abstract right. That domain comprises three sections: property, where all interactions between people and the world must take the form of ownership interests; contract, where the joint wills of property-owners are necessarily involved; and wrongdoing, where a purported choice negates the rational free will of the actor and so is not an authentic exercise of individuality (not a rational choice). Hegel recognizes that, within ethical life, institutions may arise in which persons participate otherwise than as property owners. For example, he rejects as 'disgraceful' Kant's view that marriage constitutes a property-contract.[33]

Nevertheless, at the level of abstract right (the arena in which the abstract individual will interacts with the world), rational choice is possible, Hegel appears to contend, only via property. This claim is patently false if 'property' refers to that institution which has at its core the twinned conceptions of trespassory rules and the ownership spectrum and which focuses on resources. It is indeed that institution which Hegel discusses for the most part, under the description 'property', in *The Philosophy of Right*. However, he also subsumes within the notion of property the idea of self-ownership and ownership of one's actions and capabilities which, as we saw in Chapter 11, misled both Locke and Marx in their different versions of the fruits-of-labour argument. He does so by committing the same spectacular *non sequitur* shared by those writers. Hegel speaks of a human being becoming 'his own property as distinct from that of others'.[34] (He hastens to add that his conclusions about unrestricted alienation do not apply to this sort of proprietary subject-matter.[35])

The claim that '[n]ot until he has property does the person exist as reason' is a product of the self-ownership conception. That conception facilitates a slippage between 'mine' in the sense of my activities, and 'mine' in the sense of the external things I own. If the concept of the abstractly free will is to manifest itself at all it must do so, as Hegel says, in terms of a differentiation between *meum* and *tuum*. But that 'mine' may concern only my body or my actions. Only if such things have already been smuggled into the idea of a property institution is it true that persons cannot exist as reason without property.

The misleading fourth proposition should accordingly be left to one side. It is tautologically true that no-one can act unless his actions are 'his'. It is patently false that no-one can act unless he asserts an ownership interest over some feature of the external world. The freedom argument for property concerns, not a necessary condition for being a person at all, but conditions under which persons may make a far wider range of choices than otherwise they could.

[33] *Ibid.* 105 (para. 75).   [34] *Ibid.* 86 (para. 57).   [35] *Ibid.* 96 (para. 66).

(iii) MERE PROPERTY FREEDOMS

In the tradition of political philosophy, and within recurrent political debate, property is acclaimed by some as the ally of freedom and denounced by others as its antithesis. Given the complexity and variety of property institutions, no straightforward outcome to this controversy is to be looked for. It all depends on what ranges of choice and what features of property institutions one has in mind.

On the affirmative side of the property-freedom equation, three ranges of autonomous choice may be cited. The first concerns uses of things—objects, portions of the earth's surface, ideas—and control over the use of them by others. Ownership freedoms of this sort are inherent in the idea of what we have called 'mere property' and are discussed in this section. The second concerns freedom to transmit one's bundle of use-privileges and control-powers to others, and the concomitant freedom to transmit hived-off wealth-potential in the form of money or cashable rights. Such property-transmission freedoms are inherent in full-blooded ownership and will be considered in the next section. We postpone until a later chapter discussion of a third range of autonomous choice with which property institutions are instrumentally, rather than inherently, connected—namely, the independence from social control which private holdings of wealth can bring.[36]

If a property institution exists in a society, then at least mere property over some resources must be accorded to individuals or groups with the protection of trespassory rules. Mere-property freedoms necessarily encompass an open-ended set of use-privileges and control-powers. X is free to use and (at his pleasure) to license others to use a picture, or a house, or a copyright if he has any kind of ownership interest in it—subject to any property-limitation rules there may be. If that analytical truth should turn out also to be a justificatory argument, it will be of far wider application than any of the justice reasons considered under the category of alleged natural property rights. For example, the freedoms thus vouchsafed go beyond anything which would follow from the privacy argument. Ownership, purportedly justified by freedom, extends to things with which the owner has no intimate connection. The underlying value is mere choice, not specially protected choice.

Whether mere-property freedoms should be accorded even *prima facie* value turns, in relation to particular items of social wealth, on a comparison between the application to them of the ownership spectrum and some regime of communal use. As we saw in Chapter 7, regimes of communal use may take several forms. A resource may be reserved as 'common property'. There are no trespassory rules, although there could be universalized regulations

---

[36] See Ch. 15, sect. (iv) below.

governing its use. (Recall the Forestlanders' restraints on sacrilegious treatment of sacred objects, and their rules about maintenance of the communal dwelling.) Secondly, a resource may be set aside as the subject of communitarian property. A community has the protection of trespassory rules *vis-à-vis* the rest of the world, but neither the community itself nor its individual members are vested with ownership freedoms. Instead approved uses of the resource will be referred to whatever social, ethical, or spiritual mores constitute the community. Thirdly, a resource may be the subject of a protected non-property holding, like the offices or the factories in Red Land and Contract Land. There are trespassory rules, but authorized uses are controlled by conceptions of social function without borrowing on ownership conceptions.

But by far the most widespread variant in real-world property institutions involves quasi-ownership interests being vested in social institutions, as is the case with State or public property. There will be trespassory rules conferring privileged status on social agents related to the discharge of their functions. The fact that 'ownership' is reserved to the State or to the charitable corporation or other social agency will play a part, great or small, in the elaboration of these functions, although avowed self-seekingness will not. Such an arrangement is a 'regime of communal use' in the sense that all citizens, *qua* citizens, have access on the same terms (as with a public park or highway); or all beneficiaries of the social function to be discharged have access on the same terms (as with students entering on to university premises 'owned' by an educational corporation).

If mere-property freedoms are intrinsically valuable, it must be because they contribute more to human well-being than do any of these variants of regimes of communal use. If the argument from autonomous choice to ownership were based solely on the notion of maximizing opportunities to make use of the external world it would clearly fail. Owners are armed with control-powers enabling them to exclude others. It can hardly be supposed that they will inevitably exercise them in such a way as to confer more use-opportunities than would result from any variety of communal use regime. From an abstract maximalizing standpoint, communal use is preferable. However, that is not the burden of the argument for mere-property freedoms. It has to do with channelling and policing uses which are potentially in conflict.

In a regime of communal use, competing uses are regulated either by societal norms (whether or not embodied in law) or by the exercise of official discretion. Alleged violations of societal norms are policed, formally or informally, by spontaneous social reactions or by agencies of one kind or another. Where resources are subjected to ownership interests, the regulation of competing uses is largely delegated to owners, by virtue of their inherent control-powers. Furthermore, owners become the prime movers in policing activities. This is overtly true where the property institution's trespassory rules are part of civil law, and in practice also when they are criminal prohibitions since prosecutions are unlikely unless owners complain. The 'freedom' thereby conferred on owners is obviously of value to them. It has value to the community as a whole, and thus tells in favour of the justice of the institution, if and only if it is, all things considered, a better method of channelling and policing conflicting uses than would be a regime of communal use.

If we limit our attention to tangible items and set up as the alternatives only private ownership interests or 'common property' (in the literal sense of a complete absence of trespassory rules), it may seem obvious that the ownership solution is bound to entail less social friction and waste than the free-for-all alternative. We have seen that the argument can be framed in terms of economic analysis.[37] Ownership solutions are to be preferred to regimes in which all use-channelling and policing must be settled by myriads of transactions entered into by all those effected, since they facilitate the internalization of externalities and thus produce the most 'efficient' outcome.[38] This is not, however, a universal truth which can, at an abstract level, be shown to follow merely from premises of preference-maximizing rationality.[39] Much will depend on the resource in question and the numbers of persons affected. It is not inevitably the case that the transaction costs of a shift from common property to individual ownership interests should be lower than an agreement by all concerned to limit the exercise of their use-privileges.[40]

In making the comparison the historical starting-point will often be decisive (and the alternatives will not be simply private individual ownership versus individuals transacting over that which is literally 'common property'). If in a particular society a conventional regime of communal use is already in force, for example, in relation to certain tracts of land, there are likely to be already in place smoothly-functioning conventional norms and policing procedures.[41] Disruption of these by the introduction of a property institution would not be warranted merely by virtue of that institution's use-channelling

---

[37] See Ch. 9, sect. (iii)(a) above.

[38] Harold Demsetz, 'Toward a Theory of Property Rights' (1967) 57 *American Economic Review* 347; Garrett Hardin, 'The Tragedy of the Commons', in Bruce A. Ackerman (ed.), *Economic Foundations of Property Law* (Little Brown and Co., 1975).

[39] This point is made by Frank I. Michelman, 'Ethics, Economics and the Law of Property', in J. R. Pennock and J. W. Chapman (eds.), *Nomos xxiv: Ethics, Economics and the Law* (NYUP, 1982), 3, and conceded by Harold Demsetz, 'Professor Michelman's Unnecessary and Futile Search for the Philosopher's Touchstone', *ibid.* 41.

[40] See James Buchanan, *The Limits of Liberty: Between Anarchy and Leviathan* (U. Chi.P, 1975), 22–3.

[41] See, e.g., Carl J. Dahlman, *The Open Field System and Beyond: A Property Rights Analysis of an Economic Institution* (CUP, 1980); Paolo Grossi, *An Alternative to Private Property: Collective Property in the Juridical Consciousness of the Nineteenth Century* (U. Chi.P, 1981), chs. 7–10.

and policing functions. (It might, as we shall see, be justified on the instrumental ground of creator-incentives—that is, if technological changes made it possible for individuals to add to social wealth through invention or improvement and they would not do so without being conceded ownership interest.[42])

On the other hand, if a system of ownership interests has historically evolved with regard to particular items, its replacement by any regime of communal use would necessitate the introduction of novel mechanisms to regulate and police competing uses. It is implausible to suppose that this social cost could be justified in the case of trivial objects which were widely available. In their case, use-channelling and policing via established ownership conceptions would be preferable to the *de novo* introduction of an item-by-item use-licensing system and its attendant policing costs. Even if some crisis requires that, say, clothing, furniture, or food should be rationed, decision-makers would normally be perverse if they did not deploy established ownership ideas as part of their rationing procedure, but, instead, insisted that every detail of use must be definitively stipulated and every excess policed.

It would be one thing for a clothes-rationing regime to ban trading either with clothing coupons or with the allocated garments themselves. It would be another to seek to stipulate every detail of their use, to lay down, for example, whether outworn garments could be cut up and patched for the use of other members of the recipient's family. Rational rationing regimes presuppose at least mere-property freedoms in those to whom items are supplied, even if they derogate from the conventional ownership package in specific ways. The extreme case where this would not be so would be, for example, where food is being distributed for immediate consumption amongst a starving population; for then the recipient acquires no open-ended set of use-privileges and control-powers but merely the privilege to eat what he is given. Soup-kitchen distribution amongst the starving is appropriate. To seek to dispense altogether with the use-channelling and the use-policing virtues of ownership interests would entail subjecting every item of social wealth to the soup-kitchen model.

Thus, we have an independent argument from freedom to property in respect of things which are, conventionally, already the subject of ownership interests. Clothing, furniture, books, gadgets, toys, vehicles, and many other chattels are examples. One's relationship to such things may in no sense be intimate, such as to give rise to privacy considerations,[43] let alone constitutive of personhood.[44] However, conferring (at least non-transferable) ownership privileges and powers over such things on individuals not only enlarges their domains of choice, it also saves the community the cost of instituting and

---

[42] See Ch. 15, sect. (iii) below.   [43] See Ch. 12, sect. (iii) above.
[44] See Ch. 12, section (ii) above.

policing a regime of communal use. Such a regime would multiply, for no good reason, the occasions on which community agencies make decisions about the details of citizens' lives. It would absorb effort and resources which could be expended on other community projects which justice requires.

It follows that mere-property freedoms, in relation to such things, are of value to the individual and to others and are therefore just. Only in an imaginary future society, such as William Morris's *Nowhere*[45] (in which people's wants and productive forces had been so aligned that there was always an abundance of objects which anyone might ever wish to use), would the argument cease to apply.

However, the argument to property from the use-channelling and use-policing functions of ownership interests is only an obvious winner in the case of widely available chattels. It has no purchase at all in the case of intellectual property. As we have seen, a newly invented ideational entity may, once published, be used by anyone without thereby interfering with its use by anyone else.[46] No use-channelling or use-policing instrumentality is needed. Justifications for intellectual property must be sought elsewhere.[47] It is noteworthy that Hegel was not able to explain ownership of ideas in the same terms that he applied to ownership of tangible items (percolation of an object by a person's will in such a way that the wills of others are excluded). He justifies intellectual property solely on instrumental grounds: it exists to provide authors and inventors with incentives.[48]

In the case of dwellings, on the other hand, the advantages of mere-property freedoms over regimes of communal use are considerable. Use-channelling and use-policing must be achieved somehow, and conferring open-ended use-privileges and control-powers on occupiers will, in many contexts, be the most expedient arrangement—quite apart from the privacy argument discussed in the last chapter. Even if dwellings have to be rationed, the model of Pink Land licences seems more propitious than the Red Land equivalent. There would have to be some very strong countervailing consideration before it would be justifiable for a community to saddle itself with the cost of stipulating and policing every detail of the use to which dwellings may be put.

Nevertheless, the property-freedom argument for ownership interests in dwellings does not carry the overwhelming force which it does in the case of widely available chattels. As we saw, one strand of feminist opinion condemns the view that there should be a specially protected range of autonomous choice in relation to sexual and familial relations.[49] Generalizing from such objections, it might be contended that mere-property freedoms over dwellings should not only not enjoy the special protection that privacy-claims

---

[45] See Ch. 18, sect. (i) below.   [46] See Ch. 4, sect. (i) above.
[47] See Ch. 15, sect. (iii)(c)(2) below.   [48] N. 3 above, 99–101 (para. 69).
[49] See Ch. 12, sect. (iii) above.

demand, but that they should not even exist in view of the dangers of domination by 'owners' over co-resident dependants. We return to this problem in
the next chapter.[50]

So far as major units of production or major service enterprises are concerned, the use-channelling and use-policing functions of mere-property
freedoms are inextricably enmeshed with other features of institutional
design. The complexity of interactions between users indicates that some
decision-taking regime must be in place. As we saw when discussing C. B.
MacPherson's political property-rhetoric, any suggestion that material factors of production or service-provision are to be literally 'common property'
would be wildly implausible.[51] It would mean that there were no trespassory
rules governing access to a factory and its machinery, or to a hospital and its
beds. In the practice of modern property institutions, the only regime of
communal use which has in many societies been preferred to private ownership interests is one which vests, by means of appropriate trespassory rules,
quasi-ownership interests over the unit or enterprise in a public authority.
We shall postpone further consideration of these alternatives until we reach
the anti-property-freedom arguments flowing from wealth-disparities and
domination-potential in the next chapter.

(iv) PROPERTY-TRANSMISSION FREEDOMS

We have seen that, as one moves up the ownership spectrum, there is a
significant point of discontinuity where transmission of the owners's entire
bundle of privileges and powers becomes permissible.[52] Granted that one
has already included within an ownership interest whatever range of control-
powers is required to achieve desirable use-channelling and use-policing,
where does the property-freedom argument stand so far as transmission
powers are concerned?

If, for reasons set out in the last section or for those connected with
labour-desert or privacy, a person ought to be accorded at least mere-
property freedoms over some resource, there is a distinct 'freedom' argument which entails that he should be granted transmission powers as well. A
person might choose that another should be substituted for him as the
beneficiary of trespassory rules. A property institution confers freedom to
make such choices if it empowers him to transmit his ownership interest,
whether by exchange, or by *inter vivos* or testamentary gift. Such choices are,
prima facie, as deserving of respect as any others that a person may make, so
that a society treats its citizens unjustly if it does not provide a property
institution which incorporates transmission powers. If they did not exist,

[50] See Ch. 14, sect. (iv)(b) below.   [51] See Ch. 9, sect. (iii)(d) above.
[52] See Ch. 3, sect. (vi) above.

people could make gifts of services but never of things. If they did not exist, there could be no freedom to sell or buy.

This aspect of the property-freedom argument has implications going far beyond any of those entailed by the property-specific justice reasons discussed in the last two chapters. We saw that there are no natural rights to full-blooded ownership. Yet, at least as far as widely available chattels are concerned, the present argument, combined with that of the last section, suggests that a society ought to recognize full-blooded ownership—for, as we shall see in the next chapter, it is implausible to suppose that, in the case of such chattels, anti-freedom arguments have any serious purchase.

More importantly, the present argument is the first of those we have discussed which actually supports the introduction into a property institution of money and of cashable rights. If freedom to transmit is of value in itself, merely because it confers a range of autonomous choice which would not exist without it, then people ought to be enabled to dispose of what they have by contract (as well as by gift), unless some countervailing consideration dictates otherwise. In Chapter 2 we imagined a society, Contract Land, which recognized freedom to contract as a value even though it lacked a property institution. In all real societies where freedom to bargain is accepted, ownership interests over resources are included among the bargainable items. Money is the next step.

Suppose Max has baked bread and Jane has brewed beer. Suppose that there are sufficient reasons why, in justice, there ought to be trespassory rules conferring ownership use-privileges and control-powers on Max over the bread and on Jane over the beer. Now Max and Jane wish to exchange some bread for some beer, not for immediate consumption, but in such a way that trespassory rules will confer on Jane the same privileges and powers over the bread which at present reside in Max, and the same privileges and powers over the beer in Max as now obtain for Jane. This free choice of theirs is respected if the property institution under which they live treats just such an exchange as an inherent feature of ownership.

Bring in third and fourth parties. Max wants Bill's beans and Tom's turnips, which are still in the ground. They do not want Max's bread or Jane's beer, but they want things belonging to other people who do not want the beans and the turnips. Jane wants more of Max's bread than she can swap for her beer, and knows of others who want more of her beer but who have nothing she wants. If it were possible for all to get together and make complex exchanges, each barter would be justified by the same principle of free transfer which justifies the first straightforward trade between Max and Jane. The obvious practical solution is the invention of some token of exchange, that is, money.[53] No further assumptions about autonomous choice are needed for its introduction, merely institutional invention.

[53] See Ch. 4, sect. (ii)(a) above.

The same freedom argument which justifies the incorporation within a property institution of a power to transmit ownership interests over things for ownership interests over other things or for their monetary equivalent also suffices, *prima facie*, to support freedom to contract for goods or money in the future. Then, following the same principle, a property institution may justifiably incorporate the right to call for performance of the contract, like the debt owed by a bank, as itself an exchangeable item. Such cashable rights do not confer use-privileges and control-powers over tangible things so long as they subsist as mere rights; but they have the potential of being trans-muted, within a property institution, into such ownership privileges and powers, or into money which itself can be so transmuted.[54]

Hegel takes it as axiomatic that a 'full owner' of a thing also owns its 'value', that is, has unlimited freedom to transfer its use to others; and that in consequence money and bills of exchange, as symbols of value, could be owned even though in themselves they encompass no use-freedoms.[55] This raises further problems for Waldron's psychological interpretation of Hegel's theory which was criticized in section (ii) of this Chapter. In what sense can cash or bank accounts constitute objects which can be seen, over time, to be 'registering the effects of willing'?[56]

Waldron himself argues that Hegel's central mistake was to fail to see that private property must be made available to all.[57] Everyone should have 'an amount of property sufficient for him to take seriously his responsibility for its use and management'.[58] Tantalizingly, however, Waldron fails to make clear, from first to last, whether he supposes 'property' to include money and cashable rights. As was mentioned earlier,[59] Waldron defines property as a system of rules 'governing access to and control of material resources'.[60] On the other hand, he argues that if any individual appropriates more than is necessary for the proper development of his sense of responsibility, the surplus can rightly be redistributed.[61] It is difficult to understand how satis-factory redistributive measures could be devised which did not, among other things, take property *in the form of money* from some people and give it to others. Indeed, the entire egalitarian drift of Waldron's argument is fatally compromised if we are to understand him as supposing that money and cashable rights have nothing to do with private property.

All of the instrumental property-specific justice reasons discussed later in Chapter 15 require property-holdings in the form of hived-off wealth —money and cashable rights. Quite independently of these, however, a Hegelian property-freedom argument warrants such property-holdings as necessary instruments for implementing freedom to transmit. Any just

---

[54] See Ch. 4, sect. (ii)(b) above.   [55] N. 3 above, 92–3 (para. 63 and addition).
[56] Waldron, n. 11 above, 373–4.   [57] *Ibid.* 389.
[58] *Ibid.* 5.   [59] See Ch. 7, sect. (vi) above.
[60] N. 11 above, 31.   [61] N. 11 above, 337–42.

society should afford to its citizens the power to choose between, at least, a wide range of modest items of diet, dress, and furniture, and between ordinary services of decoration, culture, and entertainment (for so long, that is, that these things are not literally abundant). In practice, tokens of some kind must be vouchsafed to enable such choices to be made. Being vested with such tokens is to own 'money'. The only alternative is the soup-kitchen society in which, however nourishing the soup, citizens, denied such choices, are, for that reason, less free. Money is indispensable to a society which seeks to expand autonomous choice.

Nevertheless, any property-freedom argument (such as Hegel's), taken in isolation, is distributionally blind. Freedom to transmit is only *prima facie* of value in the total human scale of things—in Hegel's terminology, it holds absolutely only at the 'moment' of abstract right. Since there is no such thing as a natural property right to full-blooded ownership, the individual cannot stand against the world and insist on unlimited transmission freedoms (and hence unlimited power to accumulate wealth) even should his exercise of freedom have deleterious effects on the freedom of others. There are familiar and powerful objections to unlimited powers to make inter-generational gifts and to unlimited powers to purchase resources the use of which is vital to the lives of others. To these we turn in the next chapter.

14

Against Property Freedoms

In the last chapter we investigated the contention that according ownership privileges and powers can be straightforwardly justified as extensions of the ranges of autonomous choice open to individuals or groups. Ownership freedoms should be valued for Hegelian reasons, just because they are manifestations of freedom. That explains why full-blooded ownership is sometimes described as a 'liberal' conception of ownership.

We saw that, in terms of Hegel's Philosophy of Right, that justification was, in effect, *prima facie* only. It holds at the 'moment' of abstract right, but there may be reasons for overriding ownership freedoms once that moment is taken up within the moments of morality and ethical life. It was further seen that the use-channelling and use-policing functions of ownership interests were, in most contexts, sufficient to justify mere-property freedoms in relation to ordinary chattels (and probably dwellings); that freedom to give and to make bargains entails full-blooded ownership of some things, and, more importantly, the introduction of money into a property institution; but that, in view of the distributional blindness of such arguments, a deal more had to be investigated before one could attribute an all-things-considered value to inherent property freedoms. In this Chapter we turn to various arguments against property freedoms.

(i) INTERIOR AND ULTERIOR LIMITATIONS

Those who subscribe to the view that full-blooded ownership is *prima facie* justifiable simply because it maximizes the range of autonomous choices open to owners may nevertheless argue for limitations of two kinds. They may suppose that there are some kinds of dispositions of property which are inconsistent with the very freedom which supports ownership in the first place, what may be called 'interior limitations'. Or they may appeal to independent arguments calling for restrictions on ownership freedoms ('ulterior limitations').

(a) Inherent Contradiction

The distinction between these two kinds of limitations is sometimes obscured by the suggestion that ownership conceptions contain inherent contradictions.

Charles Donahue, for example, contends that full-blooded ownership 'carries with it two inherent contradictions'. First, unlimited transmission powers would include a power to confer on someone else an interest which carries limited transmission powers. Secondly, unlimited use-privileges in one owner would restrict the use-privileges of other owners.[1]

The notion of 'inherent contradiction' is a fallacy spawned from the spurious idea of totality ownership which, as we have seen, is the source of one variant of scepticism about ownership.[2] Only if it is assumed that every owner of a resource *must* (in order to be 'owner') be able to do absolutely anything he chooses to or with the resource, does it follow that we are faced with a contradiction if the exercise by one owner of some privilege or power necessarily prevents another owner exercising a privilege or power.

So far as Donahue's second suggested 'inherent contradiction' is concerned, we saw in Chapter 3 that full-blooded ownership carries only *prima facie* unlimited use-privileges. Property-limitation rules, such as those imposed to prevent nuisances to neighbours or in the service of wider environmental objectives, may presuppose full-blooded ownership; but they do not contradict it.[3] They represent ulterior limitations. The use-privileges inherent in full-blooded ownership never carry even *prima facie* exemption from property-independent prohibitions.[4] The recognition that I am prohibited from smashing windows with my hammer does not contradict my claim to be 'full' owner of the hammer.

Donahue's other instance of 'inherent contradiction' overlooks the ownership spectrum. To be committed to a contradiction in this context one would have to assert that every resource must at all times be the subject of unlimited transmission powers. It is not a contradiction to say that X, at time T1, has *prima facie* unlimited powers of transmission over a resource (including the power to confer interests lower on the ownership spectrum), and that Y, at time T2, has, by X's direction, an ownership interest over the resource which does not comprise unlimited powers of transmission.

Nevertheless, this second alleged inherent contradiction raises important questions for the property-freedom argument. As we have seen, ownership conceptions are mutable and contestable.[5] If freedom to transmit should be vouchsafed to owners simply on the ground of respect for autonomous choice, should one not espouse something less than full-blooded ownership in order that that freedom may be as widely diffused as possible? In that sense, the property-freedom argument would recommend interior limitations on ownership conceptions. We shall consider suggestions in relation to testamentary freedom and partial or conditional gifts.

[1] Charles Donahue Jr., 'The Future of the Concept of Property Predicted from its Past', in J. Rowland Pennock and John W. Chapman (eds.), *Property: Nomos xxii* (NYUP, 1980), 28, at 33–4.

[2] See Ch. 8, sect. (ii) above.

[3] See Ch. 3, sect. (viii) above.

[4] See Ch. 3, sect. (vii) above.

[5] See Ch. 5, sects. (v) and (vi) above.

(b) Testamentary Freedom

Property institutions have, historically, been more uniform in their recognition, as an aspect of ownership, of freedom to make *inter vivos* rather than inter-generational transfers. In England land could not be devised, except through the device of the use, until the sixteenth century; and in English early and medieval law it seems that custom usually restrained the power to bequeath even personal property, where a testator was survived by dependants.[6] Over the centuries and in different cultures, complete testamentary freedom is the exception.[7] In contemporary political debates, the suggestion that testamentary gifts should be outlawed or restricted is a live issue in a way that banning *inter vivos* giving is not.[8] Supposing freedom to transfer should be valued simply as an instance of autonomous choice, why should one distinguish between *inter vivos* and testamentary gifts?

(1) Rights of Inheritance

In many cultures there have been, or still are, social conventions which prescribe that linear descendants or other relatives ought to be vested with ownership interests in resources upon the death of their previous owners. Such conventions vary in terms (that is, as to the appropriate recipients) and in strength (that is, as to the kinds of reason which may override a claim to inherit).[9] There is also variation in the extent to which they are embodied in positive law. At a particular time and place, such conventions might be as deeply embedded as those which respect ownership privileges and powers with the result that the prevailing conception of ownership does not encompass unrestricted freedom to make testamentary dispositions. If that were so, inheritance rights would constitute an interior limitation on ownership.

Where conventions of this sort exist, but are ill-defined, weak, or shared only by some members of the community, the prevailing conception of ownership may be contestable precisely to the extent that it is unsettled whether an owner, *qua* 'owner', is free to dictate how his resources should devolve on his death. Then we must raise the question whether there is any extra-conventional

---

[6] W. S. Holdsworth, *A History of English Law* (3rd edn., Methuen and Co. Ltd, 1923), ii, 93–5, iii, 550–6; George W. Keeton and L. C. B. Gower, 'Freedom of Testation in English Law' (1935) 20 *Iowa LR* 326.

[7] A. G. Guest, 'Family Provision and the Legitima Portio' (1957) 73 *LQR* 74.

[8] See D. W. Haslett, 'Is Inheritance Justified?' (1986) 15 *PPA* 122.

[9] The English Law Commission, prior to the enactment of the Inheritance (Provision for Family and Dependants) Act 1975, reported the results of a survey of public opinion. The majority of those consulted expressed the view that parents ought not to be required to make testamentary provision for offspring (Law Com. no 61, 1974).

moral basis for rights of inheritance. Nineteenth-century English liberal philosophers, like Mill and Sidgwick, argued that there was not.[10]

Various issues must be separated. Of course, if what a person has is no more
than a life interest (that is, a bundle of use-privileges and control-powers exercisable over a resource only during his lifetime), the question of testamentary
freedom does not arise. He may be empowered to transmit his limited ownership interest to someone else, thereby creating what the common law called an
'estate pur autre vie'; but the bundle terminates with his death. Furthermore,
there may be assets which are, within the terms of a property institution (legal
or social), subjected to family ownership rather than individual ownership. In
that case, whatever transmission freedoms ought to be included within the
conception of ownership inure to the family group rather than to an individual
transferor or testator. Particular institutions of feudal law presuppose that
some forms of property, especially land, are morally the joint property of a
man and his heirs. The civil law concept of a *legitima portio* (which cannot be
taken away from an heir) represents a compromise between the idea of individual and of family property. As English law came to view free testation as an
attribute of ownership, the significance of intestacy rules gradually changed.
Instead of being conceived of as rules which implemented property-claims
to which successors were already morally entitled, they came to be seen as
appropriation rules. Property which had once fully belonged to the deceased
was conferred on successors, if he made no will, by reference to what it was
presumed he would have wished.

Our present question is this. Supposing that an individual ought, as an individual, to be accorded at least mere-property freedoms over some tangible
resource (say, by virtue of labour-desert, privacy, or the concretized application of the use-channelling and use-policing argument discussed in the last
chapter), or a transferable ownership interest over money or cashable rights
(having regard to the freedom-to-bargain argument), or over some ideational
entity (because of the creator-incentive argument discussed in the next chapter), why should inter-generational gifts stand on a footing different from that
of any other gifts? Does not the individual's choice deserve as much respect in
the one case as in the other?

There are a number of grounds on which claims to the assets of deceased
persons may be advanced and incorporated within expropriation rules. The
deceased may have induced expectations upon which the claimant has relied

---

[10] John Stuart Mill, *Principles of Political Economy: With Some of their Applications to
Social Philosophy*, in J. M. Robson (ed.), *Collected Works of John Stuart Mill* (U Toronto
P, 1965), bk. II, ch. 2, ss. 3 and 4; Henry Sidgwick, *The Elements of Politics* (2nd edn.,
Macmillan, 1897), 100–1. Locke indicates that the natural right to support enjoyed by
children entails a *prima facie* right to inherit which constitutes some restraint on unfettered testation: *Second Treatise of Government* (G. W. Gough (ed.), Basil Blackwell,
1976), ch. vi, 65, 67, 72; ch. xvi, 182–3, 190, 192.

to his detriment. In that case, in English law, the doctrine of proprietary estoppel arms a court with jurisdiction to confer some (or even all) of the assets of the deceased upon the claimant (just as it could if the deceased were still alive).[11] Or there may be undischarged maintenance obligations undertaken or owed by the deceased to the claimant which appropriating a share in his wealth is the most practical means of satisfying. English legislation enables this to be done in the case of certain specified classes of dependants.[12] Or the claimant may be in a position to invoke labour-desert because social convention requires that, in the circumstances, his contribution to a relationship with the deceased should be rewarded by according him some share of the deceased's assets.[13]

Such claims depend on special obligations incurred by the deceased during his lifetime. They do not witness to any right to inherit as such. Freedom of bequest is overridden *ad hoc*, not globally challenged. For example, the Inheritance (Provision for Family and Dependants) Act 1975 empowers the court to expropriate a deceased person's estate in favour of a child[14] where the deceased has failed to make 'such financial provision as it would be reasonable in all the circumstances of the case for the applicant to receive for his maintenance'.[15] It has been held that mere blood relationship affords no basis for such a claim.[16] There may be a case for changing English law by replacing discretionary jurisdictions with a requirement that defined shares of a person's estate should pass to his dependants irrespective of his testamentary wishes. In so far as that was done as a rough-and-ready method of implementing these special obligations (one which would avoid uncertainty and litigation costs), it would confer a legal right of inheritance but would presuppose no such moral right.

Assuming that a deceased person was the individual owner of resources

---

[11] *Inwards* v. *Baker* [1965] 2 QB 20—son built bungalow on land belonging to father in expectation that he would be allowed to live there; held that an equity had been created which was enforceable against father's estate and that, to satisfy the equity, son should receive non-transferable life interest in bungalow. *Griffiths* v. *Williams* [1978] 248 EG 947—daughter spent money on improvements to mother's house in expectation that she would continue to live there after mother's death; mother left house to granddaughter; held that granddaughter not entitled to house as against daughter since daughter had acquired an equity which, in exercise of its discretion, court would satisfy by awarding daughter non-assignable lease at nominal rent (terminable on daughter's death). *Re Basham (decd.)* [1987] 1 All ER 405—deceased led step-daughter to believe she would inherit his property, in reliance upon which step-daughter and her husband performed unpaid services for deceased; held that step-daughter should receive deceased's entire estate in preference to those entitled to it under intestacy law.

[12] Inheritance (Provision for Family and Dependants) Act 1975, as amended by the Law Reform (Succession) Act 1995, s. 2.

[13] See Ch. 11, sect. (iv)(c) above.

[14] S. 1(1)(c).

[15] S. 1(2)(b).

[16] *Re Coventry (Decd.)* [1980] Ch. 461; *Re Dennis (Decd.)* [1981] 2 All ER 140; *Re Jennings (Decd.)* [1994] 3 All ER 27.

(that they were not 'family' assets), and assuming that he has fully discharged all of his special obligations, on what basis can anyone assert a natural right to become owner of what was his, merely by virtue of blood relationship or marital or other status relationship? On this matter, it is suggested, Mill and Sidgwick were right. Relationship to another person is no firmer a basis for a natural property right than are any of the other alleged bases of such rights considered and rejected in Chapters 11 and 12.

It follows that alleged rights of inheritance, as such, do not furnish a good reason for excluding testamentary freedom from conceptions of ownership. The rejection of any natural right to inherit also has implications for the way in which we should view intestacy law. Property institutions typically provide that unbequeathed resources are to be allocated to members of a deceased person's family or to surviving relatives. In England, for example, only if someone dying intestate is unmarried and is survived by no descendant of a common grandparent does his property revert to the State. Appropriation of his assets in this way may happen to implement special obligations of the kinds discussed above, or they may happen to give effect to choices he had made (albeit they were never set out in the legally approved formal manner). In so far as the appropriation rules go further than this, they confer windfall wealth (like those rules which confer full-blooded ownership on first occupants or on those who have acquired title by adverse possession).[17]

(2) *Gifts to Futurity*

One kind of disposition that might seem especially problematic concerns gifts destined for persons yet unborn, such as a person's remote descendants. While a gift to someone with whom a donor is acquainted may be thought to represent an authentic exercise of individuality, bequests to persons whose merits or characteristics must be unknown to a testator smack of arbitrariness or unacceptable dynasticism. Common law perpetuity rules can be seen, in part, as reflecting distaste for such choices. (Technically, such dispositions may be incorporated in *inter vivos* settlements as well as wills; but in substance they amount to a species of *post-mortem* benefaction.) As one English judge put it in the middle of the last century:

A man has a natural right to enjoy his property during his life and to leave it to his children at his death. But the liberty to determine how property shall be enjoyed in saecula when he who was once the owner of it is in his grave and to destine it in perpetuity to any purpose however fantastical, useless or ludicrous, so that they cannot be said to be directly contrary to religion and morality, is a right and liberty which I think cannot be claimed by any natural or divine law and which I think ought by human law to be strictly watched and regulated.[18]

[17] See Ch. 12, sect. (i)(a) above.
[18] *Jeffreys* v. *Alexander* (1869) 8 HLC 594 at 648, *per* Lord Campbell.

(3) Prima Facie *Testamentary Freedom*

Such gifts to future unknown persons aside, there seems no reason for a categorical differentiation between testamentary and other transmission freedoms. If respect for persons requires respect for autonomous choice, and transferring property is something people choose to do, then, *prima facie*, individuals should be as free to devise and bequeath that which they already justly own as they are to make *inter vivos* gifts. The *prima facie* freedom argument holds equally for both. There may, as we shall see, be substantial arguments deriving either from wealth-disparities, or from domination-potential within families, why the final conclusion we should reach about inter-generational gifts should be special. Such considerations may warrant ulterior limitations on ownership freedoms. They do not support the view that, by reference to the property-freedom argument itself, ownership interests should not carry testamentary power.

Mill recognized that this is the case. Mill left it as an open question whether individual private property, as compared to communism, was justifiable at all.[19] On the assumption that it was, testamentary freedom must, *prima facie*, be respected. Reasons must therefore be forthcoming for overriding such freedom.

Unlike inheritance *ab intestato*, bequest is one of the attributes of property: the ownership of a thing cannot be looked upon as complete without the power of bestowing it, at death or during life, at the owner's pleasure: and all the reasons, which recommend that private property should exist, recommend *pro tanto* this extension of it.[20]

Nevertheless, whether the power of bequest should be subject to limitation was an 'ulterior question of great importance'.[21] Mill concluded that, in principle, it should be limited in the following way. An owner should not be at liberty to bequeath to any single individual wealth greater than that which would be needed to afford the donee 'the means of comfortable independence'.[22] In terms of contemporary egalitarian opinion, this looks like rather a moderate restriction on the power of bequest. Mill himself justified it, not primarily as a means to break down disparities in wealth, but because 'there would be a great multiplication of persons in easy circumstances'.[23] That is, he invokes, in this context, the independence-instrumental argument for property institutions to be discussed in the next chapter.

(c) **Partial and Conditional Gifts**

Within the limits laid down by the rules against perpetuities and inalienability, the common law permitted property-owners to create limited or conditional

---

[19] See Ch. 11, sect. (iii)(b) above and sect. (iv) of the present Chapter.
[20] N. 10 above, 223.   [21] *Ibid.*   [22] *Ibid.* 225.   [23] *Ibid.* 226.

ownership interests through the instrumentalities of estates and trusts;[24] and less elaborate restrictions on donees could be created in Roman law by means of *fideicommissa* (testamentary trusts). Does it follow from the property-freedom argument that such partial or conditional gifts should not be allowed so that absence of power to make them is to be regarded as an interior limitation on full-blooded ownership? Hegel argued that this must be so. He maintained that limitations on ownership inherited from the feudal doctrine of estates and those made possible by fideicommissary gifts could all be ruled out, at the level of abstract right, on the basis of 'self-contradiction'.

If the whole extent of the use of a thing were mine, but the abstract ownership were supposed to be someone else's, the thing as mine would be wholly penetrated by my will . . ., while it would at the same time contain something impenetrable by me, i.e. the will, in fact the empty will, of someone else. As positive will, I would thus be at the same time objective and not objective to myself in the thing—a relation of absolute contradiction.—Ownership is therefore essentially *free and complete* ownership.[25]

On this will-penetration metaphysic Hegel hangs all his particular condemnations of ownership interests falling lower on the ownership spectrum than full-blooded ownership and his rejection of restraints on alienation. It is a piece of metaphysical baggage we should discard. Merely from the fact that property institutions empower choices which would not exist without them, it does not follow that this process must be seen in terms of a will going out from the agent into the thing owned. Nor does it follow that there is one true concept of property from which conclusions can be drawn about the appropriateness of positions along the ownership spectrum or of the proper content of property-limitation rules.

In any case, such conclusions, according to Hegel himself, are only provisional. As we have seen, what emerges from the analysis of property at the level of abstract right may give place to other considerations when that moment is combined with morality and/or ethical life. In the end, corporate property, mortmain, and some restraints on testation or alienation may be justified.

Right is something *utterly sacred* for the simple reason that it is the existence [*Dasein*] of the absolute concept, of self-conscious freedom. . . . In opposition to the more formal, i.e. *more abstract* and hence more limited kind of right, that sphere and stage of the spirit in which the spirit has determined and actualized within itself the further moments contained in its Idea possesses a higher right, for it is the *more concrete* sphere, richer within itself and more truly universal . . . only the right of the world spirit is absolute in an unlimited sense.[26]

---

[24] See Ch. 5, sects. (iii) and (iv) above.

[25] G. W. F. Hegel, *Elements of the Philosophy of Right* (trans. H. B. Nisbet, CUP, 1991), 90 (para. 62).

[26] *Ibid.* 59 (para. 30).

Thus, Hegel contends that, if one takes the freedom argument for property on its own, there is an interior, contradiction-obviating argument against permitting absolute owners to exercise transactional powers so as to create limited, conditional, or inalienable ownership interests. In that he was mistaken. There is nothing self-contradictory in asserting that X, by virtue of his ownership, is free to dictate, in perpetuity, how an asset should be used and that, thereafter, no-one will ever again be fully owner of that asset. Modern legal systems do not supersede ownership freedoms when they permit owners to transfer assets to the State or to dedicate them permanently to regimes of public property via charitable donations. In the hands of State organs or charitable corporations or trustees, such assets will then be the subject of quasi-ownership interests which lack the feature of avowed self-seekingness characteristic of all ownership interests proper.[27] The recognition that owners are at liberty so to remove assets from the domain of private ownership does not contradict, but rather confirms, the assumption that owners are free to do what they like with their own.

So far as the creation of private (but limited) ownership interests is concerned, there is, as we have seen, a case for denying even *prima facie* value to choices to make any kinds of gifts (complete or partial) to remote descendants of the donor. If, however, the donee is someone known to the donor (or, as the perpetuity rule would permit, the child of such a person), and the donor is taken to be free to dispose of what is his, why should he not be at liberty to dispose of half-loaves in the form of limited ownership interests? Donees can hardly complain.

Those who support transmission powers, not by reference to the property-freedom argument, but as a necessary adjunct to a functioning market may well look askance at the creation of non-transferable ownership interests. For over a century, this has been one of the rationales underlying English legislation which seeks to prevent the tying-up of land within families. It also had a considerable influence on the development of rules against inalienability.[28] Under the English property legislation of 1925, owners are for market-instrumental reasons debarred from dictating that their land shall not be sold after their deaths. They are, nevertheless, still empowered, within perpetuity limits, to ordain that the wealth-potential of what they own shall constitute a fund as to which, though its asset-base may be changed from time to time, yet successive donees shall lack the power of free disposal of capital.

If restraints on transactional freedom are desirable it is because of considerations ulterior to the property-freedom argument. They may have to do with wealth-disparities or domination-potential; or they may derive from instrumental considerations, such as the independence argument invoked by

---

[27] See Ch. 7, sect. (iii) above.
[28] See Gregory Alexander, 'The Dead Hand and the Law of Trusts in the 19th Century' (1985) 37 *Stan. LR* 1189.

Mill, or the market considerations which pervade the English 1925 property legislation.

(ii) FETISHISM

'Fetishism', literally, refers to the worship of things. It is nowadays used as a disapprobative label within political and philosophical controversy in the following way. If someone wishes to assert that a person to whose views he is opposed has erected an argument upon a concept to which that other has given an intrinsic, unexamined, and thing-like status, he announces that his opponent has made a 'fetish' out of the concept. Fetishism, as a 'boo!' word, is common coin across the political spectrum; but its popularity for this purpose probably stems from Marx's employment of the term 'commodity fetishism' in Volume 1 of *Capital*. Marx argued that political economists had assumed that exchange value was a natural quality of things, so that commodity exchange was the only mechanism through which productive labour could be organized; and such fetishistic commodification of products had served to veil the social character of the relations between producers.[29] As we saw in Chapter 11, this veiling was of particular importance, in Marx's view, when the commodity was 'labour-power'.

That unlimited powers of transmission result in great disparities of wealth and entail dangers of illegitimate domination cannot be doubted. To these matters we turn in the next two sections. Why should one suppose, however, that these consequences are veiled from (cannot be seen by) anyone who assumes that free transmissibility is an inherent attribute of property-holdings? Mill made just this assumption without, as we shall see, being blinded to the dangers of domination. 'Commodity fetishism' has an appealing rhetorical ring, but as a general diagnostic tool for the evils of property freedoms it is dispensable. (In his earlier writings, Marx preferred 'alienation' as a generalized epithet for the evils of private property: as accumulators and dealers in things, we are 'alienated' from our true human nature as cooperative social beings'.[30])

'Fetishism', in its ordinary sense of thing-veneration, is, however, a distinct ground on which it might be claimed that all the inherent qualities of ownership interests—use-privileges, control-powers, and powers of transmission—should not be considered valuable human freedoms. The object of concern is the property-owner himself. He may come to view his relation with the thing

[29] Karl Marx, *Capital* (Penguin Classics, trans. B. Fowkes, Penguin Books, 1990), i, 163–78.

[30] Karl Marx, *Economic and Philosophical Manuscripts*, in Marx, *Early Writings* (trans. Rodney Livingstone and Gregor Benton, Penguin Books, 1975), 322–34. (As to movement between Marx's earlier and later positions, see Paul Walton and Andrew Gamble, *From Alienation to Surplus Value* (Sheed and Ward, 1972).)

owned as intrinsically valuable in a way which distorts his perception of his own authentic needs and desires and which subverts his ability to form worthwhile relationships with others. The danger is not limited to tangible items. If a property institution permits free transmissibility so that a person can accumulate wealth, he may view mere money and cashable rights in the same intrinsic, distorting, and subverting way. As Marx said—using 'fetishism' this time in its ordinary sense—the miser 'sacrifices the lusts of his flesh to the fetish of gold'.[31]

Object-fetishism is, perhaps, a recognizable psychological phenomenon. A car-fetishist or a house-fetishist would love his car or his house so much that he would stint his ordinary desires and needs to preserve and maintain it. He would not drive the car on a rainy day, preferring the inconvenience of some other form of travel to the possibility of its paintwork being smirched. He would, to his own discomfort and cost, expend time and money in keeping his house pristine. He would avoid human contacts which might interfere with the all-pervading obsession with car or house. In literature, the most complete wealth-fetishist is Dickens' portrayal of Ebenezer Scrooge in *A Christmas Carol*. Scrooge loves his money so much that he subsists in painful frugality and austerity and is unable to accept human overtures which, as the story reveals, would contribute to his true happiness.

Extreme fetishism of this sort may exist in life as well as in literature. More often it is a possibility or a tendency against which the moralist rightly warns people to be on their guard. However, it should have no place in our evaluation of institutions. The simple reason for this conclusion is that it is very difficult to distinguish fetishism from perfectly acceptable self-expression through the medium of things or wealth and it would be totally impractical to reflect any such distinction in institutional design. We observe Jones lovingly attending his garden. He produces flowers and vegetables which he could undoubtedly purchase at lower cost if he employed the same productive energy in earning money. We observe that he spends time in the garden which he could have spent relating to his family or his friends. That is hardly enough to condemn his activity as fetishistic. If he is to be respected as a person, his choices to spend energies in this way should also be respected rather than denied on the ground of concern for his own true good. Even if we suspected that there was an element of fetishism in the activities of gardener Jones, it would be beyond our invention to devise property-limitation rules which would eliminate it. Even less should we deny the argument from the value of free-expression to property on this ground and conclude that, because of the dangers of fetishism, objects should never be owned.

Moral condemnations of wealth-fetishism date back at least to the Bible. St Paul lists love of money among the cardinal sins, equating it with idolatry.[32]

---

[31] Marx, n. 29 above, 231.
[32] *Ephesians*, ch. 5, v. 5; *Colossians*, ch. 3, v. 5.

He saw it as a fundamental defect of character: 'but they that would be rich fall into temptation and a snare, and into many foolish and hurtful lusts, which drown men in destruction and perdition. For the love of money is the root of all evil'.[33] Nevertheless, it was clearly not Paul's view that money is socially dispensable. Money was needed in order to discharge obligations to pay debts and taxes,[34] to provide for one's dependants,[35] and, above all, to display generosity.[36] Property institutions may incorporate these obligations, but it is impracticable to devise property-limitation or expropriation rules specifically addressed to the personal vice of wealth-fetishism. The moralist may sound the alarm, but neither social convention nor law can lay down a marker indicating the point at which the individual's day-to-day choices to spend, or not to spend, the money he owns are to be overridden solely on the ground that, in the circumstances, they exhibit the character trait of fetishism.

Fetishism should play no role whatever in property-institutional design.

(iii) DISPARITIES IN WEALTH

(a) Wealth-disparities and Property-freedoms

Property institutions confer ranges of choice upon property-owners. Exercise of such choices may lead to large disparities in holdings of wealth. Is that a good reason for denying them the status of valuable human freedoms? Hegel's answer was no.[37] A wide swathe of contemporary political opinion takes a different view. A society which tolerates enormous disparities in wealth is, for that reason alone, an unjust society. How that perception should be accommodated if one also supposes that there ought to be property freedoms is a perennial problem which, at an abstract level, has received no satisfactory answer.

Take, for example, John Rawls' contractarian theory of justice. Rawls recommends us to test the intuitions we have against an imaginary situation in which people are negotiating a structure of a society whilst not knowing what positions they will actually occupy in it. Such an exercise is designed to stimulate non-self-regarding reflection. If there seems to be a mismatch between what we, as real people, hold strongly to be just and the outcome that we suppose would be reached by the imaginary people behind their 'veil of ignorance', we may modify our intuitions or rejig the conditions of the imaginary 'original position'. The upshot to be looked for is a situation of 'reflective

[33] 1 *Timothy*, ch. 6, vs. 9 and 10.
[34] *Romans*, ch. 13, v. 7.
[35] 1 *Timothy*, ch. 5, v. 8.
[36] *Romans*, ch. 12, v. 13, ch. 15, v. 27; 1 *Corinthians*, ch. 16, v. 2; 2 *Corinthians*, ch. 9, v. 7; *Ephesians*, ch. 4, v. 28.
[37] N. 25 above, 79–81 (para. 49 and addition).

equilibrium' between our (perhaps reformed) intuitions and social arrangements which, we suppose, people who did not know what their places in society would be would have agreed to.[38]

Rawls' own conclusion is that this procedure yields a conception of justice in which 'basic liberties' are accorded priority over everything else. No-one (ignorant of his role in a society) would take the chance of being denied such liberties. Accordingly, the first principle of justice which would be chosen behind the veil of ignorance is one which provides that '[e]ach person is to have an equal right to the most extensive total system of equal basic liberties compatible with a similar system of liberty for all.'[39] Provided such basic liberties are ensured, the imaginary contractors would opt for a society which, among other things, excludes disparities of wealth save so far as these are needed (say, for incentive or market-instrumental reasons) as a means of making everyone better off. The second principle of justice is accordingly '[s]ocial and economic inequalities are to be arranged so that they are both: (a) to the greatest benefit of the least advantaged, consistent with the just savings principle, and (b) attached to offices and positions open to all under conditions of fair equality of opportunity.'[40]

These formulations have been the subject of a voluminous critical literature. We are here concerned only with one seeming paradox. If the basic liberties which are given 'lexical priority' by the first principal include property-freedoms, might not that subvert the seemingly egalitarian implications of the second principle? If basic liberties must be accorded full sway before we come to dividing up wealth, and if these liberties include freedoms whose exercise will result in enormous disparity of wealth-packages, what wealth will be left to be divided at the second stage?

One answer might be to deny, contrary to the argument of the last chapter, that property-freedoms are among the basic liberties—to contend that a society need not accord ownership privileges and powers even over chattels or dwellings, nor grant those freedoms to opt between goods and services which flow from recognizing ownership of money. That is not Rawls' position. He recognizes that the right to hold 'personal property' is among the basic liberties conceded priority by the first principle.[41] He fails to point out, however, that property freedoms differ in one important respect from the other basic liberties he lists, *viz.*, political liberties, freedom of speech and of assembly, liberty of conscience and freedom of thought, freedom of the person, freedom from arbitrary arrest.[42] Everyone comes into the world as a potential holder of opinions. Accordingly, we know roughly what is involved in demands that all should be accorded freedoms of expression and belief and that political arrangements should aim at giving equal weight to everyone's views. Everyone

---

[38] John Rawls, *A Theory of Justice* (OUP, 1972), 11–22, 46–53, 118–21, 136–42, 175–83.

[39] *Ibid.* 302.　　　　[40] *Ibid.*　　　　[41] *Ibid.* 61.　　　　[42] *Ibid.*

has a body which may be wrongfully seized, and we can understand what it is to deny to the State the power to commit such wrongs. But no-one's individual humanity attaches to him an ownership interest over any particular resource. As we saw at the end of the last chapter, however strong a property-freedom argument may be, it is necessarily distributionally blind. Rawls does not make clear what he means by 'personal property', nor whether ownership privileges and powers of all kinds are among the 'basic liberties'.

Even if all that a property institution were to afford were mere-property freedoms (that is, open-ended use-privileges and control-powers without powers of transmission), and if it granted these only in respect of widely available chattels and dwellings, unequal access to resources would result. For one thing, the chattels or the dwellings that people own may differ in their potential use-value. Further, there might be no guarantee that everyone would have an ownership interest in each item on the property list. But in any case, even if the things are roughly comparable in utility and everyone has one, the very fact that, by assumption, each 'owner' may exercise control-powers at his pleasure carries the possibility of inequality. Consider the imaginary Pink Land licensees described in Chapter 2. Each has the right, during the subsistence of the licence, to determine who shall reside with him in the licensed dwelling. Since the licensees are human individuals and not clones, some will exercise this power more generously than others. Those who are the recipients of more generosity than they themselves exercise will turn out to have more than average access.

Given the use-channelling and use-policing advantages of mere-property freedoms discussed in the last chapter, inequalities of this sort could hardly rank as a ground for not recognizing their value. No doubt Rawls' hypothetical contractors would have opted for them among the 'basic liberties' with lexical-priority status, even though none of them know what particular item will fall to his or her lot. But we need not invoke the opinions of such spectral persons. It is the actual use-channelling and use-policing functions which such freedoms perform within real property institutions which makes them valuable notwithstanding their distributional blindness. As Irving Hallowell concludes, after a wide comparative survey of property institutions in primitive and developed societies:

For human society, by definition, implies the existence of ordered relations and ordered relations mean that individuals do enjoy the security of socially sanctioned rights and obligations of various kinds. Among them we inevitably find socially recognised and sanctioned interests in valuable objects. The fact that in all human societies individuals are secured against the necessity of being constantly on the alert to defend such objects from others by physical force alone is one of the primary contributions of the institution of property to a human social order and the security of the individual.[43]

---

[43] A. Irving Hallowell, 'The Nature and Function of Property as a Social Institution', in Hallowell, *Culture and Experience* (U Pa. P, 1955), 249.

What about transmission freedoms? We argued in the last chapter that the property-freedom argument carries at least the consequence that a property institution should include money among the ownable items. Robert Nozick has advanced a well-known 'Wilt Chamberlain' argument for showing that, even if all citizens begin only with modest sums of cash, if we concede them freedom to spend as they please, large holdings of wealth may result. They may all choose to buy tickets to watch an outstanding sportsman perform so that the sportsman (Wilt Chamberlain) will end up disproportionately rich.[44] Permitting people to spend their money on National Lottery tickets or in other forms of gambling also leads to individual fortunes.

Those who see large disparities in holdings of wealth as the unacceptable side of transmission freedoms do not, generally speaking, have the idiosyncratic accumulations of gifted athletes or pop stars, or the windfalls of lucky gamblers, in mind. It is rather the persistence of a tiny percentage of the population who, from generation to generation, hold a grossly disproportionate share of wealth in the form of tangible assets or cashable rights. There is abundant evidence that, in Britain at least, inter-generational transfers are the major causes of wealth-disparity. The entrepreneur who starts with very little and then amasses a fortune through trading in his services or his products is a rarity. Most accumulations of wealth are the result of inheritance.[45]

It was argued in section (i) of this Chapter that alleged rights of inheritance were not a sufficient reason for excluding freedom of bequest from a defensible conception of ownership interests. Might it not be, however, that the disparities in wealth-holding to which this freedom has undoubtedly given rise require that it be overridden? (They would scarcely be touched merely by tinkering with intestacy rules since, as Josiah Wedgwood pointed out, most rich men make wills.[46]) As we saw, Mill recommended severe restrictions on legacies to individuals. Harold Laski would have gone much further. Modest income bequests to wives and children and small legacies to other persons should be permitted, and also charitable endowments shorn of any power to control the use to which benefactions might be put. Subject to that, freedom of bequest should be abrogated and the State assume the role of universal heir.[47]

If, however, as has been argued, inter-generational transfers (at least in favour of persons known to the donor) are as authentic an expression of autonomous choice as any other dispositions of property, none of these suggestions seems warranted if there is an alternative means of breaking down

[44] Robert Nozick, *Anarchy, State and Utopia* (Basil Blackwell, 1974), 160–4.

[45] Josiah Wedgwood, *The Economics of Inheritance* (Routledge, 1929), pt. 1; A. B. Atkinson, *Unequal Shares: Wealth in Britain* (Penguin Books, 1974); C. D. Harbury and D. M. W. N. Hitchens, *Inheritance and Wealth Inequality in Britain* (George Allen and Unwin, 1979).

[46] Wedgwood, n. 45 above, 187.

[47] Harold J. Laski, *A Grammar of Politics* (3rd edn., George Allen and Unwin, 1934), 526–33.

wealth-disparities. The obvious alternative is capital taxation. Graduated wealth taxes are aimed directly at the problem. Since when rich people die someone has to undertake the task of assembling a record of their assets, death is an administratively convenient point for imposing a wealth tax—although it also gives rise to notorious problems of tax-avoidance planning and complex legislative countermeasures.

In short, if disparity in wealth is *per se* objectionable, the answer is redistributive taxation, not some *a priori* hiving-off of a particular category of transmission power from the ownership bundle. Nobody should be banned from purchasing Wilt Chamberlain's services nor from leaving what is theirs (once all other just claims have been discharged) either to their favourite nephew or to a home for abandoned cats.

Redistributive expropriation rules presuppose that transmission freedoms, unlike mere property freedoms, do not have Rawls' 'lexical priority'.[48] They presuppose, in other words, the conclusion reached in Chapters 11 and 12, that there are no natural rights to full-blooded ownership. (Nozick suggested that taxing the fruits of labour amounts to partial servitude; but that, as we saw, was the consequence of a particular version of the self-ownership myth.[49]) Redistributive taxation, however, does not deny the *prima facie* value of transmission freedoms.

(b) What is Wrong with Wealth-disparities?

Why should we suppose that disparities in wealth are, in themselves, unjust? It is important to isolate that question from many others which are relevant to property-institutional design. We shall see in the next section that wealthy individuals who own enterprises may, by virtue of that ownership, be in a position to dominate the lives of others in an illegitimate way. To distinguish that issue from the question of wealth-disparity, assume that, in a particular society, such enterprises are not privately owned—that major holdings of wealth consist in the ownership of cashable claims over resources vested in public bodies, but that a few people have vastly more of such claims than the average citizen. We shall argue in the next chapter that the 'justice costs' for which taxing expropriation rules may rightly be imposed include the provision of basic needs for all. Assume that, in the society, all such basic needs have been discharged, but that, even so, large disparities in wealth-holding still persist. Why is disparity, as such, objectionable?

There seems to be a widely held view that the very fact that people know that others are much richer than they are is inimical to a defensible scheme of

---

[48] Rawls himself advocates both 'inheritance and gift taxes' and 'restrictions on the rights of bequest' as mechanisms for producing the distribution required by his second principle, without appreciating that this might raise problems for the priority-status of the right to hold personal property—n. 38 above, 277.

[49] See Ch. 11, sect. (ii)(b)(1) above.

human association. Stephen Munzer puts the matter as follows. People who resent the rich lack a 'sense of worth'.[50] Inequalities in wealth wound self-esteem through comparison with others.[51] A 'fully human life' therefore requires that a property institution be so designed that there is not too great a 'gap' between the wealth-holdings of individuals.[52]

Munzer's social-psychological diagnosis is highly contingent. David Hume assumed the opposite, that 'there is nothing more certain, than that we naturally esteem and respect the rich'.[53] Hume found the principal cause of this supposed phenomenon to be sympathetic entering into the pleasures of the power which other people's riches affords them.[54] Why should we assume any universal truths about psychological reactions to wealth?

In some cultures the rich may be the subject of fawning admiration, in others of dissociative envy. Should we say that in the former wealth-disparity is just while in the latter it is not? The agenda of justice presupposes a forum of debate in which there is room to ask any participant to stand back from his untutored psychological reactions and to consider whether their significance for him is relevant to any feature of just human association. If that were not so, we could not have built into our minimalist conception of justice the first and third elements (natural equality and universalized bans on unprovoked personal violence), in the teeth of the trans-historical racist and xenophobic majority.

Social phenomena of many kinds militate against that sense of common citizenship which, in a just form of human association, would enter into the individual's sense of self-worth. Property, as such, is often not the problem. Fissures arise within communities from offensive discrimination on grounds of ethnicity, gender, or physical or mental disability. Societies may be torn apart by nationalist or tribal hatred. Property comes to the fore directly when labour-desert claims are invoked on a comparative basis—X class of persons are disproportionately rewarded for their work compared with Y class; and it is indirectly relevant to demands that, given the totality of social wealth, requirement Z should be considered a basic need of all citizens, the discharge of which is a 'justice cost'. It may well be that taxation schemes needed to defray such costs will have the effect of reducing disparities in wealth. There are considerations of 'marginal utility'—that is, the assumption that the last pound removed from the wealth-holding of a rich man is less of a detriment to him than is the taking of the last pound from someone who is less rich. Bentham announced this as one of the 'pathological propositions' upon which the

[50] Stephen R. Munzer, *A Theory of Property* (CUP, 1990), 104.
[51] *Ibid*. 249–52.
[52] *Ibid*. 100–5, 181–2, 247–53, 396–8.
[53] David Hume, *A Treatise of Human Nature* (T. H. Green and T. H. Grose (eds.), Longmans, Green and Co., 1874), ii, 148.
[54] *Ibid*. 145–52.

legislator could safely rely;[55] and it is widely accepted even by those who, in other respects, dispute the feasibility of inter-personal comparison of satisfactions.

Demands for fairness in comparisons of labour-desert or for redistributive taxation to meet basic needs may be expressed as complaints against the 'unequal society'. They do not support the view that disparity in wealth, as such, is a reason for negating the effect of freedoms to transmit. The rich deserve no admiration, merely for being rich; but neither do they deserve expropriation, merely for being rich.

Disparities in wealth should play no role in property-institutional design unless, in the contingent circumstances of a particular society at a particular time, it can be shown that measures of wealth-expropriation are indispensable to producing psychological conditions for a desirable sense of common citizenship. For wealth-disparity to be shown to be non-contingently unjust, in and of itself, we would need to give a specific interpretation to the first element of our minimalist conception of justice. It would have to be argued that X is necessarily treated as less worthy than Y unless social wealth is allocated to them equally. Then it would follow, not merely that disparity was unacceptable, but that mathematical equality of resources should be considered a property-specific justice reason dominating over all features of property-institutional design. That important contention will be considered (and rejected) in Chapter 16.

(iv) DOMINATION-POTENTIAL

The most fundamental argument against justifying property from freedom alone is that such a justification ignores the nature of property institutions. There can be no property without trespassory rules. Therefore, to concede a property relationship between one person and a thing, at any point along the ownership spectrum, is to negate the liberty of the rest of mankind to use the thing without the licence of the 'owner'. The owner's say-so gives him a power over others. The person–thing relationship is always necessarily a multitude of person–person relationships in which, as to use of the thing, he is sovereign and they are subjects. The domain of domination is greatly increased if ownership is conceived of as entailing freedom to transmit, for two reasons. First, the trespassory rules now dictate, not merely that people may not use the thing without the licence of one particular X, but that they must not use it without the licence of a succession of Xs. They therefore acquire a potentially timeless duration. Secondly, power to transmit confers on the owner an additional relationship of domination with potential transferees; it is at his say-so whether or not they should acquire his dominating position.

[55] Jeremy Bentham, *Principles of the Civil Code*, Pt, 1, ch. 6, in C. K. Ogden (ed.), *Jeremy Bentham: The Theory of Legislation* (Kegan Paul, 1931).

Theorists who deplore great inequality in wealth-holdings and recommend measures to alleviate it often have in mind, not the social-psychological argument against wealth-disparities discussed in the last section, but rather inequality's resultant domination-potential. It is not disparity in bank balances that matters. It is the influence over the lives of others which large property-holdings afford. Mill, for example, who supposed that the final choice between private property and communism should be made on the basis of which system would best promote human liberty and spontaneity, had no doubt that if comparison were made between communism and the private property institutions of his day, communism would be the clear winner. The reason was that the present distribution of wealth meant that the liberties of the poor and of women were reduced to a state little better than slavery.

The restraints of Communism would be freedom in comparison with the present condition of the majority of the human race. The generality of labourers in this and most other countries, have as little choice of occupation or freedom of locomotion, are practically as dependent on fixed rules and on the will of others, as they could be on any system short of actual slavery; to say nothing of the entire domestic subjection of one half the species.[56]

At an abstract level, the argument from domination-potential can be viewed as a counter to the valuation of all freedoms inherent in property institutions. Domination-potential, and thus the denial of freedoms to non-owners, is an inherent feature of ownership interests over trivial as well as major items of social wealth. There is, however, one very good reason why the argument should not be taken at this abstract level. Mere-property freedoms and freedoms to transmit necessarily facilitate ranges of autonomous choice, whereas freedom-denying domination is only a potential concomitant of the exercise of ownership powers. Without reference to the social context in which any particular property institution holds sway, we cannot tell whether owners of particular items will, in practice, be in a position, by virtue of their ownership, to exercise unjust restraints over the liberties of non-owners. The practical significance of domination-potential depends on questions of relative scarcity, the extent to which a society discharges those just obligations to meet basic needs which we have yet to discuss, and the comparative merits of non-ownership alternatives.

If the supply of objects like clothing, furniture, and books is drastically restricted, those few who own them could dominate their fellows by the ego-centric exercise of their ownership powers to control use. On the other hand, where such chattels are widely available, the use-channelling and use-policing functions of ownership interests (discussed in the last chapter), as compared with costly and intrusive regimes of communal use, clearly out-weigh such dangers of domination. Familiar political controversies take that much for

---

[56] *Principles of Political Economy*, n. 10 above, 209.

granted. The problem of domination arises, realistically, only in two important contexts. The first concerns major enterprises, where the exercise of ownership powers may adversely affect large sectors of the life-plans of those who are dependent on them. The second concerns family life, where the vesting of ownership powers over assets needed by all family members in heads of households may facilitate and encourage unjust structures of subordination.

(a) Enterprises

Should major units of production (like factories and farms), or service-providing enterprises (like hospitals, schools, and railways) be the subject of ownership interests vested in private individuals or corporations, or should they become or remain the subject of quasi-ownership interests vested in organs of the State or other public agencies? Disputants over that question invoke (or deny) the instrumental merits of markets; but they also appeal to the significance of domination-potential, and it is that feature with which we are presently concerned. The controversy has, for a century and a half, come to be associated with the labels 'capitalism' and 'socialism'.

The disjunction, capitalist/socialist, is misleading in several respects. For one thing, theoretical socialists may oppose some other variety of communal use both to private and to State 'ownership'. As we have seen, there are, in theory, four variants of communal-use regime: common property; communitarian property; protected non-property holdings; and quasi-ownership interests.[57] Socialist aspirations as regards enterprises may envisage one of the first three or group private ownership by workers. Socialist practice has uniformly adopted public quasi-ownership interests. That was so in the former communist regimes in the Soviet Union and in Eastern Europe.[58] The same has been true of socialist governments in Western democracies.

From 1918 until 1995, the constitution of the British Labour Party contained a commitment (clause 4) in the following terms:

to secure for the workers by hand or by brain the full fruits of their industry and the most equitable distribution thereof that may be possible upon the basis of the common ownership of the means of production, distribution and exchange, and the best obtainable system of popular administration and control of each industry or service.

The expression 'common ownership' is a contradiction in terms, unless it means joint ownership by some group. An enterprise would be the subject of 'common property' if there were no trespassory rules relating to it and hence neither protected ownership nor quasi-ownership interests. Such literal

[57] See Ch. 7, sects. (ii)–(v) and Ch. 13, sect. (iii) above.
[58] Even in the former Yugoslavia—see Ivo Lapenna, *State and Law: Soviet and Yugoslav Theory* (Athlone Press, 1964), 42–51.

common property in relation to enterprises would be wildly implausible.[59] The reference to 'fruits of labour' suggests private group ownership by the workers by hand or brain, with all the product being distributed amongst them (perhaps on the basis of labour-desert). But then 'equitable distribution' may be thought to entail that some of the fruits should accrue for public use. In any case, everyday discussion of clause 4 has employed the term 'public owner-ship' as a synonym for 'common ownership', and Labour governments have put clause 4 into practice exclusively by subjecting some enterprises to quasi-ownership interests.

Furthermore, a political dispute may centre, not on whether an enterprise should be publicly 'owned', but around what kind of quasi-ownership interest should be in place. All quasi-ownership interests involve a mix of powers modelled on those of ownership interests proper and those connected with the particular function being discharged.[60] In the United Kingdom at the present day there is a party political controversy over the question whether hospitals providing the National Health Service should be vested either in local health authorities or in self-governing trusts. Either way, they will not be privately owned in the sense that management decisions can be justified on the ground that they maximize the wealth of shareholders. The dispute concerns two varie-ties of quasi-ownership interests: the one (self-governing trusts) involving more powers (particularly powers of hiring and firing) modelled on ownership interests; the other (Health Authority 'ownership') delimiting powers more rigorously by reference to the perceived function ('public accountability'). These are important questions of property-institutional design. Little is gained by labelling the opposed proposals 'capitalist' or 'socialist'.

Nevertheless, the familiar debate does encompass two sources of domination-potential which are peculiar to 'capitalist' production. Authorized self-seekingness is the differentiating characteristic of ownership interests as contrasted with quasi-ownership interests of all kinds. Decisions adversely affecting the lives of others may be frankly justified by private owners of enter-prises on the ground that they maximize private holdings of wealth. Officials exercising quasi-ownership powers are denied that particular justification. Secondly, employees of a privately owned enterprise are constantly at the mercy of economic conditions which may render it unprofitable and, ultimately, sub-ject its assets to bankruptcy expropriation. That is, characteristically not the position of their counterparts working for publicly 'owned' enterprises since bankruptcy expropriation rules do not apply in the same way to quasi-ownership interests.[61]

Capitalist owners of the nineteenth century were empowered, as owners, to submit workers to humiliating, capricious, and cruel domination over every aspect of their working lives. (That was the background for Marx's conceptual

---

[59] See Ch. 13, sect. (iii) above.   [60] See Ch. 7, sect (iii)(b) above.
[61] See Ch. 7, sect. (iii)(b) above.

blunder in insisting that every service contract *must* be a conveyance of labour-power.[62]) The common law evolved rules to restrict ownership powers where their exercise adversely affected neighbouring owners, but was powerless to draw the teeth of domination-potential. Recall the steel workers' case[63] where the court held, with regret, that owners could not be restrained, at common law, from destroying unprofitable plants even though the consequence was to deprive thousands of people of employment. The modern regulatory State has, however, enacted a raft of property-limitation and expropriation rules directed specifically at mitigating domination-potential. Use-privileges and control-powers may be curtailed by safety and health regulations and transmission powers by price controls, anti-monopoly laws, and rules governing fair wages and unfair dismissal. Expropriation rules may impose forced contributions to fund redundancy pay, pensions, and insurance against sickness or disability.

Regulatory interventions of this kind counteract the powers of owners to dominate day-to-day working lives. They are, however, no more than weak palliatives so far as security of employment is concerned. For so long as the bulk of the average person's life-chances and income stream is dependent on retaining his job, he is in a significant relationship of domination and subordination with anyone empowered to dismiss him. If he works for an enterprise which is owned by an individual or a private corporation, that power may be exercised in an avowedly self-seeking fashion and the enterprise itself may become insolvent. Security of employment was the leading saving grace of those communist regimes which have recently collapsed in Eastern Europe and the former Soviet Union. Their people's disenchantment with those regimes suggests that they concluded that exemption from that crucial aspect of domination-potential was not sufficiently valuable to outweigh other kinds of domination which flourished in those societies and the advantages in terms of increased wealth for which, they supposed, market freedoms were a necessary pre-condition.

Domination-potential (especially as regards security of employment) is an inevitable adjunct of private ownership of major industrial and service enterprises. But, of course, its absence is not a necessary incident of quasi-ownership interests. The latter are also typically entrenched within hierarchical relationships. Managers of State-owned enterprises may be vested with many powers modelled on those of ownership interests. They too may close down 'unprofitable' enterprises or dismiss 'redundant' employees, even though they cannot announce that increase in private wealth-holdings is their reason for doing so. Those who are dependent on decision-makers for services or for their livelihoods may view decisions of either capitalists or bureaucrats as equally arbitrary.

---

[62] See Ch. 11, sect. (ii)(b)(3–4) above.
[63] *United Steel Workers* v. *United States Steel Corporation*, 631 F 2d 1264 (1980), discussed in Ch. 6, sect. (ii) above.

Thus, notwithstanding the two special features of private ownership of productive and service enterprises (authorized self-seekingness and bankruptcy-risk) nothing but a case-by-case contextual comparison can settle whether ownership freedoms have more domination-potential than their quasi-ownership counterparts. Property-limitation rules may so reduce the discretion of owners, on the one hand, and delegated authority may so increase the discretion of social-agency decision-makers, on the other hand, that there is little difference in hierarchical control. Even security of employment may come out the same, especially if private owners receive subsidies from the State which are conditional upon the maintenance of an existing labour force. Furthermore, the effective power of owners or quasi-owners of enterprises to dominate the lives of workers, customers, patients, pupils, and so on will vary according to many contextual considerations unconnected with their place within property institutions. What effective choice, what political influence, do these groups have? Are the media able and willing to report complaints? How open is the society?

Given the contextual nature of the comparison and the wealth of variables which may be built into the packaging of ownership or quasi-ownership interests, it is a theoretical mistake of the first order to suppose that all social relationships take a different colour depending on whether major productive and service enterprises are or are not privately owned. There are countries in which most provision of goods and services is organized on the basis of private ownership of enterprises. But there is no such thing as a distinctly 'capitalist' society. The choice between ownership and quasi-ownership interests is an important technical question of property-institutional design but it does not deserve the pivotal role assigned to it within the socialist/capitalist disjunction.[64]

The foregoing discussion presupposes a choice between ownership or quasi-ownership interests. Both entail hierarchy in decision-making and hence domination-potential. Advocates of (as yet) untried experiments in novel forms of communitarian property may insist that all necessary use-channelling and use-policing functions over factors of production or service-provision could be maintained without any hierarchy at all. Their opponents might contend that there would then be dangers of horizontal domination. Associations

---

[64] See James Grunebaum, *Private Ownership* (Routledge, 1991), ch. 7. Grunebaum contends that the moral 'principle of autonomy' should be foundational for property institutions and draws the following conclusions. Ultimate control of land and natural resources and the income arising from them should be vested in the community, but everyone should be free to sell his labour for what it will fetch and to invest the remuneration he receives, *inter alia*, in industrial enterprises. In the result, a range of packaged ownership or quasi-ownership interests in such enterprises is permissible.

Somewhat confusingly, Grunebaum transfers the word 'autonomy' from the underlying principle to the concept of ownership itself, and treats 'autonomous ownership' as a conception competitive with 'private' or 'State' ownership. There is no sense in which one can 'autonomously' own a resource as distinct from (privately or publicly) 'owning' it.

of workers would be able to dictate the terms and duration of employment of fellow workers. It seems plausible to suppose that, as in the case of the choice which has in fact been practised, contextual considerations of many kinds would enter into the equation. The variant of 'ownership', in itself, settles very little.

We must conclude that there is no abstract argument from the value of autonomous choice as such, combined with the inherent freedom-facilitating functions of ownership interests, which provides any straightforward justification for private property in major productive and service enterprises. Different instances present too many institutional and contextual variables. The fact that such freedoms entail powers of decision over assets which play an important part in the lives of others, and hence carry the possibility of freedom-restricting domination, insures that the argument from autonomous choice will not automatically succeed. The fact that quasi-ownership alternatives also entail such powers of decision ensures that the argument will not always fail. That there is no global answer to the question whether, in this context, ownership freedoms are truly valuable, all things considered, will be no surprise to most observers of the traditional capitalist/socialist controversy.[65] It must also be borne in mind that we have here been considering that argument for ownership interests which focuses on their inherent autonomous-choice facilitation. The alleged instrumental merits of markets have yet to be considered.

(b) Families

As we have seen, Hegel supposed that the abstract concept of the free individual will, when confronted with the historically-evolved institution of private property, must entail that, at the 'moment' of 'abstract right', private property ought always to take the form of individual full-blooded ownership; but that, nevertheless, when that moment was taken up within the moment of 'ethical life', some other variant of property relations might be appropriate in 'civil society'. Of the ulterior anti-property-freedom arguments we have considered in this Chapter, Hegel makes no reference to 'fetishism', because, as he was writing before Marx, that term had not become a buzz word of political philosophy. He considers and dismisses out of hand disparity of wealth as a relevant anti-property-freedom argument.[66] He ignores domination-potential in the context of work relations; but he does admit its significance within the context of family life.[67] He says that, although unrestrained testamentary power as an exercise of free choice 'may certainly be permitted', it ought to be carefully circumscribed within ethical life since it encourages the exercise of arbitrary

---

[65] See Leszek Kolakowski and Stuart Hampshire (eds.), *The Socialist Idea: a Re-appraisal* (Quartet Books, 1977).
[66] N. 25 above, 79–81 (para. 49 and addition).
[67] *Ibid*. 218 (para. 180 and addition).

affection which 'may lead to a beneficiary being required to submit to the greatest indignities. In England, where all kinds of eccentricity are endemic, innumerable foolish notions are associated with wills'.[68]

The wealthy head of a bourgeois nuclear family, armed with despotic power over his dependants by virtue of his wealth, is a demonic figure stalking nineteenth-century life and literature. Frederick Engels read him backwards into the dawn of civilization. On the basis of highly selective and now largely discredited anthropology, Engels maintained that there had once been clans in which, whilst women worked at home caring for the nurture of children and other domestic tasks, their relationship to men was not one of oppression since their work was properly valued. Along came what? Production of items with use-value which were in excess of those required for immediate consumption. Result! Men *necessarily* asserted full-blooded private ownership over these items, and also *inevitably* wanted their biological offspring to step into their ownership interests when they died. Therefore, monogamous marriage was instituted so that males could be reasonably certain who were their 'own' children, and the domestic labour of women became degraded, exploitative, and servile. All this occurred with the first introduction of a generalized system of private property, long before the later emergence of capitalist modes of production and the modern bourgeois family. The latter is, however, the most patent exemplar of the prescription: surplus product means private-inheritable property which means domestic slavery of women through the institution of monogamous marriage—as well as the maintenance of a class system and States to defend private property against that majority of males who have not succeeded in collaring the ownable and inheritable items.[69]

Such an analysis might explain, at best, why bourgeois women are the objects of illegitimate domination, even though they are, by marriage, members of the capitalist class—who, according to a Marxist analysis, are supposed to be the exploiters. By focusing on inheritability as the crucial feature of private property which fuels exploitative relationships, the analysis is disabled from postulating that non-bourgeois males, who may happen to own a little property in the form of the only money coming into a household or perhaps a non-inheritable ownership interest in a dwelling, are, by virtue of such modest property-holdings, empowered to dominate their dependants. The analysis has even less to offer by way of explanation of domination of women by men who are altogether propertyless. If Engels were right, only rich women would ever be exploited as women. Male and female members of the proletariat would be exploited by the capitalists, but male proletarians, having nothing inheritable to own, would not foist monogamy and degradation on their female

---

[68] *Ibid*. 218 (para. 180 addition).
[69] Frederick Engels, *The Origins of the Family, Private Property and the State* (Eleanor Burke Leacock (ed.), Lawrence and Wishart, 1972).

partners—unless, perhaps, they caught the habit by imitation of the propertied classes. Not surprisingly, Engels' analysis is uncongenial from the point of view of a radical feminist critique which sees exploitation of women by men as a pervasive feature of all social arrangements.[70]

The problems associated with the internal structure of the nuclear family in modern Western societies go far beyond anything which is within the domain of property institutions. The present discussion concerns only the contribution to unjustifiable domination which may result from the fact that householders own the property which the family uses and needs. That parents ought to make at least some of the important decisions controlling activities of young children seems hardly controversial. There is such a thing as honourable dependence. It is another matter if they have, in practice, a power to dictate life-plans to older children and it is manifestly unjust if husbands have such a power over wives. Adults, at least, cannot justly be denied an equal say in matters affecting their joint lives. Yet if other members of a family are dependent on a head-of-house owner for the roof over their heads or for a share in his income to meet all their needs, the domination-potential which is inherent in his ownership interests can be viewed as a substantial argument against valuing the autonomous choices they afford him.

Full-blooded ownership would entail that a head of household could turn dependants and spouses out of doors ('cut them off without a shilling') with all the despotic implications that would follow. It would mean that he could dispose of the assets on which they depend without consulting their interests. It would carry the power to leave them destitute at his death by willing everything away from them. The latter power would be of particular significance, since it can be exercised without their knowledge and, whatever restraints might deter a living owner from despotic exercise of his ownership powers, cannot touch the cruel or eccentric testator.

These considerations are enough to demonstrate that, in this context as in that of major enterprises, there is no straightforward argument from autonomous choice which justifies the freedom-facilitation inherent in ownership interests. Domination-potential is by far the most significant of the anti-property freedom arguments. Nevertheless, it cannot serve, at an abstract level, as a complete negation of the value of ownership freedoms. Much will depend on the proprietary subject matter under consideration, the counter-domination property-limitation and expropriation rules embodied within a particular property institution and, above all, on the wider social setting.

We saw in the last chapter that, in the case of ordinary chattels, the use-channelling and use-policing advantages of ownership interests would, in most contexts, greatly outweigh the merits of any system of communal use. It is implausible to suggest that we should revise that conclusion because the owner of a book or a pair of shoes might exercise his ownership control-powers in

---

[70] See Catharine A. MacKinnon, *Toward a Feminist Theory of the State* (Harv. UP, 1989), 19–37.

such a way as to dominate the lives of his dependants. Ownership of dwellings is another matter. That a family, as a unit, should be afforded, by appropriate trespassory rules, ownership privileges and powers against the rest of the world slots into the same use-policing and use-channelling rationale that applies to chattels. But that a single head-of-household owner should, as owner, be free to dictate use of the dwelling by his dependants, or to render them homeless by disposing of it, raises a genuine spectre of illegitimate domination against which modern property institutions have sought to introduce counter-measures.

We mentioned earlier in this Chapter that the English property legislation enacted in 1925 was designed, primarily, to promote the free marketability of land, in service of the market-instrumental rationale of property institutions. Subsequent legislation and case law exhibit a fluctuating compromise between this objective and protection of dependants' security in occupation. It was held that a wife's right to occupy a dwelling owned by her husband could not bind purchasers from him.[71] That ruling was reversed by legislation[72] under which, once registered, a spousal occupation right is enforceable against most successors. The effect was to confer on the spouse with a registered occupation right a 'half-property' interest (use-privileges without control-powers).[73] If the dwelling stands at law in the name of a single individual, but some other member of his family has acquired a share in the beneficial ownership (usually, by contributing to the expenses of acquisition), the conveyancing legislation has been interpreted in such a way that a sale by the legal owner will not deprive the other family member of her right to continue in occupation.[74] If the dwelling is jointly owned, the courts have sometimes been willing to exercise their statutory discretion to grant or to refuse an order for sale[75] by declining to make the order when they can find an underlying and subsisting 'collateral purpose' of the acquisition of the property, under which the claimant is entitled to remain in occupation.[76] However, should a house-owner become insolvent, neither a registered occupation right,[77] nor (in most cases) the occupation use-privileges inherent in the beneficial interest of a family dependant,[78] will prevail against the rights of creditors represented by the trustee in bankruptcy. Furthermore, the courts have found a variety of reasons for holding that a dependent with a beneficial interest has no standing to

---

[71] *National Provincial Bank Ltd* v. *Ainsworth* [1965] AC 1175.
[72] Now contained in the Matrimonial Homes Act 1983.
[73] See Ch. 3, sect. (iv) above.
[74] *Williams and Glyn's Bank Limited* v. *Boland* [1981] AC 487.
[75] Law of Property Act 1925, s. 30.
[76] *Bull* v. *Bull* [1955] 1 QB 234; *Williams* v. *Williams* [1976] Ch. 278; *Jones* v. *Jones* [1977] 2 All ER 231; *Re Ever's Trust* [1980] 3 All ER 399; *Chhokar* v. *Chhokar* [1984] FLR 313.
[77] Matrimonial Homes Act 1983, s. 2(7).
[78] *Re Bailey* [1977] 2 All ER 26; *Re Lowrie* [1981] 3 All ER 353; *Re Citro* [1991] Ch. 142; Insolvency Act 1986, s. 336.

oppose a sale of the property by a mortgagee if the mortgage was taken out to enable the dwelling to be purchased;[79] and, as the law now stands, two legal owners may sell the property without the consent of any third party even if the latter has a share in the beneficial ownership and is occupying the dwelling as his home.[80]

We saw in the last chapter that there are overwhelming arguments for including money and cashable rights within the scope of property institutions. It is implausible to suppose that because a breadwinner may be mean to his dependants, no-one should ever be accorded the freedom to choose between goods and services which ownership of money affords. Counter-measures against domination-potential may be instituted. Law enforces obligations of maintenance and support of dependants. English law provides that, on divorce, one spouse may be expropriated of money or of other property in favour of the other spouse.[81] Case law doctrine and statutory jurisdictions enable testamentary dispositions to be set aside where there are unfulfilled maintenance obligations or obligations arising from induced expectations or, sometimes, labour- desert.[82]

Domination-potential ought to be a first consideration of property-institutional design in the family context. Few would contend that current English law satisfactorily caters for it. For example, it has not yet adjusted its counter-measures to the context of the nuclear family in which the parties are not married. In particular, neither statute nor equitable doctrine provides adequately for labour-desert claims.[83]

Whatever features of property-institutional design are, or ought to be, in place to draw the teeth of domination-potential, they have this much in common: they presuppose and seek to limit or re-distribute ownership freedoms; they do not assume that such freedoms are worthless and should be vouchsafed to no-one. Adult family members with sufficient property of their own can thumb their noses at head-of-household ownership-powers.

---

[79] An intention may be imputed to the holder of the beneficial interest whereby he agrees that the mortgage shall take priority over his interest—*Bristol and West Building Society* v. *Henning* [1985] 2 All ER 606; *Paddington Building Society* v. *Mendelsohn* [1985] 50 P and CR, 244; *Equity and Law Home Loans Ltd* v. *Prestige* [1992] 1 All ER 909. It has also been held that, in any event, on an acquisition the beneficial interest takes effect only out of the equity of redemption (that is, the net proceeds of the property once the mortgage has been discharged)—*Abbey National Building Society* v. *Cann* [1991] 1 AC 56.

[80] *City of London Building Society* v. *Flegg* [1988] 1 AC 54. The Law Commission has recommended that the law should be changed so as to provide that no sale can be made without the consent of any adult who has a share in the beneficial ownership and is in occupation of the dwelling—Law Comm. no. 188, *Overreaching: Beneficiaries in Occupation* (1989).

[81] Matrimonial Causes Act 1973, ss. 23 and 24.

[82] See Ch. 11, sect. (iv)(c) and Ch. 14, sect. (i)(b)(1) above, and Ch. 15, sect. (ii)(c) below.

[83] See Ch. 11, sect. (iv)(c) above.

In any event, the significance of property-ownership for the phenomenon of illegitimate domination within the nuclear family varies according to the social setting. Adequate public provision for education, child-care, and other basic needs diminishes the importance of the domination-potential incident to breadwinner's wealth. Effective policing and prevention of violence within the home and provision of easily accessible refuges for abused dependants would undercut the domination-potential incident to dwelling-ownership. The cruellest kinds of ill-treatment are the consequences of physical and psychological aggressiveness which have nothing whatever to do with property.

(v) ALL OWNERSHIP FREEDOMS *PRIMA FACIE* VALUABLE, NONE SACROSANCT

The conclusion which emerges from this and the last chapter is that one cannot confront 'ownership', at an abstract level, with any plausible argument which entails that some particular category of privilege or power should be excluded from the concept. John Christman has argued that we should bifurcate ownership into two distinct concepts, 'control ownership' and 'income ownership'. The first would encompass use-privileges and all unilateral exercises of powers (including gifts), and the latter all exercises of power made for consideration (hire, rent, sale, or exchange). His reason is that the former can be justified by autonomy considerations, whereas the latter has distributional consequences.[84] The bifurcation is to apply to all resources. It would follow that I 'own' the cash in my pocket in two distinct ways, one entailing that I can give it away, the other that I can spend it.

We have seen, however, that unilateral control-powers over some resources (enterprises and dwellings) are much more problematic than for others (ordinary chattels). As to distributional implications, inter-generational giving is probably more significant than sale or exchange. (Why not a third concept of ownership for major gifts?) There seems to be no good reason for hitching redistributive programmes to abstract conceptual manœuvres of this kind.

There is, in any case, no such thing as a single ownership conception, but rather a spectrum of ownership interests. The spectrum has evolved in human history and is available within property institutions as a means of conferring ranges of autonomous choice on individuals or groups. How such ownership interests should be packaged, alongside quasi-ownership interests and non-ownership proprietary interests, is a question of property institutional design which is entirely context-dependent.

On many grounds (of which domination-potential is the most pervasive) ownership freedoms may be overridden by appropriate property-limitation or expropriation rules. Since there are no convention-independent natural rights to full-blooded ownership, ownership freedoms are never immune from challenge. Situations of extreme emergency are imaginable in which all access to

---

[84] John Christman, *The Myth of Property* (OUP, 1994), pt. 3.

social wealth should be rationed without benefit of ownership freedoms—as would be the case where shipwrecked survivors in a lifeboat have to allocate meagre supplies of food and water. In normal conditions within modern societies, there could be no reason for countermanding all ownership freedoms; nor can any particular ownership freedom be hived off, abstractly, and denied *prima facie* value.

The most obvious candidate for such hiving-off is freedom of bequest and we have argued that even this historically-evolved accretion to ownership conceptions has value, although it may be overridden, *ad hoc*, on various grounds. There is no warrant for drawing a context-independent line between transmission freedoms by way of gift so as universally to exclude those which are to take effect only on death. The same applies to any suggestion that transmission freedoms by way of exchange or sale should be treated as categorically suspect.

Such a proposal has been advanced by R. M. Unger. He looks forward to a 'superliberal' society in which the intolerable relationships of domination which he finds in contemporary societies would be banished. Among the institutional innovations needed to bring about the superliberal society, Unger mentions the 'disaggregation of the consolidated property right'.[85] It would substitute for the present freedom of owners to sell their property at will a 'provisional market right' which would be subject to 'destabilization rights'.[86] Unger fails to illustrate the implications of such a move, but the suggestion appears to be that any sale transaction (and perhaps any barter transaction or any use of money to purchase services) would be open to challenge by persons vested with destabilization rights; and it seems that such rights would be conferred on any third party who could marshal arguments against allowing the transaction to proceed, whether or not his own individual interests were affected. The purpose of destabilization rights would be to smash patterns of hierarchy and differentiation, and to prevent them from re-emerging. Some agency would be empowered to prohibit the exercise of the provisional market right if it was satisfied that doing so would forward either of these objectives.[87]

As we have seen, there are provisions (arguably, inadequate ones) within English law enabling third-party occupants of family dwellings to oppose sales by owners. Perhaps existing anti-monopoly restrictions on sales of enterprises should be enlarged in such a way as to enable workers (whose employment prospects are at risk) to object to such transactions. Unger's prescription of a destabilization right as a generalized counter to the market freedoms which are inherent in all forms of the 'consolidated property right' would go much further. It would mean, presumably, that a person could not sell her house or her car to a willing purchaser without the possibility that the agency, on the

---

[85] R. M. Unger, *The Critical Legal Studies Movement* (Harv. UP, 1986), 36.
[86] *Ibid.* 39.
[87] See J. W. Harris, 'Unger's Critique of Formalism in Legal Reasoning: Hero, Hercules and Humdrum' (1989) 52 MLR 42.

application of someone wielding a destabilization right, might intervene to stop the sale.

The proposal should be rejected for two reasons. It would be grossly over-intrusive, and it is not specifically adapted to meet the problem. Property institutions at present typically regulate such transactions by imposing form-ality requirements in some cases and by allowing them to be set aside on the grounds of fraud, duress, undue influence, or mistake. The object of such regulation is to ensure that there is reliable evidence that a choice was made and that it was made authentically. So long as these conditions are met, there is no warrant for busybody intervention by society in the case of each and every exercise of this variant of ownership freedom. Furthermore, if destruction of social hierarchy and differentiation is the objective, why concentrate exclu-sively on market rights? The exercise of even mere-property freedoms may involve illegitimate domination. The head-of-household owner, or the factory owner, may exercise his control-powers unfairly *vis-à-vis* family occupants or workers, without seeking to place what he owns on the market. It can hardly follow that we should seek to disaggregate the consolidated property right by allowing any exercise of ownership freedoms to be challenged at the bar of one of Unger's novel social agencies. If my neighbour declines to lend me his lawn mower, should I be empowered to haul him before some neighbourhood col-lective or other agency of the 'superliberal' society?

The absurd implications of Unger's suggestion are symptomatic of any attempt to shackle ownership freedoms at an abstract level—to take the very idea of ownership (irrespective of the asset in question or other contextual considerations) and to make some de-contextualized global assault on a par-ticular category of ownership freedoms. Even in the case of major enterprises of production or service provision, as we have seen, 'ownership', as such, is not the unique determinant of illegitimate domination.

None of the anti-property-freedom arguments we have considered yields the conclusion that any of the freedoms vouchsafed by the ownership spectrum are, intrinsically, to be excluded from the just society. They are never sacro-sanct but, as freedoms, they have *prima facie* value.

15

The Instrumental Values of Property

What emerges from the last two chapters is that, although there are no natural rights to full-blooded ownership of any particular resource, we are nevertheless situated in a world in which property institutions have everywhere evolved and the ownership freedoms thereby vouchsafed to individuals and groups contribute to autonomous choices (the second element of our minimalist conception of justice) and are of value for that reason. However, those freedoms are susceptible of being overriden by reference to many contextually-dependent considerations relevant to human well-being, of which domination-potential is the most pervasive. Furthermore, the freedom argument for property suffers from the drawback that it is distributionally blind and may in consequence fall foul of the first element (natural equality), depending on the implications to be drawn from that notion.

The argument so far is strong enough to establish that, in most imaginable social contexts, every person has a right to insist that his society maintain a property institution of some kind. It must allow for chattel and dwelling-ownership, and for money. It cannot exclude accumulation of large holdings of private wealth merely to prevent fetishism or wealth-disparity. It must make a context-driven selection between packaged ownership interests or packaged quasi-ownership interests in major enterprises. No satisfactory reason has so far been unearthed for bringing ideas ('intellectual property') within the scope of property institutions.

It is now time to consider in what ways putative instrumental values of property institutions may be factored in, so as (perhaps) to yield a clearer idea of the kind of institution people have a right to have in place. Are there desirable social goals which cannot be achieved without property? If there are, their significance could be twofold. They might add to the pro-property side of the scale when we have to decide whether, in particular contexts, ownership freedoms are of value, all things considered—especially over the question of enterprise-ownership. Secondly, they might yield concrete distributional implications—implications about to whom property should be allocated and from whom it should be taken.

Social goals which have commonly been supposed to be dependent upon property are either material or immaterial in character. Aristotle maintained that private property has the instrumental merits both of producing greater productivity and of facilitating traits of liberality and temperance.[1] Without property, it has been contended, a society could not achieve increases in the totality of social wealth because there would be neither creator-incentives nor markets. Without property, furthermore, society would not reap rich political and cultural benefits associated with independence—the existence of citizens and groups whose private holdings of wealth enable them to advocate programmes and pursue objectives without fear of their means of subsistence being withdrawn by a disgruntled government.

The claim that incentives and markets are indispensable tools to the achievement of maximal increases in the total social-wealth pie may be false. Supposing it is true, however, what would that have to do with justice? If a society's total social wealth rises from X to X plus Y, what reason is there to suppose that any facet of just treatment can be more fully implemented than would have been the case without that increment? That question requires consideration of what will here be called 'justice costs', including those indirect justice costs which arise from alleged community obligations to discharge basic needs.

(i) DIRECT JUSTICE COSTS

The third element of our minimalist conception of justice concerns the ban on unprovoked invasions of bodily integrity. No society is just unless it subscribes to rules outlawing homicide, rape, kidnapping, and assault. Such rules were present in all the imaginary propertyless societies discussed in Chapter 2. In the primitive conditions of Forest Land and Status Land, spontaneous reactions to contraventions might be enough to enforce compliance. In Red Land and Contract Land, official agencies could have been involved in the policing and enforcing of the rules and perhaps, to that end, they might be vested with protected non-property-holdings over some resources—weapons, handcuffs, gaols, and the like. Still, since there was no money, there could not be salaried agents of law-enforcement; and none of the resources reserved to officials would entail any privileges or powers modelled on those of property institutions: there would be no State or public quasi-ownership interests.

In real modern societies, it is implausible to suppose that prohibitions required by the third element of our minimalist conception of justice could be delimited, qualified, improved, policed, and enforced without specialist agencies. Even if citizens or groups can, in justice, demand no more from their fellows than that they not be subjected to unprovoked violence, we need legislators, prosecutors, police, soldiers, judges, and social workers.

[1] Aristotle, *The Politics* (Stephen Everson (ed.), trans. Jonathan Barnes, CUP, 1988), bk. II, 5–6.

Robert Nozick has demonstrated how, even from a strictly libertarian view, a 'minimal State' may justly coerce its citizens to contribute to the support of such public agencies.[2]

We have seen that a just property institution includes money among the resources which can be owned.[3] That being so, the most practical method for achieving coerced support for these agencies is expropriatory taxation and the payment of salaries. It could hardly be contended that, whereas private citizens should receive the freedoms of choice between goods and services which money affords, those occupying necessary roles within the enforcing and policing agencies should be maintained but not paid. Expenditure required to police and enforce bans on personal violence constitutes a direct justice cost.

Direct justice costs have increased in modern societies because of changed attitudes towards violence within the family and towards male sexual violence against women. Contemporary public culture pays at least lip service to the view that such conduct falls within the scope of the third element of our minimalist conception of justice.[4] There is a strand of feminist opinion which insists that, because of the essential male-centredness of legal language and legal institutions, very little is to be expected from the law as an instrument for enforcing prohibitions of violence in this context and that, indeed, legal intervention may do more harm than good.[5] Yet, whatever may be achieved through self-help 'consciousness raising', few would suggest that the community itself should refrain from any intervention when serious incidents of this sort come to light. It is implausible to suppose that these problems can be satisfactorily addressed without the employment of salaried officials of one kind or another. Indeed, detection of, and redress for, these evils will not come cheap. A thorough-going libertarian may insist that women and children have no standing, in justice, to claim that their health or educational needs should be paid for by the community; but he cannot deny that the prevention of violence to their persons is a community cost.

If it is the case that incentives and markets enable total social wealth to be increased in such a way that direct justice costs can be met which would not otherwise be discharged, then incentives and markets are necessary features of property-institutional design, along with expropriatory taxation. Further implications also follow. Money raised by taxation cannot be instantly expended. Funds vested in public agencies will be the subject of quasi-ownership interests.[6] It would be impossible to specify every detail of the application of such funds in such a way that no borrowing need be made from the transmission freedoms which are of the essence of private owner-

---

[2] Robert Nozick, *Anarchy, State and Utopia* (Basil Blackwell, 1974), pt. 1.
[3] See Ch. 13, sect. (iv) above.   [4] See Ch. 10, sect. (iii)(c) above.
[5] See Carol Smart, *Feminism and the Power of Law* (Routledge, 1989), chs. 2 and 3.
[6] See Ch. 7, sect. (iii)(b) above.

ship of money. Other resources held as 'public property', whether chattels (books, desks, computers, and so on), or land (office buildings, defence establishments, courtrooms, and so on) could be the subject of protected non-property-holdings,[7] as they were in Red Land; but, in practice, it will usually be convenient to fill out some of the use-privileges and control-powers on the model of ownership, so that they will be the subject of quasi-ownership interests.

(ii) BASIC NEEDS

Increasing wealth and population entail greater demand for services that people need or want. It will at least sometimes be the case that such services are best supplied in the form of what economists call 'collective goods'— roads, parks, museums, and the like. There will then be quasi-ownership interests vested in public bodies and, if services cannot be provided on a fully self-financing basis, additional expropriatory taxation.

More importantly, the twentieth century has seen the emergence of a widespread consensus according to which people may justly insist that the communities in which they live meet certain of their basic needs.[8] Article 25(1) of the Universal Declaration of Human Rights (adopted by the General Assembly of the United Nations on 10 December 1948), for example, provides:

Everyone has the right to a standard of living adequate for the health and well-being of himself and of his family, including food, clothing, housing and medical care and necessary social services and the right to security in the event of unemployment, sickness, disability, widowhood, old age, or other lack of livelihood in circumstances beyond his control.

If it could be demonstrated that there are now community obligations to meet basic needs of this sort, 'justice costs' would be greatly increased. Much more extensive taxation-expropriation rules would be warranted, as would be a far wider range of quasi-ownership interests in large holdings of public funds, hospitals, schools, administrative office buildings, and so forth.

These would not be direct justice costs, in the way that policing and enforcing bans on personal violence are. Can any defensible combination of all three elements of our minimalist conception of justice (natural equality, facilitating autonomous choice, and prohibition of unprovoked invasions of bodily integrity) produce the conclusion that the community, as distinct from persons in some special relationship, has obligations to meet the basic needs of its citizens?

[7] See Ch. 7, sect. (v) above.
[8] See David Miller, *Social Justice* (Clarendon Press, 1976), ch. 4.

(a) The Libertarian Objection

Libertarian theorists, such as Robert Nozick and F. A. Hayek, contend that the current consensus, which supposes that money may justly be expropriated by the State to discharge people's basic needs, is profoundly mistaken. Private philanthropy is to be welcomed; but there are no sound arguments of 'distributive' or 'social' justice which support coerced contributions.[9]

As we saw in Chapter 11, Nozick advances an 'entitlement' theory as a version of Locke's creation-without-wrong argument for a natural property right. Granted that all resources are currently held in accordance with this theory, there is nothing left over to distribute.

The major objection to speaking of everyone's having a right *to* various things such as equality of opportunity, life, and so on, and enforcing this right, is that these 'rights' require a substructure of things and materials and actions; and *other* people may have rights and entitlements over these. . . . The particular rights over things fill the space of rights, leaving no room for general rights to be in a certain material condition.[10]

Hayek contends that, in a free society, coercion can be used only to enforce those 'rules of just conduct' which protect the private domain of individuals. The term 'social justice' is 'wholly devoid of meaning or content'.[11] It is also dangerous. It was initially invoked in favour of the destitute;[12] but it has proved 'the thin end of the wedge by which the principle of equality under the law was destroyed'.[13] It calls for demands which can only be satisfied by a totalitarian State.[14] Part of the explanation for the appeal of this chimerical notion lies in inherited dispositions of compassion towards the unfortunate which were appropriate to a face-to-face, tribal community, but which should have no place in the great society constituted by freedom and the morality of the market.[15]

It may at first seem paradoxical that the advance of morals should lead to a reduction of specific obligations towards others: yet whoever believes that the principle of equal treatment of all men, which is probably the only chance of peace, is more important than special help to visible suffering, must wish it. It admittedly means that we make our rational insight dominate over our inherited instincts. But the great moral adventure on which modern man has embarked when he launched into the Open Society is threatened when he is required to apply to all his fellow-men rules which are appropriate only to the fellow members of a tribal group.[16]

---

[9] Nozick, n. 2 above, chs. 7 and 8; F. A. Hayek, *Law, Legislation and Liberty: Vol. 2 The Mirage of Social Justice* (Routledge and Kegan Paul, 1976).

[10] Nozick, n. 2 above, 238.　　　　　　　　　　　　　[11] Hayek, n. 9 above, 96.

[12] *Ibid.* 139.　　　　　　　[13] *Ibid.* 142.　　　　　　　[14] *Ibid.* ch. 11.

[15] Market morality, in Hayek's submission, displaces any role for labour-desert, a view criticized in Ch. 11, sect. (iv)(a) above.

[16] N. 11 above, 91. Nevertheless, Hayek is willing to concede minimal State welfare. There

Both these philosophers suppose that people have moral rights to full-blooded ownership, within the sixth of the seven categories of property rights distinguished in Chapter 10, section (ii), of this book. Nozick founds himself on the creation-without-wrong argument for a natural property right, the fallacy of which was exposed in Chapter 11. Hayek appeals to the social-conventional basis of property which is criticized in the next chapter. What requires to be noticed here is a move we might call 'the libertarian trick': the unargued assumption that the same moral status holds as much for those timeless trespassory rules which protect property into whoever's hands it is voluntarily transmitted as for prohibitions of violence to the person.[17]

Hayek asserts that 'the obligation incumbent upon us, to follow certain rules derives from the benefits we owe to the order in which we live'.[18] We have argued that a society is justified in enforcing prohibitions of violence to the person even against those who do not accept that such rules are morally binding.[19] Rules of this type offer protection to the delinquent himself since he necessarily has a body which can be invaded. It is much more debatable whether the obligations which trespassory rules impose upon those without property can justly be enforced against them as though they were morally binding upon them. Rape or murder are in no way excusable because the perpetrator is destitute. It may be otherwise with theft. Contrary to the libertarian trick, trespassory obligations should not be conceived as carrying moral force for non-owners unless the social setting of the property institution is such that at least some degree of socially valuable autonomous choice is afforded to them, and that can scarcely be done unless their basic needs are met.

The question whether trespassory obligations are genuine obligations in the case of someone whose survival depends on taking another's property has perennially perplexed apologists for property institutions. For Hegel, although nothing, at the level of abstract right, could qualify that absolute ownership which is the embodiment of abstract freedom, yet, once the 'moment' of morality is taken into account, obligations which are its concomitants may, *in extremis* be modified.

---

is 'no reason why in a free society a government should not' provide a minimum 'floor' income, for those who are unable to earn an adequate maintenance in the market; and 'few will question' that public assistance may be rendered to socially deprived children (87). However, he offers no reason why those things should be done. It has nothing to do with justice nor, it seems, with compassion, for Hayek insists that the abstract order which alone may be enforced within a free society 'unfortunately cannot be based on such feelings as love' (150).

[17] Hayek, *Law, legislation and Liberty: Vol. 1 Rules and Order* (Routledge and Kegan Paul, 1973), 106–11; *Vol. 2 The Mirage of Social Justice*, n. 9 above, 38–42, 109–10, 123, and *passim*; Nozick, n. 2 above, 10–12, 268–70, 272–3, and *passim*.

[18] N. 9 above, 27.   [19] See Ch. 10, sect. (v) above.

Life, as the totality of ends, has a right in opposition to abstract right. If, for example, it can be preserved by stealing a loaf, this certainly constitutes an infringement of someone's property, but it would be wrong to regard such an action as common theft. If someone whose life is in danger were not allowed to take measures to save himself, he would be destined to forfeit all his rights; and since he would be deprived of life, his entire freedom would be negated.[20]

Blackstone supposed that the problem could be dealt with in another way. He dissented from the commonly held view of civilian writers that necessity should be recognized as a defence to theft. In England, he said, such provision was made by the poor law that '[i]t is impossible that the most needy stranger should ever be reduced to the necessity of thieving to support nature.' Whatever arguments might hold upon the continent 'where the parsimonious industry of the natives orders every one to work or starve, yet must lose all their weight and efficacy in England, where charity is reduced to a system, and interwoven in our very constitution'.[21]

Hegel's point is that it is freedom which justifies property so that trespassory obligations may be overriden where survival, the foundation of all freedom, would otherwise be negated. Blackstone's point is that the problem should be met, not by specific exceptions to trespassory rules, but by the community shouldering the obligations to provide life-sustaining sustenance. As an issue of property-institutional design, Blackstone's solution is preferable (though not his complaisance with the poor law of his day). It is preferable to discharge basic needs out of public revenue, expropriated proportionately from the population at large and taking account of marginal utility in the design of taxation rules, than to allow the burden of basic-need-satisfaction to fall, by happenstance, on whichever owner's property is to hand. Hegel, however, pointed the way to the underlying justification: historically-evolved property institutions have value by virtue of their inherent choice-facilitating qualities, so their design cannot be allowed to strip non-owners of all control over their life-plans.

Mere survival is far too parsimonious. It emerged from our discussion of the choice-facilitating advantages of ownership interests compared with regimes of communal use,[22] and the pervasive counter-consideration from domination-potential,[23] that the property-freedom argument requires a balance to be struck. For this balance to yield justifiable trespassory obligations in respect of various resources, non-owners must not be placed, by virtue of such obligations, at the mercy of owners. Contextual considerations of many kinds enter into the equation. It would seldom be enough for the community to guarantee freedom from starvation. In the conditions of a developed

---

[20] G. W. F. Hegel, *Elements of the Philosophy of Right* (trans. H. B. Nisbet, CUP, 1991), 155 (para. 127 addition).

[21] Sir William Blackstone, *Commentaries on the Laws of England* (16th edn., J. Butterworth and Son, 1825), bk. 4, 31.

[22] Ch. 13, sects. (iii) and (iv) above.   [23] Ch. 14, sect. (iv) above.

modern society, provision for the kinds of basic needs listed in the Universal Declaration is a precondition of justifiable trespassory rules. If X is to be called on to abstain from meddling with a resource to which O can show no abstract natural right, there must be sufficient reciprocity in the social bonds which have emerged to encompass them both such that X does not perceive himself as of no account *vis-à-vis* O's authorized self-seekingness over the resource. No-one can justly be expected to submit to the trespassory rules of a property institution unless the society in which the institution is situated, one way or another, caters for his basic needs.

The libertarian trick smuggles timeless trespassory rules alongside prohibitions of violence to the person, as though both were equally fundamental facets of human association. But, whereas we are all born with bodies, no-one comes into the world naturally endowed with eternally transmissible ownership of any external resource. The libertarian may consistently reject both property and compulsory charity. He cannot have the one without the other.

(b) Basic Needs and Appropriation

Trespassory obligations and community obligations to cater for basic needs have the same source in justice, the facilitation of autonomous choice. However, they implement that facet of just treatment in different ways. Trespassory obligations create and protect ownership freedoms. Basic needs may be met in kind, or they may be discharged by appropriation rules which confer ownership of money or ownership interests over other resources.

The basic needs which people have are either universal or culturally specific. The former concern physical survival, the latter what is required for a person to make his way in a particular social context. Mere survival requires some provision of food, medicine, clothing, and shelter. Beyond the sustenance of life, the material bases of autonomous living are a function partly of culture and partly of the productive capacity of a society. A community's culture may or may not, for example, entail that autonomy is denied unless a person is able to opt between different styles of clothing, is afforded some degree of privacy in his dwelling, and has access to educational facilities which will equip him with certain skills. If such assumptions are entrenched, they flesh out, for the society, the conception of what it is to be treated as a human being; and any societal decision that some sorts of people need not be afforded such facilities witnesses to a conclusion that they may receive special treatment as being persons whose humanity does not rise to the level of that of ordinary citizens. If and to the extent that there is sufficient social wealth to provide these things for all, natural equality requires that they be denied to no-one. Expropriation rules designed to finance this provision impose obligations which are just, if the trespassory obligations of the institution are just. The two sets of obligations constitute a justice package.

The discharge of all these indirect justice costs necessitates expropriation rules. Usually, it requires appropriation rules as well. Mere survival may always be insured without conferring property. The destitute could be doled out food for immediate consumption, allocated defined and non-transferable uses of garments, and herded into shelters out of the rain. Other important needs may be supplied without according property to the recipient —such as education, health-care, or recreational facilities. Often, however, people will be dehumanized unless they receive property.

In Chapter 13, we discussed the value of mere-property freedoms and transmission freedoms in relation to chattels, dwellings, and money. If a society can afford a certain, culturally-determined level of support for the aged and the involuntarily unemployed, it would treat them unjustly if it insisted on supplying all their needs in kind on the model of the soup-kitchen society, rather than appropriating to them money with which they can make transmission choices. (The English Court of Appeal has, for example, held that a recipient of welfare benefits could not be compelled to spend the money she received in discharging her rent in priority to maintaining her children.[24]) If a society can supply the disabled with chattels designed to enable them to lead more independent lives, it would be demeaning (as well as impracticable) to stipulate every permitted use. They should be vested with at least mere-property freedoms—open-ended use-privileges and control-powers. Similarly, if the involuntarily homeless are to be housed, they need dwellings over which they have mere-property freedoms. If the resources are available, shelter should include the blessings of privacy, which require open-ended use-privileges and open-ended control-powers over dwellings.

In the squatter cases discussed in Chapter 6, English courts denied any defence of necessity or other equitable restraint on the right of owners to recover dwellings. Following Blackstone's lead, they took the view that trespassory rules should be maintained as bright-line rules, not susceptible to exceptions which might be abused. They invoked ownership as a principle, even in the case of property which 'belonged' to public authorities.[25]

Bright-line rules have merits, and that may have been the right outcome. That it was so has since been strengthened by legislation, first introduced in 1977, which imposes an obligation on local authorities to provide 'accommodation' for the unintentionally homeless.[26] As that legislation has been interpreted, however, it can hardly be said to flesh out the shell of the privacy right discussed in section (iii) of Chapter 12; for 'accommodation'

---

[24] *R.* v. *Wandsworth London B.C., ex parte Hawthorne* [1995] 2 All ER 331.
[25] See Ch. 6, sect. (i) above.
[26] The Housing (Homeless Persons) Act 1977. See now the Housing Act 1985, pt. III.

has been taken to be something which may fall below even mere-property freedoms. It has been held that a family of four living in a single room of a guest house on a bed-and-breakfast basis is provided with 'accommodation' within the terms of the legislation;[27] and that there is no requirement that 'accommodation' be settled or permanent.[28] If societal opinion in England does not yet recognize day-to-day control over its living quarters as an essential background for a family's autonomous life, appeal may be made, against that conventional opinion, to the natural right of privacy. If such an assumption is already part of English culture, then the legislation, as interpreted, fails to discharge a community obligation to meet a basic need; and, since social wealth is not so restricted as to deny universal provision of it for the involuntarily homeless, this feature of property-institutional design fails the test of justice.

We have, in Chapter 2, imagined societies in which the prevailing culture did not require appropriation to its citizens either of money or of ownership interests in other resources. In all real modern societies, however, property-holdings are among the basic needs which people have.

(c) Communal and Private Obligations

The community's obligations to discharge basic needs exist alongside obligations to provide support and maintenance for dependants which are undertaken by, or justly imposed upon, private citizens. We referred to English legislation conferring jurisdiction on courts to order transfers of money or other property on divorce or death, in the contexts of our discussion of labour-desert[29] and alleged rights of inheritance.[30] These jurisdictions are one vehicle for the enforcement of private obligations to meet basic needs. Housing needs loom especially large. A court may expropriate a house-owner parent to the extent necessary to provide accommodation for children until they reach school-leaving age.[31] Or it may expropriate a house-owner spouse by vesting in the other spouse a determinable and non-transferable ownership interest for life.[32] Such obligations may extend to needs which are not 'basic', in that they are premised on the kind of provision appropriate to the relationship between the parties.[33] It may, for example, be held that the

---

[27] *Puhlhofer* v. *Hillingdon London B.C.* [1986] AC 484.
[28] *Awua* v. *Brent London B.C.* [1996] 1 AC 55.
[29] See ch. 11, sect. (iv)(c) above.   [30] See Ch. 14, sect. (i)(b)(1) above.
[31] *Mesher* v. *Mesher and Hall* [1980] 1 All ER 126.
[32] *Martin* v. *Martin* [1978] Fam. 12; *Clutton* v. *Clutton* [1991] 1 All ER 340; *In Re Moody (decd.)* [1992] 2 All ER 524.
[33] S. 25 of the Matrimonial Causes Act 1973 lists, among the factors to which the court is to have regard when ordering a lump sum payment or transfer of property on divorce, 'the standard of living enjoyed by the family before the breakdown of the marriage'. S. 3(3) of the Inheritance (Provision for Family and Dependants) Act 1975 requires the court to have

'reasonable needs' of a wife who has enjoyed a luxurious life-style justify expropriating a rich husband to the extent required to provide her with a substantial income.[34]

The exercise of these jurisdictions has seldom raised the question of how the community's obligations and these private obligations interact.[35] That is a problem which is only likely to arise where discharging a need consists in the direct payment of money, either by the community or by some private person, for then the obligations could be considered mutually substitutable. It has been generally assumed that a person cannot resile from his obligation to meet housing needs of dependants merely by pointing out that the State is already obliged to house the homeless; but in this case public provision is unlikely to be as valuable to the recipient as is continued occupation of a family dwelling. Conversely, private maintenance obligations are not considered to include reimbursement to the State of the costs of providing universal benefits in kind for dependants, such as public education or health-care. If, however, the obligations consist of money payments alone, such as those due to a mother for the support of children, the substitutability issue arises directly.

It is submitted that, in principle, a father who can afford to discharge such costs, without thereby depriving himself of the ability to meet his own basic needs or those of any other dependants, can be required to do so in priority to the community's obligation. We have suggested that trespassory obligations and the community's obligations to discharge basic needs constitute a justice package. There seems to be no sound argument to support the view that this package displaces private obligations. Fellow citizenship entails that someone can insist that others refrain from interfering with his property on the understanding that his wealth is subject to expropriatory taxation to meet the basic needs of those who, through no fault of their own, are unable to support themselves. It hardly carries the implication that persons may choose to throw the burden of their private obligations upon others.

---

regard, in the case of a child applicant, to the 'manner in which the applicant was being or in which he might expect to be educated or trained'.

[34] *In Re Besterman (decd.)* [1984] Ch. 457; *Duxbury* v. *Duxbury* [1990] 2 All ER 77.

[35] There have been occasional suggestions that it is not unreasonable for a testator to make no provision for a dependant if he knows that all he could offer will in any case be provided by State welfare—*In Re Watkins (decd.)* [1949] 1 All ER 695, *In Re E (decd.)* [1966] 2 All ER 44 (both cases decided under the Inheritance Family Provision Act 1938, the predecessor of the 1975 Act). In other cases it has been assumed that maintenance obligations are unaffected by the availability of welfare benefits—*In Re Goodwin (decd.)* [1969] 1 Ch. 283, *In Re Collins (decd.)* [1990] 2 All ER 47.

(iii) INCENTIVES AND MARKETS

(a) Market Freedoms

It emerged from our discussion of the property-freedom argument that, granted that someone ought to be conceded mere-property freedoms over some resource, he ought also, *prima facie*, to be accorded transmission freedoms as well, including freedom to transmit by way of sale.[36] We rejected R. M. Unger's suggestion that all market rights should become 'provisional'.[37] There is a case for recognizing non-transferable ownership interests in dwellings, particularly where that is the most expedient means of discharging community obligations to meet basic needs for privacy-respecting shelter. Domination-potential considerations may require that owners should not be free to dispose of dwellings without the consent of dependant partners, or restrictions on monopoly-creating transfers by owners of enterprises. Generally speaking, however, market transactions are as much manifestations of autonomous choice as are gifts. Both are policed within property institutions by doctrines of fraud, undue influence, and mistake— and sometimes by the imposition of formality requirements.

From the eighteenth century until the present day, the property-freedom argument has, in the case of sale or barter transactions (as distinct from gifts), often been combined with a market-instrumental argument. Quite apart from the respect due to autonomous choices, a multiplicity of market transactions will (it has been claimed) increase total social wealth more effectively than any other property regime. Each contractor may be motivated by private incentives, but society, as a whole, will be the richer. It follows that all resources must be the subject of ownership interests which are freely tradable. (Power to make limited gifts resulting in non-transferable ownership interests may be unobjectionable on property-freedom grounds, but it conflicts with the market-instrumental rationale for property institutions.[38])

This market-instrumental argument, taken on its own, is as distributionally blind as the property-freedom argument. It insists that transferable ownership interests be vested in individuals or groups, but it has nothing to say about how initial allocations are to be made. We have seen that there are no natural rights to full-blooded ownership. Market-instrumentalism might be combined with initial allocations based on labour-desert, first occupancy, or privacy; but we shall, in the next chapter, reject the contention that every social-conventional basis of title is immune from challenge. Apart from natural right and social convention, can the distributional blindness of a

---

[36] See Ch. 13, sect. (iv) above.
[37] See Ch. 14, sect. (v) above.
[38] See Ch. 14, sect. (i)(c) above.

pure market argument be cured by showing that individual incentives, in themselves, yield just holdings of specific resources?

(b) Forest Land, Rousseau, and Bentham

We are again in Forest Land and considering the case of the innovative tool-maker. This time he insists that his fellow tribesmen should institute tres-passory rules reserving to him an open-ended set of privileges and powers over the tool, not because he wrongs no-one in making it, nor because such an 'ownership' interest would be a fitting reward for his labour, but because, if they do not, he will not make the tool at all.

Now the tribesmen, still puzzled by the whole notion of 'property' which their returning tool-maker has brought back from abroad, set up a seance wherein to take the advice of spirits who better understand these things. They succeed in summoning up the wraiths of two philosophers, both of whom took it to be axiomatic that incentives and nothing else were the reason for creating property institutions, but whose opinions on the wisdom of taking this step are radically opposed. They are Jean-Jacques Rousseau and Jeremy Bentham.

There is a famous passage in Rousseau's *Discourse on the Origin of Inequality* in which he says that, if only the first person to fence off a plot of ground and to call it his had been denounced as an imposter and prevented from doing it, 'from how many crimes, wars, and murders, from how many horrors and misfortunes might not any one have saved mankind'.[39] However, as the rest of the *Discourse* makes clear, by the time of the imagined enclosure the damage to Man's original blessed state had already been done. The institution of property comes about only at the last stage of the state of nature. Men lived free, healthy, good, and happy lives only so long as each depended on himself alone for sustenance. From the moment one derived what he needed from the labour of another, the train was set for all the evils of inequality and property. The primary inventions which placed mankind on the road to perdition were those of metallurgy and agriculture. 'The poets tell us that it was gold and silver, but, for the philosophers, it was iron and corn, which first civilised men, and ruined humanity.'[40]

For these sciences to emerge many particular developments in human evolution were needed, including 'means of preventing others from robbing them of the fruits of their labour'.[41] If cultivation was to be possible, division was essential and property in the soil had to be protected by a 'rule of justice' in order that the labourer could be assured of reaping where he had sown. Given unequal natural talents and aptitudes, and the disproportionate bar-

[39] Jean-Jacques Rousseau, *Second Discourse*, in J. B. Brumfitt and John Hall (eds.), *The Social Contract and Discourses* (Everyman's Library, Dent, 1973), 76.
[40] *Ibid.* 83.
[41] *Ibid.* 84.

gaining power associated with different products of labour, inequalities would inevitably have arisen even if the rule of justice had been observed. There being no natural-right, but only an instrumental, argument for property in the fruits of one's labour, non-owners could justly complain even against one who had wronged no-one when he created, by his own unaided efforts, some new item of social wealth:

Who gave you your standing, it might be answered, and what right have you to demand payment of us for doing what we never asked you to do? Do you not know that numbers of your fellow creatures are starving, for want of what you have too much of? You ought to have had the express and universal consent of mankind, before appropriating more of the common subsistence than you needed for your own maintenance.[42]

But in any case rules of justice were not observed. Once there was property and its inevitable concomitant of inequality, frightful disorder was inevitable. 'Usurpations by the rich, robbery by the poor, and the unbridled passions of both, suppressed the cries of natural compassion and the still feeble voice of justice, and filled men with avarice, ambition, and vice.'[43]

Rousseau did not suppose that the clock could be put back. The pernicious sciences had arisen and, because of the indispensability of incentives, mankind was now stuck with property.[44] In the seance, however, his wraith will warn the tribesmen and recommend them to answer the tool-maker: '[i]f you won't make this useful tool unless we accord you property in it, we will do without it.'

The advice coming from Bentham's wraith will be the exact converse. In his *Principles of the Civil Code* Bentham extolled property institutions for the blessings they had conferred on mankind.[45] Property was the creation of 'law', which in this context meant prohibitions securing permanent possession of things to individuals, whether enacted by a sovereign legislator or established by custom: '[i]f we suppose the least agreement among savages to respect the acquisitions of each other, we see the introduction of a principle to which no name can be given but that of law.'[46]

Bentham asked whether the introduction of what we have called 'trespassory rules', and what Rousseau called 'rules of justice', and the proprietary rights they protect had contributed to the sum of human happiness. He was sure that they had. Many psychological satisfactions ('pleasures')

---

[42] *Ibid.* 88.   [43] *Ibid.* 87.

[44] Hence in other writings Rousseau displays attitudes towards property quite inconsistent with his sentiments expressed in the *Discourse on Inequality*—see Alan Ryan, *Property and Political Theory* (Basil Blackwell, 1986), ch. 2.

[45] Jeremy Bentham, *Principles of the Civil Code*, in C. K. Ogden (ed.), *Jeremy Bentham, The Theory of Legislation* (Kegan Paul, 1931), pt. 1, chs. 1–12.

[46] *Ibid.* 112.

resulted from security of ownership to the proprietors themselves and there were many spin-off benefits for non-owners as well:

Their labour is more uniform, but their reward is more sure; the woman's lot is far more agreeable; childhood and old age have more resources; the species multiplies in a proportion a thousand times greater,—and that alone suffices to show on which side is the superiority of happiness.[47]

Bentham, like Rousseau, assumed that there could be no incentive to engage in creative work unless the labourer was rewarded with property. But for him, since the state of propertyless competitive savagery was so bleak, the institution of property was an unparalleled achievement. 'Men universally desire to enjoy speedily—to enjoy without labour. It is that desire which is terrible; since it arms all who have not against all who have. The law which restrains that desire is the noblest triumph of humanity over itself.'[48]

On emerging from the seance, how might the tribesmen proceed? Let us assume that they will take seriously the fate of their posterity. There is a consensus between their two advisors that the institution of property is an indispensable instrument for unlocking productive forces. (If they sought further guidance from the wraiths of Marx and Engels and believed what they were told, they would conclude that full-blown capitalist private property was also such an instrument.[49]) Their decision might vary according to whether they are summing or averaging utilitarians. In the former event, they would take into account the possibility that, as Bentham had told them, the unleashed productive forces would mean that the human population could be greatly expanded. If they were averaging utilitarians, they would ask themselves whether the average satisfactions of all persons to be born were they to take the property route would be greater than that of all those to be born should they decline it. They might seek further information about the alternative futures from other spirits, before they were satisfied that Rousseau was right in supposing that it was property alone which induced crime and wars.

There is no point in speculating on how the Forestlanders could or should have arrived at a conclusion. It is one thing to invoke imaginary states of nature as a basis for testing, in the abstract, whether natural property rights can be derived from our minimalist conception of justice. It is another to suppose that one can actually recapture a historical moment at which there was a transition from literal common property to full-blooded ownership. Both Rousseau's noble, and Bentham's benighted, savages were as imaginary as our Forestlanders. We know now that primitive social arrangements cannot be analysed in terms of a simple contrast between no property institu-

---

[47] N. 45 above, 114.   [48] *Ibid.*
[49] Karl Marx and Frederick Engels, *The Manifesto of the Communist Party 1848* (trans. Samuel Moore, Progress Publishers, 1888), ch. I.

tion of any kind, on the one hand, and full-blooded ownership of resources, on the other hand.[50] Property institutions of one kind or another evolved before the dawn of recorded history and have matured in various ways. Technological developments have occurred which have utilized, among other things, the instrumentalities of incentives and markets which property institutions afford. Whether or how such innovations would have proceeded if trespassory rules and ownership interests had never entered the human consciousness is a counterfactual question beyond speculative thought. On the assumption that property was the necessary midwife of technological progress, there is little point now in trying to cast up a global moral balance sheet on the question whether mankind should have taken the technological road, as Rousseau and Bentham did. We must needs start from where we have arrived and then consider, resource-category by resource-category, whether incentives and markets are required, bearing in mind the variety of property-institutional arrangements open to us, as well as the possibility of no property whatever.

What emerges from the encounter between Forestlanders and their philo-sophical mentors is this. If, as to any resource, it really is the case that, having regard to incentives and markets, social wealth will be increased by introducing or maintaining private ownership as compared with any regime of communal use, it does not follow that such introduction or maintenance is morally required. On the up-side is the possibility that the increase can be used to discharge direct or indirect justice costs of the kinds discussed in the last two sections. However, if such costs could be fully met already, no-one has standing to insist that society must render itself as wealthy as it can. On the down-side is the contingency, discussed in section (iv) of the last chapter, that any particular package of ownership interests may entail greater dangers of illegitimate domination-potential than a possible communal-use regime alternative. In the abstract, it is impossible to reach any more precise con-clusions.

(c) Creator-incentives

(1) *Augmenting Social Wealth*

Both the property-freedom and market-instrumental arguments, taken on their own, are distributionally blind. Granted that a transaction whereby Y transfers resources to X is impeccable as between the parties, if Y's title was unjust and X knows it, X's title is also unjust. If I buy goods from a thief, or from the representatives of a military clique which has plundered a subject people, the mere fact that the purchase was itself freely negotiated does not make me the just owner of what I have bought.

[50] See Melvill Hersovits, *Economic Anthropology* (Knof, 1952); A. Irving Hallowell, *Culture and Experience* (UPa.P, 1955), ch. 12.

Assume that we do not know whether Y's title is just. That uncertainty will be carried over to X when he purchases from Y. However, if it can be shown that the transaction itself brings about an increase in social wealth which facilitates the discharge of justice costs, X can found a distinct claim to just ownership of what he has received. In that way, creator-incentives may serve as a partial cure to the distributional blindness of property-freedom and market-instrumental arguments.

Remuneration for work may be justly owned either on the basis of a conventionally-crystallized, labour-desert natural right,[51] or by virtue of in-strumental creator-incentives. For the latter to apply, something like the following conditions would have to be met:

1. X does work in consideration of a payment of Y pounds.
2. X would not have done the work for any lesser incentive.
3. On the available labour-market, no-one else could have been hired to do the work for any sum smaller than Y.
4. The work adds to total social wealth.
5. The addition enables justice costs to be discharged which could not have been met without it.

If all these conditions are satisfied, incentives and markets operate as a distinct property-specific justice reason. Increase in social wealth is not a good in and of itself. That, extrapolated from its mythological-historical setting, was Rousseau's point. Nevertheless, the community cannot justly forego an opportunity to discharge justice costs. Incentives and markets here combine as an indispensable instrument to that end. Hence, X, independent of desert, is justly the owner of the money he receives and of anything he purchases with it.

The second condition would never be met in a society in which incentives other than pay are always present to produce X's work, such as a slave-owning or feudal society. Such societies, however, require coercive measures which conflict with the third element of our minimalist conception of justice.

The third condition may or may not be fulfilled where labouring roles are allocated according to a command-economy pattern. That would depend on whether the decision-makers correctly mimic what a labour-market would have yielded. On the other hand, the third condition may or may not be met in societies which purport to be operating a free-labour market, since nepot-ism, favouritism, unproven traditions about the rate for the job, and struc-tural defects of many kinds may lead to market failings. In the United Kingdom today, there is widespread cynicism about claims that executives who receive enormous salaries do so because they alone can achieve certain wealth-maximizing operations.

'Social wealth', as we have used that expression, comprises all those things

---

[51] See Ch. 11, sect. (iv)(b) above.

and services for which there is a greater potential total demand than there is a supply. Thus the addition required by the fourth condition will only fail to materialize if X is being paid to produce something or to render some service which nobody wants or the supply of which has already reached demand-saturation.

The fifth condition may be met where X is directly engaged, either as an employee of a public institution or as an independent contractor, to discharge a communal obligation to meet basic needs. Or it may be that X's work and its remuneration have the consequence that there is a marginal diminution in basic needs which require to be discharged, in that they place persons in a position to meet their own basic needs. Most importantly, X's remuneration and that of other persons which may flow from his work can be subjected to tax-expropriation rules which contribute to public funds available to be applied in discharging basic needs. A system of just taxation will take account of both the considerations of marginal utility, referred to in section (iii) of the last chapter, and also of the overriding requirement, implicit in the fifth condition, that no-one should be taxed to the point where he is unable to discharge his own basic needs or those of his dependants.

In the general flow of property allocations resulting from work, labour-desert and creator-incentives play a real, but perennially controversial, role. There are as well standing controversies as to whether major enterprises of production or service-provision should be the subject of ownership or quasi-ownership interests. We saw in section (iv) of the last chapter that either alternative can meet the requirements of use-channelling and use-policing (in ways in which literal 'common property' could not), and that domination-potential is a variable which is heavily context-dependent. We saw, nevertheless, that there are two features peculiar to private ownership of enterprises: they are susceptible to bankruptcy expropriation; and management decisions affecting them may be frankly justified by reference to increases in the private wealth of their owners. In the terminology of an ideology which has acquired increased momentum since the demise of communist regimes in Europe, these special features are called 'the disciplines of the market'.

For such disciplines to enter into the justice equation, they must meet conditions similar to those just discussed. It must be shown that private ownership of major enterprises provides creator-incentives in a way that no comparable quasi-ownership structure, however packaged, could do; and that, in consequence, the community can discharge justice costs which otherwise it could not. No observer of the contemporary circumstances of countries now liberated from communist dictatorships could claim that such consequences have yet resulted in those countries, though they may do so in the long run.

Marx and Engels predicted that, at the historical moment at which capitalism was superseded by public ownership of major enterprises, forces of production would be unleashed which would enormously increase the total pie of social wealth beyond anything which a continuation of capitalism could have achieved.[52] Twentieth-century experience of command economies has established that, as an alleged universal truth, that prediction was erroneous. It does not follow that, in the case of each and every enterprise, competition and creator-incentives will necessarily operate in such a way that increases in wealth and consequent discharge of justice costs must inevitably tip the balance of justification in favour of private ownership. Creator-incentives must be taken into account along with necessary use-channelling and use-policing and the dangers of domination-potential on a case-by-case basis.

(2) *Intellectual Property*

Creator-incentives are of overriding significance in the context of intellectual property.[53] The use-channelling and use-policing merits of ownership or quasi-ownership interests have no bearing whatever on ideational entities once they are published since all may use them simultaneously.[54] Natural-right arguments for full-blooded ownership of at least some varieties of intellectual property have been invoked; but for reasons given in Chapters 11 and 12 they should all be rejected.

Mark Rose has examined the arguments advanced on behalf of London book-sellers in the eighteenth century in their ultimately unsuccessful bid to establish that authors of literary works have a common law right to perpetual copyright—a right which would have enabled the book-sellers to maintain a monopoly over reprinting by purchase of the right.[55] It appears from Rose's survey that the mélange of natural-right justifications appealed to during this controversy included all those we have investigated. None of them deserved to succeed.

A first occupant of a tangible resource has a right not to be evicted where eviction involves an assault on his body.[56] Nothing similar obtains for literary works. A literary work may bear the stamp of its author's personality (though hardly in all those instances in which commercial copyright is claimed). That is not the same thing as the author incorporating the work into himself like a transplanted organ, especially when he proposes to transfer rights over it to someone else. It is a *sine qua non* of personhood-constituting that that which is allegedly incorporated into a person is viewed as non-transferable.[57] Privacy warrants giving an author the say-so as to whether his manuscript is

---

[52] Marx and Engels, n. 49 above, ch. II.

[53] See Richard A. Posner, *Economic Analysis of Law* (4th edn., Little Brown and Co., 1992), 38–42 and works there cited.   [54] See Ch. 13, sect. (iii) above.

[55] Mark Rose, 'The Author as Proprietor: Donaldson v. Becket and the Genealogy of Modern Authorship', in Brad Sherman and Alain Strowel (eds.), *Of Authors and Origins* (Clarendon Press, 1994), 23–55. Roger Chartier suggests that a similar struggle was taking place in France—'Figures of the Author', *ibid.*, 7 at 12–16.

[56] See Ch. 12, sect. (i)(a) above.   [57] See Ch. 12, sect. (ii) above.

published, but nothing more.[58] Assault-analogy arguments are far-fetched, in the case of any attributed reproduction of what someone else has written, even if it is done without leave. Unattributed copying may rob an author of the credit which is rightly his; but banning plagiarism would not provide a trespassory perimeter anything near sufficient for full-blooded ownership.

Invocations of a Lockean 'fruits of labour' argument in this context, as in others, are ambiguous. In so far as they implicate self-ownership, they fall foul of the spectacular *non sequitur*.[59] Creation-without-wrong has a *prima facie* appeal in the case of ideational entities since their creation does not deplete resources.[60] However, even in their case the argument does not succeed in founding an ownership interest because non-wrongfulness of creative endeavour does not entail a unilateral power to impose new trespassory obligations.[61] The labour-desert argument is hostage to conventional acceptance that ownership of the work is the only fitting reward for the author's labour.[62] Whatever their genius or enterprise, creators of ideational entities cannot insist, as of right, on full-blooded ownership.

Yet if it can be demonstrated, for example, that a pharmaceutical corporation will invest research and development costs in the manufacture of a new drug only if it is granted a patent, or that an author or composer will create an artistic work only if he is accorded copyright, and if in either case considerations parallel to the five conditions for augmenting social wealth through incentives (set out above) apply, then justice requires that the patent or the copyright be awarded. Similarly, trade mark or 'passing off' protection law may provide incentives for manufacturers to maintain the quality of their products.[63] If, and to the extent that, they would, without such protection, produce items with a lower use-value (the marketing of which would produce fewer resources available for discharging justice costs), these aspects of intellectual property are also justified.

It is often claimed that the eighteenth-century origins of modern copyright law in common law jurisdictions, on the one hand, and in continental Europe, on the other hand, were inspired by opposed philosophical assumptions. Anglo-American legislators had instrumental considerations of public utility primarily in mind, whereas French revolutionaries proclaimed authorial ownership as a natural right. Jane Ginsburg has shown that the contrast is exaggerated. Both systems acknowledged that authors had rights which should be enforced for the public good, and only to the extent that they would promote the public good. Later continental assertions of an unqualified authorial 'moral right' were based on misreadings of earlier texts.[64] In

[58] See Ch. 12, sect. (iii) above.
[60] See Ch. 11, sect. (iii)(c) above.
[62] See Ch. 11, sect. (iv)(b) above.
[59] See Ch. 11, sect. (ii)(b)(4) above.
[61] See Ch. 11, sect. (iii)(e) above.
[63] See Posner, n. 53 above, 43–4.
[64] Jane C. Ginsburg, 'A Tale of Two Copyrights: Literary Property in Revolutionary France and America', in Sherman and Strowel (eds.), n. 55 above.

so far as claims to 'moral right' invoke a natural-right foundation other than labour-desert, they should be rejected.

Labour-desert considerations may interact with creator-incentives in the following way. Someone who creates a wonder drug or a spell-binding novel deserves recognition. There is no convention-independent reason why that recognition should take just the form of a packaged ownership interest in the ideational entity he has produced. It is creator-incentives which recommend that he be awarded intellectual property, limited to expire after a certain time, and subjected to the restricted trespassory protection we saw in Chapter 4. Once intellectual property has been in place long enough, however, it may be that desert-assumptions begin to crystallize around it. The manufacturer or the author ought to be conceded property to induce him to produce; and perhaps property is what he deserves.

Since creator-incentives are the primary (and it may be the only) justification for ideational entities being brought within the scope of property institutions, current systems of intellectual property ought to be constantly open to challenge on the grounds that the incentives are unnecessary, over-much, or insufficient. There could have been no good reason (other than bringing United Kingdom law into line with the rest of Europe) for the recent *ex post facto* extension of United Kingdom copyright protection from 50 to 70 years after the author's death. (We consider later whether property-incentives have any part to play in the context of gathered information.[65])

It might be argued that a property institution could be designed in such a way that monetary incentives, paid out of public funds, could be made available in all instances of novel creation of useful ideational entities. The drugs company or the author would contract with the government, in advance, to receive just such a sum as would provide sufficient incentive; but there would be no patent or copyright. It is evident, however, that factors relevant to the internalizing of externalities make intellectual property, in most instances, the preferable alternative. These are not those considerations which we discussed in connection with the property-freedom argument, which related to use-channelling and use-policing and which established, as we saw, that there is an overwhelming case for ownership interests in trivial chattels.[66] They have to do with the expenditure incurred if, in accordance with the advance-contract alternative, some public agency has to work out the creator's costs and the beneficial or detrimental effects of the creation on the rest of the community; as compared with allowing the creator himself to reap the beneficent externalities and to pay for the detrimental ones. Any unnecessary expenditure of resources by a public agency detracts from the pool presently available to discharge unavoidable justice costs.

It is true that there are some kinds of detrimental externalities which ought not to be fully internalized. The consequences to the public of harmful

[65] See Ch. 17, sect. (iii) below.   [66] See Ch. 13, sect. (iii) above.

new drugs are so terrible that internalization through civil liability is not enough. A publicly-financed licensing system is required as well. Perhaps also for some kinds of literary creation, there ought to be a public censorship system as well as liability for defamation. However, all these necessary regulatory regimes can be more effectively implemented, with least intrusion and least cost, if they utilize property-limitation rules which presuppose ownership interests. As a global alternative to ownership interests in ideational entities, the incentive-via-advanced-contract solution has little to recommend it. In practice it would sometimes kill off the goose that lays the golden eggs. That is why we have intellectual property.

(d) Real and Notional Markets

Real-market transactions are as much manifestations of freedom as are real gifts. Furthermore, as we have seen, real markets may combine with creator-incentives so as to yield justice-cost-discharging increases in social wealth. We must distinguish from these real transactions those envisaged within that style of economic analysis of law which has emerged over the past thirty years, which stresses the significance of hypothetical transactions in notional markets.[67] This branch of scholarship has added theoretical models to support the centuries-old assumption that markets contribute to creator-incentives and hence facilitate augmentations in social wealth. Its novelty consists in the implications which it seeks to draw from momentary, notional re-allocations within a total wealth pie taken to be fixed at a particular point of time.

Supposing we assume that the totality of goods and services available to meet insatiable demands is fixed. Let it be the case that this totality is divisible into n items, each of which is open to sale on a market. Let it further be supposed that all resources (either in the form of money or cashable rights or other resources realizable in terms of money) which may be used to purchase these items are already distributed, by no matter what process, among individuals. Then, on the assumption that each trader is a rational maximizer of his satisfactions, and on the further assumption that transaction costs are zero, instantaneous transfers will occur such that each resource comes to be owned by, and each service is placed at the disposal of, that person who will bid highest. That outcome is, within this style of scholarship, designated as the 'efficient' solution.

Because transaction costs are never zero, it may be desirable, in order that the efficient outcome be obtained, to implement features of property-institutional design which will impose a patterning of entitlements which would have been achieved under the conditions of the notional market. In a path-breaking article, R. H. Coase recommended this approach in the context of property-limitation rules. If we have to decide whether a

---

[67] See Jules Coleman, *Markets, Morals and the Law* (CUP, 1988), pt. ii.

factory-owner should or should not be enjoined from emitting smoke which interferes with the amenities of neighbouring owners, there is, Coase suggested, no reason for beginning with a prior assumption that the detrimental effects are a 'cost' to the neighbours as against regarding a restraint on emissions as a 'cost' to the factory-owner. Ask instead whether, were there an instantaneous and zero-transaction-costs market, the factory-owner would have bought out the neighbours (supposing the restraint to be in place), or the neighbours would have paid for the restraint (supposing that the general law imposed no restriction). Coase's revolutionary insight is that, on these assumptions, the answer will be the same either way. If the factory-owner is willing to pay more for the freedom to pour out the smoke than the neighbours will pay to be spared it, he will end up with the right to do it whether the legal starting-point was nuisance-liability or no nuisance-liability.[68] If that would be so on the notional market then, it seems, the factory-owner should be free to emit the smoke and the neighbours should be required to put up with it, even though, real transactions being impossible, the neighbours will receive no compensation for their detriment.

Coase's analysis has captured the imagination of an entire school of disciples precisely because it yields conclusions, based on a theoretical economic model, which, on the face of it, are counter-intuitive. The benighted layman may suppose that, even if a factory-owner's activities are, all things considered, in the public interest, he ought to bear the cost of compensating those who suffer from them. Coase's theorem demonstrates that a property institution should mimic the outcome of the notional market, let the real individual suffering be never so great.

There is a trick here. Real-market transactions are a manifestation of freedom. If a person authentically chooses (without fraud, undue influence, or mistake) to sell or purchase goods or services, he ought to be held to his bargain. But why should anyone be told that he must endure some uncompensated infraction of his welfare because he would, as a hypothetical maximizer of satisfactions, have contracted to take money for it on a notional market?

It is true that decisions about property-limitation rules in the field of nuisance law raise economic problems. Coase's example was well chosen. The reason is, however, that some kinds of restraint on ownership freedoms may detract from creator-incentives which operate within real-world markets. If the property-freedom argument were all that mattered, we should seek a property package which maximizes autonomous choice and minimizes illegitimate domination. There being no natural rights to full-blooded ownership of factories or anything else, that package would no doubt include nuisance-law restraints. It might, however, be the case that, at moments of technological innovation, creator-incentives (and attendant ability to discharge justice

[68] R. H. Coase, 'The Problem of Social Costs' (1960) 3 *Journal of Law and Economics* 1.

costs) require that owners be free to act in ways their neighbours dislike and, for one reason or another, expropriatory compensation rules may not be practical. All those real-life considerations may lead to the conclusion that neighbours must put up with the factory-owner's smoke. They ought not to be dished merely by reference to a non-existent, notional market.

It is not suggested that the elaborate models created in the genre of economic analysis of law are without value. Indeed, we have employed the terminology of 'internalizing externalities' as one way of expressing the use-channelling and use-policing advantages of ownership interests in relation to tangible resources, and as terminology peculiarly appropriate to the creator-incentives argument for intellectual property. Nor shall we enter into the question whether the notional market has some theoretical role to play in the context of rights other than property rights—although, as we have seen, such endeavours have been obfuscated by the tendency to denominate all rights 'property' rights.[69] Our suggestion is that the significance of markets, as a property-specific justice reason, is limited to real, and does not include notional, markets.

(iv) INDEPENDENCE

It was suggested at the beginning of section (iii) of Chapter 13 that three ranges of autonomous choice may be cited in connection with property institutions. The first two, mere-property freedoms and transmission freedoms, are inherent to ownership interests and their merits and demerits were discussed in the last two chapters. We now turn to a third range of autonomous choice with which property institutions are instrumentally, rather than inherently, connected. These result from the independence from social control which private holdings of wealth may afford.

(a) The Classical Argument

From Aristotle to the present day private property has been acclaimed as a source of political and cultural independence. In the nineteenth century both Mill (the recognized standard-bearer of 'negative freedom'), and Green (the acclaimed apostle of 'positive freedom'), invoked property in this context.

As we saw in the last chapter, Mill recommended ulterior limitations on the right of bequest.[70] It should be restricted to such provision as would afford the donee with 'the means of comfortable independence'.[71] His reason

---

[69] See Ch. 9, sect. (iii)(a) above.   [70] See Ch. 14, sect. (i)(b)(3) above.
[71] John Stuart Mill, *Principles of Political Economy: With Some of Their Applications to Social Philosophy*, in J. M. Robson (ed.), *Collected Works of John Stuart Mill* (U Toronto P, 1965), 225.

for this restriction presupposes that private holdings of wealth are good for society because they facilitate the independence of private projects:

> While those enormous fortunes which no one needs for any personal purpose but ostentation or improper power, would become much less numerous, there would be a great multiplication of persons in easy circumstances, with the advantages of leisure, and all the real enjoyments which wealth can give, except those of vanity; a class by whom the services which a nation having leisured classes is entitled to expect from them, either by their direct exertions or by the tone they give to the feelings and tastes of the public, would be rendered in a much more beneficial manner than at present.[72]

Mill supposed that, so long as private property existed, rights to full-blooded ownership of resources other than land could be based on creation-without-wrong.[73] Quite apart from this natural property right, however, it was (in his view) likely, once bequests to private individuals had been limited as he suggested, that accumulations of successful industry would be devoted to public uses 'either by direct bequest to the state, or by the endowment of institutions'.[74]

Green began his discussion of the rationale of private property with the assertion of a natural right based on personhood-constituting.[75] This fanciful notion is, however, unwittingly superseded, as he proceeds with the rationale, by an independence-instrumental argument. It is for the good of all that each citizen of a free State should be at liberty to pursue a free life and develop a moral character. Full-blooded ownership, including freedom to trade and to dispose of property-holdings by gift or bequest, was a necessary means to this end: '[m]oral freedom is not the same thing as a control over the outward circumstances and appliances of life. It is the end to which such control is a generally necessary means, and which gives it its value.'[76]

The clan system was defective 'from the moral point of view' because it entailed restraints on appropriation.[77]

Property is of value 'as a permanent apparatus for carrying out a plan of life, or expressing ideas of what is beautiful, or giving effect to benevolent wishes'.[78] The rationale of property is 'that everyone should be secured by society in the power of getting and keeping the means of realising a will, which in possibility is a will directed to social good'.[79] Its uncontrolled exercise

> is the condition of attainment by man of that free morality which is his highest good. It is not then a valid objection to the manner in which property is possessed among us, that its holders constantly use it in a way demoralising to themselves and others,

---

[72] N. 71 above, 226.   [73] See Ch. 11, sect. (iii)(b) above.
[74] *Ibid.*   [75] See Ch. 12, sect. (ii) above.
[76] T. H. Green, *Lectures on the principles of Political Obligation*, reprinted from *Green's Collected Works* (Longman, Green and Co., 1931), ii, 218.
[77] *Ibid.* 217–18.   [78] *Ibid.* 219.   [79] *Ibid.* 220.

any more than such misuse of any other liberties is an objection to securing men in their possession.[80]

So far as the moral character of owners themselves is concerned, Green recognizes that there is a down-side. They may be miserly and obsessed with the pursuit of gain for its own sake (the dangers we discussed under the description 'fetishism').[81] So far as non-owners are concerned, Mill stressed that they may be subjected to freedom-curtailing domination.[82] For all that, both supposed that there is a diffused spin-off advantage for society as a whole from the holding of private wealth. Whoever the owners are, a free society is better off than if there were none.

What are we to make of this classical version of the independence-instrumental argument for property institutions? Holdings of private wealth are no guarantee of independent centres of influence. There have been many societies in which people were allowed to own and accumulate property, but not to criticize the government. Other civil liberties must first be in place, as Mill was well aware. But given that they are, independence is, or has been, an instrumental merit of property institutions. If people are conceded ownership interests over accumulated wealth, they are enabled to satisfy their needs and desires without being beholden to anybody, particularly to agents of the community. They are equipped to make choices over life-plans and the disbursement of their resources which, but for their wealth, they could not make. What they choose to do or to disburse may be considered eccentric or even antisocial by their fellows or by the agencies of social decision-making. But public opinion and State organs often turn out to be wrong in such judgements. A healthy, pluralistic polity should foster, not frustrate, dissentient choice-making. It contributes to political diversity and to creative social initiatives; as well as allowing scope for the virtues of benevolence and the maintenance of non-governmental (charitable) institutions.

(b) Modern Times

Nevertheless, the argument from independence, like those from property-freedom and markets, is distributionally blind. Mill's evocation of leisured classes is the language of a Victorian gentleman. Some people who happen to have inherited wealth (albeit he would not have them excessively rich) could devote themselves to worthy objectives outside government control and, no doubt, some of them did.[83] But, as we have seen, Mill was well aware that the lives of the majority of his contemporaries were devoid of any such property-conferred independence.

---

[80] *Ibid.*   [81] See Ch. 14, sect. (ii) above.
[82] See Ch. 14, sect. (iv) above.
[83] For cynicism about this, see Josiah Wedgwood, *The Economics of Inheritance* (Routledge, 1929), 196–9.

The rich remain with us, but leisured independence is not what it was. We referred earlier to Charles Reich's call for a 'new property'.[84] Reich begins where Mill and Green left off, with the admission that property had fulfilled a crucial role in securing independence:

Thus, property performs the function of maintaining independence, dignity and pluralism in society by creating zones within which the majority has to yield to the owner. Whim, caprice, irrationality and 'antisocial' activities are given the protection of law; the owner may do what all or most of his neighbours decry.[85]

Reich, as we saw, then goes on to point out that holdings of wealth no longer secure independence from government in the modern 'public-interest State'. The reason is that a huge quantity of wealth is distributed in the form of 'government largesse'—welfare benefits, government jobs, occupational licences, State franchises, contracts and subsidies, and access to State-owned resources and to governmental services. Reich recommended measures to reduce the element of official discretion. Reformed largesse would secure the independence formally stemming from private wealth-holdings and, for that reason, Reich suggested that it should be labelled 'new property'.

We argued that the label was confusing and unnecessary. Nevertheless, Reich's point that property does not secure independence for wealthy individuals and corporations in the way it once did is well taken, as is his recommendation that officials' untrammelled discretions over many aspects of citizens' lives should be reined in (albeit that recommendation has few implications for property institutions as such).

Property today plays only a minor role in securing citizen independence, compared with freedoms of speech, political association, and demonstration of grievances, and immunities from arbitrary arrest and excessive surveillance. Nevertheless, that role is not insignificant. The wealthy individual can support unpopular or neglected causes. The affluent parent can buy education for his or her children which the organs of social decision-making deem unnecessary or undesirable. The rich entrepreneur can risk his own resources in research and development which others regard as unwise or quixotic. Even those who own nothing beyond the money they receive as wages or salaries may, if their pay exceeds the minimum requisite for subsistence, devote the surplus in support of political or philanthropic causes of their choice, or as members subscribe to trade unions, political parties, and charitable institutions.

None of the above would be possible if there were no such thing as a property institution which incorporates transmission freedoms and a consequent power to accumulate wealth in the form of money and cashable rights. This glaringly obvious instrumental advantage of property institutions is a

---

[84] See Ch. 9, sect. (iii)(b) above.
[85] Charles A. Reich, 'The New Property' (1964) 73 *YLJ* 733, at 771.

plus on the side of property freedoms in any context in which, as against the disadvantages of wealth-disparity and domination-potential, a judgement has to be formed whether such freedoms are, all things considered, valuable features of human association.

(v) THE BACKGROUND MORAL PROPERTY RIGHT

In setting our agenda in Chapter 10 we distinguished (section ii) seven categories of property rights. The first five categories concern rights internal to property institutions; categories 6 and 7 were alleged moral property rights. In Chapters 11 and 12 we rejected the possibility of free-standing natural property rights, which might have fallen within category 6. The last three chapters have established that, in a modern society, every citizen has a moral right within category 7—that is, moral standing to insist that a property institution be in place. Beginning with our minimalist conception of justice which did not include property, we have reached the conclusion that total abolition of property would treat everyone unjustly. There is a moral background right vested in each citizen of a modern society that a property institution of some kind must be maintained.

It has emerged, however, that it is not every variety of property institution which will satisfy this background right. It must incorporate certain features, and justice requires that any actual institution which does not incorporate them should be altered so that it does.

Most importantly, as we have seen in this Chapter, the social setting of the property institution must be such that the community shoulders the obligation to meet the basic needs of all citizens. The discharge of that obligation may have implications which have nothing to do with property, but it may also entail some particular requirements of property-institutional design—including expropriatory taxing rules, appropriation rules where discharge of basic needs itself requires conferring property, and quasi-ownership holdings by public agencies.

The property-freedom argument and the various instrumental arguments combine to make money and cashable rights indispensable features of a property institution. The same is true of full-blooded ownership of chattels. All dwellings must be the subject of ownership interests, the point on the ownership spectrum to be determined according to a mix of property-specific justice reasons—which includes the shell of a natural right to privacy, domination-potential in the case of family units, and incentive and market-instrumental considerations. The use-channelling and use-policing merits of property institutions, dangers of domination-potential, and market-instrumental and incentive considerations must all be taken into account on any question whether a major enterprise should be the subject of a (packaged) ownership or (packaged) quasi-ownership interest. Ownership interests over intellectual property should be recognized because, and only to the extent that, they have incentive and market-instrumental value, save where conventional assumptions about labour-desert have crystallized around them.

Irrespective of distribution, all property freedoms are *prima facie* valuable, but none sacrosanct. There is no *a priori* warrant for extracting any particular category from the bundle of ownership privileges and powers which have evolved. Nevertheless, the community does not treat owners unjustly where it imposes property-limitation or expropriation rules uniformly for the good of all (as in environmental and planning regulations); nor where it imposes them selectively, either to counter illegitimate domination or to fund the discharge of direct or indirect justice costs.

Disparity in wealth-holdings is, as such, relevant to just features of property-institutional design only in exceptional circumstances, where it results in disruptive phenomena of psychological dissociation. Even then, there may be countervailing considerations flowing from the political advantages to all of that independence from social control which private holdings of wealth afford.

Distributional questions cannot be fully determined according to any overall pattern. None the less, discharge of justice costs, and the possibility that incentives and markets are necessary adjuncts to that end, serve as pervasive property-specific justice reasons. To these must be added the convention-dependent claim to the shell of a natural right based on labour-desert and the convention-transcending shell of a natural right to privacy. Furthermore, in a few special contexts internal to the operation of an already established property institution, a right to a transmuted or improved resource may be based on creation-without-wrong.

If a historically-evolved property institution approximates to the features we have described, it constitutes a (perhaps imperfect) implementation of the moral background right. It will then be presumptively just. Its trespassory rules—against theft, criminal damage, trespass, and so forth—will be, at least, *prima facie* morally binding. Titles established under it will be presumptively morally legitimate. Any particular feature of the institution, and any category of property-holding, is, however, always open to challenge on the ground that it fails as a concretized application of the mix of property-specific justice reasons.

All property-specific justice reasons should be taken into account, where relevant, in questions of property-institutional design. There is no guarantee that indeterminacy of outcome will be eliminated. Might some snappier conclusion be available if one could find some dominating matrix within which all such particular justice reasons could be subsumed? To that question we turn in the next chapter.

16

Alleged Dominating Principles

We have reviewed a very mixed bunch of property-specific justice reasons—putative natural property rights; controversially valuable property freedoms; and instrumental merits of property institutions. An over-arching theory of justice (whether contractarian, utilitarian, or some other) concerns much else besides property. It encompasses political liberties, the proper relationship between private conceptions of the good and collective social projects, and the features of political organization which might confer legitimacy on organs of the State. 'Property' will constitute just one reference-point within any such over-arching theory.

Nevertheless, such a theory would scarcely be adequate if it failed to react, affirmatively or negatively, to the complex of justice reasons which have grown up around property institutions. Ideally, the reaction would be reciprocal. If some property-specific justice reason appears to have independent normative force, the over-arching theory of justice must make room for it. If the theory reaches a fundamental conclusion about the proper basis of human association, that may constitute a ground for upholding or rejecting or, more often, concretizing some property-specific justice reason.

We have eschewed opting between over-arching theories precisely in order that property-specific justice reasons might be displayed, with such normative force as they have, as part of the ultimate justice agenda. Might it not be the case, however, that some theory of justice could yield an all-inclusive matrix for questions of property-distribution and property-institutional design? Is there some dominating principle of just treatment under which all property-specific justice reasons must be subsumed?

We have seen that putative natural rights fail in this respect. Two other candidates for dominating principles will now be considered: equality of resources, and social convention. They represent polar opposite approaches. The advocate of equality of resources asks us to lift the totality of resources over which a property institution reigns out of its historical setting and to regard it as a cake sliceable into arithmetically equal divisions. The advocate of social convention, in contrast, recommends us to defer to the property-conventions by which people actually live. Either principle would yield moral property rights, within the sixth of our seven categories of property rights.[1] In the one case, it would be a right to an nth share of total resources. In the other

---

[1] See Ch. 10, sect. (ii) above.

case, it would be a moral right to retain whatever social convention had awarded.

(i) EQUALITY OF RESOURCES

In principle, all resources should be divided equally between the members of any relevant community.

(a) Literal Application

We have suggested that 'natural equality' carries only a negative implication: if treatment of a certain kind is due to one human being, X, nothing less is due to another person, Y, merely because Y is an inferior type of human being.[2] That might be accounted an over-restrictive notion of equality. Bernard Williams has argued that the concept of equality includes a distributional, as well as a comparative, element: people cannot be said to be treated as equals unless they receive certain goods.[3] The contention that one can spell out any substantive distributional content from 'equality' as such is notoriously controversial.[4] In accordance with the argument of this book, people's basic needs are to be met, and, given certain conditions, claims to labour-desert or to privacy are to be recognized. It might be argued that such commitments implicate no concept of equality: if we say that property-specific justice reasons are to be applied 'equally to all', is that not the same as saying that they are to be applied 'to all', the adverb 'equally' performing no more than a rhetorical role?[5]

The latter criticism would be avoided if we conceived of equality as a cake-slicer directed towards some preconceived totality, such as 'welfare' or 'overall advantage'.[6] 'Equality' would then do distinctive normative work. However, welfarist totalities may raise intricate problems of assessment. Are we to be concerned with the degree to which people are successful in fulfilling the preferences they happen to have, or the preferences which (according to some moral theory) they ought to have, or with psychological states of conscious well-being? Are expensive or deliberately manufactured preferences or tastes to count?[7] Such problems may seem to disappear if we apply the cake-slicer to

---

[2] See Ch. 10, sect. (iii)(a) above.

[3] Bernard Williams, 'The Idea of Equality', in Peter Laslett and J. G. Runciman (eds.), *Philosophy, Politics and Society* (2nd Series, Basil Blackwell, 1972), ch. 6.

[4] See D. D. Rafael, 'Equality and Equity' (1946) 21 *Philosophy* 138; Alf Ross, *On Law and Justice* (Stevens, 1958), 269–75; S. I. Benn and R. S. Peters, *Social Principles and the Democratic State* (George Allen and Unwin, 1959), ch. 5.

[5] See Joseph Raz, *The Morality of Freedom* (Clarendon Press, 1986), ch. 9.

[6] See Tony Honoré, *Making Law Bind* (Clarendon Press, 1986), ch. 9.

[7] See Ronald Dworkin, 'What is Equality? Part 1 Equality of Welfare' (1981) 10 *Phil. and Pub. Aff.* 185.

the totality of resources within the purview of a particular property institution. If there are n members of the relevant community, let each be allocated an nth share. Arithmetically equal shares of tangible resources seem eminently specific.

Literal equality of resources was advocated by P. J. Proudhon in his treatise *What is Property?*[8] The title belies its content, since Proudhon made no attempt to analyse the complex nature of property institutions as they had developed by 1840. His target was full-blooded ownership of income-bearing capital assets, especially land. He argued that rational reflection on the social instincts of men entailed the following ineluctable conclusions. All members of society are associates and hence equals. Therefore, society must concede only arithmetically equal possessory rights over land, the total area to be divided and redivided according to the population.[9] Secondly, augmentation resulting from labour arises, differences in talent or capacity notwithstanding, only from social co-operation; hence it, too, is to be divided in arithmetically equal shares between all who work.[10] (The idler should be compelled to work.[11]) Society, in principle, encompasses men the world over,[12] but not women.[13] 'Property' entails the power of individuals to assert exclusive and permanent rights to unequal shares of assets and the increase to be derived from them and so contradicts the formula 'equality in the products of nature and of labour'.[14] Therefore, 'property is theft'.[15]

There are yawning gaps in the implications we should be expected to draw from Proudhon's analysis. He calls for the 'abolition' of property.[16] Does that apply only to income-bearing assets? Ought there to be at least mere-property freedoms over dwellings or chattels for consumption and use? Are transmission freedoms of all kinds to be eliminated?[17] Above all, is money to be abolished? If all increments resulting from productive labour are equally allocated in the form of money payments, how could equality of resources be preserved in the face of differing choices about expenditure or saving? If there is to be no currency, some other mechanism for achieving equal division of products must be in place. Prodhoun addresses none of these problems.

If the principle stated at the beginning of this section were taken literally, it would mean that equality of resources must be preserved over time. If the first element of our minimalist conception of justice is understood in this way, how are we to square the circle with the second element—autonomous choice, over some range of actions open to individuals, is of value to all human beings? We

---

[8] Pierre Joseph Proudhon, *What is Property?* (trans. Donald R. Kelley and Bonnie F. Smith, CUP, 1994).
[9] *Ibid.* 66, 175, 178. [10] *Ibid.* 94–116.
[11] *Ibid.* 177. [12] *Ibid.* 165, 176–7, 178.
[13] *Ibid.* 186. [14] *Ibid.* 184.
[15] *Ibid.* 13, 14, 16, 33. [16] *Ibid.* 32, 36, 149, 187.
[17] Prodhon tells us that society should not tolerate donations of capital assets (*ibid.* 184), but that there is nothing wrong with generosity between intimates (*ibid.* 178–9).

might do that by attacking the property-freedom argument at its root, by denying that either mere-property freedoms or transmission freedoms are, all
things considered, valuable features of human association. The range of
actions open to autonomous choice should not extend to the use or control of
resources. In other words, we should aspire to a society like that of Red Land,
described in Chapter 2.[18] Or we might concede mere-property freedoms, over
widely available and roughly comparable chattels and dwellings, but eliminate
all transmission freedoms (it being their exercise which constantly threatens
any equal distribution of resources). That would be to adopt the Pink Land
model. Both proposals would require the abolition of money with all the freedom to choose between goods and services which money affords.[19] All (or
most) aspects of social wealth would be removed from the domain of private
property. Either solution would assume that the total wealth-pie could not be
increased through incentives and markets; or that, if it could, that would not
be worth the price of resources becoming unequally distributed. Either solution would repudiate the view that worthwhile cultural and political diversity
can be achieved through the medium of independent holdings of private
wealth.

It is hoped that all that has been said in the second half of this book, leading
to the conclusion about the background moral right described at the end of the
last chapter, suffices to rule out moving from where we are either to Red Land
or to Pink Land. Apart from wholesale economic reorganization, people who
now suppose that they are free to further the welfare of their families, or to
support causes they favour, by transfers of property, or to save or spend their
own money as they please, would need to be re-educated. Equality of resources, as a pattern of wealth-allocation to be literally and persistently maintained,
would require pervasive reculturalization within which conceptions of individuality which now prevail would be swamped.

(b) Squaring the Circle

Classical apologists for private property, such as Locke[20] and Hegel,[21] have
taken it for granted that equality of resources is incompatible with property-
freedoms. So did Mill. Mill envisaged colonists settling in an uninhabited
country. If they opted for a property institution at all in preference to communism, equal division would be the obvious starting-point (except that

---

[18] Proudhon's land-usufructuaries look rather like Red Land licensees. Their possessory
privileges are, it seems, subject to constant revision to ensure that fluctuations in the
number of men does not lead to unequal shares; and they are always 'under the supervision
of society' (*ibid*. 66).

[19] See Ch. 13, sect. (iv) above.

[20] John Locke, *Second Treatise of Government* (G. W. Gough (ed.), Basil Blackwell,
1976), ch. 5, 59.

[21] G. W. F. Hegel, *Elements of the Philosophy of Right* (trans. H. B. Nisbet, CUP, 1991),
79–81 (para. 49 and addition).

special allocations might be made to the disabled). But then, given different aptitudes and luck, distribution would inevitably soon become unequal.[22]

Could one interpret the first element of our minimalist conception of justice as requiring equality of resources, but nevertheless square the circle with the second element by understanding the principle stated at the beginning of this section in some less literal sense than that so far considered? Perhaps equality of resources can be recognized as a dominating principle even though people do not turn out, at every moment of time, to be vested with arithmetically equal holdings. Both Ronald Dworkin[23] and Bruce Ackerman[24] attempt this feat. They begin with the same thought-experiment as Mill—castaways on an island for Dworkin, immigrants to a new planet for Ackerman. But they hone it into an instrument for showing how equality of resources can continue as a moral base-line, whilst leaving plenty of room for property-freedoms, incentives, markets, and property-based independence.

Each author invokes a liberal argumentative strategy to answer two questions: first, how would the settlers divide the resources of the new land? Secondly, what implications do their decisions at this first stage have for their subsequent lives together and for all members of real liberal polities? Dworkin's castaways take part in an auction, beginning with an equal number of clam shells, in which each bids for a bundle of resources and takes out insurance against some future hazards. Ackerman's voyagers engage in constrained 'liberal conversation' wherein they argue for various proposals whilst observing the requirements of rationality and neutrality between theories of the good and between conceptions of personal worth. Both strategies are designed to invoke the notion of undominated choice over life-plans.

Both these thought-experiments yield the conclusion that, because of the difficulties of assessment referred to earlier in this section, equality of resources would initially be favoured over equality of welfare—with some allowance for special needs resulting from disability.[25] However, they reach different conclusions about the implications of this choice.

Dworkin suggests that the colonists would take out insurance against 'brute luck' but not against 'option luck'.[26] 'Brute luck' includes lack of income-earning talent. The colonists would insure against the contingency that they might fall below the average of talent-endowment, but not against the possibility that they might lack exceptional talents like those of a film star since, for the latter, premiums would be too high. They would not insure against the contingency that they might not be industrious or might not make wise

[22] John Stuart Mill, *Principles of Political Economy*, in J. M. Robson (ed.), *Collected Works of John Stuart Mill* (U Tor. P, 1965), 201–2.

[23] Ronald Dworkin, 'What is Equality? Part 2 Equality of Resources' (1981) 10 *Phil. and Pub. Aff.* 283.

[24] Bruce A. Ackerman, *Social Justice in the Liberal State* (NYUP, 1980), chs 2, 6, and 7.

[25] Dworkin, n. 23 above, 299–303; Ackerman, n. 24 above, 129–31, 168–9.

[26] Dworkin, n. 23 above, 292–303.

investments, these being matters of 'option luck'.[27] Equal numbers of clam shells remain after premiums have been paid. Similarly, Dworkin argues, we preserve equality of resources, in real societies, if we institute a system of income tax designed, so far as possible, to achieve the following. It expropriates the well-to-do to the extent necessary to compensate the poor for that which they have failed to earn only because they lack average talent-endowment; but it seeks no redistribution to correct inequalities resulting from exceptional talents, or from differential employments of the same talents, or from decisions to save or invest.[28]

A different conception of persisting equality of resources emerges from the liberal dialogue in which Ackerman's colonists engage; both among themselves, and with those future descendants whom they will choose to bring into existence. They take no account of differential talent-endowment. They agree that no-one should be required to disgorge any of the fruits of his industry or thrift merely because, over his lifetime, he becomes much richer than the rest.[29] However, Ackerman's colonists conclude that members of future generations will not be treated fairly unless each generation starts life on a basis of equality. Hence, in real societies, taxation schemes should be devised to neutralize the effect of inter-generational transfers,[30] but gifts made to persons other than one's offspring are unobjectionable.[31] Transfers to people who happen to be the donor's children, but not motivated by parental concern, are said to be problematic.[32] It seems that a child may retain that which he earns thanks to his being well-equipped for the world of work by parental nurture (going beyond the 'liberal education' which is to be provided for all). It is only the transfer of brute resources which is to be neutralized.

Each strategy is designed to show that we may affirm equality of resources as a dominating principle, whilst preserving worthwhile property-freedoms. Quite a deal of actual inequality of resources will continue. Both authors accept that, in principle, an exceptionally talented sportsman, like Nozick's Wilt Chamberlain,[33] may retain his earnings without violating equality of resources.[34] Gamblers of all kinds have nothing to fear. The industrious entrepreneur will be permitted to amass all he can during his lifetime, by Ackerman; but Dworkin would have him levelled down to the extent that his riches result from better-than-average (but not exceptional) talents, whilst leaving him with that 'option luck' wealth which accrues from industry or investment.

In both cases, it is difficult to resist the impression of arbitrariness. Dworkin assumes that the implications for real societies of the principle of equality of resources can be intelligently investigated while leaving to one side all

---

[27] Dworkin, n. 23 above, 304–23.

[28] *Ibid*. 323–34.

[29] Ackerman, n. 24 above, 131–2, 169.

[30] *Ibid*. 204–5, 208.

[31] *Ibid*. 184, 208–9

[32] *Ibid*. 209–12.

[33] See Ch. 14, sect. (iii) above.

[34] Dworkin, n. 23 above, 336–7; Ackerman, n. 24 above, 185.

inequalities resulting from inter-generational or other gifts.[35] Why do Dworkin's colonists insure against lack of talent, but not against being bereft of generous friends and kin? Conversely, why should Ackerman's dialogue not include an unchallengeable assertion that being born with talents is just as unfair as being born with wealthy parents? The latter unfairness Ackerman founds on a non-legatee being able to protest that, should a testator leave his wealth to another, that would be to 'deny me the good of initial equality'.[36] One had supposed, however, that Ackerman is using his dialogic strategy to establish that initial equality is a good. At this juncture, that it is as good is assumed within the dialogue.

We have argued that wealth-disparity, as such, should be taken into account in property-institutional design only in very special circumstances.[37] Dworkin and Ackerman have fastened on a particular cause of such disparity which each finds particularly unacceptable—talent-endowment and inter-generational transfers, respectively. They have contrived thought-experiments to attack the favoured target hitched, unnecessarily, to a notional base-line of persisting equality of resources.

Why should we assume that, because people coming across some new item of social wealth with which none of them has any previous connection ought to share it equally, it therefore follows that no person in any real society is treated justly unless he is (notionally) the recipient of an arithmetically equal share of resources? For one thing, distributable social wealth does not consist of an undifferentiated mass which is susceptible to cake-slicing. People have basic needs, which, as we have argued, the community must cater for, whether by transfers of money or other property, or in the form of services provided outside a property institution (but which require expropriatory taxation to fund them); and people have claims, of various sorts, which relate to differentiated and non-fungible assets. As was mentioned at the end of Chapter 1, moral evaluations of property institutions are primarily resource-centred ('lumpy').

More importantly, it is difficult to see why arithmetical equality of holdings as between X and Y should be considered relevant to the just treatment of

---

[35] Dworkin, n. 23 above, 312, n. 9, 334. In a subsequent essay Dworkin investigates the relationship between equality of resources and liberty—'What is Equality? Part 3 The Place of Liberty' (1987) 73 *Iowa LR* 1. He suggests that restraints, such as those on funding political campaigns or buying private medical care, may be justified as parts of programmes aimed at reducing inequalities, but they would have no place within a society in which the ideal of equality of resources was implemented. 'No one would be forbidden by law, in a defensible distribution, to use his resources in whatever way he chooses except in so far as necessary to protect security or to correct for different sorts of auction or market imperfection'—*ibid*. 44. The essay makes no mention of freedoms to transfer resources by way of gift. Would the distribution be 'defensible' if that was the only use of resources to be prohibited? If it was not prohibited, in what sense would the distribution ensure 'equality' of resources?

[36] Ackerman, n. 24 above, 205.

[37] See Ch. 14, sect. (iii) above.

either X or Y outside 'windfall' situations. The community's duty to meet people's basic needs directs its attention towards the objects of concern. Equality of resources is directed towards the space between people. It supposes that X is justly treated merely because there is some other person or persons, Y, Z . . . who are no worse, and no better, endowed with resources. It is a principle in which the humanity of the recipient counts only as a tag to attach to a bundle of resources.

It is true that basic needs are, as we saw in the last chapter, a function both of culture and of available productive forces. Indeterminacy in their assessment may often arise. But such questions will be nothing as compared with those thrown up by Dworkin's and Ackerman's thought-experiments—like deciding which aspect of a person's wealth came to him because of unusual (but not exceptional) talents, and which was the result of talent-independent industry or thrift; or deciding what portions of a person's wealth were parentally transferred, and which were due to exertions made feasible by parental nurture. At least questions about basic needs concern flesh-and-blood persons rather than dehumanized comparisons.

(c) Windfall Wealth

What Mill's, Dworkin's, and Ackerman's thought-experiments make clear is that, if a resource is genuine windfall wealth, equality of resources is a sound property-specific justice reason. As such it has a residual role to play over questions of distribution and property-institutional design. The uninhabited countries to which all colonists arrive simultaneously are windfalls, because nothing previously done by any of them can give a special claim. But if the property-freedom and property-instrumental arguments are to be given any force, it is both undesirable in principle, and certainly impracticable, to regard talents or benefactions as pure windfall.

The principle stated at the beginning of this section—in principle, all resources should be divided equally between the members of any relevant community—has a genuine, *faute de mieux*, role to play in various situations. It has first to be decided what the relevant community is; and then whether equal division is best achieved either by literal subdivision or by some regime of communal use. In the case, for example, of an expired copyright or patent, all mankind is the relevant community and, there being no need to channel or police uses, the appropriate communal-use regime is 'common property', that is, free-for-all. If a meteor were to fall to earth containing minerals of immense value, it is likely that the relevant community would be taken to be the citizens of the State on whose territory it fell; and the appropriate mechanism for achieving equal division would be the vesting of a quasi-ownership interest in some public agency, on terms that the minerals should be exploited for the common good. The same holds for cultural artifacts or sites to which one community, but no particular citizen, has a special claim. When oil and natural gas were discovered under the North Sea, the relevant communities were assumed to be citizens of various coastal States. An international convention provided for equal division amongst these States in advance of exploration, by drawing median lines between them. Within individual States, limited and heavily taxed extraction licences were granted to exploration companies as incentives, the goal being that all citizens should benefit equally from the receipt of revenue.[38]

Windfall wealth accrues where a group of persons is confronted with a resource to which no-one outside the group has any claim, but to which nothing gives any member of the group a better claim than any other member. Since title to most resources arises by concretized applications of the background right described at the end of the last chapter, windfall wealth comes into the picture, usually, only in the last resort. It is so invoked, occasionally, both in common law doctrine and in statutory interpretation.

English company law makes explicit and elaborate provision for the distribution of a company's assets on its winding-up. No similar regime has been invented for property held by unincorporated associations. Instead, the courts have evolved the following doctrine: when such an entity is dissolved, its members shall, in the absence of express contractual arrangements, be deemed to hold its assets on the basis of equal division amongst those who are members at the time of dissolution. Here, treating the property as windfall (and hence subject to equality of resources) is deemed to be more expedient than trying to relate each portion of the assets to the input of individual subscribers.[39] This is but a special application of the old maxim that, if no claim to any particular share can be shown, 'equality is equity'.[40]

The windfall/equality argument may crop up in the interstices of statutory construction. In a recent English case, for example, land which had been compulsorily purchased by a railway in 1846 was no longer required. On the face of nineteenth-century legislation, that meant that the successors of the original owners of the land were entitled to repurchase it at the 1846 price. The Court of Appeal rejected this construction on the ground that to accede to it would be to confer a 'vast windfall' on the plaintiffs. The Court took it to be indisputably unjust that private individuals, rather than the publicly owned British Railways Board, should reap the benefit of the increased value of the land.[41]

That which is intrinsically windfall wealth may none the less be allocated to

---

[38] See Kenneth W. Dam, 'Oil and Gas Licensing and the North Sea' (1965) 8 *Journal of Law and Economics* 51.

[39] See, e.g., *Re St Andrew's Allotments Association's Trusts* [1969] 1 All ER 147; *Re Sick and Funeral Society of St John's Sunday School Golcar* [1973] Ch. 51; *Re Bucks Constabulary Widows and Orphans Fund Friendly Society (No. 2)* [1979] 1 All ER 623; *Re GKN Bolts and Nuts Ltd Sports and Social Club* [1982] 2 All ER 855.

[40] See *Rimmer* v. *Rimmer* [1953] 1 QB 63 at 72, *per* Evershed MR.

[41] *Freedman* v. *British Railways Board, The Times,* 14 Apr. 1992.

particular individuals or groups for reasons of convenience in property-institutional design. Bright-line rules can be administered with less cost than those which require the application of individuated property-specific justice reasons. We have earlier mentioned three examples. The first occupant of a chattel or a plot of land can justly assert, at best, a right not to be turfed out by someone with no title. Yet the law confers full-blooded ownership.[42] An adverse possessor is similarly vested with full-blooded ownership even though, in his case, there is someone with a better title, but one who has delayed too long in asserting his rights.[43] Someone who takes property on the intestacy of an owner who owed him no obligations, and who did not in fact choose to transfer his property to him, receives an undoubted windfall.[44]

In all these cases there could be no just complaint if machinery could be devised for allocating the windfall to the State, on the basis that it was to be used equally for the benefit of all citizens—except that, perhaps, in the case of the first occupant some modest compensation is allowable in respect of his forgoing his right not to be evicted and, in the case of the adverse possessor, to compensate him for what might be justified reliance. In practice, other considerations make windfall treatment inexpedient. Incentive and market-instrumental factors tell in favour of the first occupant and the adverse possessor. In the case of the intestate successor, the disadvantages of costly enquiry into the testator's true intentions, and into the possible subsistence of support and maintenance obligations, recommend that some bright line be drawn.

There is another context in which a windfall/equality approach might be superior to the current law. English courts have been granted statutory jurisdictions to allocate property between spouses on divorce and death, and various equitable doctrines empower courts to allocate property on the termination of quasi-marital relationships. Claims founded on obligations to meet basic needs, labour-desert, and justified reliance have played varying roles.[45] Uncertainty and litigation costs have been the result. Might it not be better for partners to a long-standing relationship to be understood as having committed certain assets permanently to the purposes served by their association with the result that, upon its dissolution, such assets as remain are, as between them, 'windfall'? Looked on in that light, no-one outside the community constituted by the parties to the relationship has any claim, and neither of them has a claim superior to the other. In that event, equal division of these resources is the only just allocation, *faute de mieux*.

---

[42] See Ch. 12, sect. (i)(a) above.
[43] *Ibid*.
[44] See Ch. 14, sect. (i)(b)(1) above.
[45] See Ch. 11, sect. (iv)(c); ch. 14, sect. (i)(b)(1), and Ch. 15, sect. (ii)(c) above.

(ii) SOCIAL CONVENTION

In principle, everyone is morally entitled to whatever property-holdings accrue in accordance with the social conventions prevalent in any society in which there is an established property institution.

(a) Convention for Everything

Some of the property-specific justice reasons so far considered appeal, one way or another, to social conventions. Those basic needs which the community must discharge are a function of cultural assumptions as well as of available productive forces.[46] The labour-desert natural property right is entirely hostage to social convention.[47] A privacy property right can, in principle, stand independently of convention; but the all-things-considered judgment which must be made before concluding that protected choices associated with privacy are to be valued may, in turn, involve reflection on culturally-contingent assumptions about basic needs.[48]

Given that we have rejected all claims to full-blooded ownership based on natural right and have recognized the significance of social convention in these various ways, and in view of the many contingent elements which have entered into our assessment of the property-freedom argument and the instrumental values of property institutions, might it be simpler and 'more realistic' to take social convention as the direct and singular basis for the justice of property institutions, as the statement of principle at the beginning of this section suggests? Social convention is solid and reliable. It points to a way of life which flesh-and-blood people actually live by. It eschews endless normative controversy both at the level of meta-ethics and as to detailed questions of distribution and property-institutional design. It will not matter if there are no natural conditions of title so long as conventional title conditions are always to be found and we are prepared to accept their conventional status as sufficient reason for calling them 'just'.

That is the view of the eighteenth-century philosopher, David Hume. Hume provides a sketch of property institutions. What we have called 'trespassory rules', he describes as rules of 'abstinence' which secure 'stability of possession' over 'external goods' for individuals and for those to whom they choose to transfer them. These rules arise through 'human conventions'. Natural selfishness and limited generosity, together with scarcity and vulnerability of external goods, make the establishment of these conventional rules indispensable to society. Nevertheless, the public good is not the reason for their enforcement

---

[46] See Ch. 14, sect. (ii)(b) above.
[47] See Ch. 11, sect. (iv) above.
[48] See Ch. 12, sect. (iii) above.

on a day-to-day basis. Once the conventions have arisen, moral sentiment attaches directly to them. They avail the miser and the profligate. These social-conventional rules are what is meant by 'rules' or 'laws' of 'justice'.[49]

Property may be defin'd: *such a relation betwixt a person and an object as permits him, but forbids any other, the free use and possession of it, without violating the laws of justice and moral equity.*[50]

Our property is nothing but those goods, whose constant possession is establish'd by the laws of society; that is, by the laws of justice.[51]

Hume does not consider variable interests within the ownership spectrum, non-ownership proprietary interests, group or public property, property-limitation rules, or expropriation rules. He does, however, recognize that the rules of justice need to be supplemented by appropriation rules setting out specific title conditions—such as occupation, prescription, accession, succession, and transfer by delivery. In all these cases, he says, we find that determination of the concrete tends to be achieved by 'imagination' or 'fancy', there being no possibility of settling such questions by 'reason' directed to the 'public interest'.[52]

The upshot is that we must needs look to social convention, and to nothing else, as the moral basis of property and of all questions of distribution and property-institutional design.

The relation of fitness or suitableness ought never to enter into consideration, in distributing the properties of mankind; but we must govern ourselves by rules, which are more general in their application, and more free from doubt and uncertainty.[53]

Commentators differ about whether Hume shared the opinions of Adam Smith and other representatives of the Scottish enlightenment about the supreme instrumental merits of incentives and markets, or whether his position can be characterized as a species of long-run utilitarianism. It seems clear, however, that his scepticism about a faculty of practical reason which could yield determinate conclusions independently of prior assumptions about interest confirmed his view that we had better opt for the stability of enforcing whatever conventional property system we happen to have.[54]

Does it follow from Hume's position that every feature of a conventionally established property institution is immune from criticism on the ground of its alleged injustice? F. A. Hayek argues that it does not. As we saw in the last chapter, Hayek inveighs against using the notion of 'social justice' as a criterion for criticizing any state of affairs brought about by the consistent

---

[49] David Hume, *A Treatise of Human Nature* (T. H. Green and T. H. Grose (eds.), Longmans, Green and Co., 1874), ii, bk. 3, pt II, sects. ii–iv.

[50] *Ibid.* 105. [51] *Ibid.* 263–4.

[52] *Ibid.* 283–4. [53] *Ibid.* 283.

[54] See David Miller, *Social Justice* (Clarendon Press, 1976), ch. 5.

enforcement of 'rules of just conduct'. Following Hume, he insists that abstract property rules must be applied according to their content without reference to need or desert. Nevertheless, he claims, the justice of individual rules can be tested by their compatibility with other conventional rules taken to be unquestioned, the ultimate touchstone being a socially-evolved 'order of actions'.

When we say that all criticism of rules must be immanent criticism, we mean that the test by which we can judge the appropriateness of a particular rule will always be some other rule which for the purpose in hand we regard as unquestioned. The great body of rules which in this sense is tacitly accepted determines the aim which the rules being questioned must also support; and this aim, as we have seen, is not any particular event but the maintenance or restoration of an order of actions which the rules tend to bring about more or less successfully. The ultimate test is thus not consistency of the rules but compatibility of the actions of different persons which they permit or require.[55]

Hayek envisages a 'free' or 'great' society in which wide consensus exists about abstract rules protecting property. Given our perennial ignorance about variable circumstances and life-plans of multitudes of individuals, no-one could have created this order, but we are all its beneficiaries since it permits each to pursue his own goals with minimum collision. We can, however, take an individual rule and demonstrate that it does or does not harmoniously further the 'order of actions'. Any wholesale reconstruction or reform of the property system, such as that inspired by the pernicious doctrines of legal positivism, can serve only to disrupt the spontaneous evolution of this order.[56]

This roseate portrait of property is one which it is difficult to square with the problems of distribution and property-institutional design thrown up by the last two centuries. Hayek supposes that his intra-conventional immanent-critique test suffices both for judicial development and for legislative reform.[57] Are we to represent the abolition of slavery, and the enfranchisement of women as separate property-owners, merely as removing wrinkles in an otherwise smoothly functioning fabric? Is the same to be said of the wholesale statutory reforms of the archaisms of the common law concerning tenure and estates in land? We have discussed measures directed at diminishing illegitimate domination within the factory or within the home.[58] Are these all to be understood as perfecting an 'order of actions' which would enable each individual to pursue his own goals? Can problems about the ownership of commercial information be met by asking us simply to articulate new rules of just conduct which will fit smoothly with those property rules we already have?[59]

---

[55] F. A. Hayek, *Law, Legislation and Liberty, Vol. 2 The Mirage of Social Justice* (Routledge and Kegan Paul, 1976), 25.

[56] F. A. Hayek, *Law, Legislation and Liberty, Vol. 1 Rules and Order* (Routledge and Kegan Paul, 1973), 91–3; *Mirage of Social Justice*, n. 55 above, 44–8.

[57] *Rules and Order*, n. 56 above, 85–90; *The Mirage of Social Justice*, n. 55 above, 38–44.

[58] See Ch. 14, sect. (iv) above.   [59] See Ch. 17, sect. (iii)(a) below.

Does the same apply to the host of property-limitation rules imposed by planning and environmental law?[60]

The concept of 'an order of actions' is too imprecise to provide guidance in connection with any of these problems. None of them can be settled simply by appealing to convention. In any case, the property-specific justice reasons we have surveyed are as much part of our conventional heritage as are our bright-line rules about trespass or title. Hume's property sketch, and Hayek's modification of it, cannot, and should not, eliminate invocation of them. Social convention is no more a valid principle dominating all questions of distribution and property-institutional design than is equality of resources.

(b) Convention Always Relevant

Nevertheless, social convention has a pervasive, as distinct from equality-of-resources' residual, role to play. This is the consequence of problems thrown up by indeterminacy, controversy and justified reliance.

(1) Indeterminacy

We referred at the end of the last chapter to a background moral right that a property institution, with certain features, should be in place. It requires a range of property-specific justice reasons to be taken into account. Suppose that, as to a concrete question whether X should be accorded an ownership interest over some resource, or whether Y should have a non-ownership proprietary interest, or whether some property-limitation, expropriation, or appropriation rule should apply, all these reasons produce no determinate solution. Suppose also that the conventions of the society (usually embodied in law) do yield a clear answer. Changing the conventional position involves cost of some kind. By assumption, the change will produce an outcome which cannot be demonstrated to be more just than the starting-point. No change should take place.

This trite conclusion applies only to contexts in which it is admitted, on all hands, that there is nothing to choose between solutions A and B. Its significance is merely to place the onus of proof on the proponent of change.

(2) Controversy

Supposing a critic marshals all or any of the property-specific justice reasons we have considered in such a way as to demonstrate, in his view, that some feature of an existing property institution is unjust—either that there is a different determinate solution, or that there are a range of solutions none of which is embodied within the property institution under survey. Suppose that he is right, but that he fails to convince other members of his society (or the members of some other society he is criticizing). It follows from our rejection

---

[60] See Ch. 3, sect. (viii) above.

of social convention as a dominating principle that manifestly unjust conventions carry no moral force. For example, a social institution which treats
human beings as property, or one which allows some people to starve, is unjust whatever majoritarian opinion may be.

Suppose, however, that the critic favours a proposal which would, as he
thinks, be only marginally more just than the conventional solution. Then the
controversialty of the issue is significant. If he sees himself pitted against a
majority who have made a good-faith (albeit mistaken) resolution of the mix
of relevant property-specific justice reasons, he is confronted with a social
bonding which is a partial (albeit imperfect) implementation of the three
elements of our minimalist conception of justice. It is thus a matter of degree
whether a critic may claim that a conventionally-established property institution confers privileges and powers, and imposes duties, which have no, or
some, moral force.

(3) Justified Reliance

Special importance may be thought to accrue to social convention by invoking, in its support, a principle of inter-personal justice familiar to lawyers in
the context of the doctrine of estoppel. If X (even without making a promise)
deliberately or negligently creates an expectation in Y, and Y changes his position in reliance on that expectation, X treats Y unjustly if he then frustrates
that expectation. This is the principle of 'justified reliance'.

Can such an inter-personal principle be carried over into the relations
between the community and citizens, in such a way that all alterations of conventionally-established property institutions are inherently suspect? Bentham
thought that it could. He saw security of expectations as a universal blessing of
property institutions.

Property is nothing but a basis of expectation; the expectation of deriving certain
advantages from a thing which we are said to possess, in consequence of the
relation in which we stand towards it.[61]

The principle of security extends to the maintenance of all these expectations; it
requires that events, so far as they depend upon laws, should conform to the
expectations which law itself has created.[62]

Hence, even though property institutions differ from one another in the sum
of happiness they produce so that, according to Bentham's utilitarianism, some
are morally superior to others, the very fact that a particular institution has
evolved means that the law has raised expectations which ought not now to be
frustrated. The legislature may aim at maximizing utility through reducing
inequalities where no settled expectation is thereby disrupted. For example, if

---

[61] Jeremy Bentham, *Principles of the Civil Code*, in C. K. Ogden (ed.), *Jeremy Bentham:
The Theory of Legislation* (Kegan Paul, 1931), 111.
[62] *Ibid.*

there is a joint liability to meet what we have called 'justice costs', more may be taken from the rich than from the poor.[63] In general, however, so great is the utility of securing the expectations which an established system of property law has created, that no legislative redistribution is permissible, whether the property system in question is bourgeois, feudal, or even slave-owning.

In consulting the grand principle of security, what ought the legislator to decree respecting the mass of property already existing? He ought to maintain the distribution as it is actually established. It is this which, under the name of *justice*, is regarded as his first duty. This is a general and simple rule, which applies itself to all states; and which adapts itself to all places, even those of the most opposite character.[64]

It is difficult to understand how Bentham could have arrived at such a blanket conclusion from his own utilitarian standpoint. Suppose that the sum of happiness under a particular property regime is X, and a redistribution would instantly produce a sum of 2X. Why should we assume that, of necessity, the fact that such redistributions can occur will reduce (even in the long run) the happiness of all owners by a factor greater than X? The truth seems to be that Bentham has introduced the principle of justified reliance irrespective of utility, and that he has done so by personifying the law.

Suppose there are widely diffused (but false) beliefs about the justice of an established property institution and that these beliefs have given rise to settled expectations. Should such expectations be taken into account by a reformer who is proposing an enlightened change or who, for whatever reason, is empowered to bring about such a change? Members of the society have acted upon the (false) conviction that their property system deals appropriately with issues of use-control and wealth-allocation. Each member's conventional assumptions have interlocked with those of his fellows. He was acting justly by the (false) lights of his community when, for example, he arranged his affairs on the assumption that married women ought to have no separate property, or the assumption that people are entitled to accumulate wealth for their posterity and need not contribute to the basic needs of anyone else. Is it unjust to frustrate such settled expectations at a stroke? Was it right, as Mill supposed that it was, to offer compensation to slave-owners when the institution of slavery was abolished in the British Empire?[65] Are settled expectations unjustly disrupted when property-limitation rules are enacted, without compensation, in the interests of public health or amenity?[66]

For the inter-personal principle of justified reliance to be invoked, it is not

---

[63] Jeremy Bentham, n. 61 above, ch. 6.

[64] *Ibid.* 119.

[65] John Stuart Mill, *Principles of Political Economy: With Some of their Applications to Social Philosophy*, in J. M. Robson (ed.), *Collected Works of John Stuart Mill* (U Tor. P, Routledge and Kegan Paul, 1965), 233.

[66] See Ch. 6, sect. (iii) above.

enough that O (a property-owner) had settled expectations. Two further conditions must be satisfied. First, he must show that he acted in reliance on them. (Planning law usually exempts existing uses from prohibitions on development.) Secondly, he must point to some personified entity against whom an allegation of unfairness can be laid. This second condition raises tricky questions about who or what, in this context, it is legitimate to personify.

Our discussion of direct and indirect justice costs in the last chapter entailed personification of the community as the direct bearer of obligations. There seems no sound argument against personifying it also for the purpose of applying the principle of justified reliance. Nevertheless, Bentham's personification of 'the law' is unwarranted. Why should 'the community' be identified with outmoded or unpopular laws, and, more especially, with laws imposed by a minority?

If settled expectations reflect merely the conventions of a privileged minority and have arisen over an epoch during which the majority were unable to change the institutions embodying such expectations, it is difficult to see how a claim of 'justified' reliance can be levelled at the majority once it gains the power to, and does, alter the law. It is otherwise if the majority, whilst not sharing the assumptions upon which expectations are built, have nevertheless left them unchallenged when they might have challenged them. That could be seen as inducing justified reliance by default. More generally, the argument for respecting expectations has diminishing force the less conventions enjoy a breadth of social acceptance. If what was once conventionally taken for granted has for some time been the subject of increasing controversy, the less normative force can be accorded to conventionally-induced expectations.

(c) Juristic Doctrine

Because of indeterminacy, controversy, and justified reliance, social convention is always potentially relevant to the balancing of property-specific justice reasons. It is notorious, however, and to the layman a ground of weary complaint, that such questions are not settled in terms of any conventions shared by the man or woman in the street. Rather, they are referred to particularly arcane conceptual categories known only to lawyers. If it is unclear how we should decide some question in the light of the mix of property-specific justice reasons, there is a case for letting the matter be settled by popular understandings of ownership freedoms, incentives, basic needs, and the rest; but why on earth should questions of justice be hog-tied to juristic doctrine?

Max Weber represents juristic doctrine as our inevitable fate, once we permit a specialist class (whether practising lawyers or professorial scholars) a guiding hand over the evolution of our institutions.

A 'lawyers' law' has never been and never will be brought into conformity with lay expectation unless it totally renounce that formal character which is immanent in it. This is just as true of the English law which we glorify so much today, as it has been of the ancient Roman jurists or of the methods of modern continental legal thought.[67]

Weber isolated three varieties of legal reasoning: empirical-casuistic, conceptual-casuistic, and logically-formal. Casuistry ('cautelary jurisprudence') insists that the ruling in a case must be based on precedent or analogy with some earlier ruling. Casuistry may be empirical or conceptual, depending on whether precedential or analogical cogency is mediated through factual similarity or through the intrinsic meaning of the concepts in which rulings are given.[68] Logically-formal legal reasoning consists of second-order propositions under which legal concepts are subsumed at a higher level of abstraction.[69] All these variations of legal reasoning are to be contrasted with what Weber calls 'khadi justice', that is individuated conclusions which make no appeal to universalizable reasons,[70] and 'substantive rationality', where rulings are chosen by reference to their perceived moral, social, or economic consequences.[71]

Examples of all the kinds of reasoning which Weber distinguishes, both those that he considers peculiar to lawyers and those which are not, are to be found in the judgments of English courts today.[72] The court may direct its attention to broad 'policy' considerations ('substantive rationality'); or it may proceed incrementally, insisting that the case at hand must share factual similarities with previous precedents ('casuistic factual rationality'). What are of present interest, however, are instances in which courts either adopt conceptual casuistry or aspire towards logically-formal rationality, because then the reasoning, on its face, appears not to be directed towards property-specific justice reasons at all. Instead, juristic doctrine seems to acquire an independent momentum. It may, nevertheless, cater satisfactorily for problems of indeterminacy, controversy, and justified reliance in the same way that social conventions do. Thus, juristic doctrine may be seen as a specialist variety of social convention.

So far as conceptual casuistry is concerned, consider the emergence of the equity of redemption on a mortgage. From the seventeenth century onwards, the Court of Chancery took the view that contracts of a certain kind should not be enforced. Those were ones in which a mortgagor agreed that, should he be a day late in repayment of capital and interest, he should forfeit the right to redeem his property. To allow the mortgagee to exploit his ownership of

---

[67] Max Weber, *On Law in Economy and Society* (Max Rheinstein (ed.), trans. Edward Shills and Max Rheinstein, Harv. UP, 1954), 308.

[68] *Ibid.* 61–4, 73–4, 178, 198–204, 209–20, 315–18, 349–56.

[69] *Ibid.* 61–4, 145, 204–5, 220–3, 266–9, 274–9, 296–8, 303–16, 349–55.

[70] *Ibid.* 61, 229, 264, 351–2.

[71] *Ibid.* 63, 105–9, 224–6, 264–5, 279–83, 313–15, 318–21, 349–56.

[72] See J. W. Harris, 'Legal Doctrine and Interests in Land', in J. M. Eekelaar and J. Bell (eds.), *Oxford Essays in Jurisprudence 3rd Series* (Clarendon Press, 1987); 'Murphy Makes it Eight: Overruling Comes to Negligence' (1991) 11 *OJLS* 416.

money in this way placed him in a relationship of illegitimate domination over the mortgagor. Chancery took it upon itself to balance ownership freedoms against domination-potential in this context. As time went on, doctrine solidified to the point at which any contractual term inserted into a mortgage is struck down, not because it is held to be unfair, but because it is inconsistent with the nature of a mortgage—including an option for purchase of the mortgaged property entered into between businessmen negotiating at arm's length.[73]

In such a case the court is aware of the kind of reason which originally justified a facet of doctrine. It is not convinced that its present application is just, but nevertheless decides that unpicking the strands is not warranted. The proper balance of justice reasons is controversial and solidified doctrine yields a determinate (if arguably unsatisfactory) solution.

Sometimes, however, the Court may defer to juristic doctrine of the conceptual-casuistic kind even though it can see no basis in justice for it whatever. Then the justice issue is not indeterminate or controversial (in the court's view) and the only respectable excuse for doctrine-deference is the wish not to upset justified reliance. The House of Lords has recently ruled, for example, that a contractual stipulation, restraining a landlord's right to terminate a lease until the leased land was required for a road-widening scheme, must be held void as being inconsistent with the concept of a lease.[74] Lord Browne-Wilkinson, speaking for the majority of their Lordships, said of the requirement that the duration of a lease must be ascertainable from the outset:

No one has produced any satisfactory rationale for the genesis of this rule. No one has been able to point to any useful purpose that it serves at the present day. If, by overruling the existing authorities, this house were able to change the law for the future only I would have urged your Lordships to do so. But for this house to depart from a rule relating to land law which has been established for many centuries might upset long established titles.[75]

---

[73] *Samuel* v. *Jarrah Timber and Wood Paving Corporation Ltd* [1904] AC 323.

[74] *Prudential Assurance Co. Ltd.* v. *London Residuary Body* [1992] 2 AC 386.

[75] [1992] 2 AC 386 at 396–7. Lord Griffiths (at 396) and Lord Mustill (at 397) agreed with these comments. The other members of the house, Lord Templeman and Lord Goff, accepted existing doctrine and made no comment as to whether it served any useful purpose. Lord Browne-Wilkinson's excuse for not overruling the existing authorities was lame. The ancient rule seems to have fallen largely into abeyance until the CA revived it in 1944 by holding that a tenancy entered into for the duration of the war was void (*Lace* v. *Chantler* [1944] KB 368). In two subsequent decisions the CA had held that the doctrine did not render void stipulations whereby a landlord agreed to postpone his right to terminate a periodic tenancy until the happening of some uncertain event (*Re Midland Railway Company's Agreement* [1971] Ch. 725; *Ashburn Anstalt* v. *Arnold* [1989] Ch. 1) —(both decisions were overruled in the *Prudential Assurance* case.). It is not easy to see what sort of titles might have been upset if their lordships had followed their inclinations. They would have to be titles conferred on the basis that leases of uncertain duration are not allowed. The parties before the court, whose lease was made in 1930, had relied on an opposite understanding of the law and their expectations were certainly upset.

Weber suggested that the casuistic nature of common law systems meant that they had failed to develop the higher form of logically-formal rationality which was characteristic of developed continental legal thought.[76] It is indeed true that they lack the kind of abstract symmetry he had in mind. Nevertheless, common law property institutions display elements of higher-order juristic distillations wherein property-specific justice reasons are largely out of sight.

All developed property institutions presuppose what we may call the 'doctrinal cleavage'. Rights to use, to control the use of, or to extract monetary value from resources are to be classified as imposing obligations, *prima facie*, only on a particular obligor ('rights *in personam*'), or upon all-comers to the resource ('rights *in rem*'). Exceptions and qualifications are then superimposed upon this classification. Why should we not, instead, suppose a smooth curve of possibilities? If O, the owner of a resource, owes an obligation to R, let it be decided *ad hoc* whether it is just that any particular successor of O should also be required to discharge the obligation.

Such a change could only be accomplished if the agency entrusted with deciding such questions resolutely refrained from universalization in its assessment of the underlying justice reasons. It would have to conclude that R should (or should not) be able to enforce the obligation against this particular successor of O, but deny any implications for any other successor. Once universalization sets in, R's right becomes generalized as a kind of right which usually does, or does not, warrant trespassory protection—that is, should or should not be considered 'proprietary'. If we do not want khadi justice, we are stuck with the doctrinal cleavage.

That is not to say that we must abide by accrued exceptions and qualifications. Nor, more importantly, is it to say, as is generally assumed within juristic doctrine, that the distillation of property-specific justice reasons must produce the same answers to the questions whether R's right should prevail against those who succeed to the resource on O's death, or against persons who purchase the resource from O, or against O's creditors so as to be binding on his trustee in bankruptcy. Conceptual economy in property-institutional design is achieved if the proprietary/non-proprietary characterization of the right yields the same answer in all three contexts; but it may be achieved at a cost of insensitivity to the underlying justice reasons.

As we have seen, non-feudal legal systems impose a *numerus clausus* upon the category of non-ownership proprietary interests, and do not concede to owners the freedom to choose whether obligations shall be binding on their successors.[77] When the *numerus clausus* is re-asserted, English courts either simply take it for granted or else point vaguely to considerations which might be considered market-instrumental in character. Take the re-affirmation of the traditional doctrine that contractual licences do not constitute 'interests

[76] Weber, n. 67 above, 316.
[77] See Ch. 4, sect. (iii) above.

in land'.[78] The court said that the traditional view 'rested on an important and intelligible distinction between contractual obligations which gave rise to no estate or interest in the land and proprietary rights which, by definition, did.'[79] 'In matters relating to the title to land, certainty is of prime importance.'[80]

In another recent case the Court of Appeal held that a contract which purported to subject land to an easement, even though no dominant land had at the time been identified, could not bind successors to the servient land. It was said:

If one asks why the law should require that there should be a dominant tenement before there can be a grant, or a contract for the grant, of an easement sufficient to create an interest in land binding successors in title to the servient land, the answer would appear to lie in the policy against encumbering land with burdens of uncertain extent. ... A further related answer lies in the reluctance of the law to recognise new forms of burden on property conferring more than contractual rights.[81]

Bernard Rudden has argued that no convincing justification for the *numerus clausus* is to be found in terms of economic analysis. If resource-owners were free to designate novel right-bundles which were to burden their property into whoever's hands it might come, that might create additional transaction costs to be incurred on subsequent transfers; but then rational maximizers would take that into account. Why should the law curtail transactional freedom?[82]

However, market-instrumental and creator-incentive considerations are not the only property-specific justice reasons which enter into questions of property-institutional design, even in a jurisdiction predominantly committed to *laissez-faire*. Ownership freedoms, especially transmission freedoms, are, as we have seen, never sacrosanct, principally because of the pervasive counter-consideration from domination-potential.[83] Even where a right is admitted into the property category, the law may impose a visibility requirement which limits the range of trespassory protection, as did the old doctrine of notice in relation to equitable interests and as modern systems of registration seek to do, both for market-instrumental reasons and for broader ethical reasons relating to unfair surprise. More fundamentally, the mix of property-specific justice reasons may yield the conclusion that bi-party transactions ought not to impose novel trespassory obligations on all-comers to a resource even if they take with full notice.

---

[78] Discussed in Ch. 4, sect. (iv)(b) above.

[79] *Ashburn Anstalt* v. *Arnold*, n. 75 above, 22, *per* Fox LJ.

[80] *Ibid.* 26.

[81] *London and Blenheim Estates Ltd* v. *Ladbroke Retail Parks Ltd* [1993] 4 All ER 157 at 163, *per* Peter Gibson LJ.

[82] Bernard Rudden, 'Economic Theory versus Property Law: the Numerus Clausus Problem', in J. M. Eekelaar and J. Bell (eds.), *Oxford Essays in Jurisprudence* (3rd Series), n. 72 above.

[83] See Ch. 14, sects. (iv) and (v) above.

For more than a century it has been a settled feature of English land law doctrine that positive (as distinct from restrictive) covenants affecting freehold land are unenforceable against successors in title to the covenantor. The rule has been criticized both by academic commentators and by law reform bodies. In a recent case the House of Lords was invited to change it.[84] It was submitted in argument that, if the parties to a covenant intended its burden to pass, and if that burden were to affect only those who took the land with notice of it, there could be no good reason for interfering with contractual bargains. 'Less injustice would be done by affirming that covenants mean what they say than by perpetuating this injustice indefinitely.'[85]

The House of Lords affirmed received juristic doctrine. We have seen that open-ended ownership interests are incidents of estates in land.[86] Their Lordships' reasoning proceeds from this axiomatic starting-point. A conveyance 'confers on the purchaser the right to do with the land as he pleases provided that he does not interfere with the rights of others or infringe statutory restrictions'.[87] Restrictive covenants merely 'deprive the purchaser of some of the rights inherent in the ownership of unrestricted land',[88] whereas 'a positive covenant compels an owner to exercise his rights'.[89] 'To enforce a positive covenant would be to enforce a personal obligation against a person who has not covenanted. To enforce negative covenants is only to treat the land as subject to a restriction.'[90]

These citations assert the existing doctrine without actually addressing the question: why does the law police contractual undertakings in this way? It may be that behind it all is a distrust of domination-potential. If personal burdens could be attached to land at whim, then, in Rudden's words, 'feudalism is come again'.[91] (Their Lordships noted that the doctrine applicable to leaseholds, which allows positive covenants to be enforced against successors—albeit only if they 'touch and concern' the land—had led to 'social injustice'.[92]

In effect, their lordships did not see it as their business to provide a *de novo* justification for the doctrine. It was enough that there was indeterminacy and controversy as to the just outcome, as well as justified reliance on the present state of the law.

It is plain from the articles, reports and papers to which we were referred that judicial legislation to overrule the Austerberry case[93] would create a number of difficulties, anomalies and uncertainties and affect the rights and liabilities of people who have for over 100 years bought and sold land in the knowledge, imparted at an elementary stage to every student of the law of real property, that

---

[84] *Rhone* v. *Stephens* [1994] 2 AC 310.   [85] *Ibid.* 313.

[86] See Ch. 5, sect.(iii) above.

[87] *Ibid.* 317, *per* Lord Templeman.   [88] *Ibid.*

[89] *Ibid.* 318.   [90] *Ibid.* 320.

[91] Rudden, n. 82 above, 248.

[92] *Rhone* v. *Stephens*, n. 84 above at 321, *per* Lord Templeman.

[93] *Austerberry* v. *Oldham Corporation* [1885] 29 Ch. D 750 (CA).

positive covenants, affecting freehold land are not directly enforceable except against the original covenantor.[94]

In common with many of its defenders, Weber claimed for juristic doctrine the merit of affording to individuals and groups 'the possibility of predicting the legal consequences of their actions'.[95] This is a claim which it is notoriously difficult to prove. No doubt legal advice is structured in terms of the battery of concepts and second-order classifications embedded in lawyers' law. Where these juristic elements cease to reflect widespread consensus over justice reasons, however, genuine predictability may be hard to achieve. Courts will pay lip-service to doctrine whilst straining it, in a haphazard way, in the direction of the just outcome. For example, clouds of obscurity hover over current English law on informally-created interests in land. In substance, decisions have to be made as to whether, in the absence of contractual arrangements, owners' dependants ought to be awarded shares in resources by virtue of labour-desert, obligations to meet basic needs, justified reliance, or equal division of what (at the termination of a relationship) has become windfall wealth. If such an award should be made, ought it to be enforced against owners' successors, having regard to visibility requirements, unfair surprise, and the special 'none-of-my-business' argument (which suggests that successors should not be required to sort out the intimate dealings which may have given rise to such claims)? Whatever one may say of judicial attempts to solve such questions in terms of juristic categories such as resulting trusts, constructive trusts, and proprietary estoppel, predictability of outcome can scarcely be said to have been achieved.[96]

Suppose we dispensed with courts of the familiar kind and remitted questions of the sort we have been considering to some more flexible agency. That agency would not be staffed by officials whose role self-image includes the assumption that juridical reasoning stands apart from all-things-considered political controversy. Just such a development is called for by Roberto Unger as part of the programme of his 'superliberal' society.

If legal doctrine is acknowledged to be continuous with other modes of normative argument, if the institutional plan that decrees the existence of a distinct judiciary alongside only one or two other branches of government is reconstructed, and if long before this reconstruction the belief in a logic of inherent institutional roles is abandoned, legal expertise can survive only as a loose collection of different types of insight and responsibility.[97]

Such a transformation would eliminate juristic doctrine altogether. If a question arose, say, whether someone ought to vacate a dwelling, we would

---

[94] *Rhone* v. *Stephens*, n. 84 above, at 321, *per* Lord Templeman.
[95] Weber, n. 67 above at 226.
[96] See Harris, n. 72 above.
[97] R. M. Unger, *The Critical Legal Studies Movement* (Harv. UP, 1986), 111.

not—as the House of Lords did in *Street* v. *Mountford*[98]—notice that the legislature had protected 'tenants' and then go on to ask conceptual questions about what tenancies are.[99] The agency would take a view on the relative significance of market considerations, ownership freedoms, housing needs, and so forth; and to the extent that these gave no clear answer, it might consult social (non-technical) conventional opinion. How might that be done? Would the parties be free to hire 'lawyers' who would collate evidence of public opinion? Or could one assume that those staffing the new agency had privileged access to it?

One suspects that, either way, there would creep in a distinction between what public opinion appeared to be and what it ought to be taken to be, in the light of 'political correctness'. Thus, well-organized and vocal interest-groups would gain even more purchase on legal outcomes than they now have. Informal dispute-settlement has much to recommend it in particular situations. We need more experience and experimentation before we should adopt it as a total substitute for juristic doctrine.

(iii) CONCRETIZING THE MORAL BACKGROUND RIGHT

At the end of the last chapter we reached the conclusion that every citizen of a modern State has a background moral right that a property institution, with certain features, should be in place. That right required the mix of property-specific justice reasons we have surveyed to be taken into account, where relevant, over any question of distribution or of property-institutional design. We noted that there could be no assurance of determinate solutions.

In the present Chapter we have rejected the suggestion that either equality of resources or social convention may operate as a dominating principle which might displace or subsume all particular property-specific justice reasons. It is neither just nor feasible both to give due weight to ownership freedoms and to particular claims over resources, and at the same time to affirm that all resources should be and should remain equally divided. Social convention is often inconclusive and in any case typically incorporates deference to property-specific justice reasons. Furthermore, the moral background right itself requires alteration of property institutions where there is a conventional solution which clearly runs counter to the balance of property-specific justice reasons.

Nevertheless, both equality of resources and social convention retain significant, but very different, normative roles. Where the balance of justice reasons leaves some issue indeterminate, or subject to good-faith controversy, the conventional solution, if there is one, should, *prima facie*, be retained. In

[98] [1985] AC 809.
[99] See Ch. 5, sect. (iii) above.

this respect juristic doctrine, as a specialist variety of social convention, has a part to play. We could only dispense with it if we were willing to transfer settlement of disputed questions from courts of the traditional kind to an entirely novel species of social agency. Such a development, as a global response to dissatisfaction with juristic doctrine, is fraught with dangers of subjecting people to unpredictable coalescences of political interest-groups, and we should not embrace it. It is, however, the proper business of courts and of commentators to keep constantly under review the extent to which received juristic doctrine embodies defensible interpretations of the underlying property-specific justice reasons.

Social convention in general, and juristic doctrine in particular, may serve to concretize the implications of the background right, in respect of issues which would otherwise be indeterminate or controversial. For that reason, where the general features of a property institution embody the structure required by the background right, or come close to doing so, most titles to property-holdings will be, at least *prima facie*, just. Where they are not, reform needs to take account of the principle of justified reliance. That principle should, however, not be invoked indiscriminately. It is based on an analogy with an inter-personal principle and consequently requires that the community must, in some sense, be credited with having induced expectations. That is not an inference which it will be appropriate to draw whenever an out-moded or unpopular legal provision is repealed or changed.

The mix of property-specific justice reasons and its conventional or juristic interpretation has the consequence that some individual or group can found a superior claim to most of the resources within the purview of a property institution (which are not the subject of quasi-ownership interests vested in public agencies). Where that is not the case, a resource is 'windfall wealth'. In that case, equality of resources is the only applicable principle. It requires that, by some appropriate mechanism, the wealth-potential of the resource should be equally divided among the members of a relevant community. This residual role for the principle of equality of resources may operate both in the context of some item of social wealth as to which no member of the wider community has any better claim than any other member, and also as between members of a restricted community who together are entitled as against everyone else. There may, however, be practical considerations which dictate that, even though some item is in principle windfall wealth, it ought nevertheless to be allotted to some individual or group. Whether or not a resource should be regarded as intrinsically 'windfall' is one of the issues which determines the limits of property, a topic to which we turn in the next chapter.

17

The Limits of Property

Property institutions should not extend beyond anything which can be supported by the mix of property-specific justice reasons. Are there, as well, conceptual or practical limits of property? If there are, they should be taken into account, along with the relevant property-specific justice reasons, as facets of property-institutional design.

(i) RESOURCE REIFICATION

The dual functions performed by property institutions relate to the use of things and the packaging of wealth.[1] They deal in resources capable of being subjected to the twin pillars of trespassory rules and the ownership spectrum—although a resource so brought within the scope of property may then be subjected to super-structural entities in the form of cashable rights and non-ownership proprietary interests. Human well-being confronts speculative thought as a continuum. The morality and the politics of property are oriented towards lumps.

(a) Conceptual Limits

Any plausible account of human well-being will include features which are not susceptible to specific trespassory protection or participation in which cannot be guided by the organizing idea of ownership. In either case, they are, conceptually, beyond the scope of property institutions. For an entity to be a proprietary subject matter, a human subject must be distanced from it in two ways. It must be something others could be accused of 'taking' and something the subject himself could be seen to control or use as 'owner'.

Specific trespassory protection is not possible in the case of abstract features of well-being such as friendship, joy, passion, curiosity, a sense of beauty, faith, hope, and charity. We may condemn individual conduct or public programmes for neglecting, under-valuing, or even 'interfering with' these things; but we could not devise concrete rules which would mark out behaviour as amounting to their theft or invasion. 'Property' may be invoked, rhetorically, in relation to such things. 'Jane's childhood sense of

[1] See Ch. 3, sect. (iii) above.

beauty was stolen from her by the Philistines who controlled her education.' Such rhetoric builds, appropriately, on our familiarity with resources which everywhere are the subject of specific trespassory protection. But in the case of such abstract facets of well-being, no social or legal code could be devised according to which X's conduct constituted precisely, and no more than, a trespass against them.

The necessary distancing between subject and resource may also be absent even where specific trespassory protection exists. That which others are banned from meddling with may be something as to which I do not have the open-ended set of use-privileges and control-powers constitutive of mere property, let alone the transmission powers incident to full-blooded ownership.

Defamation law protects people's reputations. Yet our judgements about conduct are not guided by the notion that reputation is something one owns. If Jones scribbles in his book or paints his drawing-room in garish colours and his conduct is questioned, it will usually be a sufficient answer that his book or his house belongs to him and a man may do what he likes with his own. If Smith behaves disreputably, it could hardly be an adequate response for him to say: 'I can do what I like with my own reputation.' There are a panoply of uses of his book or of his house which Jones may authorize Brown to make as to which no third party may gainsay him, because Jones owns these things. It would be odd to say of a range of corrupt dealings between Smith and Brown that all complaints must be off-side since the reputation could be used by Brown in any way its owner, Smith, chose to authorize. And, of course, no-one can transfer his reputation to someone else. Reputations are not sufficiently distanced from their subjects such that dealings with them can be described, otherwise than rhetorically, in terms of the exercise of ownership privileges or powers.

All just legal systems prohibit torture as a means of extracting information. It does not follow from the fact that this trespassory protection is in place that the information, so long as it exists only within the skull of a potential victim, is something he 'owns'. Depending on the context, we may suppose that he has obligations to pass on, or to withhold, the information. These may be difficult moral questions, but they will not be guided by the idea that he has a set of use-privileges or control-powers somewhere along the ownership spectrum. Information once communicated may be, as we shall see later in this Chapter, a propertizable resource. So long as it is known only to a single individual, it lacks that distancing which is a precondition of an ownership interest.

The most flagrant instance in which the requisite distancing has been overlooked in the history of speculative thought about property relates to 'self-ownership'. As we have seen, the uses to which a person may put his own body, or which he may permit others to make of it, are, notwithstanding frequent invocations of property rhetoric, actually guided by what we have called the 'bodily-use freedom principle'.[2] We shall return to this topic later in this Chapter when we consider property in separated bodily parts.

The distancing between subject and resource which is a conceptual limit on property may be summarized as follows. Before any entity, material or ideational, can be subjected to a property institution it must be (1) susceptible of specific trespassory protection; and (2) a potential subject of an ownership or quasi-ownership interest; so that it is (3) reifiable as a person-independent resource.

(b) Practical Limits

We have seen that the outer perimeter of ownership interests is fixed by their trespassory protection.[3] There are uses of resources which it would be impracticable to ban, such as passers-by looking at an attractive house; and consequently such uses do not come within ownership control-powers. It is sometimes suggested that there are resources of which it would be impracticable to prohibit any uses, so that there are physical limits to property institutions. An example which has been suggested is that of a lighthouse beam, since vessels sailing nearby could not be prevented from using it.[4]

Such claims should be viewed with caution. Even if specific trespassory protection (whilst not conceptually impossible) cannot be practicably enforced, a resource may be treated as though it were the subject of an ownership interest for particular purposes. In the example of the lighthouse beam, ship-owners could be taxed on the basis that they had used a coastal State's property because they had, wittingly or not, seen the beam of light.

A parallel situation actually confronted English courts. BBC Enterprises wanted to make a profit from television programmes beamed to Western Europe. They were transmitted in encrypted form so that special decoders were needed to receive them. BBC Enterprises made arrangements for a company to manufacture the decoders and to pay to BBC Enterprises £100 on each decoder that was sold. The defendants upset this arrangement by manufacturing and selling cheaper decoders to the European market. BBC Enterprises sought an injunction to stop this. The issue turned on the interpretation of section 298 of the Copyright Designs and Patents Act 1988, which provided a remedy against any person making apparatus designed to enable people to receive transmissions when the recipients 'are not entitled to do so'.

Scott J, at first instance, held that, since reception was not prohibited, the plaintiffs could have no property rights in the waves in the ether, and he

---

[2] See Ch. 11, sect. (ii)(a) above.   [3] See Ch. 3, sect. (vi) above.
[4] Jeremy Waldron, 'Can Communal Goods be Human Rights?' (1987) 28 *Arch. Europ. Sociol.* 296 at 304; Kevin Gray, 'Property in Thin Air' (1991) 50 *CLJ* 252 at 269.

dismissed the action.[5] The Court of Appeal reversed his decision,[6] and the House of Lords upheld the Court of Appeal.[7] The judgments of the appellate courts lack lucidity. They held, in effect, that since Parliament must have supposed that creator-incentives warranted moral protection of the programmes, its language must be interpreted as if reception on the continent without the plaintiff's consent was not allowed—that is, as though ether waves were the subject of a protected ownership interest.

There may be many reasons, having to do with the content of the necessary trespassory rules, why an otherwise arguable case for creating an ownership or quasi-ownership interest is overridden. It may be that the restraints run counter to some valued freedom. Or perhaps they would entail excessive policing costs. Literal impossibility will, however, be rare.

We have seen that a resource must normally be scarce before there is any point in introducing trespassory protection.[8] However, it is always possible to create artificial scarcity, as intellectual property regimes do in the case of published ideas.[9] Seawater and sunlight are not scarce, but a lunatic tyrant might seek to establish a monopoly of these things by attempting to ban their use without his permission. He could make no progress if he sought to extend the prohibition to atmospheric oxygen. Yet, even here, he could impose a tax on breathing premised on the assumption that oxygen belonged exclusively to him.

(c) Justice Limits

Genuine problems concerning the limits of property are unlikely to raise the conceptual and practical issues so far considered. No-one will suggest placing abstract features of human well-being on the property agenda; and the tyrannical regimes we encounter have easier ways of despoiling their subjects without instituting impracticable trespassory rules. The limits are met, in practice, when some category of resource is encountered as to which we presently lack any clear guidance, from social convention or juristic doctrine, as to how the mix of property justice reasons is to be applied. It is not now, as it once was, a matter of public debate whether human beings should be the subject of proprietary interests. But persistent controversy surrounds the question whether patents should be granted in respect of animals created in the furtherance of biotechnological research.[10]

It may be clear enough that a resource should be allocated to someone, but who that is to be is a wide open question. Or it may be that the resource

---

[5] *BBC Enterprises Ltd* v. *Hi-Tech Xtravision Ltd*, *The Times*, 28 Nov. 1989.
[6] *BBC Enterprises Ltd* v. *Hi-Tech Xtravision Ltd* [1990] 2 All ER 118.
[7] *BBC Enterprises Ltd* v. *Hi-Tech Xtravision Ltd* [1991] 3 All ER 257.
[8] See Ch. 3, sect. (i) above.   [9] See Ch. 4, sect. (i) above.
[10] See Deryck Beyleveld and Roger Brownsword, *Mice, Morality and Patents* (Common Law Institute of Intellectual Property, 1993).

could be subjected to ownership protection, but might better be left as common property. Or it may be that the alternatives include ownership interests, quasi-ownership interests, or protected non-property holdings.[11] We shall in the rest of this Chapter consider three kinds of resource which illustrate these problems: the fruits of wrong-doing; information; and separated bodily parts. These topics raise very different issues at the margins of property. In each case, however, the difficulties have to do with assessing the strength of applicable property-specific justice reasons. No other conceptual or practical problems are involved.

(ii) THE FRUITS OF WRONG-DOING

If W engages in a course of conduct which both (1) constitutes a legal wrong as against V, and (2) results in W acquiring title to some resource (R), then V should be regarded as the owner of R and accordingly be protected against all-comers to R.

Suppose someone seeks a short cut across my land (a trespass) and only by shortening his journey in this way is he able to keep a business appointment at which he makes a profitable deal, Or suppose a contractor delivers merchandise to me one day later than the date fixed by our agreement, because, on the contract date, he was using his lorry for another highly profitable transaction. Or suppose a thug has been paid a large sum by my enemy to break my windows. The above-stated principle would support the contention that, in all three cases, I am justly the owner of the resource represented by the profits of the trespasser and of the contractor, as well as the money paid to the thug. This being a proprietary claim, it would, so the principle claims, prevail against any of these people's creditors and any successor in title of theirs, except (perhaps) a good-faith purchaser without notice.

Any reader of this book who is unacquainted with the recent burgeoning literature in common law jurisdictions on the topic of restitution will, it is thought, find these conclusions surprising—at least so far as the first two examples are concerned. That literature has built upon two facets of property institutions to which we have referred. The first is that restitutionary protection is an important species of trespassory protection afforded to ownership interests.[12] The second is the 'fruits doctrine': if someone is already justly the owner of some resource, he ought to be treated as owner of any accretion to that resource which comes about without wronging anyone else.[13] It is not difficult to see how juristic doctrine may combine these

---

[11] The use of these terms is explained in Ch. 7, sects. (iii), (iv), and (v) above.
[12] See Ch. 3, sect. (ii) and Ch. 4, sect. (ii)(b)(1) above.
[13] See Ch. 11, sect. (iii)(e) above.

two elements so as to conclude that an owner ought to have restored to him, not merely property which is (or once was) his, but also any accrued fruits which were produced by someone making wrongful use of his property. From there the step has been taken towards constructing a category known as 'restitution for wrongs', whereby that which is to be 'restored' never did belong to the claimant but is the result of some kind of wrongful action directed towards him. It was an enrichment achieved 'at his expense'. At its most extreme, juristic synthesist reaches the principle stated at the beginning of this section.[14]

Current English law does not approach this extreme version of restitution for wrongs. The Court of Appeal has recently held, for example, that a defendant who makes a profit by adopting a course of conduct which constitutes a technical breach of contract need account for none of his profits to the other party; he is liable merely to compensate for the loss he has occasioned, if any.[15] Tortfeasors are usually liable to pay only reparatory damages, save in special circumstances, such as defamation, where exemplary damages are awarded as a deterrent.[16] The fruits doctrine typically founds restitutionary relief where someone has wrongly sold another's property, in which case the owner may opt between seeking damages for the tort of conversion, or else adopting the transaction and recovering the sale proceeds (so long as they are identifiable).[17] In such a case the owner recovers that which has been substituted for his property and the terminology of 'restitution' is not inappropriate. What we are here concerned with are instances in which W's holding consists of a resource which neither is, nor represents, anything V ever owned; but the fact that V is W's victim is alleged sufficient warrant for treating V as the true owner of the resource.

There are three possibilities. Perhaps W should be allowed to retain what he holds. In our examples of the technical trespasser or contract-breaker, that is surely the right outcome. Market-instrumental, creator-incentive, and property-freedom arguments combine to suggest that the trespasser or the lorry-owner ought to be free to keep the profits of their transactions. No doubt they must pay damages for their technical wrongs if any loss has been caused, but that is all. If, however, there is some good reason why W should

[14] See Gbolahan Elias, *Explaining Constructive Trusts* (Clarendon Press, 1990), 24–6, 76–8. Elias criticizes those writers who have failed to expand the principle of restitution for wrongs to this point. All he offers by way of a rationale for the principle is: '[t]hat the plaintiff has suffered is bad enough. That his suffering of loss should have been translated into a gain which the defendant can insist on keeping would be incongruous' (16). This is bare assertion. The incongruity arises once a jurist has decided to adopt the principle. It does not explain why he should adopt it.
[15] *Surrey County Council* v. *Bredero Homes Ltd* [1993] 3 All ER 705.
[16] *Rookes* v. *Barnard* [1964] AC 129; *Cassell and Co. Ltd* v. *Broome* [1972] AC 1027.
[17] *In Re Hallett's Estate* (1880) 13 Ch.D 696 at 708–9, 710, *per* Jessell MR; *United Australia, Limited* v. *Barclays Bank, Limited* [1941] AC 1.

not retain the fruit of his wrong-doing, then the resource he holds may be expropriated in favour of either V or the community.

How should we choose between these latter alternatives? If V can show a moral claim to the resource which W now holds, he should have it. Otherwise, it stands as an item of social wealth to which no-one has a claim and is hence 'windfall wealth' in the sense discussed in the last chapter. In that case, the principle of equality of resources plays its residual, *faute-de-mieux* role. The relevant community is constituted by all citizens of the jurisdiction. Hence, forfeiture to the State is the appropriate proprietary mechanism.

For three centuries common law systems have applied a special expropriatory rule to the relationship between a fiduciary and his principal. If a fiduciary makes a profit while exercising his fiduciary role, he must account to the principal for that profit. The rule was devised as a deterrent to meet the situation in which a fiduciary's duty of loyalty to his principal might conflict with his own interest in taking up some business opportunity. It started life as a bright-line rule which will be applied wherever the fiduciary profits out of his position, even if his conduct is in no sense discreditable, and even if neglecting to pursue his own interest would, on the particular facts, have been of no advantage to the principal.[18] Some modifications have been introduced, notably, in English law, the recognition of a labour-desert claim in the case of a fiduciary whose conduct is in fact beyond reproach. He will still be expropriated of the profit he has made, but there will be deducted an allowance for his 'work and skill', to be calculated 'on a liberal scale'.[19]

This rule confers the windfall constituted by the fiduciary's profit, not on the community, but on his principal. There are obvious reasons relevant to property-institutional design why that should be so. It would be impracticable and wasteful for any public agency to search out these occasions, to determine what remains over after the principal has been compensated for any actual loss he has sustained, and then to forfeit the balance. Supposing the deterrent rule to be justifiable in the first place and hence that the fiduciary must be expropriated in favour of someone, his principal is the person most likely to learn of what has happened, and if the windfall is to come to him, he will have an incentive to institute the necessary civil proceedings. However, there is no good reason for deeming the profit already to belong to the principal before expropriation takes place, with the consequence that he is entitled to claim it against the rest of the world (including the fiduciary's creditors). If the fiduciary is insolvent, he will not keep the gain in any event. Why should the principal take a windfall in priority to those to whom the fiduciary owes purchased obligations.

Common law jurisdictions are armed with a flexible mechanism known as the 'constructive trust' whereby the rule just discussed could be extended to

---

[18] *Keech* v. *Sandford* (1726) Sel. Cas. Ch. 61.
[19] *Boardman* v. *Phipps* [1967] AC 46.

all situations in which the court deems it just that fruits should be taken from a wrong-doer and paid over to his victim.[20] Thus, in the case of the thug hired to smash V's windows, beneficial ownership of the thug's reward could be vested in V. English law has not yet taken that step. Should it do so?

Consider two recent decisions which indicate opposed approaches to this problem. The Judicial Committee of the Privy Council has ruled that where an employee takes a bribe in circumstances amounting to a crime, the bribe is at once held on constructive trust for the employer. If the bribe is then invested, the trust persists.[21] In consequence, if the criminal employee becomes bankrupt, having nothing in his name but a fortune which represents the product of the invested bribe then, even if the employer can show no pecuniary loss, the employer is to scoop the pool and all others to whom the criminal owed debts—his family, the revenue, or whoever—must go whistle for their money.[22] On the other hand, the Court of Appeal has held that, where a crook fraudulently induced a building society to grant him a mortgage loan and the society (exercising its power of sale) recovered more than it was owed, the balance of the sale proceeds was not to be held on constructive trust for the society but was, rather, to be forfeit to the Crown.[23]

It is suggested that the Court of Appeal's approach is very much to be preferred. As was said in the last chapter, juristic doctrine has a proper role to play as a specialist variety of social convention; but it ought to be kept constantly under review in the light of the underlying property-specific justice reasons. Nothing is achieved by assertions about the availability or unavailability of constructive trusts, for they are mechanisms to be used to

---

[20] *Metall und Rohstoff AG* v. *Donaldson Lufkin and Jenrette Inc.* [1990] 1 QB 391 at 478–9, *per* Slade LJ.

[21] *Attorney-General for Hong Kong* v. *Reid* [1994] 1 AC 324.

[22] The PC decided not to follow a decision of the CA which, for over a century, had been taken to establish the rule that a principal might recover, as a debt, bribes paid to his agent, but had no proprietary claim to them—*Lister and Co.* v. *Stubbs* (1890) 45 Ch.D 1. The CA considered that to rule otherwise would have 'startling' consequences, one of which was that, should the agent become bankrupt, any property purchased with the bribe would be withheld from the mass of his creditors—*ibid.* 15, *per* Lindley LJ. The PC found this consequence to be perfectly in order—[1994] 1 AC 324 at 336. One reason was that the creditors could have no claim to property which belongs in equity to the principal—*ibid.* 331–2. That is question-begging since the legal question before the Judicial Committee was precisely whether the bribe should be treated as the principal's property or whether, as had been ruled in *Lister and Co.* v. *Stubbs*, it constituted merely a debt. The PC also invoked an arcane maxim of juristic doctrine to the effect that 'equity considers as done that which ought to have been done' (*ibid.* 331). If taken literally, the maxim would turn all debts into proprietary rights. Their Lordships' chief reason was that a criminal should make no profit at all from his crime (*ibid.* 330–1). However, as was pointed out in argument, a civil action could lie in debt in favour of the principal both as to the bribe itself and as to any gain he makes out of it (*ibid.* 328). Where the principal has incurred no quantifiable loss, it would be better still to invoke criminal forfeiture rules if available. Such rules can be tailored to take account of other people's just claims—see *R.* v. *Robson, The Times*, 7 Aug. 1990; *R.* v. *Gregory, The Times*, 31 Oct. 1995.

[23] *Halifax Building Society* v. *Thomas* [1995] 4 All ER 673.

implement defensible principles. Nor does it help to try to squeeze all the situations discussed in this section under an all-embracing category of supposed 'restitution for wrongs'.

We begin with a functioning property institution in which it is taken for granted that people are justly the owners of resources to which, according to the prevailing conventions, they have acquired title. Were that questioned, some amalgam of property-specific justice reasons could no doubt be invoked. Perhaps V purchased a resource, R 1, on a market (which itself is a desirable feature of the property institution) from someone who was entitled to it by virtue of labour-desert or creator-incentives. Or perhaps he was given R 1, via the exercise of a worthwhile ownership freedom, by such a person. Or V may himself have a labour-desert or creator-incentive claim to R 1.

Our question is this. Assuming that V has a just concretized right to ownership of R 1 in the sense discussed at the end of the last chapter, do the relevant property-specific justice reasons, whatever they are, carry over in such a way that he ought to be regarded as owner of some other resource, R 2? If R 2 is the product of R 1, achieved by the exercise of a transmission freedom which V himself either chose to exercise or now chooses to adopt, carry-over is plausible. By assumption, V was entitled to trespassory protection as regards R 1 and he now chooses, without wronging any third party, that R 2 should be substituted for R 1. The term 'restitution' is employed in a sense similar to that in which V is entitled to claim back R 1 itself—because, for example, his exercise of a transmission freedom in respect of it is, for some reason, defective. What is restored to him is the product of that which he once owned and ought still to own.

Where someone makes a profit and ought not to be allowed to retain it, as is supposed to be the case with all fiduciaries and is certainly the case with criminals, there is no such carry-over. Nothing V owns is represented by the (to be expropriated) profit. To speak of 'restitution' is a juristic sleight of hand. The practical considerations which support expropriation in V's favour where the fiduciary's misfeasance is no more than a falling below standards of loyalty do not apply where the crime has already brought him before the courts for punishment. Then it is perfectly feasible for the property institution to operate criminal-forfeiture expropriation rules. That should always be done if possible, since the profit, having been taken from W and being something to which neither V nor anyone else has any just claim, is windfall wealth. Only if a jurisdiction lacks suitable forfeiture rules should V come in as the next best bet. It is better that he should take the profits of criminal wrong-doing than that the criminal should keep them. Even then, however, there is nothing to warrant his priority over the criminal's creditors.

The principle stated at the beginning of this section is, as a general principle, indefensible.

(iii) INFORMATION

A person who creates or gathers information which, but for his initiative, would not have been collated ought to be regarded as its owner.

Few things are more distinctive of the modern world than the explosion in what is often called the 'information industry'. Gathered information is the subject of much piecemeal legal protection. It is encompassed within various forms of intellectual property. It is the subject of criminal prohibitions against 'insider dealing', or 'hacking' of computerized data. Might we not, as a matter of property-institutional design, achieve conceptual sublimation and normative consistency by recognizing a broad principle such as that set out above?[24]

Would not that be a worthy contribution of modern juristic doctrine to Weberian 'logically formal' rationality?[25]

In assessing how far the law implicitly already recognizes property in information, the basic question of ownership has to be disentangled from other issues. There are many instances in which duties are imposed against communicating information where the information has been acquired in the course of a contractual or fiduciary relationship. Courts have, in addition, been prepared to grant *prima facie* injunctive relief (or damages in lieu) against those who knowingly receive such information in breach of contract or confidence,[26] subject to a 'public interest' defence.[27] Sometimes this extension of the obligation is spoken of as a recognition of 'property' in the information.[28] We mentioned in the last section the rule that a fiduciary who makes a profit from his fiduciary role is expropriated of it in favour of his principal. The normal justification for that rule is deterrence against fiduciaries preferring their interest to their duty of loyalty. But sometimes an alternative 'fruits' rationale is floated, by suggesting that the information

---

[24] For arguments to this effect, see D. F. Libling, 'The Concept of Property: Property in Intangibles' (1978) 94 *LQR* 103; Arnold S. Weinrib, 'Information and Property' (1988) 38 *UTor. LJ* 117. [25] See Ch. 16, sect. (ii)(c) above.

[26] *Argyle* v. *Argyle* [1967] Ch. 302; *Seager* v. *Copydex Ltd* [1967] 2 All ER 415; *Fraser* v. *Evans* [1969] 1 QB 349; *Schering Chemicals Ltd* v. *Falkman Ltd* [1982] QB 1; *Roger Boulevant Ltd* v. *Ellis* [1987] ICR 464; *Universal Thermosensors Ltd* v. *Hidden* [1992] 3 All ER 257.

[27] *Initial Services Ltd* v. *Putterill* [1968] 1 QB 396; *Lyon Laboratories Ltd* v. *Evans* [1985] QB 526; *Attorney-General* v. *Guardian Newspapers Ltd (No. 2)* [1990] 1 AC 109.

[28] See, e.g., *Exchange Telegraph Co. Ltd* v. *Central News* [1897] 2 Ch. 48, *per* Stirling J; *Exchange Telegraph Co. Ltd* v. *Howard and Manchester Press Agency Ltd* (1906) 22 TLR 375, *per* Buckley J; *F.C.T.* v. *United Aircraft Corporation* (1943) 68 CLR 525 at 548, *per* Williams J, dissenting.

acquired in the course of such a relationship is 'property' already belonging to the principal.[29]

The principle set out at the beginning of this section affirms that, quite apart from such special relationships and remedies, a person who creates or gathers information should be regarded as its owner. He should be granted generalized trespassory protection, civil and criminal, in respect of uses of it against all-comers; and he himself should be accorded an open-ended set of use-privileges, control-powers, and powers of transmission over it, at some point along the ownership spectrum. That is what is meant by 'owning' gathered information.

It is sometimes suggested that the conceptual objection examined in the last section applies. Information cannot be distanced from the minds of individuals and so is intrinsically non-propertizable. Latham CJ said in a tax case heard by the High Court of Australia: 'knowledge is neither real nor personal property. A man with a richly stored mind is not for that reason a man of property.'[30]

There is no force in this objection. It is true that the contents of the human memory fail the distancing test which is a necessary, conceptual precondition of property. Nevertheless, information, once communicated, can be regarded as a distinct ideational entity whose use by all except some favoured 'owner' could be banned.

The use-policing and use-channelling advantages of mere-property freedoms which apply to tangible assets have no bearing on information, any more than on any other ideational entities.[31] All may use information simultaneously. The vast majority of indicative propositions are, and always have been, in the public domain—'common property'. What we have to consider is whether there are property-specific justice reasons sufficient to warrant the creation of artificial scarcity, as with other forms of intellectual property, by the enactment of specialized trespassory rules in the case of collated information.

(a) Commercial Information

Common law courts have seldom isolated the ownership question. There are, however, two frequently cited rulings which may be taken to support the following proposition: if an enterprise collates information the value of which would be augmented were it unavailable to commercial rivals, then,

---

[29] See, e.g., *Boardman* v. *Phipps* [1967] 2 AC 46 at 107, *per* Lord Hodson.

[30] *F.C.T.* v. *United Aircraft Corporation*, n. 28 above, at 534. The question at issue was whether the communication of information about the manufacture of aircraft engines by an American company to an Australian company could be regarded as a transfer of property, so that payments made by the recipient company, out of profits achieved by using the information, could be treated as derived from a source in Australia. The majority answered no to this question.   [31] See Ch. 13, sect. (iii) above.

for so long as the information has this character, it should be accorded civil trespassory protection against competitors. The proposition does not extend to criminal trespassory protection, nor to civil trespassory protection against persons other than commercial rivals; and it presupposes ownership use-privileges, control-powers, and powers of transmission relating only to commercial exploitation. It thus accords a limited ownership interest with circumscribed trespassory protection.

In *Exchange Telegraph Co. Ltd* v. *Gregory and Co.*,[32] the committee of the London Stock Exchange had collected daily information about the prices of stocks and shares quoted on their exchange and they had assigned the right of exclusive dissemination of that information to the plaintiff news agency. The Court of Appeal upheld an injunction to restrain the defendant broker from publishing the information, on the ground that the information was the plaintiffs' property.[33]

The Court of Appeal said nothing about the nature of the ownership interest which the plaintiffs had acquired. The United States Supreme Court was more explicit in its celebrated ruling in *International News Service* v. *Associated Press*.[34] The majority of the Court held that a news agency was entitled to an injunction restraining a rival agency from selling news taken from bulletins issued by the complainant, Associated Press, or from newspapers published by its members. Pitney J, delivering the leading judgment, said that information gathered about events of public interest was not 'susceptible of ownership or dominion in the absolute sense'.[35] The gatherer had no right against the public at large that they should not make any use they wished of such information. In that sense, news was 'common property'.[36] On the other hand, there was a right to restrain use of the news by a commercial rival. As between the complainant and the defendant, fresh news must be regarded as 'quasi-property'.[37] 'It has all the attributes of property necessary for determining that a misappropriation of it by a competitor is unfair competition.'[38]

There are two rulings of common law courts which are commonly cited against the proposition that commercial information can be the subject of any kind of ownership interest, but in which that question was largely sidetracked by discussion of land-owners' rights. In *Sports and General Press Agency Ltd* v. *'Our Dogs' Publishing Co. Ltd*,[39] the Ladies' Kennel Club had promoted a dog show on land which it had leased for the day. It had purported to assign the exclusive right to take photographs of the show, ultimately, to the plaintiffs. The plaintiffs sought an injunction to prevent publication by the defendants of photographs taken at the show by a free-lance photographer. The Court of Appeal upheld the dismissal of the action

[32] [1896] 1 QB 147.   [33] *Ibid.* 152, *per* Lord Evershed MR.
[34] 284 US 215 (1918).   [35] *Ibid.* 236.   [36] *Ibid.* 235.
[37] *Ibid.* 236.   [38] *Ibid.* 240.   [39] [1917] 2 KB 125.

by Horridge J.[40] The issue was seen, both at first instance and in the Court of Appeal, as raising the limits of the control-powers incident to an ownership interest in land. Since these did not include power to prevent anyone off the premises from taking photographs, it followed that the right to take photographs was not a proprietary subject-matter. Although the *Exchange Telegraph* case was cited in argument, the Court did not address the question whether information about the show could be the subject of limited protection against commercial competitors, which might have included a prohibition against commercial rivals disseminating such information in the form of published photographs.

In *Victoria Park Racing and Recreational Grounds Ltd* v. *Taylor*,[41] the majority of the High Court of Australia held that no legal right of the owners of a racecourse had been infringed when live commentaries on the races were broadcast over the radio by a commentator standing on an observation platform specially erected on a neighbour's land. For the most part, the judgments of both the majority and the minority were directed to the question whether the conduct of the defendants could be brought within the law of nuisance so that power to control this activity would be an incident of the plaintiffs' ownership of their land.[42] There was some reference to 'property in a spectacle'.[43] This was as much a red herring as the exclusive right to take photographs had been in the *'Our Dogs'* case. The plaintiff was not seeking to prevent neighbours watching the races if they could put themselves in a position to look over the fence. What it sought to have enjoined was the dissemination to the public of information about the starting-positions and the winners, since that would encourage potential customers to stay at home. It was not suggested that use of such information, without the plaintiff's permission, should be universally banned; but only that a particular kind of use by a commercial competitor should be prohibited. The plaintiff was thus asserting what the United States Supreme Court in the *International News* case had called 'quasi-property' in this information. That case was cited to the Court. Latham CJ, dismissed the notion of 'quasi-property' on conceptual grounds. If there was 'property' in the information, how could it be material whether it was communicated to many or to few?[44] That is a dogmatic assertion to the effect that trespassory protection must be all-or-nothing. If one cannot justify a universal prohibition against use of informa-

---

[40] [1916] 2 KB 880.   [41] [1937] 58 CLR 479.

[42] The majority ruled that it could not—*ibid.* 493–6, *per* Latham CJ, 506–8, *per* Dixon J, 523–6, *per* Mactiernan J. The minority ruled that it did—*ibid.* 501–4, *per* Riche J, 513–18, *per* Evatt J. Mactiernan J approved the reasoning in *'Our Dogs'* (*ibid.* 526). Dixon J approved Brandeis J's dissenting opinion in the *International News* case (*ibid.* 509). Brandeis J had cited *'Our Dogs'* with approval—*International News Service* v. *Associated Press*, n. 34 above, at 255–6.

[43] *Ibid.* 483, Counsel for appellant, 488, Counsel for respondents, 496–7, *per* Latham CJ.

[44] *Ibid.* at 496–7.

tion, one cannot contend that it should be prohibited in the case of commercial rivals. However, as we have seen with other forms of intellectual property, there is nothing inconsistent between the notion of an ownership interest and merely circumscribed trespassory protection.[45]

In particular, the law might recognize a limited ownership interest over commercial information whilst reserving its protection to civil, rather than criminal, trespassory rules. In the United States judges have come to speak of property in information in the same terms as property in anything else. A trade secret has been held to be 'property' for the purpose of the takings clause of the Constitution.[46] Criminal legislation protecting property has accordingly been interpreted as including information. In *Carpenter* v. *United States*,[47] the Supreme Court ruled that an employee of a newspaper, who disclosed information about its investment advice column prior to publication, could be convicted of fraudulently obtaining 'property'. The court invoked the *International News* case, but without any of the qualifications contained in that decision.

A different view on whether criminal trespassory protection must necessarily accompany civil trespassory protection prevails in England and Canada. The Divisional Court ruled that, whatever might be its proprietary status for the purpose of civil law, information is not 'intangible property' for the purposes of the Theft Act 1968, so that a student who got hold of a proof of an examination paper could not be convicted of stealing the information it contained.[48] The Supreme Court of Canada held that confidential information was not 'anything, whether animate or inanimate' within the Criminal Code, so that someone who sought to bribe a hotel security guard to supply him with a list of the hotel's employees could not be convicted of counselling theft.[49] It was said that, whereas liability in civil law may be tailored to meet a balancing of considerations in different contexts, the criminal law allocates responsibility in black-and-white terms.[50]

Not only is it open to a property institution to provide merely circumscribed trespassory protection for an ownership interest in commercial information, but it may also reserve ownership privileges and powers only over commercially exploitative uses. That possibility may be overlooked if ownership of such information is invoked as a principle by analogy with 'ownership' of any other resource. The mistaken inference would run: '[t]here are reasons for granting trespassory protection against commercial competition. Therefore, the enterprise owns the information. Therefore, it has the right

---

[45] See Ch. 4, sect. (i) above.

[46] *Ruckelshaus* v. *Monsanto*, 104 SCt. 2862 (1984).   [47] 108 SCt. 316 (1987).

[48] *Oxford* v. *Moss* [1978] 68 Cr.App.R 181.

[49] *Stewart* v. *R.* [1988] 58 DLR (4th) 1.

[50] *Ibid.* at 12, *per* Lamer J, citing with approval Grant Hammond, 'Theft of Information' (1984) 100 *LQR* 252. See also John T. Cross, 'Protecting Confidential Information under the Criminal Law of Theft and Fraud' (1991) 11 *OJLS* 264.

to control any use of it, whether that is required for its commercial viability or not.' The United States Supreme Court committed this mistake in the *Carpenter* case:

The confidential information was generated from the business and the business had the right to decide how to use it prior to disclosing it to the public. . . . it is sufficient that the journal has been deprived of its right to exclusive use of the information for exclusivity is an important aspect of confidential business information (and most private property for that matter).[51]

The appropriate degree of trespassory protection and the appropriate range of the ownership interest, if any, which should be reserved over confidential information turns, like all other questions of property-institutional design, on the relevant underlying property-specific justice reasons. If it were a matter of natural right, no doubt the former should be wide and the latter extensive. But it cannot be a matter of natural right for reasons which have been given in this part of this book.

In the *Exchange Telegraph* case, the Court of Appeal simply asserted that one who collates commercially valuable information must be its owner:

The committee say we will not allow this valuable information to be given to certain persons who are outside brokers and who are not subject to the rules of the Stock Exchange. They chose to refuse and they had the right to refuse to allow the information to be given to those outside brokers. . . . If this information, this collecting together of materials so as to give knowledge of all that has been done on the Stock Exchange, is something which can be sold, it is property and being sold to the plaintiffs it was their property.[52]

This assertion might be understood as an invocation of the argument we have called 'creation-without-wrong'. The creator or gatherer of the information has created something of value and has infringed no-one's rights in doing so. Therefore, he ought to own it.

However, as we have seen, creation-without-wrong cannot stand on its own as the basis for a natural property right. It does not follow from the mere fact that I have created or gathered information that I am entitled to insist that my community institute rules imposing obligations on everyone not to use it without my say-so, just as the Forest Land tool-maker could not insist that such rules should be created to give him ownership of the tool. Unilateral creative interaction with the world does not, in itself, carry such far-reaching moral consequences.[53]

---

[51] *Carpenter* v. *United States*, n. 47 above, 321 *per* White J. Arnold Weinrib makes the same mistake: '[i]f something is property it is generally not a function of the legal system to second guess the owner as to the appropriate use of that property'—'Information and Property' (1988) 34 *UTor.LJ* 117 at 143. Weinrib is here arguing inconsistently with his earlier assertion that 'property' is merely a 'conclusary' term—*ibid.* 120.

[52] *Exchange Telegraph Co. Ltd* v. *Gregory and Co.* [1896] 1 QB, 147 at 152, *per* Lord Evershed MR. [53] See Ch. 11, sect. (iii)(d) above.

There are passages in the judgment of the majority in the *International News* case which appear to invoke a labour-desert argument. Pitney J said that unfair business competition would be committed by any competitor who endeavoured 'to reap where it has not sown'.[54] The defendant agency was seeking to divert a material proportion of the profit 'from those who had earned it'.[55]

However, as we have seen, a labour-desert argument for a property right will not work in the absence of conventions which dictate that the morally appropriate reward for creative endeavour is ownership of the thing created rather than something else.[56] It may be that such conventions do exist, say, for artistic creations. But it is implausible that this is so of all information-gathering activities.[57] Informal property rhetoric about 'pinching ideas without acknowledgement' is too vague and unfocused to provide a labour-desert claim to information-ownership. If an investigative journalist digs out important information, he deserves acclaim, but surely not the power personally to control and commercially exploit all uses of the information.

The only argument which can be invoked for ownership of commercial information is, as with other forms of property in ideational entities, the instrumental one from creator-incentives. It may be obvious in particular contexts that a person or enterprise will not create or gather information unless its exploitation of the information is protected against commercial rivals. That instrumental argument will, as we have seen, enter into the mix of property-specific justice reasons if the item so created and marketed increases social wealth in such a way that justice costs can be more fully discharged.[58] In the case of information it may also be that what is created contributes directly to human well-being on the ground that knowledge has value for its own sake. That was the principal ground relied on in the *International News* case. Pitney J said that the complainant association was providing a valuable service in bringing information about the daily events of the world to the breakfast table of the millions. The trifling payments made by its ultimate customers were sufficient in the aggregate to afford compensation for the cost of gathering and distributing the news 'with the added profit so necessary as an incentive to effective action in the commercial world'.[59]

That being the sole reason for recognizing an ownership interest in commercial information, it follows that the kind of interest in question and the

[54] *International News Service* v. *Associated Press*, 284 US 215 (1918), at 239.

[55] *Ibid.* 240. These comments were cited with approval by Evatt J in his dissenting judgment in *Victoria Park Racing and Recreational Grounds Ltd* v. *Taylor* (1937) 58 CLR 479 at 518.

[56] See Ch. 11, sect. (iv) above.

[57] In his dissenting opinion, Brandeis J pointed out that, apart from special cases like copyright and patent, a product of the human mind, even if it has 'cost its producer money and labour', becomes, after voluntary communication to others, 'free as the air to common use'—*International News Service* v. *Associated Press*, n. 54 above, 250.

[58] See Ch. 15, sect. (iii)(c) above.

[59] *International News Service* v. *Associated Press*, n. 54 above, 238.

degree of trespassory protection need to be tailored precisely to what is required, and no more than is required, to provide the necessary incentive. The requisite ownership interest will, in one sense, be high on the ownership spectrum since it must carry powers of transmission for value. Without marketability the incentive will almost certainly be absent. On the other hand, it need not include ordinary control-powers associated with ownership of tangible resources. So long as the 'owner' can control commercial exploitation, he will have the incentive to create or gather the information even if he is not armed with control over many non-commercial uses. It will still be 'ownership' of a sort, since ownership will play the role of an organizing idea from which an open-ended set of exploitation powers may be inferred. Similarly, trespassory protection need extend only to prohibitions against competing commercial uses. There may be a case for criminal prohibitions in particular contexts, where certain kinds of data misuse ought to be excluded as a background to ownership interests over many kinds of information and leaving each owner to seek a civil remedy might be wasteful. The vandal who spreads computer viruses is a menace to everyone. But there need be no *a priori* assumption that, wherever the incentive argument supports a limited ownership interest, civil infringements must always be accompanied by criminal offences.

Thus, the principle stated at the beginning of this section can be accepted, in the case of commercial information where the incentive argument applies, only if 'owning' is understood in a special sense peculiar to the subject matter—as the Supreme Court recognized in the *International News* case. It is a mistake to assume that either we must align property in information with property in other resources, or else we must exclude information from the property agenda. Property-institutional design may be and should be much more flexible than these alternatives allow.

(b) Government Secrets

There is a further reason for withholding an unqualified assent to the principle stated at the beginning of this section. It is sometimes desirable, for example for reasons connected with national security or the administration of justice, that there be trespassory protection (usually criminal in nature) in respect of information held by public agencies. Such restrictions need to be kept to a minimum and they involve a constant (and often controversial) balancing between vital public interests in secrecy and the countervailing argument for openness within a free society. However that balance should be struck, it should not be settled by invocations of the open-ended privileges and powers characteristic of ownership. Restrictions over, and official uses of, such information should be dictated exclusively by the particular function served. It follows that, unless the public agency is itself a player on the commercial scene and requires incentives in the same fashion as other enterprises, the relevant trespassory protection should accord to government, not a quasi-ownership interest, but a protected non-property holding.

Take, for example, the notorious litigation which arose out of Peter Wright's book *Spycatcher*. Wright, a former member of the British security service, wrote a book disclosing operational details of his former department and making sensational accusations. It was not disputed, in the English litigation, that he thereby breached a duty of secrecy owed to the Crown. None the less, *Spycatcher* had been published abroad and it was easily obtainable within the United Kingdom. In those circumstances, was the Crown entitled to prevent anyone, apart from Wright himself and his agents, from publishing the book? Scott J answered no, and his decision was upheld by the Court of Appeal and the House of Lords.[60] Now that the damage to security had been done by publishing abroad, nothing was to be gained by banning publication in the United Kingdom.

The cogent reasons for reaching this conclusion were set out by Scott J. He indicated, however, that he would have decided otherwise if the following ownership argument had been deployed by the Crown. The rule to which we referred in the last section (which expropriates a fiduciary's profits to prevent conflict of duty and interest) was applicable. Therefore, the product of Wright's breach of duty, the copyright in *Spycatcher*, could be regarded as 'belonging in equity to the Crown'. It would follow that the Crown would be entitled to prevent further publication of the book by anyone 'on straightforward proprietary grounds. The equitable owner of copyright in a book can choose to suppress the book and forego any profits therefrom if he chooses.'[61]

If we were to accept that anyone, including government, who creates or gathers information which, but for his initiative, would not have been collated thereby becomes owner of the information, there would be no need to invoke the special rule relating to expropriation of profits. State 'ownership' could always be invoked as a principle giving open-ended use-privileges and control-powers. It is true that the information, as public property, would be the subject of a quasi-ownership interest which, as we have seen, entails a combination of ownership privileges and powers with those referable to the particular function to be discharged.[62] However, if State information is regarded as the subject merely of a protected non-property holding, no

---

[60] *A.-G.* v. *Guardian Newspapers Ltd (No 2)* [1990] 1 AC 109.

[61] *Ibid.* 139–40. Bingham LJ in the CA (*ibid.* 210), and in the HL Lord Keith (*ibid.* 262), Lord Griffiths (*ibid.* 276), and Lord Goff (*ibid.* 288), agreed that there was a strong arguable case for the Crown to claim equitable copyright, but without drawing Scott J's conclusion about a consequent right to prevent publication. Sir John Donaldson MR in the CA, who did refer to that conclusion, inclined to the view that a claim to equitable copyright would not have succeeded (*ibid.* 194–5).

[62] See Ch. 7, sect. (iii)(b) above.

ownership-invocations at all will be in order.[63] That is the preferable option. The balancing problem between security and openness is difficult enough as it is. The last thing we need is for that balancing to be upset by a proprietary loose cannon.

(c) Information and Privacy

In Chapter 12 we considered the argument that, where a person's privacy can be effectively guaranteed only if he is granted an open-ended set of use-privileges and control-powers over some resource with which he is intimately connected, he ought to be regarded as owner of that resource. We concluded that privacy constitutes the basis for a shell of a natural property right. It is dependent on a balance between the requirement of a range of specially protected autonomous choice and necessary intervention by the community to prevent abuse.[64]

Where the resource in question is information about the intimate affairs of an individual, there is a strong case for affirming that, contrary to the present state of English law, publication of that information by others should, *prima facie*, be prohibited without his or her consent. Such trespassory protection would reserve to the individual what amounts to mere-property freedoms in respect of the information on grounds which have nothing to do with those contained in the principle set out at the beginning of this section. The limited ownership interest would be entirely unlike that which has emerged for commercial information. It would ban intermeddling by persons generally, not merely commercial rivals; but it would not encompass transmission powers.

The law of contract enables a person to sell 'his story' (intimate information about his affairs) to that newspaper which will pay him most. If, following such authorized publication, other newspapers repeat the story, it would be manifestly absurd for the person to complain on privacy grounds. No-one can simultaneously assert both that he is entitled to keep information about himself private, and at the same time commercially to exploit publication of that information. Claims over information based on commercial incentives and those based on privacy yield different ownership interests and should not be confused.

Comparable confusion should be avoided in the case of photographic reproductions of a person or of his activities. Courts have ruled, with regret, that English law gives no redress to a person whose photograph is published against his will.[65] One might, on privacy grounds, suggest that the law should be changed: subject no doubt to exceptions, no-one should be free to publish

---

[63] See Ch. 7, sect. (v) above.

[64] See Ch. 12, sect. (iii) above.

[65] *Tolly* v. *J. S. Fry and Sons Ltd* [1930] 1 KB 467; *Kaye* v. *Robertson* [1991] FSR 62.

a person's photograph against his will. We might express that conclusion by affirming that a person has 'mere property' use-privileges and control-powers over his own image. It would not follow, on privacy grounds, that he could sell an exclusive right to publish his photograph.[66] A person who wishes his image to be published for reward does not want to keep it private. Commercial propertization of images can be supported, if at all, only on creator-incentive grounds, not on natural right; unless, that is, one supposes that those rights which we have over our own bodies somehow carry over into full-blooded ownership of detached parts of our bodies. To that problem we turn in the next section.

(iv) SEPARATED BODILY PARTS

Every person ought to be regarded as the owner of any separated part of his body.

(a) The Alternatives

Developments in medical science have forced a novel question of property-institutional design on to the agenda of property-specific justice reasons. Who, if anyone, ought to be regarded as the owner of tissues or substances taken from a human body? The consequence of refusing ownership to anyone is not, as with information in the public domain, 'common property'. Information may be used by all simultaneously, without treading on each other's toes. It could hardly be suggested that separated bodily parts should be permanently open to a common scramble. Trespassory rules are obviously required. The alternative to according ownership or quasi-ownership interests is, as with secret information held by government, what we have called 'protected non-property holdings'.

This has traditionally been the pattern in most societies so far as corpses are concerned. Respectful abstention from meddlesome interference was demanded of all, except next-of-kin, religious functionaries, or public authorities. Any of the latter might be vested with special disposal-powers or subjected to role-duties in the interest of decency, sacred observance, or public health; but they were not clothed with ownership privileges and powers. Corpses could not be owned at common law.[67]

Protected non-property holdings have in modern English law been established in relation to some separated bodily parts. As we have seen, the

[66] Cf. the ruling of the Sup. Ct. of California that Bela Lugosi had a sufficient 'proprietary interest' in his name, face, and Count Dracula persona to enable him to sell licences to reproduce his likeness and to enjoin unlicensed use of it—*Lugosi* v. *Universal Pictures*, 160 Cal. Rptr. 323 (1979).

[67] See J. C. Smith, *The Law of Theft* (7th edn., Butterworths, 1993), 32.

regulatory regime set up under the Human Fertilisation and Embryology Act 1990 includes generalized prohibitions and specific duties relating to the storage of embryos and live gametes without reserving ownership privileges or powers over these things to anyone.[68] Similarly, the regulatory regime set up under the Human Organ Transplants Act 1989 makes no assumptions about ownership. It renders the commercial sale or purchase of organs for transplantation criminal, but that is a property-independent prohibition—it is not addressed to 'owners'. It is perfectly feasible in the case of these highly sensitive separated parts to ban intermeddling by outsiders and to dictate what is to be done during storage without making anyone their owner and without infusing into official roles any privileges or powers modelled on ownership.

It is important to bear in mind the distinction to which we have already drawn attention between commodification and propertization.[69] It is arguable that any sale by a human being of parts of his or her body is such an affront to our fundamental notions of human dignity that it ought not to be permitted.[70] That is a reason against organs being admitted into the category of commodities. Supposing, however, we thought that the Organ Transplants Act constituted an infringement of what we have called the 'bodily-use freedom principle',[71] and that people ought to be free to sell their organs if they wished. Then organs would be a commodity; but it would not follow that they were property. The fact that I might be empowered to sell a kidney does not entail that, while it is still in me, I have an open-ended set of use-privileges and control-powers over it modelled on those of an ownership interest over any other chattel. It does not even entail that the purchaser should be granted an ownership interest, for we might stipulate that sales were to take place only in favour of institutions which would retain the purchased organs as protected non-property holdings. In the United Kingdom the Surrogacy Arrangements Act 1985 prohibits commercial surrogacy as a means of supplying childless parents with babies. Supposing one thought that this was also an unwarranted interference with the freedom of potential surrogate mothers. That would mean that surrogacy services ought to be recognized as a commodity; but it would hardly entail that either the surrogate mother or the purchaser was to be armed with ownership privileges and powers over the foetus or the baby.

The principle stated at the beginning of this section affirms nothing either way about whether services involving the supply of organs or surrogacy ought to become commodities, nor as to the proper disposal of corpses or any parts thereof. It asserts that if some part of a body becomes separated, by surgery

[68] See Ch. 7, sect. (v) above.

[69] See Ch. 11, sect. (ii)(b)(3) above.

[70] See Stephen R. Munzer, 'An Uneasy Case Against Property Rights in Body Parts', in Ellen Frankel Paul, Fred D. Miller, and Jeffrey Paul (eds.), *Property Rights* (CUP, 1994).

[71] See Ch. 11, sect. (ii)(a) above.

or otherwise, its human source ought to be recognized as its owner. After separation, the necessary distancing between human source and owned object (to which we referred in section 1 of this Chapter) would be present, so there would be no conceptual difficulty in implementing the principle. Trespassory rules, civil or criminal, could ban everyone else from intermeddling with the new chattel; and its human source could be accorded an open-ended set of privileges and powers over it, at some point along the ownership spectrum.

If the principle were supposed to be of universal application, it would follow that the Human Transplants Act and the Human Embryology and Fertilisation Act deprive people of property without compensation. But then it might be contended that the principle is subject to exceptions in the case of materials essential to survival or reproduction. It ought to apply only to useful bits and pieces which are not specially charged with morally sensitive issues.

Suppose we are confronted with a piece of excised human tissue (T) of which three things are true: (1) T is not an organ vital to the survival of a recipient, nor is it connected with human reproduction; (2) T is susceptible of permanent exploitation for a wide variety of therapeutic purposes with great commercial potential; (3) it is not practical to realize T's potential unless someone is accorded ownership privileges and powers over it—that is, no enumeration of all beneficial uses can be attained, so it is necessary to invoke that familiar organizing idea which property institutions provide— 'ownership'. The third condition rules out protected non-property holdings. Someone must own T, but who?[72]

As a general question of property-institutional design, such as a legislature might face, there are three possibilities. First, ownership of T could be vested in its human source. Secondly, ownership might be conferred on the person who first gets hold of T knowing of its therapeutic potential—call him 'the first knowing appropriator'. Thirdly, a quasi-ownership interest over T might be vested in some emanation of the community, with a mandate to exploit it to the maximum for the equal benefit of all citizens.

(b) The *Moore* Case

California courts had the opportunity to choose between solutions 1 and 2 in the celebrated litigation brought by John Moore.[73] Their judgments repay

---

[72] See R. Hardiman, 'Toward the Right of Commerciality: Recognising Property Rights in the Commercial Value of Human Tissue' (1986) 34 *UCLA LR* 207; O. Danforth, 'Cells, Sales and Royalties: The Patient's Right to a Portion of the Profits' (1988) 6 *Yale Law and Pol. Rev.* 169; Barry Hoffmaster, 'Between the Sacred and the Profane: Bodies, Property and Patents in the Moore Case' (1992) 71 *Int. Prop. J.* 115.

[73] *Moore* v. *Regents of the University of California*, 249 Cal. Rptr. 494 (1988, Court of Appeals); 271 Cal. Rptr. 146 (1990, California Sup. Ct.).

careful attention since they illustrate the way in which, at the margins of property, common law adjudication invokes the mix of property-specific justice reasons.

John Moore went to the Medical Centre of the University of California in Los Angeles in 1976. He was diagnosed by Dr Golde (an employee of the University) as having an enlarged and diseased spleen. He was advised that the spleen should be removed, and the operation was duly carried out. During the next seven years Moore attended at the centre where samples of his blood and other bodily substances were taken. Eventually, he learned that Dr Golde and an associate, also employed by the University, had developed a cell-line from the excised spleen and the other extracted substances. Owing to a unique peculiarity of these materials, the cell-line created from them had great therapeutic potential. By a process of recombinant generation, it constituted an immortal product. In 1984 the University registered a patent of the cell-line. Drug companies purchased licences from the patentees. By 1990 the cell-line was said to be the basis of a three-billion-dollar industry.

Moore sued Dr Golde, his associate, the Regents of the University, and two of the licensee drug companies for the tort of conversion. A person commits that civil wrong, *inter alia*, if he exercises dominion over a chattel which is owned by someone else. Dominion had certainly been exercised over the materials taken from Moore's body in order to create the cell-line. The question for the court to decide was whether Moore or the University was the owner. The Court of Appeals found for Moore. The Supreme Court of California, by a majority, found for the University.

Technically, the Supreme Court had only to decide against Moore's ownership in order to dismiss his claim. Nevertheless, their reasoning was premised on the assumption that ownership ought to be accorded to the employers of the first knowing appropriator. 'The theory of liability that Moore urges us to endorse threatens to destroy the economic incentive to conduct important medical research.'[74] That incentive would, of course, also be absent unless the institution engaging in research and development itself enjoyed a protected ownership interest. As Broussard J pointed out in his dissent:

if, for example, another medical center or drug company had stolen all of the cells in question from the UCLA Medical Center Laboratory and had used them for its own benefit, there would be no question but that a cause of action for conversion would properly lie against the thief, and the majority opinion does not suggest otherwise.[75]

---

[74] 271 Cal. Rptr. 146 (1990), at 162.

[75] *Ibid.* 168. The majority opinion refers to legislation which drastically restricts powers of disposal of such materials and requires them to be destroyed once research is terminated— *ibid.* at 158–9. These provisions did not entail that the cells were no-one's property, since evidently they did not restrain the university from exercising ownership privileges and powers for research and profit. They were thus property-limitation rules.

In the view of the Court of Appeals: '[d]efendants' position that plaintiff cannot own his tissue, but that they can, is fraught with irony.'[76]

Consequentialist reasoning occupied a considerable part of the judgments in both courts, some broadly social, but mostly economic. The majority of the Supreme Court pointed to the undesirability of patients shopping around, if they owned their tissues, to the detriment of their best medical interests.[77] The Court of Appeals, in contrast, surmised that medical institutions might themselves be corrupted in making clinical judgments if they knew that surgery might bring a shower of gold.[78] Much more attention was directed to those incentive and market-instrumental merits of property institutions which we discussed in Chapter 15.[79] Manufacture of drugs from the cell-line would add to the social wealth available to meet justice costs and would in any case contribute directly to the well-being of the patients who would use them. It was generally accepted in the litigation that, for the community to reap such benefits, incentives had to be provided, and that could only be done if ownership was vested in someone.[80] The majority of the Supreme Court were impressed by the argument that if patient-sources were conceded ownership, researchers would be inhibited by the danger of being subjected to civil liability.[81] The Court of Appeals and the minority in the Supreme Court maintained, however, that an owner-patient would sell his precious extracted tissue to someone so that, with appropriate record-keeping, there would be no uncertainty as to title.[82]

Granted the crucial significance of incentives in this instance, the economic argument is inconclusive. If we assume that both the human source and the first knowing appropriator are rational maximizers, the cells will end up with those willing to pay most for them whichever of these two is granted the first title. In this situation the distributional blindness, which, as we have seen, is a characteristic of pure market-instrumental arguments,[83] is not cured.

In the judgments of the courts, intermingled with the consequentialist claims, different views were expressed about the moral base-line. The Court of Appeals and the minority in the California Supreme Court supposed that a person has what amounts to a natural property right over materials taken from his body. The majority of the Supreme Court denied this. Arguments

[76] N. 73 above (CA), at 507.   [77] N. 74 above, at 151.
[78] N. 73 above (CA), at 508–9.   [79] See Ch. 15, sect. (iii) above.
[80] Only Broussard J seems to have contemplated that a protected non-property holding might be appropriate. 'It is certainly arguable that as a matter of policy or morality it would be wiser to prohibit any private individual or entity from profiting from the fortuitous value that adheres in a part of a human body and instead to require all valuable excised body parts to be deposited in a public repository which would make such materials freely available to all scientists for the betterment of society as a whole.' (N. 74 above, at 172.)
[81] *Ibid.* at 154–5, 160–3.
[82] N. 73 above (CA), at 508–9; n. 74 above, at 171–3, *per* Broussard J, 180–2, *per* Mosk J.
[83] See Ch. 15, sect. (iii)(a) above.

for or against such a right were not systematically addressed. In effect, however, three in its favour emerged founded, respectively, on privacy, self-ownership, and creation-without-wrong. The Supreme Court majority countered the privacy argument and ignored the other two.

The privacy argument floated in the Court of Appeals was to this effect. Medical treatment offered to a person without fully informing him of all the consequences of the operation, including any possible therapeutic and commercial potential of materials to be taken from him, is an invasion of his privacy. Therefore, he ought to be regarded as owner of whatever is excised. 'A patient must have the ultimate power to control what becomes of his or her tissues. To hold otherwise would open the door to a massive invasion of human privacy and dignity in the name of medical progress.'[84]

The majority of the Supreme Court considered that the privacy right would be sufficiently safeguarded by imposing a duty of full disclosure upon the medical practitioner. They said that if it could be proved that Dr Golde had been aware of the potential at the time of the splenectomy and had withheld that information from Moore, Moore would have an action against Golde personally for failing in his duty.[85] Privacy considerations did not, however, entail that Moore should be accorded ownership of the excised spleen and its product, with a consequent right to sue for conversion anyone who, at any time, intermeddled with the cell-line without his leave. 'Yet one may earnestly wish to protect privacy and dignity without accepting the extremely problematic conclusion that interference with those interests amounts to a conversion of personal property.'[86]

We have seen that it is possible to found the shell of a natural property right on privacy in the case of resources with which a person is intimately connected.[87] That might suffice to yield mere-property use-privileges and control-powers in the case of separated bodily parts which are visibly identifiable as having come from a particular individual. Y should not be allowed to put on display X's beautiful and easily recognizable locks after they have been cut off, without X's consent. But if Y comes across a piece of anonymous diseased tissue which once formed part of X's body it is far-fetched to suggest that anything Y may do with the material constitutes an invasion of X's privacy. Privacy is thus not an adequate justificatory basis for anything approaching full-blooded ownership over all separated bodily parts.

A self-ownership argument for ownership of separated bodily parts would run as follows:

---

[84] N. 73 above (CA), at 504.

[85] N. 74 above, at 150–5, 156–8, 160, 163–4. They did not make it clear whether such an action would enable Moore to expropriate some of Golde's profits, in accordance with that rule of equity which provides for such expropriation where a fiduciary makes a profit out of his position. Broussard J interpreted the ruling as having this effect (*ibid.* 167). Mosk J disagreed (*ibid.* 187).

[86] *Ibid.* 158.   [87] See Ch. 12, sect. (iii) above.

1. If I am not a slave, nobody else owns my body. Therefore
2. I must own my own body and each and every part of it. Therefore
3. If any part of my body is separated from me, I continue to own that separated bodily part.

Just such an argument, albeit more cryptically expressed, surfaced in the Moore judgments. The Court of Appeals stated that there is 'a dramatic difference between having property rights in one's own body and being the property of another';[88] and that the rights which a person has to determine uses of his own body 'are so akin to property interests that it would be a subterfuge to call them something else'.[89] That is to say, if nobody else owns me, the rights over my body which follow from the bodily-use freedom principle must be regarded as constituting an ownership interest over my body vested in me; from which it follows that a patient-source must own every part of his body both before and after separation.

Mosk J, in his dissenting judgment in the Supreme Court, decided that 'every individual has a legally protectable property interest in his own body and its products'.[90] To reach that conclusion, he ran the three-step argument backwards. He noted that our society acknowledges a profound ethical imperative to respect the human body 'as the physical and temporal expression of the unique human persona'.[91] That respect was manifested, *inter alia*, by the disappearance of slavery and other institutions of servility. 'Yet their specter haunts the laboratories and boardrooms of today's biotechnological research-industrial complex.'[92] In other words, if those conducting research and development with materials taken from human beings deny that they are owned by the people they came from (step 3), they are implicitly denying that those people own their bodies (step 2), and that is tantamount to regarding them as slaves (step 1).

If the three-step argument were sound, it might be inferred that a legal system which denies full-blooded ownership of embryos or gametes to the persons from whom they came is somehow implying that such people are the community's slaves. It is not sound. As we have seen, the move from steps 1 to 2 commits a spectacular *non sequitur*. From the fact that I am not a slave it does not follow that I own myself. No-one owns me.[93] Those engaged in biotechnological research do not, merely by seeking to acquire ownership interests in waste human products, raise the spectre of slavery. It is not a subterfuge to deny that the rights which flow from the bodily-use freedom principle are internal to the operation of property institutions.[94]

The creation-without-wrong argument for a natural property right maintains that, if a person (1) creates a new item of social wealth, and (2) wrongs

---

[88] N. 73 above, at 504. [89] *Ibid.* at 505.
[90] N. 74 above, at 182. [91] *Ibid.* [92] *Ibid.*
[93] See Ch. 11, sect. (ii)(b)(4) above.
[94] See Ch. 11, sect. (ii)(a) above.

no-one in doing so, then (3) he ought to be accorded ownership of that new item.[95] How might that argument apply to Moore's case?

It is important to distinguish the cell-line as a tangible entity (a collection of living cells capable of being made, through recombinant genetic engin- eering, into an eternal organism), from the cell-line which became the sub- ject of the University's patent. The latter comprised inventive ideas about how the cells could be made to reproduce themselves and be harvested from time to time for products of therapeutic value. Those ideas may well be justly owned by the patentees on creator-incentive grounds.[96] Moore laid no claim to them. He claimed to own the cells from the moment they were excised and his loss would have been measured by reference to their golden potential at that time.

According to the creation-without-wrong argument, Moore must be recognized as owner of the physical materials taken from his body since, without his consent to the splenectomy and the other operations, no such things would have been added to the store of valuable resources. Moore, rather than the surgeon, should be regarded as the creator of this new item because his participation has the greater causal significance. Any other competent surgeon could have excised the spleen. No operation on any other patient could have produced the golden cell-line. In the words of the Court of Appeals judgment: '[w]ithout these small indispensable pieces of plaintiff, there could have been no three billion dollar cell-line.'[97] In the words of Mosk J: 'for all their expertise, defendants do not claim that they could have extracted the MO cell line out of thin air'.[98]

We have seen that creation-without-wrong cannot serve as an abstract argument for a natural property right since it involves a unilateral power to create new trespassory obligations; but that it may serve as an argument internal to property institutions where the creative activity serves merely to concretize existing trespassory obligations.[99] It can similarly be invoked in the case of separated bodily parts because, by virtue of the third element of our minimalist conception of justice, there must already be trespassory rules protecting the human body from which the part comes. If X consents to surgical removal of tissue and insists that others refrain from meddling with it after its excision, he does not purport to impose new obligations, but merely to concretize those rules which already prohibit interfering with the whole of his body.

However, the argument yields, not full-blooded ownership, but only mere property over the separated bodily part. Moore had the right that no-one else should make use of his spleen without his consent, both before and after its removal. That trespassory perimeter reserved to him, for what it was

---

[95] See Ch. 11, sect. (iii) above.   [96] See Ch. 15, sect. (iii)(c)(2) above.
[97] N. 73 above, at 507.   [98] N. 74 above, at 178.
[99] See Ch. 11, sect. (iii)(d) above.

worth, an open-ended set of use-privileges and control-powers over the spleen. Full-blooded ownership would entail that trespassory obligations surround the spleen into whosoever's hands Moore chooses to transmit it by way of sale, hire, or gift. No such exploitative powers of transmission, and their concomitant extended trespassory obligations, applied to the spleen before it was excised merely by virtue of the bodily-use freedom principle. The fact of excision cannot, *ipso facto*, have created them.

The courts in Moore's case were not in a position to construct a *de novo* solution to the general problem of property in separated bodily parts. They had to allocate ownership either to the human source or to the first knowing appropriator; and the conversion claim meant that they had to fit their answer into the common law which, for the purposes of this action, recognizes only full-blooded ownership of chattels. The choice was between awarding full-blooded ownership, carrying commercial exploitation powers, either to someone who, by virtue of creation-without-wrong, had a right to mere property in the tissues, or to someone who had no right whatever. Given those constraints, Moore should have won.

(c) Windfall

As a general question of property-institutional design, there is a third alternative. Supposing ownership powers are needed, a quasi-ownership interest over separated bodily parts might be thought to accrue to the community.

The majority of the California Supreme Court opined that if Moore could sue for conversion, that would enable him to recover a 'highly theoretical windfall'.[100] But their disposal of the case conferred the same windfall on the defendants. The university medical centre happened to be the place where the diseased spleen was removed. If the university acquires full-blooded ownership merely because it was one of its employees who spotted the commercial potential, its luck outstrips even the most fortunate strikes of the forty-niners in the California Gold Rush.

We saw in the last chapter that accretions to social wealth to which no-one has any claim are 'windfall wealth' to which all members of the relevant community are equally entitled. In the case of separated bodily parts with commercial potential, the human source has a claim only to mere property. That entitles him to make such uses as he pleases of his bits and pieces and to permit others to do so, but does not carry the transmission powers essential for commercial exploitation. The source may or may not attach significance to this ownership interest, but, being unsaleable, it possesses no measurable monetary value. Perhaps he should be awarded a small solatium for loss of this limited interest. (The same might be said in the case of important bodily products which the law subjects to protected non-property

[100] N. 74 above, at 163.

holdings vested in public agencies.) Subject to that, the windfall wealth consequent on the by-products of necessary surgical operations should be the subject of a quasi-ownership interest vested in some appropriate agency mandated to exploit them to swell the public coffers.[101]

We have seen that there are instances in which that which is in principle windfall wealth may nevertheless be justly allocated to particular individuals or groups for reasons unconnected with natural right. Could it be that necessary creator-incentives dictate that this should be so in the case of separated bodily parts with commercial potential? So far as the human source is concerned, that could hardly apply to the waste products of surgery to which a patient must consent if his life is to be saved, as in Moore's case. If the first knowing appropriator is the surgeon, it is likely that incentives to watch out for tissues with exceptional qualities can be provided without going to the lengths of conferring ownership of them on one who otherwise has no right to them. Whether, in the case of bodily parts whose removal is not required for the patient's health, the patient needs ownership as an inducement to contribute them to some worthy object will depend upon the social context. If people will donate organs or blood, so much the better. Even if they must be paid for the service of supplying such materials, it does not follow that they need to be vested with ownership of them once removed from their bodies.

(d) Mere-Property at Best

The principle stated at the beginning of this section is unacceptable if 'ownership' is taken to mean full-blooded ownership. Every invasion of a person's bodily security without his consent, including removing any part of his body, is, *prima facie*, an assault. It does not follow that he becomes full owner of anything taken from him. He does acquire mere property over any part or tissue unless he consents, expressly or impliedly, to waive any such right.

He has a natural right to mere property by virtue of creation-without-wrong. The materials, being now separated, pass the conceptual distancing test discussed in the first section of this Chapter and hence may constitute a proprietary subject-matter. Those rules which previously protected the whole of his body crystallize around what is taken from it. He is responsible for creating the new item if he consents to the removal and he may, if it was taken without consent, adopt the wrongful removal for the purposes of

---

[101] The state of California advance no claim in the *Moore* case. Conceivably, it might have done so by extension of the *bona vacantia* doctrine. That doctrine requires that, where property lacks an owner because its previous owner has died intestate and without heirs, the property vests in the State. Here it would have to be argued that property should vest in the State in respect of newly created things as to which no-one has a just claim to full-blooded ownership.

asserting his mere-property interest. (In the case of items which are identifiably former parts of his body, he may pray in aid a privacy right as well.) Full-blooded ownership would arise only where it constitutes an indispensable incentive for the creation of some new and valuable item of social wealth.

Such a mere-property right, since it does not carry transmission powers, expires with the death of the human source (supposing he has not previously abandoned it). We may respect the wishes of persons who indicate, during their lifetimes, that they want to 'donate' their bodies, or parts of them, for medical research or transplant surgery. We do so by extension of the bodily-use freedom principle, not by supposing that their bodies, or parts of them, are among the chattels they own to which open-ended ownership transmission-freedoms apply. The same is true when we respect people's wishes about their mode of burial or cremation. As with other uses to which people may put their bodies, the limits are not set by invocations of ownership as an organizing idea or as a principle.

As against a human source who insists on his mere-property right, first appropriators acquire no right. Some kind of ownership or quasi-ownership interest, or protected non-property holding, may be needed in the case of items such as anatomical specimens, or fluid-samples collected for forensic purposes. If so, special title conditions may be laid down, or first occupancy, or even labour-desert,[102] may be invoked.

Most separated bits of human beings are of no value to anyone and questions about the property in them will not arise. Where they are of value, pecuniary or otherwise, literal common property is inappropriate. Trespassory rules of some kind must be in place, whether they end up as the subject of full-blooded ownership, mere property, quasi-ownership, or protected non-property holdings. In England, such protection will be afforded by the law of theft which has now been extended to encompass possession and control, as well as 'ownership'.[103] In the case of specially sensitive items connected with reproduction or survival, further trespassory protection has been introduced by the relevant regulatory regimes.

Questions relating to the commodification of the supply of human organic materials involve combinations of economic and social issues which will vary from one kind of material to another. So far as property-institutional design is concerned, the alternatives of ownership, quasi-ownership, or protected non-property holding are to be selected against the following moral background. The human source is entitled to mere property over separated bodily parts. Any further value that they may have is windfall wealth and, one way or another, should accrue to the community.

---

[102] It has been suggested that a proprietary interest in a corpse could be acquired by someone who expends time and skill on it with a view to its preservation on scientific or other grounds—*Doodeward* v. *Spence* (1908) 6 CLR 406.   [103] See Theft Act 1968, s. 5(1).

18

Property is Just, to a Degree, Sometimes

Every property institution, whatever else it comprises, includes trespassory rules and reserved ownership use-privileges and control-powers. Modern property institutions confer ownership transmission powers which facilitate more or less extensive mechanisms for hiving off and accumulating wealth, and also subject some resources to quasi-ownership interests. All historical instances of property institutions include property-limitation, expropriation, and appropriation rules. (In Chapter 9 we contend that, if property was to be confronted with justice, expansive employments of the word 'property', unconnected with the actual operation of the rules of property institutions, were to be rejected.)

A judgement about the relative justice or injustice of a particular property institution, taken as a whole, must be addressed to the total package of privileges, powers, rights, obligations, liabilities, and immunities to which it gives rise, set in the social context in which it obtains. A conclusion that no property institution of any kind could be justified would entail that obligations imposed by trespassory rules are never genuine moral obligations and that claims to exercise ownership privileges and powers are never morally sound.

(i) NOWHERE

At the end of Chapter 15 we reached the conclusion that there is a moral background right vested in each citizen of a modern society that a property institution, of some kind, must be maintained, and that questions of distribution and property-institutional design be structured in terms of a mix of property-specific justice reasons. At the end of Chapter 16 we noted that, as to questions which were the subject of indeterminacy or good-faith controversy, the right might be concretized by social convention and especially by juristic doctrine. That is a historically situated right. Might the future unfold in such a way that this right would disappear?

Marx and Proudhon supposed that capitalist private property was in terminal decline but, as we have seen, it is unclear whether any, and if so what kind of, property institution they envisaged as its successor.[1] For a vision of a

---

[1] See Ch. 7, sect. (vii) and Ch. 16, sect. (i)(a) above.

future propertyless society, we may turn to the idyllic world conjured up by William Morris in *News from Nowhere*.[2]

Morris, writing at the end of the nineteenth century, presents a time-traveller from his day visiting an England of the twenty-first century. In Nowhere, 'pure communism' has been achieved. There is no property of any kind.

Whatever else may be said of the novel, Morris is conceptually consistent. There are no trespassory rules, not even those such as we imagined in Red Land safeguarding protected non-property holdings.[3] No-one who wishes to go into a factory or any other centre of production and there to operate the machinery is debarred from doing so. There is no such thing as 'group', 'collective', or 'public' property. Anyone may take up residence in buildings large and small, all of them architectural gems. The mutual goodwill of the inhabitants is such that notions of exclusive living-space associated with current ideas of privacy are, it seems, unknown. Beautifully handicrafted chattels exist in profusion, so there is, of course, no conception of theft. In a propertyless society, as we have seen, the notion of 'common property' is redundant;[4] and this term is never used in Morris's novel.

Without trespassory rules, that other pillar of property institutions, the ownership spectrum, must also be absent, and so it is. We saw in Chapter 5 that, however institutions may differ in their technical terminology, countless day-to-day interchanges are influenced by taken-for-granted assumptions about ownership interests. In Nowhere, by contrast, no trace remains of ownership as an organizing idea, much to the puzzlement of the time-traveller. Morris describes an encounter in which the traveller wants to acquire a tobacco pipe. He goes into a 'shop' where such artefacts are distributed. He is presented with a wondrously decorated pipe. He protests to the child who supplies it that he is an absent-minded fellow and he is afraid he might lose the lovely object. She patiently explains to him that, if he does, someone else will find it and use it and he (the traveller) can always come back for another.[5]

The three elements of our minimalist conception of justice are implemented in Nowhere, without benefit of property. All are equally free to offer and to accept services—although there can be no question of 'giving' things, in our sense of transferring ownership of them from one person to another. Autonomy is extended to children who learn what they like, when they like—no need for ownership interests in family dwellings or quasi-ownership interests in schools. Personal violence is unacceptable; but then it rarely occurs now that property has gone. When it does, as when one man kills another in a fight engendered by sexual jealousy, the slayer is left to his repentance. There is no

[2] William Morris, *News from Nowhere and other Writings* (Clive Wilmer (ed.), Penguin Books, 1993).
[3] See Ch. 2, sect. (iii) and Ch.7, sect. (v) above.
[4] See Ch. 7, sect. (iv) above.
[5] N. 2 above, ch. 6.

civil or criminal law, no courts, no police, no government, no communally organized obligations and hence no 'justice costs'.

There is an abundance of all material resources that any citizen of Nowhere might want—including houses with ample gardens, well-tended woods and parks, gorgeous apparel, fine wines, and the best tobacco. Hence the use-channelling and use-policing functions of property institutions are redundant. Since there is also an abundance of services, no-one is constrained to make selections among his preferences and so there is no money. The abundance is brought about because people choose to work for pleasure, at building, road-repairing, transportation, growing and conveying food to where it is wanted, and so forth. They need no material incentives. Praise might make sense as a response to their inherently enjoyable labour, but 'desert' would not. Wants always match supply because the old-style capitalist market economy has disappeared, so that desires for unnecessary products are no longer being artificially created. The inhabitants live long and healthy lives in more or less perfect amity with their neighbours.

If the future could produce a society like Nowhere, would it be more just than one which fully met the conditions of the background moral property right (one which discharged basic needs completely and which in every other respect took proper account of relevant property-specific justice reasons)? Some readers might not share Morris's arcadian preferences for rural and semi-rural life, or his tastes in architecture and design. Some might hanker after an ability to make gifts to friends and loved-ones of things that are (relatively) scarce, which would disappear with conditions of literal abundance. Some might value privacy-conferring exclusivity, or the challenge of incentives to undertake, or the satisfaction of rewarding, disagreeable labour. Some might even suppose that a degree of market competition adds spice to life. Above all, Morris does not tell us what are those things and services for which the old market system created artificial needs and which the inhabitants of Nowhere have no wish to receive. They might include items which Morris thought worthless but we do not.

However that might be, from a bird's eye view the society of Nowhere is preferable to the ones we know with their wars, mayhem, intolerance, intra-family violence, social strife, and poverty. If the abolition of property is both necessary and sufficient to bring it about, let property be abolished.

To suppose that to be true, we must make a number of assumptions. First, production of goods and services, on the one hand, and reining in of wants, on the other, can so evolve that abundance will result. Secondly, wants will cease to include exclusivity over anything. Thirdly, people will be found to perform all necessary tasks, motivated only by the inherent pleasure of the work. Fourthly, there will be a smooth and spontaneous matching of supply and wants on a day-to-day basis. Fifthly, there will be no need to regulate access to factors of production or of service provision. Sixthly, when all this is achieved, all tribalism, clannishness, xenophobia, inter-generational conflict, sexual harassment, work-place bullying, envy, egotism, frustration, and all the other springs of human dissension will (virtually) disappear.

Although no-one can prophesy the future of humanity, it can be said that these assumptions, individually, require acts of faith for which there is no historical warrant: and that, collectively, they amount to the wildest implausibility. Given the people we are and are likely to remain, and the practicable configurations of our interchanges over the multifarious items of social wealth, each of us has a right to insist that a property institution be maintained. In that sense, the answer to the question 'Is property a just institution?' is 'yes'.

We must begin with that answer and work out particular questions of distribution and property-institutional design in its light. To that end, we have cleared the normative undergrowth by eliminating some hoary philosophical dead wood. Property institutions cannot be erected on natural rights to full-blooded ownership, because there are none. 'Self-ownership' may have a (rhetorical) role to play in the context of the bodily-use freedom principle, but its invocation in the context of external resources is illegitimate.[6] The notion that persons constitute themselves by absorbing everything they own is a bizarre fancy.[7] Speculative assertions about the real pre-history of property have little to contribute.[8] The question whether enterprises should be the subject of either packaged ownership, or packaged quasi-ownership, interests ought not to be elevated to the status of a social-typological definition.[9]

We have sorted other normative considerations into an ordering of approximate significance. Thing-fetishism is relevant to moral aspiration, not to the legislator.[10] Equality of resources has a role to play only in the context of that which is genuinely 'windfall' wealth.[11] Domination-potential is of pervasive significance, wealth-disparity is not.[12] Social convention, including juristic doctrine, has inescapable importance, but is never conclusive.[13]

In the end, we are left with a mix of property-specific justice reasons—property freedoms, labour-desert, privacy, incentives and markets, independence, and basic needs. None of these imports precise, context-free considerations, and their mix can do no more than structure our answers to general or specific problems. On the contested planes of politics or adjudication, there can be no such thing as judgement-free determinacy. In any case, property questions are inseparably affected by the social setting in which a property institution exists. For example, whether ownership of resources of itself arms the owner with powers of illegitimate domination, or whether a class of citizens' basic needs are adequately catered for, may turn on cultural and political arrangements outside the purview of property.

---

[6] See Ch. 11, sect. (ii) above.
[7] See Ch. 12, sect. (ii) above.
[8] See Ch. 15, sect. (iii)(b) above.
[9] See Ch. 14, sect. (iv)(a) above.
[10] See Ch. 14, sect. (ii) above.
[11] See Ch.16, sect. (i)(c) above.
[12] See Ch. 14, sects. (iii) and (iv) above.
[13] See Ch. 16, sect. (ii) above.

Macro or micro problems of distribution and property-institutional design are what we face. Morris's vision may serve to reinforce condemnations of unattractive consumerism and wealth-fetishism and to uplift yearnings towards a more co-operative kind of human fellowship. As a total package, however, Nowhere is so implausible that, for any future we can foresee, we must lay it reverently aside.

(ii) THE JUSTICE THRESHOLD

If we suppose that, in a particular society, problems of distribution and property-institutional design have been addressed, more or less, in terms of the relevant property-specific justice reasons, and that the solutions reached (albeit imperfect) are arrived at in good faith, the society's property institution is, to a degree, just. If, on the other hand, we conclude that important property-specific justice reasons are systematically neglected—that, for example, the necessary property freedoms of daily life are denied to many, or no consideration is given to counteracting the domination-potential of ownership or quasi-ownership interests within family or industrial life, or that conventionally-established conceptions of labour-desert are ignored by those who administer the system, or that the basic needs of a particular class of citizens count for nothing—the property institution falls below what we may call 'the justice threshold'.

That may be a difficult judgement. For one thing, systematic failure in one respect might be compensated for by full implementation in another. Then the judgement can never be entirely ahistorical. As we have seen, what constitutes labour-desert is always hostage to convention,[14] some basic needs are a function of culture and of the productive capacity of a society,[15] and what counts as 'illegitimate' domination turns partly on how people view their own aspirations and life-plans.[16] On the other hand, we need not defer abjectly to cultural relativism. There is more than enough information for us to conclude that the property institutions of slave-owning, feudal, untrammelled private-enterprise, or ruthless command-economy societies are radically unjust.

The justice threshold is inevitably imprecise, but it is of the first moral consequence. If it is not attained, a property institution dissolves into a coercive machine for subjecting social wealth to the control of a privileged clique —as was the case, for example, when an international crime syndicate established a feudal property institution in England in 1066, or when Joseph Stalin imposed centralized collectivisation in the Soviet Union during the 1920s and 1930s. Both pillars of the institution suffer moral disintegration. Not only are holdings of wealth illegitimate, but the trespassory rules which underpin all ownership and quasi-ownership interests lack moral bindingness.

---

[14] See Ch. 11, sect. (iv) above.
[15] See Ch. 15, sect. (ii)(b) above.
[16] See Ch. 14, sect. (iv) above.

If a society rises above the justice threshold, stealing is always, *prima facie*, wrongful. That is so because of the way in which trespassory rules underlie the institution as a whole. It would be rare for anyone to conclude that the distributional consequences of a property institution are ideal. Suppose that, nevertheless, it represents a good-faith aspiration towards implementing the background moral right that derives from (and calls for problem-solving by reference to) the mix of property-specific justice reasons. Then every citizen is morally obligated to support it as an institution, whilst calling for distributional readjustments or changes in property-institutional design. A flat refusal to recognize any category of trespassory rules to be binding would be inconsistent with this obligation to support the institution. The obligation derives from society's partial implementation of the background right, and rests on the moral integrity to be looked for in any morally concerned person.

Imagine a citizen named Critic. She supposes that she (and everyone else) has a right to have in place social arrangements of the following kinds. There should be money which people can spend in making choices between goods and services, rather than all such things being allocated according to the discretion of a social agency. There ought to be chattels for daily use which people can dispose of as they please, being answerable to no-one. Privacy in dwellings is to be treated as a value. For some kinds of work, rewards in the shape of money, shares in tangible assets, or intellectual property should be regarded as deserved. Sometimes, incentives and markets are an appropriate mechanism for increasing the total pie of social wealth. People ought to be free to exchange or sell their things, or to purchase services, without the prior consent of a social agency, and to make donations to individuals or political causes of their choice.

Critic recognizes that the property institution of her society makes such arrangements possible. Nevertheless, she considers that, as the institution currently works out, rewards are grossly disproportional to desert; that in particular, women's work within the family home is under-valued; that many enterprises presently in private ownership ought to be transferred to quasi-ownership control, since that would not in fact reduce production and would better protect workers from welfare-threatening domination; that political culture is distorted because of the excessive influence of the rich; that the basic needs of many citizens are imperfectly met. Suppose she is right in all these critical judgements. It does not follow that she is morally free to shop lift, or to vandalize public telephone boxes. Her recognition that the property institution partially implements her background moral right entails that she would lack moral integrity if she simultaneously disavowed the institution's trespassory rules.

On the other hand, if a society's property institution does not rise above the justice threshold, the moral quality of its trespassory rules crumbles away. Theft or criminal damage which hurts particular individuals may be condemned *ad hoc*—as when mobs of the disadvantaged pillage or burn the property of those who are little better off than they are; but social rulers who demand universal compliance with rules protecting property merely have force, not right, on their side. Biblical prohibitions of theft and covetousness are combined with injunctions to care for the widow and the orphan and the stranger within the gate, to render due reward, and to abstain from using riches to oppress.

This connection between the threshold of justice and the moral obligatoriness of trespassory rules is commonly ignored by libertarians and liberal egalitarians alike. The libertarian trick consists of asserting, as a premise, that property-protecting obligations are of the same pre-social (natural) kind as are obligations against violence to the person.[17] The egalitarian who proclaims the radical injustice of contemporary societies for their failure to respect equality of resources seldom goes on to draw the inference—'so steal, whenever you can get away with it, so long as you don't injure someone as disadvantaged as you are yourself!'[18] We are more likely to draw the conclusion that the property institutions of the societies we know rise above the justice threshold if we take the test to be, as we should, whether they embody good-faith attempts to meet basic needs and to counter illegitimate domination than if we abstract social wealth as a cake and assume, mistakenly, that justice is merely a function of how it is sliced.

Lawyers and judges in their daily work do not, and are in no position to, raise their eyes to overall yes/no questions about whether their society's property institution is, to the requisite degree, just. Yet they inevitably swim within the mix of property-specific justice reasons. They have to deal with micro questions of distribution and property-institutional design. Juristic doctrine ought not to be dismissed as unworthy logic-chopping, since, like other aspects of social convention, it has a *prima facie* normative status in view of indeterminacy, good-faith controversy, and justified reliance.[19] On the other hand, in relation to most difficult questions, the underlying justice reasons ought to be unearthed, much more often than they are when, in legal reasoning, 'ownership' is invoked as a principle.[20] We have provided some illustrations of how this might be done in the last chapter and in earlier sections of this book.[21]

Finally, we must remember that the justness of a property institution, or of particular aspects of it, is only part of the justice agenda. *Pace* Marxist predictions, most of the terrible conflicts which have arisen in this century have not been primarily triggered by dissatisfaction with property institutions. A

[17] See Ch. 15, sect. (ii)(a) above.
[18] See the discussion of Dworkin and Ackerman in Ch. 16, sect. (ii)(b) above. Neither writer considers this inference.
[19] See Ch. 16, sect. (ii) above.
[20] See Ch. 6 above.
[21] See Ch. 11, sect. (iv)(c); Ch. 12, sects. (i) and (iii); Ch. 14, sects. (i)(b)(1) and (iv)(b); Ch. 15, sect. (ii)(b)–(c); Ch. 16, sects. (i)(c) and (ii)(c) above.

just, or fairly just, property institution does not guarantee that people will find particular forms of government tolerable, that individuals and groups will suppose their identities and diversities receive due consideration and respect, or that a society's prior duty to repress inter-personal violence will be discharged. A just property institution is but one of the hallmarks of a just society.

Bibliography

ACKERMAN, BRUCE A., *Private Property and the Constitution* (Yale University Press, 1977).
—— *Social Justice in the Liberal State* (Yale University Press, 1980).
ACKERMAN, SUSAN ROSE, 'Inalienability and the Theory of Property Rules' (1985) *Columbia Law Review*, 931.
ALCHIAN, ARMEN, A. and DEMSETZ, HAROLD, 'The Property Rights Paradigm' (1973) 33 *Journal of Economic History* 16.
ALEXANDER, BARRY, 'All or Nothing at All: The Intentions of Authorities and the Authority of Intentions', in Andrei Marmor (ed.), *Law and Interpretation* (OUP, 1995).
ALEXANDER, E. R., 'The Canadian Charter of Rights and Freedoms in the Supreme Court of Canada' (1989) 105 *Law Quarterly Review* 561.
ALEXANDER, GREGORY, 'The Dead Hand and the Law of Trusts in the 19th Century' (1985) 37 *Stanford Law Review* 1189.
ANOUILH, JEAN, *L'Invitation au Château* (La Table Rond, Paris).
ARISTOTLE, *The Politics* (ed. Steven Everson, trans. Jonathan Barnes, CUP, 1988).
ATKINSON, A. B., *Unequal Shares: Wealth in Britain* (Penguin Books, 1974).
AVINERI, SHLOMO and DE-SHALIT, AVNER (eds.), *Communitarianism and Individualism* (OUP, 1992).
BARZEL, YORAM, *Economic Analysis of Property Rights* (CUP, 1989).
BECKER, LAWRENCE C., 'The Moral Basis of Property Rights' in J. Rowland Pennock and John W. Chapman (eds.), *Property: Nomos XXII* (New York University Press, 1980).
—— *Property Rights: Philosophic Foundations* (Routledge and Kegan Paul, 1977).
BEDDARD, R., *Human Rights and Europe* (3rd edn., CUP 1993).
BENN, S. I. and PETERS R. S., *Social Principles and the Democratic State* (George Allen and Unwin, 1959).
BENTHAM, JEREMY, *Principles of the Civil Code*, in C. K. Ogden (ed.), *Jeremy Bentham: The Theory of Legislation* (Kegan Paul, 1931).
—— *Of Laws in General* (Athlone Press, 1970).
—— *An Introduction to the Principles of Morals and Legislation* (J. Burns and H. L. A. Hart (eds.), Athlone Press, 1970).
BERLE, JR., ADOLF A. and MEANS, GARDINER C., *The Modern Corporation and Private Property* (Commerce Clearing House, 1932).
BEYLEVELD, DERYCK and BROWNSWORD, ROGER, *Mice, Morality and Patents* (Common Law Institute of Intellectual Property, 1993).
BIRKS, PETER, 'The Roman Law Concept of Dominium and the Idea of Absolute Ownership' (1986) *Acta Juridica* 1.
BLACKSTONE, SIR WILLIAM, *Commentaries on the Laws of England* (16th edn., J. Butterworth and Son, 1825).
BOUCKAERT, BOUDEWIJN, 'What is Property?' (1990) 13 *Harvard Journal of Public Policy* 775.

BRADER, ROCHELLE, *Rochelle's Place* (Kiwi Pacific Records Ltd, 1986).

BRINK, DAVID, *Moral Realism and the Foundation of Ethics* (CUP, 1989).

BROWNLIE, IAN, *Principles of Public International Law* (4th edn., Clarendon Press, 1990).

BUCHANAN, JAMES, *The Limits of Liberty: Between Anarchy and Leviathan* (University of Chicago Press, 1975).

BUCKLAND, W. W. and MCNAIR, ARNOLD D., *Roman Law and Common Law* (2nd edn., revised by F. H. Lawson, CUP, 1952).

BUCKLE, STEPHEN, *Natural Law and the Theory of Property: Grotius to Hume* (Clarendon Press, 1991).

CALABRESI, GUIDO and MELLAMED, DOUGLAS A., 'Property Rules, Liability Rules and Inalienability: One View of the Cathedral' (1972) 85 *Harvard Law Review* 1089.

CALDWELL, LINTON K., 'Rights of Ownership or Rights of Use: The Need for a New Conceptual Basis for Land Use Policy' (1974) 15 *William and Mary Law Review* 759.

CHALLIS, H. W., *Law of Real Property* (3rd edn., Charles Sweet, 1911).

CHARTIER, ROGER, 'Figures of the Author' in Brad Sherman and Alain Strowel (eds.), *Of Authors and Origins* (Clarendon Press, 1994).

CHRISTMAN, JOHN (ed), *The Inner Citadel: Essays on Individual Autonomy* (OUP, 1989).

—— *The Myth of Property* (OUP, 1994).

CICERO, *De Finibus*.

CLARKE, LORENNE M. F., 'Privacy, Property, Freedom, and the Family' in Richard Bronaugh (ed.), *Philosophical Law* (Greenwood Press, 1978).

CLAUDE, R. P. and WESTON, B. H. (eds.), *Human Rights in the World Community* (2nd edn, University of Pennsylvania Press, 1992).

COASE, R. H., 'The Problem of Social Cost' (1960) 3 *Journal of Law and Economics* 1.

COHEN, G. A., *Self-Ownership, Freedom, and Equality* (CUP, 1995).

COLEMAN, JULES, *Markets, Morals and the Law* (CUP, 1988).

COPP, DAVID and ZIMMERMAN, DAVID (eds.), *Morality, Reason and Truth* (Rowman and Allen Held, 1985).

COVAL, S., SMITH, J. C. and COVAL, SIMON, 'The Foundations of Property and Property Law' (1986) 45 *Cambridge Law Journal 457*.

CROSS, JOHN T., 'Protecting Confidential Information under the Criminal Law of Theft and Fraud' (1991) 11 *Oxford Journal of Legal Studies* 264.

DAHLMAN, CARL J., *The Open Field System and Beyond: A Property Rights Analysis of an Economic Institution* (CUP, 1980).

DAM, KENNETH W., 'Oil and Gas Licensing and the North Sea' (1965) 8 *Journal of Law and Economics* 51.

DANFORTH, O., 'Cells, Sales and Royalties: The Patient's Right to a Portion of the Profits' (1988) 6 *Yale Law and Political Review* 169.

DEMSETZ, HAROLD, 'Toward a Theory of Property Rights' (1967) 57 *American Economic Review* 347.

—— 'Professor Michelman's Unnecessary and Futile Search for the Philosopher's Touchstone' in J. Rowland Pennock and John W. Chapman (eds.), *Nomos XXIV: Ethics, Economics and the Law* (New York University Press, 1982).

DICKENS, CHARLES, *Dombey and Son* (Chapman and Hall Ltd, 1892).

DONAHUE, CHARLES JR., 'The Future of the Concept of Property Predicted from its Past' in J. Rowland Pennock and John W. Chapman (eds.), *Property: Nomos XXII* (New York University Press, 1980).

DWORKIN, R. M., *Taking Rights Seriously* (Duckworth, 1978).

—— 'What is Equality? Part 1 Equality of Welfare' (1981) 10 *Philosophy and Public Affairs* 185.

—— 'What is Equality? Part 2 Equality of Resources' (1981) 10 *Philosophy and Public Affairs* 283.

—— 'What is Equality? Part 3 The Place of Liberty' (1987) *Iowa Law Review* 1.

ELIAS, GBOLAHAN, *Explaining Constructive Trusts* (Clarendon Press, 1990).

ENGELS, FREDERICK, *The Origins of the Family, Private Property and State* (Eleanor Burke Leacock (ed.), Lawrence and Wishart, 1972).

FEINBERG, JOEL, *Doing and Deserving* (Princeton University Press, 1970).

FISH, STANLEY, *Doing What Comes Naturally: Change, Rhetoric and the Practice of Theory in Literary and Legal Studies* (Clarendon Press, 1989).

FITZGERALD, P. J. (ed.), *Salmond on Jurisprudence* (12th edn., Sweet and Maxwell, 1966).

FOOT, PHILIPPA, 'Moral Realism and Moral Dilemma' (1983) 80 *Journal of Philosophy* 379.

GOLDBERG, JEFFREY D., 'Involuntary Servitudes: A Property-Based Notion of Abortion Choice' (1991) 38 *University of California at Los Angeles Law Review* 1597.

GRAY, KEVIN, 'Property in Thin Air' (1991) 50 *Cambridge Law Journal* 252.

GREY, THOMAS C., 'The Disintegration of Property' in J. Rowland Pennock and John W. Chapman (eds.), *Property: Nomos XXII* (New York University Press, 1980).

GARDBAUM, S., 'Law, Politics, and the Claims of Community' (1992) 90 *Michigan Law Review* 685.

GEORGE, ROBERT (ed.) *Natural Law Theory* (Clarendon Press, 1992).

GIBBARD, ALAN, 'Natural Property Rights' (1976) 10 *Nous* 77.

GINSBURG, JANE C., 'A Tale of Two Copyrights: Literary Property in Revolutionary France and America', in Brad Sherman and Alain Strowel (eds.), *Of Authors And Origins* (Clarendon Press, 1994).

GREEN, THOMAS HILL, *Lectures on the Principles of Political Obligation,* reprinted from *Green's Philosophical Works* (Longman, Green and Co., 1931), ii.

GROSSI, PAOLO, *An Alternative to Private Property: Collective Property in the Juridical Consciousness of the Nineteenth Century* (trans. Lydia G. Cochrane, University of Chicago Press, 1981).

GROTIUS, HUGO, *De Jure Belli ac Pacis* (trans. F. W. Kelsey, Oceana Publications, 1964).

GRUNEBAUM, JAMES, *Private Ownership* (Routledge, 1991).

GUEST, A. G., 'Family Provision and the Legitima Portio' (1957) 73 *Law Quarterly Review*, 74.

GUTTERIDGE, H. C., 'Abuse of Rights' (1933–5) 5 *Cambridge Law Journal* 22.

HAGERSTRÖM, A., *Enquiries into the Nature of Law and Morals* (trans. C. D. Broad, Almqvist and Wikfell, 1953).

HALLOWELL, IRVING A., 'The Nature and Function of Property as a Social Institution' in Hallowell, *Culture and Experience* (University of Pennsylvania Press, 1955).

HAMMOND, G., 'Theft of Information' (1984) 100 *Law Quarterly Review* 252.

HAND, CATHERINE, 'The Statutory Tenancy: An Unrecognised Proprietary Interest?' (1980) *Conveyancer* 351.

HARBURY, C. D. and HITCHENS, C. M. W. N., *Inheritance and Wealth Inequality in Britain* (George Allen and Unwin, 1979).

HARDIMAN, R., 'Toward the Right of Commerciality: Recognising Property Rights in the Commercial Value of Human Tissue' (1986) *UCLA Law Review* 207.

HARDIN, GARRETT, 'The Tragedy of the Commons' in Bruce A. Ackerman (ed.), *Economic Foundations of Property Law* (Little Brown and Co., 1975).

HARGREAVES, A. D., 'Terminology and Title in Ejectment' (1940) 56 *Law Quarterly Review* 376.

—— 'Modern Real Property' (1956) 19 *Modern Law Review* 14.

HARMAN, GILBERT, 'Is There a Single True Morality?' in D. Copp and D. Zimmerman, (eds.), *Morality, Reason and Truth* (Rowman and Allen Held, 1985).

HARRIS, D. R., 'The Concept of Possession in English Law' in A. G. Guest (ed.), *Oxford Essays in Jurisprudence* (OUP, 1961).

HARRIS, J. W., *Variation of Trusts* (Sweet and Maxwell, 1975).

—— *Law and Legal Science* (Clarendon Press, 1979).

—— *Legal Philosophies* (Butterworths, 1980).

—— 'Olivecrona on Law and Language—The Search for Legal Culture' (1982), *Tiddsskrift för Rettsvitenskap* 625.

—— 'Ownership of Land in English Law' in N. MacCormick and P. Birks (eds.), *The Legal Mind* (Clarendon Press, 1986).

—— 'Legal Doctrine and Interests in Land' in J. M. Eekelaar and J. Bell (eds.), *Oxford Essays in Jurisprudence, 3rd Series* (Clarendon Press, 1987).

—— 'Unger's Critique of Formalism in Legal Reasoning: Hero, Hercules and Humdrum' (1989) 52 *Modern Law Review* 42.

—— 'Murphy Makes it Eight: Overruling Comes to Negligence' (1991) 11 *Oxford Journal of Legal Studies* 416.

—— 'Private and Non-Private Property: What is the Difference?' (1995) 111 *Law Quarterly Review* 421.

—— 'Who Owns My Body?' (1996) 16 *Oxford Journal Of Legal Studies* 55.

HART, H. L. A., *Essays on Bentham: Studies in Jurisprudence and Political Theory* (Clarendon Press, 1982).

—— *The Concept of Law* (2nd edn., Clarendon Press, 1994).

HASLETT, D. W., 'Is Inheritance Justified?' (1986) 15 *Philosophy and Public Affairs* 122.

HAYEK, F. A., *Law, Legislation and Liberty: Vol. 1 Rules and Order* (Routledge and Kegan Paul, 1973).

—— *Law, Legislation and Liberty: Vol. 2 The Mirage of Social Justice* (Routledge and Kegan Paul, 1976).

HAYTON, D. J., 'Equity and Trusts' in G. G. Jowell and J. P. W. McAuslan (eds.) *Lord Denning: The Judge and the Law* (Sweet and Maxwell, 1984).

HEGEL, G. W. F., *Elements of the Philosophy of Right* (trans. H. B. Nisbet, CUP, 1991).

HOBBES, THOMAS, *Leviathan* (C. B. MacPherson (ed.), Penguin Books, 1968).

HOFFMASTER, BARRY, 'Between the Sacred and the Profane: Bodies, Property and Patents in the Moore Case' (1992) 71 *Intellectual Property Journal* 115.

HOHFELD, WESLEY NEWCOMB, 'Relations Between Equity and Law' (1913) 11 *Michigan Law Review* 537.

—— *Fundamental Legal Conceptions as Applied in Judicial Reasoning* (Yale University Press, 1919).

HOLDSWORTH, W. S., *A History of English Law* (3rd edn., Methuen and Co. Ltd., 1923).

—— 'Terminology and Title in Ejectment—A Reply' (1940) 56 *Law Quarterly Review* 479.

HONDERICH, TED (ed.), *Morality and Objectivity* (Routledge and Kegan Paul, 1985).

HONORÉ, A. M., *Making Law Bind* (Clarendon Press, 1987).

HUGHES, JUSTIN, 'The Philosophy of Intellectual Property' (1988) 77 *Georgia Law Journal* 287.

HUME, DAVID, *A Treatise of Human Nature* (T. H. Green and T. H. Grose, (eds), Longman Green and Co., 1874).

JONES, J. W., 'Forms of Ownership' (1947) 22 *Tulane Law Review* 82.

KAMENKA, E. and TAY, A. E. S. (eds), *Human Rights* (Edward Arnold, 1979).

KANT, I., *Critique of Practical Reason and Other Works on the Theory of Ethics* (trans. Thomas Kingmill Abbott, Longman Green and Co., 1879).

KEETON, GEORGE, W. and GOWER, L. C. B., 'Freedom of Testation in English Law' (1935) 20 *Iowa Law Review* 326.

KNOWLES, DUDLEY, 'Hegel on Property and Personality' (1983) *Philosophical Quarterly* 45.

KOLAKOWSKI, LESZEK, and HAMPSHIRE, STUART (eds.), *The Socialist Idea: A Re-appraisal* (Quartet Books, 1977).

LAPENNA, IVO, *State and Law: Soviet and Yugoslav Theory* (Athlone Press, 1964).

LASKI, HAROLD J., *A Grammar of Politics* (3rd edn., George Allen and Unwin, 1934).

LAW COMMISSION, *Trusts of Land* (Law Comm. no. 181, 1989).

—— *Overreaching: Beneficiaries in Occupation* (Law Comm. no. 188, 1989).

LAWSON, F. H., *Negligence in the Civil Law* (Clarendon Press, 1950).

—— and RUDDEN, BERNARD, *The Law of Property* (2nd edn., Clarendon Press, 1982).

LENIN, V. I., *The State and Revolution* (Progress Publishers, 1949).

LIBLING, D. F., 'The Concept of Property: Property in Intangibles' (1978) 94 *Law Quarterly Review* 103.

LOCKE, JOHN, *The Second Treatise of Government* (G. W. Gough (ed.), Basil Blackwell, 1976).

LUCAS, J. R., *On Justice* (Clarendon Press, 1980).

LYCAN, WILLIAM G., *Judgment and Justification* (CUP, 1988).

MACCORMICK, NEIL, 'Rights in Legislation' in P. M. S. Hacker and Joseph Raz (eds.) *Law, Morality and Society* (Clarendon Press, 1977).

MACINTYRE, ALASDAIR, *After Virtue: A Study in Moral Theory* (Duckworth, 1981).

MACKIE, J. L., *Ethics: Inventing Right and Wrong* (Penguin Books, 1977).

MACKINNON, CATHARINE A., *Toward a Feminist Theory of the State* (Harvard University Press, 1989).

MACPHERSON, C. B., *The Political Theory of Possessive Individualism: Hobbes to Locke* (OUP, 1962).

—— 'Capitalism and the Changing Concept of Property' in E. Kamenka and R. S. Neale (eds.), *Feudalism, Capitalism and Beyond* (Edward Arnold, 1975).

MacPHERSON, C. B. *Property: Mainstream and Critical Positions* (Basil Blackwell, 1978).

MAINE, SIR HENRY SUMNER, *Ancient Law* (Pollock revised edn., John Murray, 1906).

MAITLAND, F. W., *Equity* (J. Brunyate (ed.), CUP, 1936).

—— *The Forms of Action at Common Law* (CUP, 1936).

MANN, F. A., *The Legal Aspect of Money* (5th edn., Clarendon Press, 1992).

MARX, KARL, *Economic and Philosophical Manuscripts*, in Marx, *Early Writings* (trans. Rodney Livingstone and Gregor Benton, Penguin Books, 1975).

—— *Capital* (Penguin Classics, trans. B. Fowkes, Penguin Books, 1990), i.

—— and ENGELS, FREDERICK, *The Manifesto of the Communist Party 1848* (trans. Samuel Moore, Progress Publishers, 1888).

McNEIL, KENT, *Common Law Aboriginal Title* (Clarendon Press, 1989).

MICHELMAN, FRANK I., 'Ethics, Economics and the Law of Property' in J. Rowland Pennock and John W. Chapman (eds.), *Nomos XXIV: Ethics, Economics and the Law* (New York University Press, 1982).

MILL, JOHN STUART, *Principles of Political Economy: With Some of their Applications to Social Philosophy*, in J. M. Robson (ed.), *Collected Works of John Stuart Mill* (University of Toronto Press, Routledge and Kegan Paul, 1965).

MILLER, DAVID, *Social Justice* (Clarendon Press, 1976).

MILSOM, S. F. C., *The Legal Framework of English Feudalism* (CUP, 1976).

MINOGUE, KENNETH, 'The Conception of Property and its Contemporary Significance' in J. Rowland Pennock and John W. Chapman (eds.), *Property: Nomos XXII* (New York University Press, 1980).

MOORE, MICHAEL, 'Moral Reality' (1982) *Wisconsin Law Review* 1061.

—— 'A Natural Law Theory of Interpretation' (1985) 58 *Southern California Law Review* 277.

MORRIS, WILLIAM, *News from Nowhere and other Writings* (Penguin Books, 1993).

MUNZER, STEPHEN R., 'Realistic Limits on Realist Interpretation' (1985) 58 *Southern California Law Review* 459.

—— *A Theory of Property* (CUP, 1990).

—— 'An Uneasy Case Against Property Rights in Body Parts' in Ellen Frankel Paul, Fred D. Miller, and Jeffrey Paul (eds.), *Property Rights* (CUP, 1994).

NAGEL, THOMAS, *The View From Nowhere* (OUP, 1985).

NINO, C. S., *The Ethics of Human Rights* (Clarendon Press, 1991).

(NOTE), 'Who Owns the Clouds?' (1948) 1 *Stanford Law Review* 43.

NOZICK, ROBERT, *Anarchy, State and Utopia* (Basil Blackwell, 1974).

OLIVECRONA, KARL, 'Legal Language and Reality' in R. Newman (ed.), *Essays in Jurisprudence in Honor of Roscoe Pound* (The Bobbs-Merrill Co., 1962).

—— *Law as Fact* (2nd edn., Stevens, 1971).

—— 'Locke's Theory of Appropriation' (1974) 24 *Philosophical Quarterly* 222.

PENNER, JAMES, *The Idea of Property in Law* (OUP, forthcoming).

POLLOCK, SIR FREDERICK and MAITLAND, F. W., *History of English Law* (CUP, 1911).

POSNER, RICHARD A., *Economic Analysis of Law* (4th edn., Little Brown and Co., 1992).

POTTAGE, ALAIN, 'Property: Re-appropriating Hegel' (1990) 53 *Modern Law Review* 259.

PROUDHON, JOSEPH PIERRE, *What is Property?* (trans. Donald R. Kelley and Bonnie G. Smith, CUP, 1994).

PUFENDORF, SAMUEL, *De Jure Naturae et Gentium* (trans. C. H. and W. A. Oldfather, Clarendon Press, 1934).

RADIN, MARGARET JANE, 'Property and Personhood' (1982) 34 *Stanford Law Review* 957.

—— *Reinterpreting Property* (University of Chicago Press, 1993).

RAFAEL, D. D., 'Equality and Equity' (1946) 21 *Philosophy* 138.

RAWLS, JOHN, *A Theory of Justice* (OUP, 1972).

—— *Political Liberalism* (Columbia University Press, 1993).

RAZ, JOSEPH, *The Morality of Freedom* (Clarendon Press, 1986).

—— *Ethics in the Public Domain* (Clarendon Press, 1994).

REEVE, ANDREW, *Property* (Macmillan, 1985).

REICH, CHARLES A., 'The New Property' (1964) 73 *Yale Law Journal* 733.

Report on Human Fertilisation and Embryology (Cmnd. 9314, 1984).

ROSE, C. M., 'The Comedy of the Commons: Custom, Commerce and Inherently Public Property' (1986) 53 *University of Chicago Law Review* 711.

ROSE, MARK, 'The Author as Proprietor: Donaldson *v.* Becket and the Genealogy of Modern Authorship' in Brad Sherman and Alain Strowel (eds.) *Of Authors and Origins* (Clarendon Press, 1994).

ROSS, A., 'tu-tu' (1957) 70 *Harvard Law Review* 812.

—— *On Law and Justice* (Stevens, 1958).

ROTHBARD, MURRAY N., 'Justice and Property Rights' in Samuel L. Blumenfeld, (ed.), *Property in a Humane Economy* (Open Court, 1974).

ROUSSEAU, JEAN-JACQUES, *Second Discourse*, in J. B. Brumfitt and John Hall (eds.), *The Social Contract and Discourses* (Everyman's Library, Dent, 1973).

RUBENFELD, JED, 'On Usings' (1993) 102 *Yale Law Journal* 1077.

RUDDEN, BERNARD, 'The Terminology of Title' (1964) 80 *Law Quarterly Review* 63.

—— 'Notes Towards a Grammar of Property' (1980) *Conveyancer* 325.

—— 'Economic Theory Versus Property Law: The *Numerus Clausus* Problem' in J. Eekelaar and J. Bell (eds.), *Oxford Essays in Jurisprudence, 3rd series* (Clarendon Press, 1987).

RYAN, ALAN (ed.), *The Idea of Freedom: Essays in Honour of Isaiah Berlin* (OUP, 1979).

—— *Property and Political Theory* (Basil Blackwell, 1986).

SALMOND, SIR JOHN, *Salmond on Jurisprudence* (7th edn., Sweet and Maxwell, 1924).

SANDEL, MICHAEL J., *Liberallism and the Limits of Justice* (CUP, 1982).

SAYRE-MCCORD, GEOFFREY, *Essays in Moral Realism* (Cornell University Press, 1988).

SCHLATTER, RICHARD, *Private Property: The History of an Idea* (George Allen and Unwin, 1951).

SENECA, *De Beneficiis*.

SHERR, GEORGE, *Desert* (Princeton University Press, 1987).

SIDGWICK, HENRY, *The Elements of Politics* (2nd edn., Macmillan, 1897).

SIMPSON, A. W. B., *A History of the Land Law* (2nd edn., Clarendon Press, 1986).

SINGER, JOSEPH W., 'The Reliance Interest in Property' (1988) 40 *Stanford Law Review* 611.

SMART, CAROL, *Feminism and the Power of Law* (Routledge, 1989).

SMITH, J. C., *The Law of Theft* (7th edn., Butterworths, 1993).

SNARE, FRANK, 'The Concept of Property' (1972) 9 *American Philosophical Quarterly* 200.

STEPHEN, SIR JAMES FITZJAMES, *History of the Criminal Law of England* (Macmillan, 1883).

STRAWSON, P. F., *Individuals* (Methuen and Co. Ltd, 1959).

TAYLOR, CHARLES, *Sources of the Self: The Making of the Modern Identity* (Harvard University Press, 1989).

TUCK, RICHARD, *Natural Rights Theories* (CUP, 1979).

TURNER, J. W. C., 'Some Reflections on Ownership in English Law' (1941) 19 *Canadian Bar Review* 342.

TWAIN, MARK, *The Adventures of Huckleberry Finn* (Chatto and Windus, 1912).

UNGER, R. M., *The Critical Legal Studies Movement* (Harvard University Press, 1986).

VAN ALSTYNE, WILLIAM, 'Cracks in the "New Property": Adjudicative Due Process in the Administrative State' (1977) 62 *Cornell Law Review* 445.

VINOGRADOFF, P., *Outlines of Historical Jurisprudence* (OUP, 1920), i.

VON DER HEYDTE, F. A. F., 'Discovery, Symbolic Annexation and Virtual Effectiveness in International Law' (1935) 29 *American Journal of International Law* 448.

WALDRON, JEREMY, 'What is Private Property?' (1985) 5 *Oxford Journal of Legal Studies* 313.

—— 'Can Communal Goods be Human Rights?' (1987) 28 *Archives Européennes de Sociologie* 296.

—— *The Right to Private Property* (Clarendon Press, 1988).

WALTON, PAUL and GAMBLE, ANDREW, *From Alienation to Surplus Value* (Sheed and Ward, 1972).

WALZER, MICHAEL, *Spheres of Justice: A Defence of Pluralism and Equality* (Basic Books, 1982).

WARREN, SAMUEL and BRANDEIS, LOUIS, 'The Right to Privacy' (1890) 4 *Harvard Law Review* 193.

WEBER, MAX, *On Law in Economy and Society* (Max Rheinstein (ed.), trans. Edward Shills and Max Rheinstein, Harvard University Press, 1954).

WEDGWOOD, JOSIAH, *The Economics of Inheritance* (Routledge, 1929).

WEINRIB, ARNOLD S., 'Information and Property' (1988) 38 *University of Toronto Law Journal* 117.

WHEELER, SAMUEL C., 'Natural Property Rights as Body Rights' (1980) 14 *Nous* 171.

WHELAN, FREDERICK H., 'Property as Artifice: Hume and Blackstone' in J. Rowland Pennock and John W. Chapman (eds.), *Property: Nomos XXII* (New York University Press, 1980).

WILLIAMS, BERNARD, 'The Idea of Equality' in Peter Laslett and J. G. Runciman (eds.), *Philosophy, Politics and Society* (2nd Series, Basil Blackwell, 1972).

—— *Ethics and the Limits of Philosophy* (3rd edn., Fontana, 1993).

WOLF, CLARK, 'Contemporary Property Rights: Lockean Provisos and the Interests of Future Generations' (1995) 105 *Ethics* 791.

Index